The Spanish in the Mississippi Valley 1762-1804

The Spanish

in the

Mississippi

Valley

1762-1804

—◆—

EDITED BY

John Francis McDermott

—◆—

University of Illinois Press

Urbana   Chicago   London

To

John S. Rendleman

President

Southern Illinois University, Edwardsville

in admiration

Foreword

————◆◦◆————

$\mathcal{O}$N November 5, 1762, France by secret treaty ceded to Spain the "island" of New Orleans and all of Louisiana west of the Mississippi River. Though rumors of the cession were current in the summer of 1764, it was not until September 10 that sealed orders from Versailles reached Director General Jean-Jacques-Blaise d'Abbadie in the colonial capital. He prepared to deliver Louisiana to Spanish officials but died on February 4, 1765. On March 5, 1766, Don Antonio de Ulloa, the first Spanish governor, arrived at New Orleans with a small military force, but the formal transfer was made only on January 20, 1767. In the face of much dissidence, Ulloa, having quite inadequate military support, was hesitant to take over full control, and in October, 1768, a revolution forced him to withdraw to Cuba. The rebels, however, were soon suppressed by General Alexandro O'Reilly, who took firm possession of the colony on August 18, 1769.

Delays occurred also in establishing Spanish rule in the Western Illinois country (later to be called Upper Louisiana). The first plan of the Spanish officials called for the building of forts at the mouth of the Missouri River, with the intention of fixing there the center of government for the entire northern part of Louisiana. A military party dispatched by Governor Ulloa in the spring of 1767 under the command of Captain Francisco Riú passed through three-year-old St. Louis without orders to take possession of it. The officers and the engineer in charge of the expedition discovered the impracticability of constructing the forts as planned and soon the idea of establishing a District of the Missouri was dropped. St. Louis was recognized as the seat of government for the Western Illinois, and on November 19, 1769, its inhabitants took the oath of allegiance before Captain Louis St. Ange, the commandant. The first Spanish lieutenant governor, Captain Pedro Piernas, arrived the following year.

Spanish ownership of Louisiana continued until 1801, when, again by secret treaty, the territory was ceded back to France. Transfer was again slow. A military expedition under General Victor, planned in 1802 for the repossession of the colony, never sailed. Pierre-Clément de Laussat, appointed *préfet colonial* of Louisiana, arrived at New Orleans in March, 1803, prepared for a long stay, only to learn in June that the territory had been sold to the United States on April 30, 1803. Actual transfer was made by Spain to France at New Orleans on November 30, 1803. Three weeks later (December 20) Laussat made over Louisiana to the United States.

In Upper Louisiana the transfer from Spain to France, made on March 9, 1804, marked the close of Spanish rule. Captain Amos Stoddard of the U.S. army, who acted that day in the name of France, on March 10 received the district from France for the United States.

It was to stimulate interest and to encourage research in the issues and incidents, the practices and personalities of these four decades when the French Mississippi Valley was under the dominance of Spain that a meeting of scholars was arranged in 1970. Like earlier conferences on the French in the Mississippi Valley in 1964 and 1967 and on the western frontier in 1966 and 1968, this one, centered on Spanish activities, was designed for the consideration of whatever problems or subjects aroused the curiosity of the individual researcher. No theme or point of view was imposed on the members of the conference—no common conclusion was sought. We merely wished to make contributions that would enlarge knowledge and understanding of that period and might stir others to further investigation.

To this end we present in this volume sixteen papers on subjects varying from John Francis Bannon's broad introductory look at Spanish beginnings in this vast Mississippi Valley, stretching from mountains to mountains and from Canada to the Gulf of Mexico, to my detailed reconsideration of the case against the long-denounced Lieutenant Governor Fernando de Leyba, which I think will vindicate him as a conscientious and able defender of the town of St. Louis at the time of the British-Indian attack in 1780.

Between these extremes a wide variety of subjects have been explored. C. Richard Arena has written on land settlement policies and practices in Spanish Louisiana, William S. Coker on the Bruin family and the formulation of Spanish immigration policy in the Old Southwest in 1787–88, John Preston Moore on Anglo-Spanish border conflicts following the transfer of Louisiana to Great Britain and Spain, Robert L. Gold on Governor Gálvez and Spanish espionage in Pensacola in 1777.

Noel M. Loomis has traced Philip Nolan's activities in Texas in 1800. A. P. Nasatir has presented another diary of Pedro Vial, the explorer of the Santa Fe Trail. John G. Clark, in summing up the role of city government in the economic development of New Orleans, has been specifically concerned with the role of the cabildo and the city council from 1787 to 1812. Jack D. L. Holmes has reported in detail the regulations by the Spaniards of taverns and the liquor trade in the Mississippi Valley. Samuel Wilson, Jr., in another of his pioneering studies in architectural history, has contributed a detailed account of Andrés Almonester as builder and philanthropist in late eighteenth-century New Orleans. Carl H. Chapman has provided new information about the "indomitable Osage" and new insight into their behavior in the Spanish Illinois between 1763 and 1804. John C. Ewers has illuminated the importance of the symbols of chiefly authority in Indian-white relations. Charles E. O'Neill has reported on the present state of studies on Spanish colonial Louisiana. C. Harvey Gardiner has exposed the riches of the Mexican archives for the historiography of the Spanish Mississippi Valley. A. Otis Hébert, Jr., has described the resources in various archives in the state of Louisiana for the study of Spanish activities in the period of interest to us.

These papers were originally presented (some of them in much briefer form) at a three-day conference on "The Spanish in the Mississippi Valley" sponsored by Southern Illinois University, Edwardsville. Joining with the university as co-sponsors were the Missouri Historical Society, the Spanish International Pavilion Foundation, the Alliance-Française (Groupe de St. Louis), La Société Française de St. Louis, La Sociedad Hispano-Americana de St. Louis, the American Association of Teachers of French (St. Louis Chapter), the American Association of Teachers of Spanish (St. Louis Chapter), and the Sons of the Revolution (St. Louis Chapter).

The first day's sessions, on April 9, 1970, held on the university campus, were chaired by George R. Brooks, director of the Missouri Historical Society, and Richard S. Brownlee, director of the State Historical Society of Missouri at Columbia. Chairman of the Friday meetings at the Spanish Pavilion in St. Louis were Alejandro Ramirez, professor of Romance languages at Washington University, and Dan Romani, assistant professor of Spanish at Southern Illinois University. On Saturday morning at the Spanish Pavilion Richard L. Millett, assistant professor of history at SIU, presided. John S. Rendleman, then chancellor, now president of Southern Illinois University, Edwardsville, was chairman of the dinner session on Saturday evening at the Spanish Pavilion. Guests of honor at the dinner meeting were His Excellency Dr. Carlos Manzanares, then minister of Spain to the United States and consul general at Chicago, Mr. Eduardo S. de Erici, commercial attaché at Chicago, and Mrs. Erici, Mr. José Alvarez, Spanish consul at St. Louis, and Mrs. Alvarez. Clare (Mrs. Chris) Condon and Alexandra and Richardson Usher were good enough to entertain with folksongs of the early Mississippi Valley. Dr. Manzanares delivered an interesting address on the great dramatist, Calderón.

Once again my colleagues and I thank Southern Illinois University for its sponsorship of this conference and of the volume which has resulted from it as well as our friends and associates who were interested and kind enough to preside at the six sessions. I personally was delighted to have all these visiting scholars come to our campus and to have so many good papers to offer to readers. I am grateful to Doña Rosario Parra Cala, director of the Archive of the Indies at Seville, for permission to print documents under her care. I cannot cease to marvel at the patience of all my friends at the University of Illinois Press, and I am most happy at their skill in putting these papers into such handsome dress. Finally, there is once more my gratitude, which I have expressed thirty or forty times before, to Mary Stephanie McDermott, my wife, for her virtues of commission and of omission, which have been as important to me in this conference and this book as at any time before.

JOHN FRANCIS MCDERMOTT
Southern Illinois University
Edwardsville

Contents

———◆•◆———

xi

The Spanish in the Mississippi Valley 1762-1804

The Spaniards
in the Mississippi Valley —
An Introduction

———◆———

JOHN FRANCIS BANNON, S.J.

SPAIN was in the Mississippi Valley, officially and as the sovereign power, just a few weeks short of thirty-eight years. The first Treaty of San Ildefonso was drawn on November 5, 1762; the second of the same name, and as secret as the first, came on October 1, 1800. It is true that the Spanish officials stayed on at their posts several years more, until late 1803 in the south and until the spring of 1804 in St. Louis, but they were during those last years only caretakers for France. In round figures, then, one can say that the Spaniards were in the Valley during the last four decades of the eighteenth century.

Spanish excursions into mid-continent North America run through a considerably longer period. In this rapid introductory survey attention will be directed more broadly to mid-continent, rather than limit itself simply to the Mississippi Valley proper. The area embraced will be that from the western watershed of the Appalachian highland to the eastern slopes of the Rocky Mountain cordillera. Stretching things a bit geographically this can be considered the great Mississippi Valley, even though most of the rivers in Texas and those in Spanish West Florida do flow into the Gulf. Historically, Spanish activity in this broader area is basic to an understanding of Spain in the Valley.

Spain's first contact with mid-continent, and it was not an intimate one, dates from 1519, when Alonso Pineda ran the Gulf of Mexico coastline. At one point, around 90° longitude, he noted a sufficient flow of fresh water entering the Gulf to conclude that he must be passing the mouth of a sizable river. This river he named Río del Espíritu Santo. It was the Hernando de Soto party, in 1541, which really put this Río del Espíritu Santo on the map, when the weary but still hopeful Spaniards reached its banks, somewhere in northwestern Mississippi or southwestern Tennessee, and crossed over to the farther bank into the future Arkansas. For almost two years these Spaniards were in the Trans-Mississippi, probing fruitlessly for precious-metal riches, burying their captain in the great river, testing a possible land route into New Spain, and, finally, sailing off to Pánuco in makeshift boats, thus closing, rather ingloriously, the first chapter of Spain in the Valley. Their reports of the lands which they had traveled, on either side of the river, were hardly enthusiastic enough to draw other Spaniards into mid-continent North America.

Cabeza de Vaca and his three companions, a few years before, had given no better press to the lands which they had traversed, Texas and westward. Again, the men of Coronado had little good to say of the "buffalo plains" or of Quivira. Juan de Oñate, early in the seventeenth century, retraced Coronado's steps onto the "buffalo plains" but could paint no brighter picture. Periodically thereafter the Spaniards talked of Gran Teguayo and Gran Quivira and even of a supposedly fabulous Kingdom of Texas, but this talk was much too vague to launch expeditions or to entice potential investors to test the reality of the dreams.

Until late in the seventeenth century the Spaniards showed little or no active interest in mid-continent, which to them meant everything beyond the Rio Grande, or at best the Pecos River. They seemed willing to leave the area to the Indians, the buffalo, the prairie dogs, and the rattlesnakes. The Franciscan missionaries of Nuevo León and Coahuila, such as the famous Fray Juan Larios, were about the only Spaniards who ventured far beyond the lower Rio Grande. But their *entradas* had no immediate influence in changing Spanish expansionist policies in an easterly direction, no more than did the very occasional sallies out of New Mexico.

Doubling back chronologically, one should recall that the seventeenth century saw the North American continent become a mite cluttered. Through the previous century Spain had the continent to herself, save for a very occasional intrusion by other Europeans. But early in the 1600s came the interlopers, poaching on her exclusivist claims. The English, the French, the Dutch, and a few Swedes, unimpressed by

Spain's monopoly claims and not at all overawed by the papal donation of 1493, began to carve out North American empires. By the third quarter of that seventeenth century, however, Spain's North American rivals had been reduced to two, the French and the English. The Dutch had eliminated the Swedes and been in turn pushed out by the English. Spain was not pleased at having to share her continent but did not feel herself seriously threatened by either, although the foundation of South Carolina, in the 1670s, did not augur well for the future peace and lasting security of Spanish Florida. Even so, it would not be the English who were destined to be Spain's initial worry.

The French, from their northern bases, made the first moves into the Valley and mid-continent in general. Even before Louis Jolliet and Jacques Marquette, in 1673, made their trip down the Mississippi, French *coureurs de bois* had edged westward beyond the farther Great Lakes, Michigan and Superior. The Jolliet-Marquette expedition was but a logical follow-up of these earlier westward moves. Spain does not seem to have been immediately aware of this first "trespass" onto De Soto's Río del Espíritu Santo. Whether the Spaniards actually heard at the time of the La Salle trespass of 1682 is equally doubtful. The Spaniards in those early years of the 1680s had a North American problem of their own about which to fret, the loss of Nuevo México following the highly successful Pueblo revolt of 1680. Had the Spaniards known of the all-embracing claims which La Salle made for France at the mouth of the Mississippi, they might well have been perturbed and at the same time forewarned of future trouble. La Salle had, as the expression goes, "tagged all the bases" when he staked French claims to "the seas, harbors, ports, bays, adjacent straits, and all the nations, people, provinces, towns, villages, mines, minerals, fisheries, streams, and rivers within the extent of said Louisiana." He was, at the very least, making certain that all of mid-continent belonged to France.

With La Salle's next move, however, the Spaniards were quickly acquainted. Rumors that he was sailing, with a complement of colonists, to make a French foundation on the Gulf of Mexico reached the court of Spain and brought fast action in her Indies. Between 1685 and 1687 four expeditions went out by sea to scout the Gulf Coast in search of the French, two out of Florida and the other two out of Veracruz. Three found no signs of the French; the fourth, the second out of Veracruz, did sight the wrecks of French vessels in Matagorda Bay. However, seeing no Frenchmen around, the Spaniards concluded that they had perished and so returned to the home base with this intelligence.

Complementing the search by sea were as many expeditions by land,

5

these led by Alonso de León, between 1686 and 1689. In 1686 he set out from Monterrey (Nuevo León), reached the Rio Grande, followed it downstream to its mouth, then moved eastward along the coast a short distance before returning. The next year, again out of Monterrey, León penetrated into Texas as far as the Río Salado, but found nothing disturbing. At this juncture León was named governor of Coahuila but was ordered to continue his search for the French. Now, from his provincial capital of Monclova, in late 1688, he went off to verify, if possible, the story that there was a white man among the tribes east of the Rio Grande. Friendly Indians had so reported. This third expedition netted the governor one Jean Jarri. The Frenchman had deserted several years before and hence did not know what had happened to La Salle and his former companions; but he did furnish the Spaniards with information concerning the location of Fort Saint-Louis. Accordingly, in 1689 León went off again. This time he found the sorry remains of La Salle's little settlement, several miles up Garcitas Creek. Further, he picked up a couple of survivors among the tribes, one of whom was young Jean l'Archevêque, and from them heard the fuller story of the tragedy.

Alonso de León, after scouting a bit more, believed the assertion of L'Archevêque that the survivors had fled northward to New France or had scattered among the Indians. He so reported to his superiors in Mexico City. But Viceroy Gaspar de la Cerda Sandoval Silva y Mendoza, Conde de Galve, still worried. The next year (1690) León was sent back into Texas with a small party, including several Franciscans, among whom were Fray Damián Massanet and Fray Francisco Hidalgo. They had orders to occupy the country, to counter or to forestall the French. Two missions were founded among the Hasinai on the Neches River. In 1691 Domingo de Terán was named governor of Texas. He came up with more personnel to strengthen and expand the Spanish position. It was he who founded the first presidio, San Francisco de los Tejas. Terán explored as far as the Red but found no evidence of French occupation or penetration.

This Texas venture, Spain's first real advance into mid-continent, lasted only a short time longer. Maintenance costs were high; immediate missionary results were far from encouraging; and, most of all, the French seemed to have lost interest. Accordingly, the Texas posts were withdrawn in 1693—much to the relief of the Mexican officials, particularly of the Real Hacienda (treasury department), but much to the distress of the Franciscan missionaries. One of their number, Fray Francisco Hidalgo, obediently pulled back but began immediately to work for a re-establishment of the Hasinai missions. A letter of Hidalgo to the governor of Louisiana a dozen or so years later may have had some influence on the French action of 1713—this is a moot point in the history of Spanish Texas, but the details are not wholly germane to this rapid survey.

After 1693 Spain decided on a policy of watchful waiting. Meanwhile, she sought to re-establish control in Nuevo México—Don Diego de Vargas had the *reconquista* well under way. Farther down the Rio Grande she sought to strengthen her then northeast frontier with new missionary effort in Coahuila and Nuevo León.

Not many years passed, however, before Spain was rudely shaken from her complacency and had to act, and act quickly. The French had not lost interest in the Gulf Coast. In 1698 intelligence out of France concerning French designs on Louisiana reached the Spanish court. Pierre LeMoyne, Sieur d'Iberville, was preparing to head an expedition designed to accomplish what La Salle had failed to achieve: French possession of mid-continent North America at its southern end. Orders went out, this time to Florida, to forestall or at least to checkmate the French intrusion.

About the time the Spaniards of New Spain were abandoning Texas, in 1693, Andrés de Pez was exploring Pensacola and Mobile bays, with an eye to possible occupation. But there, too, Spain pulled back. Now, in 1698, action was ordered. Accordingly, Andrés de Arriola moved out of Florida in November, founded a post at Pensacola, and girded his little garrison for the possible advent of the French. The Spaniards did not have to wait long. In January, 1699, the ships of Iberville sailed into the bay but, on finding the Spaniards already in possession, chose not to challenge them, at least for the moment, and went westward to Biloxi, which became their first Louisiana foundation. Three years later Iberville transferred to a more strategically located and more easily defensible position on Mobile Bay, where he laid the foundation of another Saint-Louis.

Spain noted this encroachment toward her Florida but waited for the next French move. France, for the moment, seemed more intent on trying to win the friendship and trade of the Indians inland. Besides, during the next years both Spain and France had prime concerns at home in Europe, where both were involved in the War of the Spanish Succession. Also, France had her hands full in the Americas, in the conflict with England known as Queen Anne's War. Spain, too, had American worries, especially on the Atlantic side of Florida, where she was being badgered by aggressive Englishmen out of Carolina.

The war was ending and the Peace of Utrecht was in the making in

1713, when the Louisiana French made a next move. Though still centered at Mobile, the French had eyes on the lands and the Indians beyond the Mississippi. Louis Juchereau de Saint-Denis, acting on orders from Cadillac, governor for the new Louisiana proprietor, Antoine Crozat, moved over to the Red River and founded the trading post of Natchitoches. This could be a base from which to bid for the trade of the Caddo peoples and other tribes to the north and west of the Red.

Spain took as a challenge the appearance of Saint-Denis and companions at San Juan Bautista on the Rio Grande in 1714. France quite evidently would not be content to deal simply with the Indians of the Mississippi Valley. Arrested and sent south to Mexico City for further questioning, Saint-Denis became the symbol of this challenge. Even though he disclaimed motives other than the desire to buy horses for the governor of Louisiana and to let Fray Francisco Hidalgo know that the Hasinai still thought kindly of their former Spanish missionaries, officialdom of New Spain was disturbed. A *junta de guerra*, meeting in the viceregal capital on August 12, 1715, voted for the immediate reoccupation of Texas, authorizing missions, a presidio, and a settler colony.

Domingo Ramón, in February, 1716, led a small party out of Saltillo. Two months later, with enough additions to raise the total complement to sixty-five, the Spaniards pushed across the Rio Grande from San Juan Bautista. Before the end of the summer there were four missions on or near the Neches and the Angelina, and Ramón had laid the foundations of the Presidio de Dolores. Two groups of Franciscans shared the missionary burdens of the enterprise. Fray Isidro Félix Espinosa was the *padre presidente* of the friars from the missionary college of Querétaro; the saintly Fray Antonio Margil de Jesús headed the contingent from the Colegio de Propaganda Fide de Zacatecas.

Spain was back in Texas, and incidentally in mid-content; but her hold was not exactly secure. The East Texas establishments were hundreds of difficult miles away from the nearest Spanish post, San Juan Bautista. There were rumors that Saint-Denis and his Frenchmen were planning another trading expedition westward. And equally worrisome was the report that the French were minded to move their capital to a base on the lower Mississippi—New Orleans, as time proved, was no more than a year or two into the future.

From the beginning of the Texas venture the Franciscans, and especially Fray Francisco Olivares, had been agitating for an intermediate base in the new province, which might also serve as the center for expanded missionary activity. A December, 1716, *junta de guerra* seconded the general idea. Martín de Alarcón was named governor and was authorized to found a presidio-mission-settlement complex at a convenient middle location. San Antonio de Béxar was the result.

During his short term as governor Alarcón visited the east and planted two more missions; one of the farthest of these, among the Adai, soon developed into the historic Los Adaes, set just about a dozen miles to the west of the offending French post of Natchitoches. Los Adaes, close to the Red River, was really the first Spanish post in the Mississippi watershed proper.

For the next decades, down to the end of 1762, the Spaniards and the French sparred and feinted on that Texas-Louisiana frontier. Los Adaes became for a time the "capital" of Texas; the French won East Texas during the 1719–21 altercation between the two mother countries in Europe; the Marqués de Aguayo won it back quickly; Inspector General Pedro de Rivera in the late 1720s allowed Los Adaes and a few other eastern missions to remain but ordered the rest to be transferred to the San Antonio area; a few folk from New Spain and a dozen families from the Canary Islands, imported precisely for the purpose, founded the civilian settlement of San Fernando de Béxar in the San Antonio complex. With the Texas-Louisiana frontier quiet, the Spaniards turned attention to the Apache-Comanche problems, which were upsetting the peace elsewhere in Texas. The French, too, could look farther afield. Their interest shifted westward; it stemmed largely from their positions in the Illinois country, and their "new west" became the Great Plains. The Treaty of San Ildefonso of 1762 removed the French and put the Spaniards on the banks of the Mississippi.

But before advancing the story to 1762–63, note should be taken of Spanish attention to the Great Plains in the first half of the eighteenth century; this had a New Mexican base. The infiltration of the French into the upper and middle Mississippi Valley, particularly their establishment at Cahokia in the last year of the seventeenth century and at Kaskaskia early in the new century, very quickly had the Spaniards at Santa Fe on the alert. Spanish thinking and policy had to adopt a northeasterly orientation.

Early in the new century reports of white men on the Plains drifted into Taos, at fair time, and into the New Mexican capital. Officials were concerned. They became distinctly upset when a bit later they learned that these white men, who almost certainly had to be French, were trafficking in guns. One did not have to be overly smart to realize that guns in the hands of the plainsmen might very well upset the already precarious balance of power among the tribes to the north and northeast of New Mexico. The province was already beginning to have its troubles with the tribes which ringed it round, the Navaho, the Ute, and particularly the too-numerous Apache nations. New Mexicans could envision the Comanche with guns pressuring Apache rivals and these in turn, on the run, threatening the Spanish frontiers. It was anything but a reassuring vision of the future.

In 1719 officials in the viceregal capital, so far removed from the realities of the farther frontier, laid out a plan of action. They ordered that a presidio be established on the Plains, with El Cuartelejo (in southwestern Kansas) as the site. They further commanded the governor of New Mexico to take an expedition beyond and to end the reported westward encroachment of the French. Wiser heads in New Mexico rejected the presidio proposal as impractical. The second order launched the ill-fated Villasur expedition of 1720, defeated and disastrously mauled on the Platte. After that reverse New Mexico was in a state of real fear for the next few years.

After the immediate danger seemed to have passed, New Mexico fretted. Little could be done save to contain Apache, Navaho, Ute, and Comanche raiders, and to make an occasional sally onto the Plains, in order to recover stock or to bring back truant Indians to their pueblos. These were years, however, when Bernard de La Harpe was on the lower Arkansas, Claude du Tisné in the Osage country, and the resourceful Sieur de Bourgmont actually breaching the Comanche barrier. Fortunately, during the early years of the century's second quarter the French of the Illinois country were distracted by the Fox wars, which threatened their lines of communication with Canada, and thus were not able to follow up the contacts which Bourgmont had made on the Plains.

Whether they liked it or not, the Spaniards were forced to keep mid-continent in their thinking. French traders, edging westward along the Gulf Coast and making contact with the Bidai and the Orcoquiza, kept the Spaniards in Texas on the alert. Then, farther north, the arrival of the Mallet brothers and party in Santa Fe, in 1739, seemed to herald fresh troubles from the Mississippi Valley. Especially, when in the next years other Frenchmen showed up in the northern capital, Spain had to recognize that New Mexico was becoming as much a defensive borderland against the French as Texas and Pensacola had been from their beginnings. But the situation was due for a drastic change.

As of 1763 the mid-continent picture, territorially at least, was altered very considerably. Only Spain and England figured in the "new look," France having been squeezed out of the Mississippi Valley by her own Treaty of San Ildefonso of late 1762 and more completely by the Treaty of Paris of the next year. Spain, overnight, became a Valley power, and so did Great Britain. At first the Great River was the dividing line. Then a second Treaty of Paris, twenty years later, saw England replaced in the Trans-Allegheny by the young United States, and this same international agreement brought Spain back into the Floridas, East and West, thus giving her control of the entire Gulf of Mexico coastline from the Florida keys to the peninsula of Yucatan.

Here, then, are some of the salient points of the pre-1763 Spanish background for mid-continent North America. They can constitute a backdrop, so to speak, against which the more specific events of the Spanish decades in the Mississippi Valley can be acted out. Many of these specific events and/or developments make up the topics of this volume. Let me close this introductory survey with a few general remarks or observations on the post-1763 decades.

The first may be out of place, but it is probably worth making. It is more correct to talk of the "Spanish years" in the Mississippi Valley than of the Spaniards there. Actually, relatively few Spaniards were in the Valley during those last four decades of the eighteenth century—top officials and their entourage, some of the soldiery, occasional merchants and clerics, and a small assortment of others. For example, only four of the lieutenant governors of Spanish Illinois or Upper Louisiana were Spanish; by the 1790s Spain was appointing Frenchmen to that post. Several Frenchmen held the post of governor of the entire province. The Spaniards left few notable marks on the Valley. Their laws and regulations did at times have influence on the preponderant French population; but even these did not quite Hispanicize life, customs, manners, or language. Later, Americans had to wrestle with Spanish land grants after 1803; but they had as much trouble with French grants. There are a few buildings in New Orleans dating back to Spanish days; there are almost none in the middle Valley which can be said to be Spanish. The Spanish years did add another flag to the New Orleans and St. Louis "collections"—by tallying the fleur-de-lys of the Bourbons, the tricolor of the Revolution and/or the First Consulate, and the later Stars and Stripes, the number can run to four. Perhaps significantly, the Spaniards left almost no place names in the Valley, or even any notable number of street names in the towns which once were Spanish. Basically, the Spanish years did little more than prolong the Latin and the Catholic character of the nearer Trans-Mississippi for another four decades after the British victory of 1763, which was really only the first stage of the ultimate Anglo takeover in the first half of the nineteenth century.

Even so, there were significant, if not always purely Spanish, developments in the Valley and the Trans-Mississippi during those last eighteenth-century decades. The Spanish years reinforced the orientation of the Valley toward the Gulf of Mexico and the Caribbean. This had always been true of French Louisiana. During these years the middle Valley, which in French days looked northward to Canada as well as toward New Orleans, received a quite exclusive southward pointing. Had the Spaniards remained some years more in the Valley, the future Missouri connection with the Southwest might have dated from Spanish days. The 1792–93 trek of Pedro Vial from Santa Fe to St. Louis and back might have made a Santa Fe Trail a dozen or more years before it became an American reality.

Although *Luisiana* immediately became a Spanish borderland, like Florida she was never reckoned among Spain's Provincias Internas. The new province was attached administratively to the captaincy general of Havana, and was only indirectly tied to New Spain. This, again, contributed to the Gulf-Caribbean orientation. *Luisiana's* borderland character had much more than passing influence on later eighteenth-century developments within the province. At first the very size of the newly acquired province staggered the Spaniards. As of mid-eighteenth century Spain's northern frontiers were already far extended; as of 1763 they seemed almost hopelessly and impossibly so. However, Spain did recognize, even as she reluctantly accepted the territory from France, that possession of the Trans-Mississippi could serve a valuable, if somewhat expensive, defensive purpose. The British prior to 1762 had been comfortably removed, save on the Florida frontier. But in 1763 there was no longer a Spanish Florida, and the fearsome Englishmen were soon to be into the very heart of mid-continent. It was an advantage to have a sizable buffer zone against them, and *Luisiana* could serve that purpose. Spain knew that she would hardly be able to put many of her own Spaniards therein; but the Frenchmen might supply that deficiency. They might not be enthusiastic "Spaniards," but Spain could count on them to dislike and distrust English neighbors. This was amply proved very soon, when the English took over the Illinois posts. Many Frenchmen went scurrying to the west bank, thus contributing to an early "population explosion" in newly founded St. Louis. The Spanish Illinois, particularly, became a Spanish bastion against the new lords of the Trans-Allegheny.

One very interesting aspect of the Spanish years in the Valley evidenced a hitherto almost unsuspected ability of Spanish officialdom to adapt to new situations—Spain for so long had been so inflexible in maintaining and applying her colonial policies. At first Spain was minded to make new French subjects conform to her traditional imperial patterns. Soon, however, she found herself sanctioning adaptations, administrative and economic, changes in immigration policies, and very notably changes in Indian policies. Athanase de Mézières, and others like him, taught the Spaniards the secrets which the French had learned in their long dealings with the semi-nomadic Indians of North America—Spain had inherited subject tribesmen of this stamp in frightening numbers when she acquired the Trans-Mississippi. Already her Texas experience had caused Spain to lose some confidence in what she had previously thought to be the universal applicability of the mission as her frontier institution of expansion and control. How well the Spaniards learned the trade-and-presents approach can be read in the very enlightening *Instrucción* which Viceroy Bernardo de Gálvez sent to his *comandante general* of the Provincias Internas, Jacobo Ugarte y Loyola, in 1786. Again, Spanish officials learned to count on the St. Louis traders, ranging up the Missouri, to forestall the British in the Upper Missouri country and thus prevent a potential Anglo threat to New Mexico and the provinces to the south, which might have come down from the high plains. These traders, however, had to be accorded much more freedom than would have been normal in earlier Spanish practice.

The main themes for the Spanish years in the middle Valley were defense, trade, and Indian policies. These elements were in the story of the lower Valley, but there were others as well. Worthy of note, but not allowing more than mention in this survey, were the post-1783 frictions with the young United States, which grew into the so-called Mississippi Question; another was the story of Spanish intrigue with overly ambitious, callously unscrupulous, and not infrequently dissatisfied "westerners" in the Trans-Allegheny. In the handling of neither of these problems was the Spanish performance particularly gratifying to national pride. Spain may, in a sense, have been glad enough to have France take over in 1800. She possibly welcomed the chance to exit gracefully from Louisiana and to retire behind the frontiers of her Provincias Internas. The diplomatic double-cross of Napoleon, in 1803, which gave her the aggressive Americans as too-close neighbors in the Trans-Mississippi, did not allow her long to enjoy a period of worry-free calm. Americans beyond the east bank of the Mississippi could be one thing; Americans in the Trans-Mississippi quite another. Again to indulge a conjecture, one may wonder whether, after living for a dozen and a half years with the Americans in the Trans-Mississippi, Spain may not have been somewhat less than unwilling to pass on the problems of her Provincias Internas to self-willed and obstreperous Mexican children in 1821.

One last generality on the Spaniards in the Mississippi Valley to conclude this introductory survey. Bolton had a thesis which neither leisure nor length of days gave him the opportunity to develop fully, but one which might have some real bearing on the present topic. Writing to Verner W. Crane, on August 11, 1913, he confided: "I have a thesis up my sleeve—where it may remain—to the effect that the great struggle for the continent of North America was not between France and England after all, but between England and Spain, and extended all the way from the Caribbean to the Pacific Ocean. . . ." If this thesis is demonstrable, a number of the studies in this volume might well fit into "proof" thereof. One of the confrontations of the Spanish and the English was in the Mississippi Valley; this could be added to their earlier contest in Georgia-Florida and their long-standing rivalry in the Caribbean. And this Valley confrontation was, in a way, an immediate preliminary to the final showdown. Interestingly, however, neither of the original principals was on hand in the last stages of the contest. In both instances the second generation resolved the struggle for North America at mid-nineteenth century, when the Anglo-Americans of the United States overpowered the Spanish-Americans of Mexico and came off with a sizable segment of the continent. Had the Spaniards never been in the Mississippi Valley, Anglo predominance would hardly have been so long delayed.

BIBLIOGRAPHICAL NOTE

Rather than load a rapid survey with dozens of footnotes, it seems more practical simply to mention a few of the works on which it has relied for its data and interpretation. Two general borderland studies should be recalled first: Herbert E. Bolton, *The Spanish Borderlands: A Chronicle of Old Florida and the Southwest* (New Haven, 1921), and John Francis Bannon, *The Spanish Borderlands Frontier, 1513–1821* (New York, 1970). This latter volume has a quite extensive bibliography, noting, besides the major works, a sizable number of journal articles. Two general treatments of the French in the Mississippi Valley, which can serve as background for the Spanish years: Joseph H. Schlarman, *From Quebec to New Orleans* (Belleville, Ill., 1929), and John Anthony Caruso, *The Mississippi Valley Frontier: The Age of French Exploration and Settlement* (Indianapolis, 1966). A conference similar to the present one produced a series of papers which were published under the editorship of John Francis McDermott in a volume entitled *The French in the Mississippi Valley* (Urbana, Ill., 1965).

The lengthy introduction to the two-volume collection of documents offered by Abraham P. Nasatir in *Before Lewis and Clark* (St. Louis, 1952) is one of the best survey pieces on the Spaniards in the Mississippi Valley. More recently Nasatir, teaming with Noel M. Loomis, produced another study, *Pedro Vial and the Roads to Santa Fe* (Norman, 1967), which is rich with data on the Spaniards in the Valley. Very helpful and informative, too, is Henry Folmer, *Franco-Spanish Rivalry in North America* (Glendale, Calif., 1952); the earlier phases of the Franco-Spanish contest are explored by William E. Dunn, *Spanish and French Rivalry in the Gulf Region of the United States, 1678–1702* (Austin, 1917). Clarence W. Alvord, *The Illinois Country* (Springfield, Ill., 1920) can be used with profit.

A valuable documentary collection is Lawrence Kinnaird, ed., *Spain in the Mississippi Valley, 1765–1794* (3 vols., Washington, 1946–49). One should not overlook John Francis McDermott, ed., *The Early Histories of Saint Louis* (St. Louis, 1952), nor the stories of two of the Spanish governors, *Bernardo de Gálvez in Louisiana, 1776–1783* (Berkeley, 1934), by John W. Caughey, and *Gayoso: The Life of a Spanish Governor in the Mississippi Valley, 1789–1799* (Baton Rouge, 1965), by Jack D. L. Holmes.

Many other studies which might be noted here will be recalled in the references and bibliographies of the other papers in this volume; duplication would seem rather useless.

The State of Studies
on Spanish Colonial Louisiana

CHARLES EDWARDS O'NEILL, S.J.

THE president of the United States gives the State of the Union address. The presidents of universities have taken to giving state-of-the-university addresses. It is as a private citizen of the once-Spanish Mississippi Valley and as one of the "students" that I venture to survey the state of studies on Spanish colonial Louisiana.

The development and distribution of these studies have been uneven. The research and publications have come in starts and spurts with lulls in between. It seems we are presently in a "spurt period," but, before justifying that estimate, let us review the "history of the history" of the Spanish in colonial Louisiana.

In this report I omit references to unpublished dissertations; the capable young doctor of history can rewrite his dissertation for publication in entirety or he can extract selected materials for articles in scholarly journals. Moreover, it is only in this way that the work can be put to the test of reviews—and thus enter into the stream of studies. Also, I will generally omit reference to books and articles which reproduce documents with brief comments from the author.

Before beginning with the studies, however, let me list major collections of documents: Louis Houck, ed., *The Spanish Régime in Missouri* (2 vols., Chicago, 1909). Manuel Serrano y Sanz, *Documentos históricos de la Florida y la Luisiana, siglos XVI al XVIII* (Madrid, 1912). Lawrence Kinnaird, ed., *Spain in the Mississippi Valley, 1765-1794* (translations of materials from Spanish archives in the Bancroft Library), published by the American Historical Association, 1946–49, in three parts: *Revolutionary Period, 1765–81; Post-War Decade, 1782–91;* and *Problems of Frontier Defense, 1792–94.* Abraham P. Nasatir, *Before Lewis and Clark: Documents Illustrating the History of the Missouri, 1785–1804,* published by the St. Louis Historical Documents Foundation, 1952, in two volumes. Jack D. L. Holmes, *Documentos inéditos para la historia de la Luisiana, 1792–1810* (Madrid, 1963), in the Porrúa Colección Chimalistac.

Over the years 1923–48 résumés-in-translation of the Spanish Judicial Records of Louisiana appeared in the *Louisiana Historical Quarterly* (vols. VI-XXXI).

Of the few scholarly full-fledged books in the field of Spanish colonial Louisiana, the majority have focused on governors—their lives and administrations. In 1934 John Walton Caughey, a Bolton disciple, gave us *Bernardo de Gálvez in Louisiana, 1776–1783* (Berkeley). It was a work of Caughey's youth and of love, but he did not remain in the study of the northeast borderland. There is a general work by Guillermo Porras Muñoz on *Bernardo de Gálvez* (Madrid, 1952).

Less known than Caughey's was Caroline Maude Burson's *The Stewardship of Don Esteban Miró, 1782–1792,* an admirable book in spite of the limitation acknowledged in the subtitle: "A Study of Louisiana Based Largely on Documents in New Orleans." Her book suffered the fate of obscurity which befalls many a locally published work (New Orleans: American Printing Company, 1940).

Twenty-five years went by before Jack D. L. Holmes published his study of Gayoso, both as Natchez governor and as governor of the entire colony: *Gayoso: The Life of a Spanish Governor in the Mississippi Valley, 1789–1799* (Baton Rouge, 1965).

The latest biographical work on a Spanish Louisiana administrator is Bibiano Torres Ramirez's *Alejandro O'Reilly en las Indias,* which Seville's Escuela de Estudios Hispano-Americanos published in 1969. The fourth part of this little volume covers the official action of O'Reilly in Louisiana.

Among articles in the field David K. Bjork did a chapter on "Alexander O'Reilly and the Spanish Occupation of Louisiana, 1769–1770," in George P. Hammond, ed., *New Spain and the Anglo-American West,* a Bolton festschrift offering (2 vols., Lancaster, Pa., 1932), I, 165–182.

John Preston Moore added to our biographical knowledge of Ulloa in sketching "A Profile of the First Spanish Governor of Louisiana,"

Louisiana History, VIII (1967), 189–218. Professor Moore is presently preparing a full biography of Ulloa.

The most popular approach to the field has been political, with these subdivisions: the 1768 revolution, the successive-boundary questions, and relations with the expanding United States of America.

Vicente Rodríguez Casado reoriented the study of the 1768 revolution by the publication of his patriotic *Primeros años de dominación española en la Luisiana* (Madrid, 1942), which superseded James E. Winston, "The Cause and Results of the Revolution of 1768 in Louisiana," *Louisiana Historical Quarterly*, XV (1932), 181–213. Rodríguez furthered his thesis on the self-interest of the debtor leaders of the anti-Ulloa rising when he touched on the "Proyecto del Banco del Monte de Piedad de Nueva Orleans [1768]," *Anuario de Historia del Derecho Español*, XIV (1942–43), 629–635. Later, however, Rodríguez, like Caughey, developed other interests, and did not pursue the field of his youthful research. Just recently David Kerr Texada published his dissertation on *Alejandro O'Reilly and the New Orleans Rebels* (Lafayette, La., 1970).

In 1927 Arthur Preston Whitaker brought out his study of *The Spanish-American Frontier: 1783–1795* (Boston); in 1934 he pursued the topic further with *The Mississippi Question 1795–1803: A Study in Trade, Politics, and Diplomacy* (New York). His viewpoint is that of an American looking out at Louisiana; events reach a point in time when he judges that any Spaniard should have seen that this part of the empire was held by the merest thread, easily cut.

Among Americans who have studied the boundary questions we find: Richard Stenberg, "The Boundaries of the Louisiana Purchase," *Hispanic American Historical Review*, XIV (1934), 32–64; and D. C. Corbitt, "James Colbert and the Spanish Claims to the East Bank of the Mississippi," *Mississippi Valley Historical Review*, XXIV (1938), 457–472. More recently Jack D. L. Holmes described the tense situation of 1805 in his article on "The Marqués de Casa-Calvo, Nicolás de Finiels, and the 1805 Spanish Expedition through East Texas and Louisiana," *Southwestern Historical Quarterly*, LXIX (1966), 324–339.

Beyond the question of boundaries as such, Abraham P. Nasatir has long been interested in "Anglo-Spanish Rivalry on the Upper Missouri," *Mississippi Valley Historical Review*, XVI (1929–30), 359–382, 507–528; Dr. Nasatir also delivered Louisiana State University's Walter Lynwood Fleming Lecture for 1970 on "The Shifting Frontiers of Spanish Louisiana."

Then and now Spanish officials and Spanish researchers have seen these matters from a different angle. Pichardo's *Treatise on the Limits of Louisiana and Texas* was edited by Charles W. Hackett between 1931 and 1946 in four volumes (Austin). *Athanase de Mézières and the Louisiana-Texas Frontier, 1768–1780* was Bolton's own contribution to the historiography of this borderland (2 vols., Cleveland, 1914).

In our day Fernando Solano Costa has looked at "Los problemas diplomáticas de las fronteras de la Luisiana" in the *Cuadernos de Historia Diplomática* (Zaragoza, 1958), III, 51–95; IV, 121–154. And Jaime Delgado judges American expansionism in "Una polémica en 1805 sobre los límites de la Luisiana" as he reviews James Monroe's mission to Spain in the *Revista de Archivos, Bibliotecas y Museos*, LIV (1948), 403–433.

For the anniversary of the accession of Charles III, Fernando de Armas Medina recalled the hopes of Spain for vast "Luisiana en el reinado de Carlos III," *Estudios Americanos*, no. 100 (1960), 67–92.

In religious-life history Roger Baudier chronicled the Spanish years in some chapters of his *Catholic Church in Louisiana* (New Orleans, 1939). Closely related to the topic is M. J. Curley's *Church and State in the Spanish Floridas* [*1783–1822*] (Washington, 1940).

There is a tentative biography of Père Antoine entitled *La Luisiana española y el Padre Sedella* by Capuchin Father Antonio de Castillo (San Juan, P.R., [1929]).

Recently Jack Holmes published an article on "Irish Priests in Spanish Natchez," *Journal of Mississippi History*, XXIX (1967), 169–180.

In the writings on immigration one finds reference to Protestant entry and presence in the Spanish colony. Rabbi Bertram W. Korn has given us the best documented pages on Jews in Spanish Louisiana in his *The Early Jews of New Orleans* (Waltham, Mass., 1969).

The researcher might be pleased to know that the Genealogical Research Society of New Orleans has published some valuable sources, such as the *Confirmaciones* records of St. Louis Parish in New Orleans (New Orleans, 1967).

Immigration has drawn increasing attention. Oscar William Winzerling in *Acadian Odyssey* (Baton Rouge, 1955) gave a solid account of the benevolent efficiency of Spain in aiding the homeless exiles to settle on the Mississippi. Fernando Solano Costa had discussed "La emigración acadiana a la Luisiana española (1783–1785)" the year before in the *Cuadernos de Historia Jerónimo Zurita*, II (1954), 85–125.

19

Earlier, back in 1928, Francis P. Burns used a U.S. federal compilation of documents to tell of "The Spanish Land Laws of Louisiana" that applied to settlers in *Louisiana Historical Quarterly*, XI, 557–581. Lawrence Kinnaird had a chapter on "American Penetration into Spanish Louisiana" in Hammond, ed., *New Spain and the Anglo-American West*, I, 211–237.

More recently Gilbert C. Din, who presented a doctoral dissertation to the University of Madrid in 1960 on "Colonización en la Luisiana española: proyectos de emigración en la Luisiana del siglo XVIII," published this past year an article on "The Immigration Policy of Governor Esteban Miró in Spanish Louisiana," *Southwestern Historical Quarterly*, LXXIII (1969), 155–175, wherein he finds Miró most positively favorable to American in-migration. Irene D. Neu pointed to Irish immigration in "From Kilkenny to Louisiana. Notes on Eighteenth-Century Irish Immigration," *Mid-America*, LXIX (1967), 101–114.

Government financial affairs have been treated briefly in articles, but mainly by reproducing typical documents: Charles H. Cunningham, ed., "Financial Reports Relating to Louisiana, 1766–1788," *Mississippi Valley Historical Review*, VI (1919), 381–397. Abraham P. Nasatir, "Government Employees and Salaries in Spanish Louisiana," *Louisiana Historical Quarterly*, XXIX (1946), 885–1040. Jack D. L. Holmes, "Some Economic Problems of Spanish Governors of Louisiana," *Hispanic American Historical Review*, XLII (1962), 521–543.

Commerce has been but little treated also: A. P. Whitaker, "The Commerce of Louisiana and the Floridas at the End of the Eighteenth Century," *Hispanic American Historical Review*, VIII (1928), 190–203. C. Richard Arena, "Philadelphia–Spanish New Orleans Trade in the 1790's," *Louisiana History*, II (1961), 429–445, written mainly from the Philadelphia viewpoint. Vicente Rodríguez Casado examined an abortive bank proposal which would have used as collateral the gross product of the colony (see page 18 above).

A few writers have treated of the Indian in Spanish Louisiana. Jane M. Berry studied "The Indian Policy of Spain in the Southwest, 1783–1795," *Mississippi Valley Historical Review*, III (1917), 462–477. Frank Delfina did the same in "Mestizos y blancos en la política india de la Luisiana y la Florida del siglo XVIII," *Revista de Indias*, XXVI (1966), no. 103–104, 59–77. Vicenta Cortes Alonso looked at Indian and European population movements in "Geopolítica del sureste de los Estados Unidos (1750–1800)," *Revista de Indias*, XII (1952), no. 47,

23–49. "Spanish Treaties with West Florida Indians, 1784–1802" was the subject of a recent article by Jack D. L. Holmes in *Florida Historical Quarterly*, XLVIII (1969), 140–154.

The founding of particular posts has drawn the attention of several historians:

Fort Miró: J. Fair Hardin, "Don Juan Filhiol and the Founding of Fort Miró, the Modern Monroe, Louisiana," *Louisiana Historical Quarterly*, XX (1937), 463–485.

The Bastrop Concession in the same area: Jennie O'Kelly Mitchell and Robert Dabney Calhoun, "The Marquis de Maison Rouge, the Baron de Bastrop, and Colonel Abraham Morhouse: Three Ouachita Valley Soldiers of Fortune. The Maison Rouge and Bastrop Spanish Land Grants," *Louisiana Historical Quarterly*, XX (1937), 289–462.

"The Arkansas Post of Louisiana: Spanish Domination"—the continuation of Stanley Faye's article on the French period—*Louisiana Historical Quarterly*, XXVII (1944), 629–716.

New Madrid: Max Savelle, "The Founding of New Madrid," *Mississippi Valley Historical Review*, XIX (1932), 30–56. Fernando Solano Costa, "La Fundación de Nuevo Madrid," *Cuadernos de Historia Jerónimo Zurita*, II (1954), 85–125; IV–V (1956), 91–108.

Another popular topic for researchers has been the intrigues linking Spanish Louisiana and the American West. The name that comes first to mind is that of General James Wilkinson. Among others, Isaac Joslin Cox, Arthur Preston Whitaker, and the general's twentieth-century namesake James Wilkinson have studied the matter. Isaac Joslin Cox, "The Pan-American Policy of Jefferson and Wilkinson," *Mississippi Valley Historical Review*, I (1914), 212–239, and "The Louisiana-Texas Frontier during the Burr Conspiracy," *Mississippi Valley Historical Review*, X (1923), 274–284. James Wilkinson, "General James Wilkinson," *Louisiana Historical Quarterly*, I (1917), 79–166. A. P. Whitaker, "Spanish Intrigue in the Old Southwest: An Episode, 1788–89," *Mississippi Valley Historical Review*, XII (1925), 155–176. Thomas Robson Hay, "Some Reflections on the Career of General James Wilkinson," *Mississippi Valley Historical Review*, XXI (1935), 471–494, and "General James Wilkinson—the Last Phase," *Louisiana Historical Quarterly*, XIX (1936), 407–435.

Two Spanish historians, José Navarro Latorre and Fernando Solano Costa, co-authored *¿Conspiración española?* (Zaragoza, 1949), in which they play down Spain's role in the frontier plotting.

The military has formed the subject of two books. By land Jack D. L. Holmes in *Honor and Fidelity* reported on *The Louisiana Infantry Regiment and the Louisiana Militia Companies, 1766–1821* (Birmingham, 1965). By water Abraham P. Nasatir covered *Spanish War Vessels on the Mississippi, 1792–1796* (New Haven, 1968).

Spain's Mississippi Valley role in the American Revolution was of particular interest to James Alton James, who published three studies between 1917 and 1932: "Spanish Influence in the West during the American Revolution," *Mississippi Valley Historical Review*, IV (1917), 193–208; "Oliver Pollock, Financier of the Revolution in the West," *Mississippi Valley Historical Review*, XVI (1929), 67–80; "Oliver Pollock and the Free Navigation of the Mississippi River," *Mississippi Valley Historical Review*, XIX (1932), 331–347.

I consider West Florida operations as extraneous to the topic of this volume.

As early as 1898 Frederick Jackson Turner wrote about "The Origin of Genêt's Projected Attack on Louisiana and the Floridas," *American Historical Review*, III (1898), 650–671. Again in 1905 Turner took up the topic with "The Policy of France toward the Mississippi Valley in the period of Washington and Adams," *American Historical Review*, X (1905), 249–279. In this article as well as in the 1898 Genêt article Turner rings a tone of expansionism and imperialism. Since that time France's influence and interest in Spanish colonial Louisiana have merited the attention of several serious articles:

"Correspondence of the Comte de Moustier with the Comte de Montmorin, 1787–1789," *American Historical Review*, VIII (1903), 709–733.

"George Rogers Clarke['s Letter] to Genêt, [Louisville, April 28,] 1794," *American Historical Review*, XVIII (1913), 780–783.

"Letter of Thomas Paine re George Rogers Clarke's Plan to Revolutionize Louisiana in 1792," *American Historical Review*, XXIX (1924), 501–505.

E. Merton Coulter, "The Efforts of the Democratic Societies of the West to Open the Navigation of the Mississippi," *Mississippi Valley Historical Review*, XI (1924), 376–389.

Mildred S. Fletcher, "Louisiana as a Factor in French Diplomacy from 1763 to 1800," *Mississippi Valley Historical Review*, XVII (1930), 367–376.

Louise P. Kellogg, "France and the Mississippi Valley: A Résumé," *Mississippi Valley Historical Review*, XVIII (1931), 3–22.

A. P. Whitaker, "Spain and the Retrocession of Louisiana," *American Historical Review*, XXXIX (1934), 454–476.

Allan Christelow, "Proposals for a French Company for Spanish Louisiana, 1763–1764," *Mississippi Valley Historical Review*, XXVII (1941), 603–611.

Ernest Liljegren showed interest in this field and wrote of "Jacobinism in Spanish Louisiana," *Louisiana Historical Quarterly*, XXII (1939), 47–97, as well as of "French Education in Spanish Louisiana," *Missouri Historical Review*, XXXV (1941), 345–372. Strangely, after 1941 interest disappeared in this fascinating feature of late eighteenth-century Louisiana.

The First New Orleans Theatre 1792–1803 was carefully studied by René J. Le Gardeur, Jr. (New Orleans, 1963). Although 1809 was the year of the first performance of Paul Louis Le Blanc de Villeneufve's play, colonial Louisiana was its seedbed; Mathé Allain researched the author and his work for her translation of *The Festival of the Young Corn, or the Heroism of Poucha-Houmma by Le Blanc de Villeneufve* (Lafayette, La., 1964).

The process whereby Spain obtained Louisiana in 1762–63 was minutely treated by Arthur S. Aiton in "The Diplomacy of the Louisiana Cession," *American Historical Review*, XXXVI (1931), 701–720. And "Spain's [lingering] Farewell to Louisiana 1803–1821" was narrated by Philip C. Brooks in *Mississippi Valley Historical Review*, XXVII (1940), 29–42.

So they came, and so they went, these Spanish of the Mississippi Valley. This is as far as historians in their published works have gone in describing and analyzing their presence and accomplishments. What conclusions might one draw on opportunities for study?

To begin with, in all of the categories reviewed above in this paper, there is room for revision of work done a few decades ago when original sources were not as readily available through travel or through microfilm. I have been disappointed by a number of generalizations in this literature that seem quite unfounded; for example, a snap judgment on a given official that sounds as if the historian were in an electoral campaign against him. Another example—the acceptance of a Parisian press story on the origin of the New Orleans fire of 1788, printed long after the fire—points to the need for a more critical use of sources.

Then there is a dearth of studies on down-to-earth real life. Minter

Wood attempted such a work, but drew on secondary general historical sources: "Life in New Orleans in the Spanish Period," *Louisiana Historical Quarterly*, XXII (1939), 642–709. After reading of boundaries and governors and diplomacy and dioceses, what can we learn of the people's way of life—in the fashion of John Bach McMaster?

In this era of black studies one awaits fuller treatment of the black Louisianian who could be a militiaman in 1790—but not fifty or a hundred years later.

In this era when "quantitative history" is in vogue, some scholars must dig out the numerical data available in the archives on population density, taxes, trade, life expectancy, meteorology.

Where are the biographical studies of Unzaga, Carondelet, Salcedo, Casa Calvo? Of second-echelon key figures like Martín Navarro or Juan Ventura Morales? Of mysterious personalities like Padre Antonio de Sedella? Some Namier-style study of Spanish Louisiana should be very revealing.

There is need for a descriptive analysis of the functioning of the governmental machinery. What precisely in Louisiana did this and that official do?

The cartography of Spanish Louisiana should attract some enterprising researchers. One student, I know, is pursuing the history of maps of the Mississippi River.

To encourage aspiring scholars and to complete this survey of the state of studies, let me conclude with information on the archival catalogs that are available. These indispensable tools have been provided over the years: William R. Shepherd, *Guide to the Materials for the History of the United States in Spanish Archives (Simancas, the Archivo Histórico Nacional, and Seville)* (Washington, 1907). James Alexander Robertson, *List of Documents in Spanish Archives Relating to the History of the United States, Which Have Been Printed or of Which Transcripts Are Preserved in American Libraries* (Washington, 1910). Roscoe R. Hill, *Descriptive Catalogue of the Documents Relating to the History of the United States in the Papeles Procedentes de Cuba Deposited in the Archivo General de Indias at Seville* (Washington, 1916). Julian Paz, *Catálogo de manuscritos de América existentes en la Biblioteca Nacional* (Madrid, 1933). Jesús Dominguez Bordona, *Manuscritos de América* (Madrid, 1935). Miguel Gómez del Campillo, *Relaciones diplomáticas entre España y los Estados Unidos según los documentos del Archivo Histórico Nacional* (2 vols., Madrid, 1944–46). Cristóbal Bermúdez Plata, *Catálogo de documentos de la sección novena del Archivo General de Indias*, vol. I, ser. 1 and 2: *Santo Domingo,*

Cuba, Puerto Rico, Luisiana, Florida y Mexico (Seville, 1949). José
Tudela de la Orden, *Los manuscritos de América en las bibliotecas de
España* (Madrid, 1954).

Let me mention in detail the latest such catalog and the latest work to
enter this state-of-the-studies address. Fr. Ernest J. Burrus, D. José
de la Peña, Srta. María Teresa García, and *su servidor* have collaborated
in preparing a catalog of the Louisiana papers in the *Audiencia de Santo
Domingo* subsection of the *Gobierno* section (fifth) of the Archivo
General de Indias: *Catálogo de documentos del Archivo General de
Indias (Sección V, Gobierno. Audiencia de Santo Domingo) sobre la
epoca española de Luisiana* (2 vols., Madrid and New Orleans, 1969). It
is a descriptive catalog that introduces the researcher into a mass of
about 140,000 pages of manuscript sources in 148 *legajos*. Part I utilizes
two kinds of description: when presenting an official's correspondence,
it lists sender, addressee, and the earliest and latest dates; when presenting a packet of material on a given case or problem, it lists topic and
date. Part II contains *indices de remisión*. We have let the sender give
résumés of his own correspondence! Through these résumés one can
quickly survey a long series of correspondence in order to plunge in at
the particular point desired. A microfilm copy of these documents is
available in the Loyola University Library. In New Orleans no copies
can be made; however, one can quickly obtain them from Seville.

After receiving reviewers' opinions on techniques we have utilized,
Loyola University intends to continue its cooperation with Spanish
archivists in cataloging the immense documentary treasures of Spanish
colonial Louisiana.

The conference from which this volume grew is a sign of broad
interest in the Spanish period of the Mississippi Valley, and has provided
an apt forum to review the historiography of this period-area. In conclud-
ing this state-of-the-studies report, I voice the hope that this volume
and the above-mentioned publications of the 1960s will be part not of a
quick spurt but rather of a continuing flow—like the Great River itself.

Resources in Louisiana Depositories

for the Study

of Spanish Activities in Louisiana

A. OTIS HÉBERT, JR.

$\mathcal{L}$OUISIANA's history is richer than that of many other states in the Union. It has been under ten flags; yet its past is less well known than that of most of the states. At least a partial explanation of this anomaly is the fact that Louisiana, until very recently, has neglected the preservation of its early records. If a scholar wanted to study Louisiana's colonial period, it was almost imperative for him to travel to France or Spain in order to search original documents. Official concern has at best been sporadic. Charles E. A. Gayarré, the noted Louisiana historian who became secretary of state in 1846, made the first active effort to organize and bring together the state's colonial and territorial archives. Much of his fine work, however, was lost after he left the secretary of state's office in 1852. In the 1880s the state's colonial records were placed in the custody of the Louisiana Historical Society. After the establishment of the Louisiana State Museum in the early 1900s, that organization was given the Louisiana records. During the curatorship of Robert Glenk, despite meager appropriations, progress was made in cleaning, repairing, cataloging, and preserving these valuable chronicles of Louisiana's past. Later, unfortunately, the documents fell into a condition as bad as that of the historic old Cabildo building in which they were housed. The result was that many wasted away, fell into the hands of "interested parties" or curiosity seekers, or otherwise deteriorated.[1]

It was 1956 before Louisiana created an official state archival agency, and for twenty-two months the department had no money with which to operate. When the State Archives and Records Service did obtain money in 1958, it had no home. For over a year it was housed in the hallway of the sub-basement of the Louisiana State Capitol. Needless to say, the department had no space to store records, and thus it served only as an agency for state departments which wanted their records microfilmed and had the necessary funds to pay for this service. In 1959 the department found shelter in the old Peabody Hall behind the Louisiana State Library. Its home, at first, was the hallway of the first floor of this building, dating prior to 1900, which had been condemned by the state fire marshal as a fire trap. Later, one-half of the second floor of Old Peabody was obtained and the State Archives and Records Service was able to begin to accumulate some records depicting Louisiana's rich and fabulous past. In 1967 the Archives and Records Service acquired as its home a building approximately two miles from the State Capitol. Formerly a hardware store, this building serves well as a low-cost records center and will have to satisfy the needs of an archival building until one can be built.[2]

The point was well taken by my good friend Winston DeVille at the conference on "The French in the Mississippi Valley" here in St. Louis in 1964. In discussing "Manuscript Sources in Louisiana for the History of the French in the Mississippi Valley," he observed that Louisiana's colonial records, although essential to researchers in French colonial history, were among the least studied. "In most cases," he commented, "their pages were last read over two centuries ago by the men who

[1] For a detailed account of the development of Louisiana archives see A. Otis Hébert, Jr., "Keeping Louisiana's Records," *McNeese Review*, XVIII (1967), 27–38. See also Edwin A. Davis, "Archival Development in the Lower Mississippi Valley," *American Archivist*, IV (1940), 44; John C. L. Andreassen and Edwin A. Davis, *Louisiana Archives Survey Report No. 1: Survey of Public Records* ([Baton Rouge], 1956); and John C. L. Andreassen and Edwin A. Davis, *Louisiana Archives Survey Report No. 2: Finding and Recommendations* ([Baton Rouge], 1956).

[2] State of Louisiana, *Acts 1956* (Baton Rouge, 1956), Act 337, pp. 689–696; Hébert, "Keeping Louisiana's Records," 33–36; Minutes, State Archives and Records Commission, Feb. 20, 1957, Mar. 7, July 12, Nov. 12, 1958, Mar. 30, 1960, Nov. 3, Dec. 1, 1966, Jan. 19, 1967; Minutes, Board of Liquidation of State Debt, Nov. 2, 1966; John C. L. Andreassen, *First Report of the State Archives and Records Commission* ([Baton Rouge], 1959); Andreassen, *Second Report of the State Archives and Records Commission* ([Baton Rouge], 1960); John E. Regard, *Biennial Report of the Louisiana Archives and Records* ([Baton Rouge], 1962).

wrote them."[3] To say the same of those records dealing with the Spanish domination of Louisiana would not be an exaggeration.

Now that I have given the background for the lack of study of Louisiana's colonial records, let us turn our attention to those records that do exist for the years of Spain's domination of Louisiana, 1762–1803. But first a word of explanation is in order. Although Spain officially was given Louisiana in 1762, the colony remained French in every way except governmentally. The French language continued to be spoken and in fact was the dominant language throughout the Spanish period. It is no wonder then that many records dealing with Spanish Louisiana are written in French.

Perhaps the most valuable group of records dealing with Spanish Louisiana are the Spanish Judicial Records. These papers are part of a larger group commonly known as the "Cabildo Records." The cabildo documents total over 15,000 pieces; approximately 4,400 of them form the Spanish Judicial Records. These records, in the custody of the Louisiana State Museum, are housed in a fireproof, temperature- and humidity-controlled vault in the recently renovated Presbytère, 751 Chartres Street, New Orleans (opposite Jackson Square). Unfortunately they are not available to researchers at this time. The reason for this fact is the sad condition of these extremely valuable records. A beginning has been made in restoring them so that they can be preserved for future generations of scholars. But the task is a slow and tedious one, as well as costly. In some cases there are as many as ten or twelve layers of scotch tape to be removed. Then needed repairs must be made. The next step is the microfilming of these valuable chronicles. The Louisiana State Museum has made application to the federal government for a grant to carry the program to fruition, but so far no federal money has been forthcoming. The work of rehabilitation and microfilming will be done by the State Archives and Records Service.[4]

A calendar of the Spanish Judicial Records to August 9, 1785, prepared by Laura L. Porteus, appeared in the *Louisiana Historical Quarterly*, volumes VI–XXXI. Each entry contains the date, identification of the case, number of pages in the document, a brief abstract of the case, and, in some instances, marginal notes pointing out what procedure is illustrated, and whether the case illustrates anything unusual. The

---

[3] Winston DeVille, "Manuscript Sources in Louisiana for the History of the French in the Mississippi Valley," in John Francis McDermott, ed., *The French in the Mississippi Valley* (Urbana, Ill., 1965), 217.

[4] Hébert, "Keeping Louisiana's Records," 29–30; DeVille, "Manuscript Sources in Louisiana," 218–220.

usefulness of this guide is impaired since the index to the *Louisiana Historical Quarterly*, published in 1956, does not include the Spanish Judicial Records.[5]

When Alexandro O'Reilly took physical possession of Louisiana for the Spanish monarch on August 18, 1769, the French Superior Council, which functioned right up to the moment of O'Reilly's arrival, ceased to exist as an institution of government. A blank occurs in the colonial judicial records of Louisiana until September 18, 1769, when Bartholomew Robert, carpenter, petitioned "His Excellency Señor O'Reilly, Captain and Governor General of the Province of Louisiana," for leave to open his (Robert's) wife's succession. Governor O'Reilly ordered Joseph Ducros and Jean B. Garic to act for him, and to them he referred the petitioner's case for action. This rule of procedure was followed until the reorganization of the judiciary in November, 1769.[6]

The first paper in the archives after O'Reilly's arrival is the original oath of allegiance to the Spanish government of the inhabitants of Pointe Coupee and False River on September 10, 1769. This is also the first document found in the calendar in the *Louisiana Historical Quarterly*. Other documents include a number of original notarial acts that were found among the court records. Some of these acts were sewed together in paper covers and evidently had been overlooked when, years before, the other French and Spanish notarial acts of the colonial period were bound and turned over to the custodian of notarial records in the new courthouse in New Orelans.[7]

A more complete guide to the original records is available in the so-called "Black Books," ninety-four small ring binders, located in the Louisiana State Museum Library opposite the Presbytère. The entries are essentially the same as the calendar in the *Louisiana Historical Quarterly*. A typical entry includes document number, date, document title, and a two- or three-line description. The principal parties in the document appear in capital letters and those who signed are listed last. If the document was listed in the *Louisiana Historical Quarterly* calendar, that fact is stated. These "Black Books" have been printed in *New Orleans Genesis*, the publication of the Genealogical Research Society of New Orleans.[8] For reasons unknown not every document summarized in the

[5] *Louisiana Historical Quarterly*, VI (1923)–XXXI (1949); DeVille, "Manuscript Sources in Louisiana," 220.

[6] "Index to the Spanish Judicial Records of Louisiana," *Louisiana Historical Quarterly*, VI (1923), 145.

[7] *Ibid.*; DeVille, "Manuscript Sources in Louisiana," 217–218.

[8] *New Orleans Genesis*, VI (1967)–VIII (1970); DeVille, "Manuscript Sources in Louisiana," 220–221.

"Black Books" was published in the *Louisiana Historical Quarterly*.

Other legal records of importance are safeguarded in the New Orleans Notarial Archives, now in the civil courts building in the new civic center. Although many such documents have not survived, one can find here sixteen volumes of the papers of Andrés Almonester (1770–82), a portion of the records drawn up by J. B. Garic in 1766, 1767, and 1779, as well as the files of Charles J. Maison for 1766–69.

The Louisiana State Museum Library contains many Works Progress Administration typescripts, translations, and copies of early documents pertaining to Louisiana's past as a colony of Spain. Notable among these are typescript translations of twenty-five volumes of dispatches of the governors of Spanish Louisiana to their superiors made from photostats of the originals of Seville and of eleven volumes of the dispatches of the Baron de Carondelet.

An extremely valuable collection, initiated in 1961 by Loyola University of New Orleans, will be devoted to the reproduction of material from the relatively unknown section of the Audiencia de Santo Domingo pertaining to the Spanish epoch in Louisiana. I shall not dwell on the project, since the Reverend Charles O'Neill, S.J., is describing it in his contribution to this volume.[9] Here I should add also a reference to another project of the future: the University of Southwestern Louisiana, under the direction of Mr. Glenn R. Conrad, director of archives, plans to microfilm all material in the Archivo General de Indias at Seville (described in Roscoe R. Hill's *Calendar*) that concerns eighteenth-century Louisiana.

The New Orleans Public Library, officially designated as the archives depository of the city of New Orleans, possesses many documents of the period of Spain's domination of Louisiana. Here are the city council records and deliberations of the cabildo from August 18, 1769, to November 18, 1803, in ten bound books, some of them in the original handwritten state. Two volumes of petitions, decrees, and letters of the cabildo, 1770–99, are also found in the Louisiana Room of the New Orleans Public Library. Among other Spanish Louisiana documents in this depository are: one volume of miscellaneous Spanish records; the succession of Gilberto Antonio de St. Maxent; notarial books of Carlos Ximenes (1768–70); various court cases (1795–1808); a volume of documents and letters of Pierre-Clément de Laussat (November 30,

---

[9] A descriptive catalog published jointly by Loyola University of New Orleans and the Spanish Archives Administration, *Catálogo de documentos del Archivo General de Indias (Sección V, Gobierno. Audiencia de Santo Domingo) sobre la epoca española de Luisiana*, is available from the Spanish Documents Project, Loyola University, New Orleans.

1803–March 31, 1804).[10] A program to put these documents on micro-film has been instituted with the aid of the State Archives and Records Service.

The Special Collections Division of the Howard-Tilton Memorial Library, Tulane University, contains a number of collections and private papers dealing with the Spanish period of Louisiana history. The Favrot Family Papers (1695–1935), consisting of 2,005 pieces, contain letters from Carlos de Grand Pré, Juan Ventura Morales, Armesto y López, José de Gálvez, Bernardo de Gálvez, Baron de Carondelet, Chevalier de Kerlérec, Alexander McGillivray, and other prominent figures of colonial Louisiana. Eight volumes of transcriptions of these papers, prepared by the Louisiana Historical Records Survey of the W.P.A., were published in 1941 and 1942 (volumes I–VII and IX). The work was later resumed by the Howard-Tilton Memorial Library. Volume VIII was published in 1961, and volumes X, XI, and XII, carrying the project through 1815, have been published and are available through the library's Special Collections Division. The Rosemonde E. and Emile Kuntz Collection (1655–1878) consists of some 420 French and Spanish manuscripts dealing with the families of Bouligny, Dauterive, Maison Rouge, de Villemont, Villars, and de Grand Pré, the government of New Orleans and Louisiana, and the revolution of 1768.

Other collections at Tulane dealing with family groups of the Spanish period include the Chesnier-Duchesne-Smith family, 1780–1892 (151 pieces); the De la Vigne family, 1797–1840 (69 pieces); the Grima family, 1783–1931 (1,320 pieces); the Augustine D. Tureaud family, 1754–1955 (37 pieces); the Hébert-Kirkland family, 1793–1881 (113 pieces); the Peters-LeMonnier-Lastrapes family, 1711–1933 (700 pieces); the Charest-DeGournay-DuBourg family, 1715–1952 (159 pieces); the Bringier family, 1771–1942 (501 pieces).

Papers of individuals include those of Joseph Lakanal, educator, 1793–95 (30 pieces); Marie Drivin Girard, teacher and writer, 1777–1902 (61 pieces); John McDonogh, merchant and philanthropist, 1802–73 (6,950 pieces); Father Antonio de Sedella, priest, 1798–1807 (6 volumes); Prosper Foy, St. Charles planter, 1790–1878 (196 pieces); Julien Poydras, Pointe Coupee planter, 1792–1822 (3 pieces and 2 volumes).

[10] In surveying the archives in the New Orleans Public Library, I found many documents still unclassified. It is felt that some of these most certainly go back to the Spanish period of Louisiana history; for example, ship lists and registers. It was pleasing, however, to find that these records are being classified as rapidly as possible.

Papers of persons prominent in government during the period of Spanish domination include those of Francisco Bouligny (Bouligny-Baldwin Papers), 1710–1863 (167 pieces); Baron de Carondelet, 1793–97 (85 pieces); Marqués de Casa Calvo, 1800–1803 (10 pieces); Bernardo de Gálvez, 1779–81 (17 pieces); Manuel Gayoso de Lemos, 1797–99 (10 pieces); Esteban Miró, 1779–91 (32 pieces); Pierre-Clément de Laussat, 1803–04 (19 pieces); W. C. C. Claiborne, 1800–1818 (20 pieces).[11]

In the capital city of Baton Rouge, the State Archives and Records Service has collections which are invaluable to the scholar studying the Spanish domination of Louisiana. Among them are the colonial documents of Avoyelles, dating from 1786, which consist of some 430 items. The records cover land grants, land sales, slave sales, marriage contracts, concessions, wills, and even a petition for legal separation. These documents have been cataloged and a calendar is available at $1.75. The catalog contains an index, but the number of pages in each document is omitted. Although all records date from the Spanish period, 97 percent are written in French. The remaining 3 percent are in Spanish. Corinne Saucier has abstracted the Avoyelles colonial records in her *History of Avoyelles Parish, Louisiana* (1943). A comparison of the two lists reveals that from 1943 until 1961, when the original documents were transferred to the State Archives, many were lost.[12]

Clerk of Court Gradney Couvillion, in commenting on why he consented to being the first in Louisiana to agree to transfer his colonial records to the State Archives, said many old records of Avoyelles Parish had been lost when the clerk of court's office had been moved from the old courthouse to the present building and then later from the second to the ground floor. Realizing that eventually all records could be lost, he wanted to preserve his parish's part in Louisiana's written heritage.[13]

St. Landry Parish colonial records, dating from 1764, also were transferred to the State Archives in 1961. In all there are approximately twenty-five linear feet of records and twelve bound volumes. Those

[11] For detailed descriptions of the holdings of the Special Collections Division, Howard-Tilton Memorial Library, Tulane University, see Connie G. Griffith, "Collections in the Manuscript Sections of Howard-Tilton Memorial Library, Tulane University," *Louisiana History*, I (Fall, 1960), 320–327.

[12] Winston DeVille, *Calendar of Louisiana Colonial Documents*, vol. 1: *Avoyelles Parish* ([Baton Rouge]: State Archives and Records Commission, 1961), 50 pp.; Corinne Saucier, *History of Avoyelles Parish, Louisiana* (New Orleans, 1943), 542 pp.

[13] Baton Rouge *Morning Advocate*, Dec. 9, 1961; Marksville *Weekly Press*, Dec. 14, 1961.

documents covering the years 1764–85, consisting of 457 items, have been calendared. The calendar (now out of print) is an improvement over that of Avoyelles in that it contains the number of pages in the document, but it suffers from the lack of an index.[14] The documents from 1786–89 are in the process of being calendared. Those after 1789 have been arranged and are waiting their turn.

Microfilm copies of the St. Charles Parish colonial records, dating as early as 1734 in the French period, are also in the State Archives. The documents up to 1769, the D'Arensbourg Records, have been cataloged. The fifty-one-page catalog (available at $2.00) covers 181 items and is much superior to the other two calendars in that the documents have been abstracted in much greater detail. Each decipherable name mentioned appears in the abstract. Likewise, the comprehensive index includes each name with a clear indication of the multiple variants under which it appears. Microfilm copies of these documents are available through the office of the St. Charles Parish clerk of court.[15]

Recently transferred into the State Archives and Records Service are the records of East Feliciana Parish and some 900,000 items from nineteen state departments which were formerly in the Louisiana State University Department of Archives and Manuscripts. Created by legislative act in 1936, the LSU Archives was authorized to "receive and collect public records or documents and materials bearing upon the history of the state." The act further provided that state, parish, and other officials could turn over to the LSU Archives for preservation "any books, records, documents, newspaper files, original papers, or manuscripts not in current use in their offices."[16] As the number of manuscript collections increased, these state and parish records were housed in the old Hill Memorial Library building, where they were not available to scholars. For this reason and also because it was realized that all archives of the state should be under one agency, if possible, an agreement was made between the LSU Department of Archives and the State Archives and Records Service whereby all state and parish archives were transferred to the State Archives. The records of East Feliciana are presently being cleaned and put in order preparatory to being microfilmed.

[14] Winston DeVille, *Calendar of Louisiana Colonial Documents*, vol. II: *St. Landry Parish* ([Baton Rouge]: Louisiana State Archives and Records Commission, 1964), 33 pp.

[15] Elizabeth Becker Gianelloni, *Calendar of Louisiana Colonial Documents*, vol. III: *St. Charles Parish, Part One: The D'Arensbourg Records, 1734–1769* ([Baton Rouge]: Louisiana State Archives and Records Commission, n.d.), 51 pp.

[16] State of Louisiana, *Acts 1936* ([Baton Rouge], 1936), Act 258, pp. 669–670.

Other parishes retain custody of their colonial records in the local courthouses.[17] The State Archives and Records Service is cooperating with these fourteen parishes in preserving these valuable documents and making them available to the public. In most of the parishes the records are in good shape, well cataloged, and readily accessible. Why are not all these chronicles transferred to the State Archives and Records Service? The Archives at the present time is not equipped or staffed to handle all of them. Furthermore, some local clerks of court have gone to great expense with their records and are now reaping some returns by making copies available to interested persons. And in some cases interested local residents and groups are strongly opposed to permitting the removal of their records to Baton Rouge. Presently negotiations are under way with two parishes, and it is to be hoped that shortly their records will be transferred to the State Archives. Microfilm copies will, of course, be made available to the local parish.

The LSU Department of Archives and Manuscripts still contains numerous collections dealing with Spanish Louisiana. The Carondelet Papers (1791–1819) include ten letters of Francisco Luis Héctor, Baron de Carondelet; sixteen rules of commerce by Carondelet and Andrés López de Armesto, governing the trade of the Spanish colonies; a farmer's claim against the government for land used in making a canal in 1791; and documents relating to the boundary between the districts of Avoyelles and Rapides.

The Gayoso de Lemos Papers (1797–99) consist of only three pieces, but are very interesting. One is a letter dated 1797, in Spanish, from Governor Gayoso to Luis DeBlanc, commandant of the German Coast of Louisiana, concerning Bonato Trahan's bequest of one-fifth of his estate to a free Negro, Venus.

The Joseph Vidal Papers (1795–1936) contain 768 pieces. They include the business and legal papers of José Vidal, secretary to Manuel Gayoso de Lemos, governor of the District of Natchez, 1787–97, and later commandant of the post of Concordia, Louisiana. The early part of the collection embodies a number of documents in Spanish concerning land grants, transfers, and surveys issued by the Spaniards during the last years of the eighteenth century.

The Felipe E. N. Bastrop Collection (1796–1819) contains thirty-five

[17] Parishes still retaining custody of records locally that date to the period of Spanish Louisiana are: Assumption (1781), East Baton Rouge (1782), Iberville (1770), Lafayette (1799), Lafourche (1796), Natchitoches (1716), Ouachita (1785), Plaquemines (1792), Pointe Coupee (1762), St. Bernard (1788), St. James (1782), St. John the Baptist (1753), St. Martin (1760), and West Feliciana (1787).

different items. The letters and papers pertain to the land grants of the Baron de Bastrop and others in the Ouachita River valley of Louisiana. The collection includes ten letters exchanged by Bastrop and Carondelet, 1796–97, concerning land grants in the Ouachita River basin. The collection also includes a plat of Bastrop's land grant from the Spanish government.

Other collections of private papers also deal with the years of Spanish domination of Louisiana. The Meullion Family Papers (1776–1906) are the papers of a Louisiana free Negro family (121 pieces). Included are manumission papers in Spanish issued in 1776 by Luis Augustín Meullion to María Juana and her son. There are also land deeds dated 1786 and 1796.

The William J. Minor and Family Collection (1748–1898), consisting of 409 pieces and 38 volumes, contains papers of Stephen Minor, a military leader during the Spanish rule and also first president of the Bank of Mississippi.

The Charles E. A. Gayarré Collection (588 pieces and 5 volumes) contains the legal, business, literary, and personal papers (1720–1895) of the Louisiana historian, jurist, and statesman. Among the papers are genealogical data on the Gayarré, DeBoré, and de Grand Pré families.

The John McCarty and Family Papers (1764–1935) contain a forty-page inventory, dated 1764, describing the family residence on Conti Street. Here is a description of the house furnishings, linen, and silver; French and Spanish coins; and letters of credit and exchange with M. Bureau and M. Goquet of La Rochelle, France. In a series of four French documents, Mme Françoise Trepanier Macarty, widow of Jean Macarty, and Jean Trudeau were appointed natural tutor and subjugate tutor, respectively, of the minor daughters of the deceased.

The John Walker Papers (1769), consisting of three pieces, include a British land grant and a certificate for a tract near Pointe Coupee. A plat of the land is enclosed.[18]

One other archival depository in Baton Rouge remains—the Department of History and Archives of the Catholic Diocese of Baton Rouge. The Diocese of Baton Rouge, created November 8, 1961, is the most recently established diocese from the historic Province of New Orleans.

[18] For detailed descriptions of the holdings of the Department of Archives and Manuscripts, Louisiana State University, see William Ranson Hogan, ed., *Guide to Manuscript Collections in Louisiana*, vol. I: *The Department of Archives, Louisiana State University* (University, La., 1940), and V. L. Bedsole, "Collections in the Department of Archives and Manuscripts, Louisiana State University," *Louisiana History*, I (Fall, 1960), 328–334.

The first church in what is now the Diocese of Baton Rouge was St. Francis of Pointe Coupee, built in 1738, but the religious history of the area commences in 1722, when it was served, along with other French river posts, by the Capuchin father Philibert de Viauden. Shortly after his installation as ordinary of the diocese, Bishop Robert E. Tracy, acting upon the advice of a group of Catholic Louisiana historians, established the Department of History and Archives. Dr. Elisabeth Joan Doyle, then a professor of history at Southeastern Louisiana College, Hammond, was employed as archivist on a part-time basis.

A thorough inventory was made of all the records held in the parishes founded before 1870. Following this, Bishop Tracy called in all church records which antedated this date. Those in need of repair were sent to an expert in such work and have now been so treated that it is estimated they will survive for many years more, since they are stored in a temperature- and humidity-controlled vault. In all, over 200 items—birth, marriage, and death records—are now stored in the vault. *A Guide to Archival Materials* deals with the records and provides a descriptive catalog of the items held by the department. In addition, the department has an impressive group of records brought to Louisiana by the Acadians. The records of the parish church of St. Charles-aux-Mines at Grand Pré, dating back to 1707, and carefully nursed by the parishioners through their long journey from Canada, survive because of the keen interest and historic foresight of Bishop Tracy. A list of the parish churches and the date of the earliest record follows:

> St. Joseph Cathedral, Baton Rouge, 1793
> St. John the Baptist, Brusly, 1840
> St. Michael's, Convent, 1808
> Ascension Church, Donaldsonville, 1772
> St. Philomena, Labadieville, 1848
> Immaculate Conception, Lakeland, 1861
> St. Francis of Pointe Coupee, New Roads, 1728
> St. Elizabeth, Paincourtville, 1839
> St. John the Evangelist, Plaquemine, 1845
> Assumption Church, Plattenville, 1793
> St. Gabriel, St. Gabriel, 1773
> St. James, St. James, 1757
> Our Lady of Peace, Vacherie, 1864
> (Chapel of Notre Dame, 1856)[19]

[19] Elisabeth Joan Doyle, *A Guide to Archival Materials Held by the Catholic Diocese of Baton Rouge Department of History and Archives* (Baton Rouge: Department of History and Archives, Diocese of Baton Rouge), 70 pp.

A considerable amount of personal and private papers are still retained by individuals throughout the state of Louisiana. The archival and manuscript depositories in the state are actively engaged in collecting these for preservation and use by scholars. Other libraries and public institutions, besides those mentioned in this paper, especially the libraries of universities and colleges, are today collecting archival material and manuscripts dealing with Louisiana. With this reawakening to the value of archives in Louisiana, fewer and fewer materials are slipping out of the state to depositories in Texas, California, or North Carolina or are falling prey to fire, wind, dust, fowls, vermin, and insects.

The Mexican Archives and the
Historiography of the Mississippi Valley
in the Spanish Period[1]

———— ◆ ————

C. HARVEY GARDINER

*T*HE flow of both man and river suggests a natural and persistent relationship between Mexico and the Mississippi Valley. However, in a given interval of time history introduces more variables than does a given geographic setting. Man and his activities frequently defy, even nullify, the pull of the contiguous. Put quite simply, the Mexican factor in the history of the Mississippi Valley is not what at first it might appear to be. By extension then, as we explore the Valley historiographically, we are led to wonder whether the Mexican archival factor is a promise unfulfilled.

Three powers, Spain, France, and England, moved into the Valley. Spain came from the southwest and south, France from the north and northeast, England from the east. Some would add to their varying timetables and individual directions fundamentally different motives. Be that as it may, neither restatement nor reinterpretation of those historical chapters is the issue at hand. Ours is rather the recognition that the three centuries, the sixteenth, seventeenth, and eighteenth, that rooted three

[1] Research in Mexico during the summer of 1967 was made possible by Grant 4566 of the Penrose Fund of the American Philosophical Society. That assistance is gratefully acknowledged.

empires in the Valley guaranteed at least a three-way dispersal of pertinent records.

And yet the approach to the historiography of the Valley is not that simple. Whereas considerable unity of place attends the student's effort to get at French archives, such is not the case with the English and Spanish manuscripts. As an independent heir of the British and as possessor of the Valley in nineteenth- and twentieth-century years, the United States is herself a primary focus. But it is left to the first Europeans in the Valley to present the widest dispersal, and simultaneously the greatest confusion and availability, of its relevant records. Anyone aware of the pattern of Spanish imperial administration, aware of the insistence of Spanish bureaucracy upon numerous copies of various kinds of documents, aware of the hit-and-miss routing and delivery of records, aware of the faulty handling by so-called archivists of those papers that escaped wind, water, enemy, insect, and all else, aware of the numerous regulations concerning the documentary spheres of interest of repositories in widely separated parts of Spain—anyone aware of this multiplicity of obstacles between researcher and record is desirous of guidance.

Without guidance precursor Charles Gayarré[2] and a few others had turned their hands to Valley history in nineteenth-century years, but the wave of significant research and publication came only in the wake of certain twentieth-century trailblazers, men who eased the way to the archives. Many things, in happy combination as this century dawned, led to the historians' increased awareness of archives. Along with our coming of age as a world power, the founding of regional and national historical societies, and the expansion of graduate education, one organization, the Carnegie Institution of Washington, brought a sharp focus to bear upon archives.

When William R. Shepherd declared in 1907 that the *Papeles de Cuba* in the Archivo General de Indias in Seville "provide the materials for a detailed study of Louisiana and Florida under Spanish rule,"[3] he established the primacy of that Spanish archive for the telling of the history of Spain in the Mississippi Valley. A related archival perspective was

[2] Preliminary to Charles Etienne Arthur Gayarré's *History of Louisiana: The Spanish Domination* (New York, 1854) was that author's research in Spain; see Henry P. Dart, ed., "Gayarré's Report on Louisiana Archives in Spain," *Louisiana Historical Quarterly*, IV (Oct., 1921), 464–480.

[3] William R. Shepherd, *Guide to the Materials for the History of the United States in Spanish Archives (Simancas, the Archivo Histórico Nacional, and Seville)* (Washington, 1907), 77.

gained in 1913 when Herbert E. Bolton published his guide to the sources in Mexico.[4] The date borne by Bolton's volume eloquently reminds us of obstacles he faced. Yet his guide, as a mammoth, initial effort, is especially noteworthy. At times archival regulations hampered his labors; and on other occasions his own interests predetermined his emphases. However, his report clearly indicated that certain sections of the Archivo General de la Nación, namely *Historia, Provincias Internas,* and *Marina,* were the most promising concerning the Mississippi Valley. Conversely he hazarded the guess that the mammoth section named *Tierras,* counting thousands upon thousands of volumes of manuscripts to which he did not have free access, would offer very little. In addition to concentrating upon the national archive in Mexico City, as most historians have done, with good reason, ever since, Bolton did offer assistance regarding lesser archives south of the border.

In the aggregate Bolton suggested a paucity of materials in Mexico while Shepherd's encouraging words about Seville invited more attention to Spain. The result was Roscoe R. Hill's full-volume treatment of the *Papeles de Cuba,*[5] which, ever since this wider publicity, have been a prime magnet to the historically-minded. So named because of their transfer from Cuba to Spain in 1888–89, the *Papeles de Cuba* count "2375 legajos and about a million and a quarter individual documents." More than one-third of the twenty-three series into which they are divided treat political, military, economic, social, religious, fiscal, and judicial aspects of the history of the Mississippi Valley.[6] The significance and popularity of the *Papeles de Cuba* speedily encouraged a photoduplication program which, in turn, has enabled many individuals who have never set foot inside the famed storehouse in Seville to shed light upon Spanish activity in the Mississippi Valley by recourse to copies in Washington, D.C., New York City, North Carolina, Illinois, Mississippi,

[4] Herbert E. Bolton, *Guide to Materials for the History of the United States in the Principal Archives of Mexico* (Washington, 1913). For a full account of the labor related to this work, see John Francis Bannon, "Herbert Eugene Bolton: His *Guide* in the Making," *Southwestern Historical Quarterly,* LXXIII (July, 1969), 35–55.

[5] Roscoe R. Hill, *Descriptive Catalogue of the Documents Relating to the History of the United States in the Papeles Procedentes de Cuba Deposited in the Archivo General de Indias at Seville* (Washington, 1916).

[6] *Ibid.,* xi–xiii. A terse, recent statement concerning the *Papeles de Cuba* is in E. J. Burrus, "An Introduction to Bibliographical Tools in Spanish Archives and Manuscript Collections Relating to Hispanic America," *Hispanic American Historical Review,* XXXV (Nov., 1955), 458.

Another helpful guide, in reference to the Mississippi Valley in the Spanish period, is Luis Marino Pérez, *Guide to the Materials for American History in Cuban Archives* (Washington, 1907), 76–104.

Missouri, Tennessee, California, Louisiana, Wisconsin, Texas, Florida, and elsewhere.

Meanwhile, in the same opening decades of the century that produced these guides, scholarly research related to the Valley counted a thin line that included Shepherd, Isaac Joslin Cox, Louis Houck, James Alexander Robertson, and Thomas Maitland Marshall.[7] As Cox's doctoral study at Pennsylvania in 1904,[8] with but very slight dependence upon Mexican archives, was possibly the only dissertation of that decade regarding Mississippi Valley history, so that of Marshall at Berkeley in 1914, without recourse to any Mexican archive, was probably the only Valley-related dissertation of the second decade of this century.[9]

During the 1920s, however, historical awareness of the Valley came into full flower. Five men then turned their attention to Spain in the Mississippi Valley for varying portions of the interval between 1762 and 1803. In 1923, at Berkeley, David K. Bjork presented a dissertation entitled "The Establishment of Spanish Rule in the Province of Louisiana,

[7] During the first two decades of this century Shepherd published (a) "Wilkinson and the Beginnings of the Spanish Conspiracy," *American Historical Review*, IX (Apr., 1904), 490–506; (b) "Papers Bearing on James Wilkinson's Relations with Spain, 1787–1789," *ibid.* (July, 1904), 748–766; (c) "The Cession of Louisiana to Spain," *Political Science Quarterly*, XIX (1904), 439–458. All of these studies drew upon Spanish archives; none utilized Mexican archives.

In the same period Isaac Joslin Cox published (a) *The Early Exploration of Louisiana* (Cincinnati, 1906); (b) "The Louisiana–Texas Frontier," *Texas Historical Association Quarterly*, X (July, 1906), 1–75; (c) "The Significance of the Louisiana Frontier," *Mississippi Valley Historical Association Proceedings*, III (1909–10), 198–213; (d) "The Louisiana–Texas Frontier," *Southwestern Historical Quarterly*, XVII (July–Oct., 1913), 1–42, 140–187; (e) "Wilkinson's First Break with the Spaniards," *Ohio Valley Historical Association Report*, VIII (1910–14), 49–61; (f) "General Wilkinson and His Later Intrigues with the Spaniards," *American Historical Review*, XIX (July, 1914), 794–812; (g) "The Pan-American Policy of Jefferson and Wilkinson," *Mississippi Valley Historical Review*, I (Sept., 1914), 212–239; (h) *The West Florida Controversy, 1798–1813* (Baltimore, 1918). For items (a), (d), (f), and (g), Cox used Mexican archival material.

Louis Houck, ed., *The Spanish Régime in Missouri* (2 vols., Chicago, 1909), offered 128 documents, all of which were drawn from Spain.

James Alexander Robertson's publications in this period included (a) *Louisiana under the Rule of Spain, France, and the United States, 1785–1807* (2 vols., Cleveland, 1911); and (b) "Spanish Correspondence Concerning the American Revolution," *Hispanic American Historical Review*, I (Aug., 1918), 299–316. Both items drew heavily upon Spanish archives; neither utilized Mexican archival material.

In this period Thomas Maitland Marshall published *A History of the Western Boundary of the Louisiana Purchase 1819–1841* (Berkeley, 1914), a work which treats a post-Spanish period and indicates no use of Mexican archives.

[8] The dissertation of 1904 bore the same title as the book of 1906, for which see n. 7.

[9] Marshall's dissertation bore the same title as his book of the same year, 1914; see n. 7.

1762–1770."[10] The following year, at Harvard, Arthur P. Whitaker concluded his dissertation, "The Expansion of the Old Southwest, 1783–91." Two years later, in 1926, Abraham P. Nasatir offered his dissertation "Indian Trade and Diplomacy in the Spanish Illinois 1763–1792" to the faculty at Berkeley. At the same institution, in 1928, two more dissertations concerning Valley history emerged, that of Lawrence Kinnaird entitled "American Penetration into Spanish Territory, 1776–1803"[11] and that of John W. Caughey bearing the title "Louisiana under Spain, 1762–1783."[12] For every one of these five doctoral studies the *Papeles de Cuba* were most important but the Mexican archives, unvisited, were unmentioned.

No other decade can match the 1920s in the production of scholars dedicated to long-term immersion in the history of Spain in the Valley. In the 1930s three doctoral dissertations on that general theme, those of Ruth King at Illinois, Max Savelle at Columbia, and P. C. Brooks at Berkeley,[13] exhibited the same patterns of archival use and disuse as had

[10] Bjork's post-doctoral publications related to the Mississippi Valley include (a) "Documents Relating to Alexandro O'Reilly and an Expedition Sent Out by Him from New Orleans to Natchitoches, 1769–1770," *Louisiana Historical Quarterly*, VII (Jan., 1924), 20–39; (b) "Documents Relating to the Establishment of Schools in Louisiana, 1771," *Mississippi Valley Historical Review*, XI (Mar., 1925), 561–569; (c) "Documents Regarding Indian Affairs in the Lower Mississippi Valley, 1771–1772," *ibid.*, XIII (Dec., 1926), 398–410; (d) "Alexander O'Reilly and the Spanish Occupation of Louisiana, 1769–1770," in George P. Hammond, ed., *New Spain and the Anglo-American West* (2 vols., Lancaster, Pa., 1932), I, 165–182.

[11] Kinnaird's post-doctoral publications related to the Mississippi Valley include (a) "International Rivalry in the Creek Country, Part I: The Ascendancy of Alexander McGillivray, 1783–1789," *Florida Historical Society Quarterly*, X (1931), 59–85; (b) "American Penetration into Spanish Louisiana," in Hammond, ed., *New Spain and the Anglo-American West*, I, 211–237; (c) "The Spanish Expedition against Fort St. Joseph in 1781, a New Interpretation," *Mississippi Valley Historical Review*, XIX (Sept., 1932), 173–191; (d) "Clark-Leyba Papers," *American Historical Review*, XLI (Oct., 1935), 92–112; (e) *Spain in the Mississippi Valley, 1765–1794* (3 vols., Washington, 1946–49). No Mexican archival materials are used in any of these works.

[12] Caughey's post-doctoral publications related to the Mississippi Valley include (a) "The Panis Mission to Pensacola, 1778," *Hispanic American Historical Review*, X (Nov., 1930), 480–489; (b) "Willing's Expedition down the Mississippi, 1778," *Louisiana Historical Quarterly*, XV (Jan., 1932), 5–36; (c) "Bernardo de Gálvez and the English Smugglers on the Mississippi, 1777," *Hispanic American Historical Review*, XII (Feb., 1932), 46–58; (d) "Alexander McGillivray and the Creek Crisis, 1783–1784," in Hammond, ed., *New Spain and the Anglo-American West*, I, 263–288; (e) "The Natchez Rebellion of 1781 and Its Aftermath," *Louisiana Historical Quarterly*, XVI (Jan., 1933), 57–83; (f) *Bernardo de Gálvez in Louisiana, 1776–1783* (Berkeley, 1934); (g) *McGillivray of the Creeks* (Norman, 1938). Heavily dependent upon Spanish archives, these works utilize no Mexican archival material.

[13] The three dissertations are: Ruth King, "Social and Economic Life in Spanish Louisiana" (1931); Max Savelle, "George Morgan, Colony Builder" (1932), under which title it was published (New York, 1932); and Philip C. Brooks, "The Adams-Onis

those of the 1920s. In the 1940s academic interest regarding Spain in the Mississippi Valley diminished further,[14] to be revived late in the 1950s by the dissertations of C. Richard Arena at Pennsylvania and Jack D. L. Holmes at Texas, both in 1959.[15]

To three men, persistently published students of Spain in the Valley over a considerable period of time, attention is now drawn in reference to sources employed. Following his dissertation of 1924, and before he shifted his riverine interests to the Plata, Arthur P. Whitaker published, in the course of a dozen years, at least three books and a half-score articles about the Mississippi Valley.[16] No Mexican archival

---

Treaty of 1819 as a Territorial Agreement" (1933), which is the forerunner of *Diplomacy and the Borderlands: The Adams-Onis Treaty of 1819* (Berkeley, 1939).

[14] The dissertations in this decade were Sister Mary A. M. O'Callaghan's "The Indian Policy of Carondelet in Spanish Louisiana, 1792–1797" (University of California, Berkeley, 1942) and John Villasana Haggard's "The Neutral Ground between Louisiana and Texas" (University of Texas, 1942). Related to the first of these dissertations is that author's article "An Indian Removal Policy in Spanish Louisiana," in *Greater America* (Berkeley, 1945), 281–294. In dissertation and article, O'Callaghan's work exhibits no use of Mexican archival material. Haggard's "The Neutral Ground between Louisiana and Texas, 1806–1821," *Louisiana Historical Quarterly*, XXVIII (Oct., 1945), 1001–1128, is essentially the dissertation of 1942. Its only recourse to Mexican archival material, which is slight, is by means of transcripts made by Bolton and Hackett (see pp. 1076–78).

[15] These dissertations were: C. Richard Arena, "Philadelphia–Spanish New Orleans Trade in the 1790's," and Jack D. L. Holmes, "Gallant Emissary: The Political Career of Manuel Gayoso de Lemos in the Mississippi Valley, 1789–1799." Titled the same as his dissertation is Arena's "Philadelphia–Spanish New Orleans Trade in the 1790's," *Louisiana History*, II (Fall, 1961), 429–445, which is unrelated to Mexican archival materials. Related to his dissertation is Jack D. L. Holmes's *Gayoso: The Life of a Spanish Governor in the Mississippi Valley, 1789–1799* (Baton Rouge, 1965), which does employ Mexican archival materials, namely, volumes in the section of *Historia* of the Archivo General de la Nación (Mexico City) and items in the Archivo Histórico de Sonora (Hermosillo).

[16] Whitaker's published writings related to the Mississippi Valley include (a) "Spanish Intrigue in the Old Southwest: An Episode, 1788–89," *Mississippi Valley Historical Review*, XII (Sept., 1925), 155–176; (b) "The Muscle Shoals Speculation, 1783–1789," *ibid.*, XIII (Dec., 1926), 365–386; (c) "Spain and the Cherokee Indians, 1783–98," *North Carolina Historical Review*, IV (July, 1927), 252–269; (d) *The Spanish-American Frontier: 1783–1795; the Westward Movement and the Spanish Retreat in the Mississippi Valley* (Boston, 1927); (e) "James Wilkinson's First Descent to New Orleans in 1787," *Hispanic American Historical Review*, VIII (Feb., 1928), 82–97; (f) "Alexander McGillivray, 1783–1789," *North Carolina Historical Review*, V (Apr., 1928), 181–203; (g) "The Commerce of Louisiana and the Floridas at the End of the Eighteenth Century," *Hispanic American Historical Review*, VIII (May, 1928), 190–203; (h) "Alexander McGillivray, 1789–1793," *North Carolina Historical Review*, V (July, 1928), 289–309; (i) "Harry Innes and the Spanish Intrigue: 1794–1795," *Mississippi Valley Historical Review*, XV (Sept., 1928), 236–248; (j) "New Light on the Treaty of San Lorenzo: An Essay in Historical Criticism," *ibid.* (Mar., 1929), 435–454; (k) *Documents Relating to the Commercial Policy of Spain in the Floridas, with Incidental Reference to Louisi-*

material is cited in any of those writings. From multi-national perspectives no American scholar has dedicated his energies more consistently to fathoming Valley history than has A. P. Nasatir. How many cigars Abe has reduced to ashes may be unknown but not so the publications that include at least three books and a dozen and a half articles between 1927 and 1968 on Spanish aspects of the Valley's history alone.[17] More is in the offing, continuing proof that Nasatir, the dean of Mississippi Valley historians, has fixed a lifetime of scholarly affection upon our river. Yet in only one Nasatir item, that concerning Pedro Vial, is there reference to a Mexican archive. Beyond recourse to European archives it should be added, in reference to Nasatir, that the wellsprings of the Bancroft Library have never run dry. The third persistently published specialist in Mississippi Valley history, the youngster of the trio and

ana (Deland, Fla., 1931); (l) *The Mississippi Question 1795–1803: A Study in Trade, Politics, and Diplomacy* (New York, 1934); (m) "Antonio de Ulloa," *Hispanic American Historical Review*, XV (May, 1935), 155–194; (n) "Reed and Forde: Merchant Adventurers of Philadelphia," *Pennsylvania Magazine of History and Biography*, LXI (July, 1937), 237–262.

[17] Nasatir's published writings regarding the Spanish in the Mississippi Valley include (a) "Jacques D'Eglise on the Upper Missouri, 1791–1795," *Mississippi Valley Historical Review*, XIV (June, 1927), 47–56; (b) "Spanish Exploration of the Upper Missouri," *ibid.*, 57–71; (c) "The Anglo-Spanish Frontier in the Illinois Country during the American Revolution, 1779–1783," *Illinois State Historical Society Journal*, XXI (Oct., 1928), 291–358; (d) "Ducharme's Invasion of Missouri: An Incident in the Anglo-Spanish Rivalry for the Indian Trade of Upper Louisiana," *Missouri Historical Review*, XXIV (Oct., 1929, Jan.–Apr., 1930), 3–25, 238–260, 420–439; (e) "Anglo-Spanish Rivalry on the Upper Missouri," *Mississippi Valley Historical Review*, XVI (Dec., 1929, Mar., 1930), 359–382, 507–528; (f) "An Account of Spanish Louisiana, 1785," *Missouri Historical Review*, XXIV (July, 1930), 521–536; (g) "Anglo-Spanish Rivalry in the Iowa Country 1797–1798," *Iowa Journal of History and Politics*, XXVIII (July, 1930), 337–389; (h) "The Formation of the Missouri Company," *Missouri Historical Review*, XXV (Oct., 1930), 10–22; (i) "John Evans, Explorer and Surveyor," *ibid.* (Jan.–July, 1931), 219–239, 432–460, 585–608; (j) "The Anglo-Spanish Frontier on the Upper Mississippi 1786–1796," *Iowa Journal of History and Politics*, XXIX (Apr., 1931), 155–232; (k) "St. Louis during the British Attack of 1780," in Hammond, ed., *New Spain and the Anglo-American West*, I, 239–261; (l) "Materials Relating to the History of the Mississippi Valley from the Minutes of the Spanish Supreme Councils of State, 1787–1797," *Louisiana Historical Quarterly*, XXI (Jan., 1938), 5–75; (m) "Jacques Clamorgan: Colonial Promoter of the Northern Border of New Spain," *New Mexico Historical Review*, XVII (Apr., 1942), 101–112; (n) "Government Employees and Salaries in Spanish Louisiana," *Louisiana Historical Quarterly*, XXIX (Oct., 1946), 885–1040; (o) *Before Lewis and Clark: Documents Illustrating the History of the Missouri, 1785–1804* (2 vols., St. Louis, 1952); (p) "An Opposition to the Sale of Louisiana," *Louisiana History*, III (Summer, 1962), 192–201; (q) "The Shifting Borderlands," *Pacific Historical Review*, XXXIV (Feb., 1965), 1–20; (r) "Jacques Clamorgan," *Mountain Men*, II (1965), 81–94; (s) "Jacques Deglise," *ibid.*, 123–134; (t) with Noel M. Loomis, *Pedro Vial and the Roads to Santa Fe* (Norman, 1967); (u) *Spanish War Vessels on the Mississippi, 1792–1796* (New Haven, 1968).

quite possibly the only person at our conference offering a course concerning the Mississippi Valley in colonial times, is Jack D. L. Holmes. Since that dissertation of 1959, Holmes has published four volumes and approximately twoscore articles distinctly related to the Valley in the Spanish period.[18] While Holmes's work, like that of Nasatir and

[18] Holmes's published writings regarding Spain in the Valley include (a) "Fort Ferdinand of the Bluffs: Life on the Spanish-American Frontier, 1795–1797," *West Tennessee Historical Society Papers*, XIII (1959), 38–54; (b) "The Two Series of the *Moniteur de la Louisiane*," *Bulletin of the New York Public Library*, LXIV (June, 1960), 323–328; (c) "A 1795 Inspection of Spanish Missouri," *Missouri Historical Review*, LV (Oct., 1960), 5–17; (d) "Livestock in Spanish Natchez," *Journal of Mississippi History*, XXIII (Jan., 1961), 15–37; (e) "The *Moniteur de la Louisiane* in 1798," *Louisiana History*, II (Spring, 1961), 230–253; (f) "La última barrera: la Luisiana y la Nueva España," *Historia Mexicana*, X (Apr.–June, 1961), 637–649; (g) "The First Laws of Memphis: Instructions for the Commandant of San Fernando de las Barrancas, 1795," *West Tennessee Historical Society Papers*, XV (1961), 93–104; (h) "Some Economic Problems of Spanish Governors of Louisiana," *Hispanic American Historical Review*, XLII (Nov., 1962), 521–543; (i) "Research Opportunities in the Spanish Borderlands: Louisiana and the Old Southwest," *Louisiana Studies*, I (Winter, 1962), 1–19; (j) "Joseph Piernas and a Proposed Settlement on the Calcasieu River, 1795," *McNeese Review*, XIII (1962), 59–80; (k) "The Spanish-American Struggle for Chickasaw Bluffs, 1780–1795," *East Tennessee Historical Society Publications*, no. 34 (1962), 26–57; (l) "Law and Order in Spanish Natchez, 1781–1798," *Journal of Mississippi History*, XXV (July, 1963), 186–201; (m) "Maps, Plans and Charts of Louisiana in Spanish and Cuban Archives: A Checklist," *Louisiana Studies*, II (Winter, 1963), 183–203; (n) *Documentos inéditos para la historia de la Luisiana, 1792–1810* (Madrid, 1963); (o) "Showdown on the Sabine: General James Wilkinson vs. Lieutenant Colonel Simón de Herrera," *Louisiana Studies*, III (Spring, 1964), 46–76; (p) "Natchitoches Revolt," *ibid.*, 117–132; (q) "Robert Moss' Plan for an English Invasion of Louisiana in 1782," *Louisiana History*, V (Spring, 1964), 161–177; (r) "Medical Practice in the Lower Mississippi Valley during the Spanish Period, 1769–1803," *Alabama Journal of Medical Sciences*, I (July, 1964), 332–338; (s) "Gallegos notables en la Luisiana," *Cuadernos de Estudios Gallegos*, XIX (1964), 103–123; (t) "Three Early Memphis Commandants: Beauregard, Deville Degoutin, and Folch," *West Tennessee Historical Society Papers*, XVIII (1964), 5–38; (u) "The Ebb-Tide of Spanish Military Power on the Mississippi: Fort San Fernando de las Barrancas, 1795–1798," *East Tennessee Historical Society Publications*, no. 36 (1964), 23–44; (v) "Some Irish Officers in Spanish Louisiana," *The Irish Sword*, VI (Winter, 1964), 234–247; (w) "The New Orleans Yellow Fever Epidemic of 1796 as Seen by the Baron de Pontalba," *Alabama Journal of Medical Sciences*, II (Apr., 1965), 205–215; (x) "Manuel Gayoso de Lemos: Genealogical and Heraldic Notes," *Genealogical Register* (Louisiana), XII (June–Sept., 1965), 37, 46–49; (y) "O'Reilly's Regulations on Booze, Boarding Houses, and Billiards," *Louisiana History*, VI (Summer, 1965), 293–300; (z) "Notes on the Spanish Fort San Esteban de Tombecbé," *Alabama Review*, XVIII (Oct., 1965), 281–290; (aa) "Some French Engineers in Spanish Louisiana," in John Francis McDermott, ed., *The French in the Mississippi Valley* (Urbana, Ill., 1965), 123–142; (bb) *José de Evia y sus reconocimientos del Golfo de México, 1783–1796* (Madrid, 1965); (cc) *Honor and Fidelity: The Louisiana Infantry Regiment and the Louisiana Militia Companies, 1766–1821* (Birmingham, 1965); (dd) *Gayoso: The Life of a Spanish Governor in the Mississippi Valley, 1789–1799* (Baton Rouge, 1965); (ee) "The Marqués de Casa-Calvo, Nicolás de Finiels, and the 1805 Spanish Expedition through East Texas and Louisiana," *Southwestern Historical*

Whitaker, is basically dependent upon European archives, it nonetheless does know marginal assists from Mexican archival material.[19] However, no scholar concerned with Mississippi Valley history in the Spanish period has ever produced a wide-ranging work that exhibits major dependence upon Mexican archives.

This raises a question which will be answered variously: what do the Mexican archives hold for the historian of the Spanish in the Mississippi Valley? To begin with, those archives once had more to attract the scholar than they presently have, a circumstance that invites explanation. In 1906, when Bolton was in the early stages of his survey of the Mexican archives and Cox was already deep in his study of early exploration of Louisiana, the latter expressed the hope that the confiscated journal and papers of Zebulon Pike would be found.[20] Bolton did locate those materials, in the Ministry of Foreign Relations.[21] Three years later, in 1910, Mexican authorities honored the official request of the United States that they be returned, and they were soon transferred to Washington. More recently still, thanks to the labors of Donald Jackson, those papers have been published in full.[22] Accordingly, records that once

---

Quarterly, LXIX (Jan., 1966), 324–339; (ff) "Louisiana in 1795: The Earliest Extant Issue of the *Moniteur de la Louisiane*," *Louisiana History*, VII (Spring, 1966), 133–151; (gg) "Spanish Military Commanders in Colonial Alabama," *Journal of the Alabama Academy of Science*, XXXVII (Jan., 1966), 55–67; (hh) "1797 Alabama Census According to Spanish Records," *Alabama Genealogical Register*, VIII (Sept., 1966), 123–124; (ii) "Joseph Piernas and the Nascent Cattle Industry of Southwest Louisiana," *McNeese Review*, XVII (1966), 13–26; (jj) "Father Francis Lennan and His Activities in Spanish Louisiana and West Florida," *Louisiana Studies*, V (Winter, 1966), 255–268; (kk) "De México a Nueva Orléans en 1801: el diario inédito de Fortier y St. Maxent," *Historia Mexicana*, XVI (July–Sept., 1966), 48–70; (ll) *"Dramatis Personae* in Spanish Louisiana," *Louisiana Studies*, VI (Summer, 1967), 149–185; "Irish Priests in Spanish Natchez," *Journal of Mississippi History*, XXIX (Aug., 1967), 169–180; (nn) "Indigo in Colonial Louisiana and the Floridas," *Louisiana History*, VIII (Fall, 1967), 329–349; (oo) "Genealogical and Historical Sources for Spanish Alabama, 1780–1813," *Deep South Genealogical Quarterly*, V (Feb., 1968), 130–138; (pp) "Andrés Almonester y Roxas: Saint or Scoundrel?," *Louisiana Studies*, VII (Spring, 1968), 47–64; (qq) "The Calcasieu Promoter: Joseph Piernas and His 1799 Proposal," *Louisiana History*, IX (Spring, 1968), 163–167; (rr) "The Choctaws in 1795," *Alabama Historical Quarterly*, XX (Spring, 1968), 33–49.

19 Items (f), (h), (dd), and (kk) in the preceding note cite materials from Mexican archives. In item (i) Holmes says, "For materials on Louisiana, Mississippi and the Old Southwest, the most important archives and libraries are located in Madrid, Seville, Simancas and Segovia" (pp. 6–7).

20 Cox, *The Early Exploration of Louisiana*, 154.

21 Herbert E. Bolton, "Material for Southwestern History in the Central Archives of Mexico," *American Historical Review*, XIII (Apr., 1908), 523.

22 Donald Jackson, ed., *The Journals of Zebulon Montgomery Pike, with Letters and Related Documents* (2 vols., Norman, 1966). A brief history of the Pike papers is given therein (see II, 191).

would have taken the researcher to Mexico City or later to Washington, D.C., are now at his fingertips in printed form.

Another Bolton discovery at the Ministry of Foreign Relations in Mexico City concerns the Pichardo papers. Opportunity to assess this ponderous study of the Texas-Louisiana boundary issue had been desired by more than one historian. A logical consequence of this scholarly interest was the four-volume translation of Pichardo's writing by Charles Wilson Hackett.[23] Needless to say, those volumes, containing another jewel of the Mexican archival collection, further diminish the indispensability of the archives themselves.

Other such instances might be cited but suffice it to say that as photo-duplication has made the historian less dependent upon Seville for the *Papeles de Cuba*, so publication has reduced dependence upon Mexico for the telling of Valley history.[24] Yet even as we discount those once Mexican-based manuscripts that are now freely available to us in this country, the question remains: what is still in Mexico for the historian of the Spanish era in the Mississippi Valley?

A recent trip to Mexico was undertaken for the precise purpose of exploring the relationship of the Archivo General de la Nación to our Valley theme. Begun with the humility that becomes anyone undertaking an archival assessment, and concluded in like vein, some of the results of the survey are now briefly set forth.

The 576-volume section of the archives denominated *Historia* is the richest regarding the Mississippi Valley. Therein are limited amounts of material concerning geography, exploration and travel, boundaries, defense, Indian questions, trade, finance, and supplies. The interrelated themes of geography, exploration, and travel can lead one to volumes 27, 41, 43, and 62. Volume 43, incidentally, has been one of the most frequent resorts of historians of the Valley. As early as 1906 Cox needed it; and Nasatir has cited it as recently as 1967.[25]

On the rich theme of boundaries, wherein majority emphasis is on the Texas-Louisiana line, the following volumes of *Historia* offer information: 43, 72, 298, 299, 301, 302, 321, and the run of volumes beginning

---

[23] Charles Wilson Hackett, trans. and ed., *Pichardo's Treatise on the Limits of Louisiana and Texas* (4 vols., Austin, 1931–46).

[24] For an impressive proof of reduced direct dependence upon archives, see James Alexander Robertson, *List of Documents in Spanish Archives Relating to the History of the United States, Which Have Been Printed or of Which Transscripts Are Preserved in American Libraries* (Washington, 1910). Quite possibly activities of the last half-century would double the size of this work were it brought up to date.

[25] Cox, *The Early Exploration of Louisiana*, 154, and Loomis and Nasatir, *Pedro Vial and the Roads to Santa Fe*, xvii.

with 543 and continuing through 588. Another Valley theme spread through a number of volumes in *Historia* is defense, which is treated in volumes 161, 162, 214, 401, 415, and 430. To some it may come as a surprise to learn that the Indians per se tread very lightly in the records, volume 431 of *Historia* offering a rare instance of their presence. For matters commercial and financial, attention is directed to volumes 43, 93, 401, 413, 430, and 431 of *Historia*.

Among these various volumes of *Historia* are materials that represent instances of overlapping and duplication. For example, volume 72, a summary of a segment of Father Pichardo's work, is related to items in the Ministry of Foreign Relations and to documents in volumes 543–558 of *Historia* as well as to Hackett's published work. Duplication of material in the archives may be illustrated by reference to certain writings concerning the boundary question by Padre Talamante which may be found in both volumes 43 and 302. Similarly, certain documents concerning trade between Louisiana and Texas are found in two places, the originals in volumes 182 and 183 of the section of the archives named *Provincias Internas* and copies thereof in volumes 43, 93, and 298 of *Historia*.[26] In sum, it follows that duplication joins publication as a fact of life reducing, from a quantitative standpoint, the significance of the total collection at the AGN. Translation is another factor affecting, diminishing, the significance of the archival holdings. Certain of the geographical notes on Louisiana found in volume 43 are translations from English into Spanish. Similarly volume 62 of *Historia* is a Spanish translation of a text the original of which is in French.

The 228-volume section of the archive termed *Provincias Internas*, despite the fact that it should not, by geographic definition, include the Mississippi Valley, is nonetheless the second most fruitful area of the collection for our purposes. Therein such themes as military affairs—with special emphasis upon defense—trade, exploration, religion, boundaries, and justice can be studied. Of these subjects, military affairs is the most persistent one in the records.[27] In the aggregate, however, one is disappointed by the limited support given the study of the Spanish in the Mississippi Valley by the documentation ensconced in *Provincias Internas*.

---

[26] Herbert E. Bolton, ed., *Athanase de Mézières and the Louisiana-Texas Frontier, 1768–1780* (2 vols., Cleveland, 1914), offers additional instances of the duplication of materials between *Historia* and *Provincias Internas* in the AGN.

[27] By subject, *Provincias Internas* offers material on military affairs, with emphasis on defense (vols. 20, 99, 133, 162, 163, 181, 182, 200, 201), on trade (vols. 181, 182, 183, 187), on exploration (vols. 100, 183), on religious life (vol. 182), on boundaries (vol. 183), and on justice (vol. 187).

A third area of the AGN deserving our attention is that named *Marina*, a collection of 316 volumes. They offer data on trade—both legal and illegal—the regulation of the *situado*,[28] defense of the realm, and the movements of such individuals as Burr and Wilkinson. Cox, in his treatment of the Wilkinson theme, made early use of material from this sector of the archives.[29]

The numerous other divisions of the archive in the National Palace in Mexico City are either totally unrelated to the Mississippi Valley, as, for example, are *Colegios, Hospital de Jesús* and *Minería*, or they represent the most unlikely of needle-in-haystack prospects. In the latter category, perhaps most prominently so, is the section termed *Tierras*. No sane person would categorically insist that the 3,692 volumes (give or take a few) in this section are totally unrelated to the Valley. On the other hand, no one possessed of a single lifetime would attempt close study of all those volumes. Via pages of the *Boletín del Archivo General de la Nación*,[30] which since its inception in 1930 has cast much light on the contents of most of *Tierras*. The result underscores the truth of the statement an administrator made to Bolton more than a half-century ago, namely, "that the number of expedientes relating to grants in the United States is small."[31] In reference to the Mississippi Valley that number is well-nigh nonexistent.

Incidentally the forementioned *Boletín del Archivo General de la Nación*, in an oft-present section, lists the names of researchers and the volumes and themes that drew their attention in the archive. This listing additionally indicates which materials have been copied or photographed, and for whom.[32]

In conclusion, the contribution the Archivo General de la Nación can make to our understanding of the Valley during the period of Spanish authority is a small one, a disappointingly small one. However, in

[28] The *situado* was a subsidy. In the assignment of them Spain underwrote operations in less productive areas of the empire.

[29] Cox, "General Wilkinson and His Later Intrigues with the Spaniards," 809, 812, and "The Pan-American Policy of Jefferson and Wilkinson," 216.

[30] An overview of the holdings of the AGN is given in [Luis González Obregón], "Lista de los ramos que comprenden el Archivo General de la Nación," *Boletín del Archivo General de la Nación*, I (Sept.–Oct., 1930), 113–118.

[31] Bolton, *Guide to Materials for the History of the United States in the Principal Archives of Mexico*, 191. Beginning with *Boletín del Archivo General de la Nación*, II (May–June, 1931), 352, and continuing in succeeding issues of that publication with great regularity for decades, an index of *Tierras* has been published.

[32] A published record of the use and duplication of materials in *Historia* appears in many issues of the *Boletín del Archivo General de la Nación*; see, for example, II (July–Aug., 1931), 623–630; *ibid.* (Sept.–Oct., 1931), 777–792; *ibid.* (Nov.–Dec., 1931), 939–944.

view of the multi-national focus on the area, the peripheral and limited role it played in the Spanish empire, and the flow of documentation established by higher authority, this circumstance is rather to be expected. Transfer, duplication, publication, and translation have combined to lessen further the significance of the aggregate collection.

However, even as isolated edited documents continue to flow to state journals and articles on narrow themes are published and graduate theses are written, ours also is a time, in this season of sesquicentennials up and down the Valley that easily merge into a national bicentennial, that invites a larger statement of the history of Spain in the Mississippi Valley. When that major synthesis is undertaken and areas such as Mississippi and Missouri, Louisiana and Illinois, and others too are made to fit into the huge geographical-historical jigsaw that is the Valley, then too a melding of the resources of all the archives will be in order.

Who, I ask, is working on this broad historical canvas that places demands upon all the archives, including the Mexican?

Land Settlement Policies and Practices in Spanish Louisiana

———◦•◦———

C. RICHARD ARENA

$\mathcal{L}$OUISIANA represented a special colonial problem in America for the Spanish monarchs because of her frontier status and French heritage. During the entire period of Spanish domination, 1762 to 1803, these two factors were to weigh heavily in every action undertaken by the officials entrusted with this vast and vaguely defined province. The precise boundaries of Louisiana refused definite limits from the very beginning of French occupation to the final United States–Spanish Transcontinental Treaty, concluded during the wars of independence throughout Latin America. In 1712 France claimed an area which stretched "from the source of the Mississippi, as far as the place where that river empties into the Gulf of Mexico."[1] The extent of the northern and western limits was equally vague. The French had never really occupied the Texas territory whose plains La Salle had penetrated in 1684, except for some scattered posts that were erected along the Red and Missouri rivers. According to Samuel F. Bemis, "the only reasonable limits which might be argued historically for western and northern Louisiana would be the western and northern watershed of the Mississippi."[2]

In the Treaty of Paris of 1763 England received whatever claim France had had to West Florida, thereby eliminating all of Florida as part of the previous year's secret cession of Louisiana to Spain by the

[1] M. de Vergennes, *Mémoire historique et politique sur la Louisiane* (Paris, 1802), 33.
[2] Samuel F. Bemis, *A Diplomatic History of the United States* (3rd ed., New York, 1951), 180–181.

51

French monarch. The Spanish legalists, moreover, considered the ill-defined Louisiana cession as nothing more than the "repossession" of her old territory, inasmuch as she had once claimed title to all of the New World by right of discovery.[3]

Under French occupation, Louisiana, before the coming of the Spaniards, did not develop consistent political institutions. It was a colony of the crown at first, later it emerged as a proprietary province under the exclusive ownership of Antoine Crozat for the French Company of the Indies, and finally returned, after 1731, to its original status as a crown colony. The French therefore tended to delegate extensive authority to private individuals, a procedure that contrasted sharply with the absolute paternalism normal to the Spanish political rule in the Americas. The French had even delegated landownership authority to private parties, such as the Company of the Indies, along with extensive military and political powers, something the Spanish monarchs very carefully tried to avoid at all costs. Under the French, therefore, the Company of the Indies was granted "ownership of all lands it put into cultivation; the right to grant lands to its individual stock-holders upon condition that these grants be settled and improved, ownership of all forts and government property; power to raise troops and make war upon the Indians when necessary, and finally the right to nominate governors and officers."[4]

But in spite of differences of orientation, both French and Spanish colonial regimes had the same ends and even basic assumptions. Thus a basis existed for the facile assimilation of the French colony into the Spanish empire. The religion of the Louisianians, for example, was Roman Catholic, and both nations were ruled by absolute and divine-right monarchs. Not having experienced any self-government as subjects of the French crown, when it was "not even desired,"[5] the colonists could not claim the loss of any such privilege as a result of their rather cold-blooded transfer to a new sovereign. Most significant for the purposes of this paper, it should be noted that Roman law was the foundation of the juridical systems of both societies. Hence the *coutume de Paris*, which served as the basis of the French legal system in Louisiana,[6] was replaced by Spanish codes which were as similarly grounded in Roman law as was the *coutume*.

[3] *Ibid.*, 11.
[4] Henry E. Chambers, *Mississippi Valley Beginnings: An Outline of the Early History of the Earlier West* (New York, 1922), 60–63.
[5] Peter J. Hamilton, *Colonial Mobile* (New York, 1910), 181.
[6] *Ibid.*, 180 ff.

With the arrival of the determined Don Alexandro O'Reilly in New Orleans on August 18, 1796, Spanish royal authority was firmly established in the Louisiana province. Governor O'Reilly arrived, it will be recalled, in the wake of a serious colonial uprising against the Spanish government under the first governor, Don Antonio de Ulloa, an eighteenth-century scientist and *philosophe*.[7] His measures, which now 3,000 Spanish soldiers stood ready to enforce, were intended to inculcate a permanent respect for the Spanish crown on the part of the new subjects. Governor O'Reilly skillfully blended the use of intimidation and peaceful persuasion into an effective policy designed to achieve his aims.[8]

Many official positions were given to native Frenchmen, such as those of the all-important government surveyors and frontier post *comandantes*. Former French officials were allowed to remain in office and their acts during the interval when the colony was changing sovereigns were confirmed. Typical was the case of the *comandante* St. Ange, who was in command of the post of St. Louis when the Spaniards took over Upper Louisiana. His official acts, such as the granting of land concessions, "were never questioned by the Spanish authorities."[9]

Although the *Recopilación de las leyes de los reynos de las Indias* was declared the basic code and Spanish the official language of the province, the practical politician O'Reilly did not ignore the importance of the French laws and practices of long usage. He published a summary of the Spanish code in French, which language he continued to use when communicating with the various French-speaking post *comandantes*.[10] Whenever possible he even settled local disputes in accordance with the local customs of the place where they occurred, without referring them to the proper judicial tribunals. In the more isolated regions of Upper Louisiana the inhabitants continued to abide by the *coutume de Paris* for all practical purposes throughout the entire Spanish domination.[11]

The land tenure systems of both the French and Spanish were remarkably similar in many basic aspects. The use of *comunales* (community-owned lands), for example, was known and practiced by the French

[7] In 1768 a "bloodless" revolution against the first Spanish Governor, Don Antonio de Ulloa, was successfully executed by several important French colonists, officials as well as men of property.

[8] For his harsh measures he earned the title of "Bloody" O'Reilly from later Louisiana historians.

[9] Louis Houck, *A History of Missouri, from the Earliest Explorations and Settlements until the Admission of the State into the Union* (3 vols., Chicago, 1908), II, 23.

[10] Chambers, *Mississippi Valley Beginnings*, 110.

[11] Houck, *History of Missouri*, II, 197.

Louisiana settlers before the coming of the Spaniards. Governor Ulloa was compelled to abandon his attempt to build fortifications on a plot of commons because the French vehemently protested that the land in question "belonged exclusively to them."[12] Moreover, the official policy of France and Spain regarding speculation in land was the same—both sovereigns condemned the practice. On one occasion the French monarch, upon being informed after the event that the early colony builder Bienville and other officials were guilty of fraudulently withholding lands for the purpose of speculation instead of dividing them among the settlers, "annulled the concessions granted them."[13] Neither the French nor the Spanish colonial governments ever sold any of the public land in Upper Louisiana. "The first sale of land by the sovereign of the soil in Upper Louisiana was made by the United States."[14]

In addition to the large body of accumulated, formal legislation on the subject, the various Spanish governors were permitted to issue their own laws that applied to their jurisdiction in Louisiana. The result was the emergence of a very complicated collection of land laws consisting of Spanish codes compiled prior to the cession of Louisiana to Spain and the separate decrees of the governors. For a brief period, moreover, the power to distribute land in Louisiana was actually lifted from the governor and deposited in the hands of the intendant, who also issued his own regulations with the force of law, thus further adding to the legal confusion.

Among the basic codes of Spain that applied to Louisiana were the *Fuero viejo de Castilla,* published by Count Don Sancho García around the end of the tenth century; the *Fuero real* by King Alonso V (and important because it included within its jurisdiction the kingdom of León, Galicia, and part of Portugal); and, in 1348, the famous code of *Las siete partidas,* originally prepared by King Alonso the Wise and issued by King Alonso XI. The *Partidas,* made up in large part of Roman laws, canon law, and papal bulls, represented an attempt to adapt the "customs and *fueros* of the nation, hoping to produce a legal body which was perfect and peculiar to . . . Spain: but this object, so important, was not completely attained."[15] In defining the various types of land grants, the social historian should take note, the *Partidas* served to

12 Vicente Rodríguez Casado, *Primeros años de dominación española en la Luisiana* (Madrid, 1942), 196.

13 Charles T. Soniat, "The Title to the Jesuits' Plantation," *Louisiana Historical Society Publications,* V (1911), 1–12.

14 Houck, *History of Missouri,* II, 214–215.

15 José María Álvarez, *Instituciones de derecho real de Castilla y de Indias* (4 vols., Guatemala, 1818–20), I, 11–13.

denote the legal social status of the owner and tenants who occupied the land.[16] Moreover, this same code stresses that the king is the source of all land titles, those of the clergy as well as the nobles; the "prelates and churches, and the authorities of monastic foundations" were subject to the code.[17] Then there is the all-embracing *Recopilación de las leyes de los reynos de las Indias*. Begun under the order of Philip II of Spain in 1570, the code was not completed until 1680, and it embodied all of the various rules, orders, and separate instructions which the Spanish rulers had issued pertaining to the American colonies. This, along with the rest of the codes cited already, applied to Louisiana.

Among the different types of landholdings which were provided for by the Spanish land laws in Louisiana was the nonprivate type of holding. The *Recopilación de las leyes de los reynos de las Indias* made mention of several, actually: *exidos*, *dehesas*, and *propios*. As customary, original title to such lands was claimed by the Spanish crown on the grounds that it had inherited completely "the dominion of the Indies."[18] The *exidos*, or commons, were those lands about the town which were owned jointly by the inhabitants and cultivated by them. The various laws dealing with the *exidos* were quite specific. Their exact distance from the limits of the town, for example, was determined to allow for the future expansion of the town.[19] Moreover, no other land grants were permitted around a new settlement, until the officials had made due provision for the laying out of the *exidos*.[20]

Another form of public landholding was the *dehesa*, which was land set aside for the use of the townspeople who owned cattle, thereby insuring sufficient land for pasture.[21] The *valdíos* (unappropriated public lands of the towns, as David Weeks calls them) were claimed by the crown for a special purpose. Again, with an eye to the future development of the town, the crown made it mandatory that certain lands be reserved for later distribution among new settlers of the town. Hence these lands were to remain "empty" (*valdías*).[22] Town planning, evidently, is not a "Yankee first" in America!

[16] *Las siete partidas del Rey don Alfonso el Sabio, cotejadas con various codices antiguos por la Real Academia de la Historia* (3 vols., Madrid, 1807). See *La cuarta partida, título* XXV, *ley* i, and *título* XXVI, *leyes* i–iv.

[17] *Ibid., La primera partida, tít.* VI, *ley* xiii.

[18] *Recopilación de las leyes de los reynos de las Indias* (1681) (5th ed., 4 vols., Madrid, 1841), *libro* IV, *título* XII, *ley* xiv (hereafter cited as *Recopilación*).

[19] *Ibid., lib.* IV, *tít.* VII, *ley* xiii.

[20] *Ibid., ley* xiv.

[21] *Ibid., ley* vii, ". . . y dehesa en que pueda pastar abundantemente el ganado que han de tener los vecinos."

[22] *Ibid., ley* xiv.

Finally, as a type of nonprivate landholding under the law there was the land set aside for towns already established but which lacked any public lands of their own. Such lands were designated as *propios*, and were taken from the *valdíos* of other towns.[23] And the town receiving such lands was granted the right to sell them, using the revenue so gained as a means for paying the salaries of certain designated public officials.[24]

Don Antonio de Ulloa, the very first Spanish governor of Louisiana, was acting in perfect accord with the *Recopilación* when he issued the following regulation for the establishment of a new town in Louisiana: "Corn plantations or fields large enough to be of great relief shall be made immediately, and that will provide against famine. Later when the settlement has some stability fields of wheat shall be planted as well as of other grains, for the common welfare, all the people sharing in them in common."[25]

What about the rights of the Indians under the land laws? In complying with the *Recopilación* on this all-important question, Governor Ulloa ordered the leaders of an expedition into Indian territory in Spanish Louisiana around 1767–68 to respect the land rights of this group.[26] To the very end of their stay, the Spaniards officially tried to live up to the law. Article 31 of Morales's land laws, toward the end of Spanish domination in the province, clearly stated that the "Indians shall be protected in their holdings."[27]

In Louisiana the Spaniards made a distinction in landholding rights between the "civilized or Christian" and the non-Christian Indian. An Indian who received Christian baptism could legally hold land on a basis of equality with white settlers, but the non-Christian native was permitted to transfer his land title to someone else only with the written approval of the governor.[28] It should be noted, however, that the non-Christian Indian otherwise enjoyed legal privileges identical with those of the Christian Indian. By way of contrast, the U.S. Government insisted that "the states and the United States were firm in the determina-

23 *Ibid.*, ". . . y de estas tierras hagan . . . separar las que parecieren convenientes para propios de los pueblos que no los tuvieren."

24 *Ibid.*

25 Rule 71 of Governor Ulloa's "Rules for Establishing a Spanish Settlement in Illinois," cited in Louis Houck, ed., *The Spanish Régime in Missouri* (2 vols., Chicago, 1909), I, 16–19.

26 *Ibid.*, rule 17.

27 Art. 31 of Morales's land laws, cited in Francis P. Burns, "The Spanish Land Laws of Louisiana," *Louisiana Historical Quarterly*, XI (1938), 573.

28 Burns, "Spanish Land Laws," 564–567. The author cites *The American State Papers, Public Lands*, III, 83.

tion to deny the power of the Indian tribes to alienate any portion of the soil to private parties."[29]

It is not surprising that the Spanish land laws reflected the same duality of interests that characterized their theologian-jurist framers. Under the *Recopilación* only those "approved in Christianity" were permitted to establish new settlements.[30] Sites were to be granted for the use of monasteries and other religious purposes, although in the case of monasteries it was specifically provided that only the space actually needed was to be granted.[31] Because partial religious toleration prevailed in the province, an important—really radical—modification of one of Spain's basic principles in the New World on the exclusion of all but Roman Catholics was extended. American Protestants, desirous of receiving land grants in Louisiana, were permitted freedom of conscience, but Governor Gayoso's law stipulated that "the privilege of enjoying liberty of conscience is not to extend beyond the first generation. The children of those who enjoy it must positively be Catholics."[32]

The *Recopilación*, by requiring that religious institutions and societies be established in all new settlements, provided the legal wedge that enabled the Church to acquire its principal holdings of real property in Louisiana. At the same time, however, the laws limited the sphere of real estate transactions in which the Church could participate and function. One law, for example, forbade the sale of lands by new settlers directly "to a church, or monastery, or any other ecclesiastical person."[33] Church holdings were also to be limited under the law to the extent that they actually fulfilled the needs of the religious parties making use of them.[34]

The prospect of liberal land grants, provided for in the Spanish land laws, was one of the chief devices employed by the crown to induce loyal subjects to emigrate to the New World, especially Louisiana, which was considered dangerously underpopulated. A common technique of colonization was to offer contracts to individuals, guaranteeing extensive landholdings as well as social preeminence in the newly formed

[29] Houck, *History of Missouri*, II, 109–110.

[30] *Recopilación*, lib. IV, tít. I, ley ii.

[31] *Ibid.*, lib. I, tít. III, ley i.

[32] Number 5 of Governor Gayoso's land laws, cited in *The American State Papers. Documents, Legislative and Executive, of the Congress of the United States, in Relation to the Public Lands, from the First Session of the First Congress to the First Session of the Twenty-third Congress: March 4, 1789 to June 15, 1834* (8 vols., Washington, 1832–61), V, 730.

[33] *Recopilación*, lib. IV, tít. XII, ley x, ". . . no las puedan vender a iglesia, ni monasterio ni a otra persona eclesiástica, pena de que las hayan perdido. . . ."

[34] *Ibid.*, lib. I, tít. III, ley ii.

community. The laws included the necessary qualifications for a pioneer ready to undertake the founding of a new community; he was called a *poblador,* a "populator."[35] The law establishing such contracts is worth quoting in full:

> The boundary and territory, which are given under the contract to the *poblador,* shall be divided in the following manner: they shall first provide for the residential sections of the town with sufficient commons, and *dehesa,* which shall provide an abundant pasture for the cattle of the townspeople, and an equally sufficient amount for the private lands of the town: the rest of the territory and boundary shall be divided into four parts; one part of which shall go to the one responsible for founding the settlement, he choosing it himself, and the remaining three parts shall be divided into equal lots for the settlers.[36]

This law was the crown's method, of course, of rewarding the private enterpriser who was ready to develop the main resources that the crown had in the New World—land. No less than one-fourth of the total settlement, excluding the public domain or commons, was no mean reward, especially when Louisiana had vast frontier stretches that needed "populating." It is very easy to see how Louisiana under Spain could develop that widespread economic, political, and social problem so plaguing the history of Latin Americans and known as *latifundia*—most of the land in the hands of a few.

Such rewards even attracted citizens from the United States, including such legendary characters as Daniel Boone, who, upon electing to become a Spanish subject, received a grant of 1,000 arpents on the Missouri River. This tract became considerably augmented when his "services" in coaxing an additional 100 Kentucky and Virginia families to settle in Louisiana were recognized, to the tune of a further grant of 10,000 arpents.[37] Another interesting case of an emigrant from the United States moving to the Spanish territory is that of Bryan Bruin of Virginia, who, on March, 31, 1787, petitioned Governor Miró for the right to settle, along with several other families, "in whatever part of this province on the Mississippi which Y. E. [Your Excellency] would think more convenient." Bruin and his fellow Virginians offered the following explanation for their earnest desire to become Louisiana immigrants: "The

[35] *Ibid., lib.* II, *tít.* XXXIII, *ley* xix.
[36] *Ibid., lib.* IV, *tít.* VII, *ley* vii.
[37] Chambers, *Mississippi Valley Beginnings,* 128.

only reason which prompts . . . [the] petitioners to take such a step is that they do profess the roman religion and . . . the free exercise of the said religion is not allowed by the Constitution of the U.S."[38]

Following the intent of the framers of the laws regarding land settlement in Louisiana, the various Spanish governors sincerely engaged in the task of promoting more settlements and more agricultural production. In addition to the usual free grant of land, new settlers were offered other attractive inducements: tax exemption privileges, free farming tools, and, on occasion, financial subsidies. On February 19, 1778, Governor Gálvez issued the decree that the government would provide each immigrant farmer with an ax, a hoe, a scythe or sickle, a spade, two hens, a cock, and a two-month-old pig, plus a specific allotment of maize for each member of the family.[39]

In spite of the liberal land laws and the sincere efforts of the officials, Spanish Louisiana did not achieve agrricultural self-sufficiency during the period in question. Foodstuffs were constantly being imported from outside sources. The shortage is shown by the various strict regulations that were enacted to control the situation: price regulation, prohibition of food exports, and elaborate measures for storing scarce food items.

As early as the governorship of Alexandro O'Reilly it had been necessary to institute government price control over agricultural products. This action, according to the Louisiana historian Charles Gayarré, affected the "inhabitants in almost every district."[40] In 1796 the cabildo still had to enact regulations for the prices and hours of sale of the rice being cultivated in the province.[41] During the same year the cabildo was equally worried over the failure of the expected arrival of imports from "las Provincias de Kintuquis" (Kentucky territory), where U.S. western pioneers had been working to supply the New Orleans market with flour and corn.[42] What was truly alarming to the members of the cabildo was the tendency of the local rice growers to take advantage of the good export prices being paid and ship their product abroad. The cabildo then sought to prohibit the exportation in the future as a defensive measure against the shortage of foodstuffs within the province.[43] This action

[38] Bryan Bruin to Governor Miró, Mar. 31, 1787, MS, Taliaferro Papers, Department of Archives, Louisiana State University, Baton Rouge.

[39] Houck, ed., *The Spanish Régime in Missouri,* I, 155–156.

[40] Charles Gayarré, *History of Louisiana* (4 vols., New York, 1867), II, 29.

[41] "Actas de cabildo," MS, minutes of Apr. 1, 1796, New Orleans Public Library.

[42] *Ibid.,* minutes of Apr. 26, 1796.

[43] *Ibid.,* minutes of Mar. 11, 1796.

was followed by the inevitable preparations of the cabildo to look after the storage of these items, such as flour and rice, "the new branch of industry," as it was described in 1796.[44]

Because Louisiana was lacking in population and abundantly rich in virgin farmland, Spain employed a land tenure policy precisely suited to resolve the crisis evolving from this sad state of affairs. It was a policy that had been developing for nearly 300 years in the Caribbean and continental possessions, juridically precise and conscientiously applied with realism and no false assumptions where Louisiana was concerned.

Large landholdings were encouraged and held out as inducements to private individuals who would undertake the founding of new settlements. Such persons could expect further aid and substantial rewards from the Spanish officials, who did so in their functions as lawful executors under the crown, which was backing this policy all the way. David Weeks, in commenting on the Spanish land laws and the wisdom with which they were conceived, said that they "anticipated the homestead act of the United States by three centuries."[45]

The big landowners, who were fostered in part by the Spanish colonial land settlement program, made up the local cabildo government and, not surprisingly, developed into an important stronghold of landed aristocrats. In Louisiana this group was well aware of its economic vested interests, of its rooted juridical status, and expertly dominated every means to advance through the cabildo these same interests.

The Spanish land policy and laws also held out some practical prospects for the development of a class of small farmers, capable of satisfying the domestic food needs of the colony. This bright economic vision never materialized, however, as the Spanish officials discovered to their sorrow. Of the two types of landowners which the Spanish land tenure system helped to develop, only one—the plantation owners—had secured enough political power to maintain their leadership over the other class, the small landholding class.

[44] *Ibid.*, minutes of June 17, 1774, Mar. 11, 1796.
[45] David Weeks, "The Agrarian System of the Spanish American Colonies," *Journal of Land and Public Utility Economics*, XXIII (1947), 153–168.

The Bruins and the Formulation
of Spanish Immigration Policy
in the Old Southwest,
1787-88

WILLIAM S. COKER

*U*NTIL recently not much was known about Bryan Bruin and little more about his son, Peter Bryan Bruin. A few biographical sketches noted that they had emigrated to the Natchez district from Virginia in 1787–88.[1] Arthur Preston Whitaker once characterized the younger Bruin as an insolvent planter quite willing to betray his oath of loyalty to Spain by supporting the American bid for control of the Natchez area.[2] Peter Bruin also gained some notoriety as one of Mississippi's first territorial judges, but has generally been relegated to obscurity as a drunken old sot who fell asleep while sitting on the bench.[3]

[1] J. F. H. Claiborne, *Mississippi as a Province, Territory and State, with Biographical Notices of Eminent Citizens* (Jackson, Miss., 1880), 161n; Dunbar Rowland, *Mississippi: Comprising Sketches of Counties, Towns, Events, Institutions, and Persons, Arranged in Cyclopedic Form* (3 vols., Atlanta, 1907), I, 319–320.

[2] Arthur Preston Whitaker, *The Mississippi Question 1795–1803: A Study in Trade, Politics, and Diplomacy* (Gloucester, Mass., 1962), 63, 381, n. 28. William Baskerville Hamilton intimates the same: *Thomas Rodney: Revolutionary and Builder of the West* (Durham, N.C., 1953), 73.

[3] William Baskerville Hamilton, *Anglo-American Law on the Frontier: Thomas Rodney and His Territorial Cases* (Durham, N.C., 1953), 238–239; D. Clayton James, *Antebellum Natchez* (Baton Rouge, 1968), 108.

A closer examination of Peter Bryan Bruin, however, reveals that he made a significant contribution to the independence movement as an officer during the Revolutionary War. He became a prominent Spanish citizen during the last ten years of Spain's occupation of Natchez, played an important part in the transition from Spanish to U.S. government north of the thirty-first parallel, and exerted an influence on early territorial law and justice in Mississippi. His father emerges as a large-scale land speculator on Virginia's colonial frontier and as a seminal figure in the change of Spanish immigration policy in the lower Mississippi Valley in the late 1780s. Unfortunately, time and space will not permit a review of all these interesting facets of their lives. This oversight will be corrected, it is hoped, in the not too distant future with publication of a full-length biography of Peter Bryan Bruin.[4] The present study, however, is limited to the roles played by the Bruins in the development of Spanish immigration policy in the Old Southwest.

In 1783, with the questions of freedom of transit on the Mississippi River and the boundary between Spanish West Florida and the American West unresolved, Spain and the United States stood toe to toe in the lower Mississippi Valley. The American colonists made this confrontation very real to the Spanish by their rapid westward expansion during and after the war. In order to strangle the American frontier settlements, which it considered a direct threat to West Florida and Louisiana, Spain closed the Mississippi River to navigation by American ships. Spanish officials occasionally permitted exceptions to this policy.[5]

[4] William S. Coker, "Peter Bruin: Record as Soldier, Judge, Settler," *Natchez Democrat*, Sesquicentennial edition, Jan., 1968, 8–10; Coker, "Peter Bryan Bruin of Bath: Soldier, Judge and Frontiersman," *West Virginia History*, XXX (July, 1969), 579–585. Some confusion has also resulted from the similarity of the names of the father and son, Bryan Bruin and Peter Bryan Bruin. The son helped to further confuse the situation by signing his name "P. Bryan Bruin," but with the *P* and *B* written as one character, thus making it appear to the unwary as "Bryan Bruin." The following reproduction of his signature is from a letter he wrote to Winthrop Sargent, governor of Mississippi Territory, Mar. 12, 1801. The original is in the Winthrop Sargent Papers, Massachusetts Historical Society, Boston.

[5] These questions are thoroughly discussed in Samuel Flagg Bemis, *Pinckney's Treaty: America's Advantage from Europe's Distress, 1783–1800* (New Haven, 1960), 1–59, and Bemis, *Jay's Treaty: A Study in Commerce and Diplomacy* (rev. ed., New Haven, 1962).

Further, to erect a wall of alien territory between the Spanish-American frontiers, Spain negotiated a series of treaties with the southern Indian tribes, who would serve as military bastions on the northern periphery. The fur trade with them would bolster the economy of the Floridas and Louisiana. Behind this defensive wall Spain planned to develop those regions through a program of immigration. But only Spaniards or other Catholics were eligible immigrants, and it must be admitted that Spanish immigration policy to 1786–87 had been a distinct failure.[6] There matters stood on the eve of Bryan Bruin's first visit to New Orleans.

Rather mysteriously—no apparent reason can be found in the records in Virginia—Bryan Bruin sold everything he owned, including his land, household goods, guns, saddles, and even one old horse.[7] Then he left Virginia for the Louisiana country in the summer of 1786.

The reason for Bruin's choice of Louisiana became clear in October after he reached New Orleans. Bruin filed suit in the Spanish court against Luke Collins, Sr., of Opelousas, Louisiana, an old acquaintance and former resident of Virginia. In July, 1772, Collins borrowed £250 and Bryan Bruin signed as security. Collins subsequently left Virginia without paying the loan. Bruin eventually paid it, but thirteen years and five months had elapsed and the note with interest came to £622 8s., or

---

In spite of Spanish policy to the contrary, the Mississippi River was not entirely closed to American traders. Some boats which came down the river were confiscated while others were not. The most notable exception to this rule was the arrival of General James Wilkinson and his cargo at New Orleans in the summer of 1787. See Dawson A. Phelps, "Travel on the Natchez Trace: A Study of the Economic Aspects," *Journal of Mississippi History*, XV (1953), 157–159; Miguel Gómez del Campillo, *Relaciones diplomáticas entre España y los Estados Unidos según los documentos del Archivo Histórico Nacional* (2 vols., Madrid, 1944–45), I, 57.

An interesting contemporary evaluation of America's chances for free transit of the Mississippi River is found in Thomas Hutchins, *An Historical Narrative and Topographical Description of Louisiana and West-Florida*, facsimile of the 1784 edition with introduction and index by Joseph G. Tregle, Jr. (Gainesville, 1968), xiv, xliii–xliv.

[6] Jack D. L. Holmes provides census figures which show that in 1769 the Spanish reported a total population of 13,538 for Louisiana. In 1788 it had increased to 42,611 including 6,376 in the seven West Florida posts. He suggests the increase was admirable by Spanish standards, but when compared to the population in the United States, the Spanish colonies were "virtually a 'desert.'" *Gayoso: The Life of a Spanish Governor in the Mississippi Valley, 1789–1799* (Baton Rouge, 1965), 22. For a select bibliography of immigration proposals and schemes in English and Spanish see *ibid.*, 23, n. 62; Caroline Maude Burson, *The Stewardship of Don Esteban Miró, 1782–1792* (New Orleans, 1940), 124–127; Arthur Preston Whitaker, *The Spanish-American Frontier: 1783–1795; the Westward Movement and the Spanish Retreat in the Mississippi Valley* (Boston, 1927), 90–107; Whitaker, "Spanish Intrigue in the Old Southwest: An Episode, 1788–89," *Mississippi Valley Historical Review*, XII (1925), 155–158. See also n. 30 below.

[7] Frederick County Deed Book (Winchester, Va.), XX, 376, XXI, 128.

2,077 *pesos*, 4 *reales* ($2,077.50). The court, with Governor General Esteban Miró serving as judge, found in Bruin's favor. Miró instructed the commandant at Opelousas to order Collins to pay Bruin or, if he refused, to seize his property to satisfy the debt. Collins agreed to pay Bruin 2,500 *pesos*—a bonus of over 400 *pesos*—1,000 as a down payment and the balance the following March.[8]

The speedy justice which he received from the Spanish government pleased Bruin, as did the treatment accorded him by Governor Miró. The climate, the richness of the soil, and the large areas of unoccupied land on both sides of the Mississippi River also favorably impressed him, and he wrote his son several letters extolling the virtues of the country. On March 31, 1787, Bryan Bruin petitioned Governor Miró for permission to bring Peter and nine or ten families to settle in the Spanish province. Their main reason for leaving Virginia, he asserted, was that they were all Catholics and did not have freedom of worship under the "Constitution of the United States." They desired to live in a country where its citizens enjoyed peace and quiet and in which they could worship without fear or suspicion. He asked that they be permitted to bring all the equipment and implements needed for farming, their household goods, and provisions enough to last a year. They also desired to bring their firearms and fishing equipment; a number of "horses, stallions, and mares to establish the breeding of saddle and draft horses, some sheep, rams and ewes," and all their Negro slaves. He asked Miró to let him know how many acres of land each family could expect to receive in any of several specific locations: Bayou Pierre, Homochitto, Thompson's Creek, Baton Rouge, Barrancas Blancas, or Manchac.[9]

---

[8] Collins had known Bruin since 1761 when he bought a lot from him in Winchester. Frederick County Deed Book, VI, 306–310; "Case of Don Bryan Bruin versus Lucas Collins," Oct. 2, 1786, file 69, doc. 1397, box 47, Louisiana State Museum, New Orleans. This is a two-page English translation and condensation of the case. The original in Spanish covers fifty-four pages. A paper entitled "Luke Collins, Sr., and Family of Opelousas: An Overview," read by this author at the Attakapas Historical Society meeting, Lafayette, Louisiana, Nov. 6, 1971, and soon to be published by *Louisiana History*, provides additional data on this court case.

Peter later wrote that his father had left Virginia to chase a man to West Florida, obviously Collins, who had absconded owing him a large sum of money. Peter Bryan Bruin to Diego de Gardoqui, Spanish chargé d'affaires to the United States, Bath, July 15, 1787, Archivo Histórico Nacional, Madrid (hereafter cited as AHN), *Estado, legajo* 3893.

In general, *pesos* and dollars in 1786 were exchanged on the basis of 1:1. Conversion from colonial pounds and shillings to dollars was figured at 3⅓ dollars to the pound. W. G. Sumner, "The Spanish Dollar and the Colonial Shilling," *American Historical Review*, III (1898), 607–619.

[9] Bryan Bruin to Governor Esteban Miró, Mar. 31, 1787, AHN, *Estado*, leg. 3888. A copy of this letter may also be found in Lawrence Kinnaird, "American Penetration

Three weeks later Miró approved Bruin's request. He specified that they could settle in any of the places designated provided the land was vacant. Each family would be given a tract of land 20 by 40 arpents. This 800 arpents amounted to about 680 acres.[10] Miró promised a second tract if they satisfactorily settled the first grant. They could bring all of the goods, equipment, and animals mentioned, but only enough sugar and brandy to last the journey as those articles could not be imported from foreign countries.[11]

On May 1, Miró advised the minister of the Indies, the Marquis of Sonora (José de Gálvez), of his action. Miró believed that immigration under such conditions would populate the province at no expense to the crown. He did not think that the Spanish had anything to fear from this class of people, and he recommended that the 6 percent import duty be waived on the goods they would bring with them.[12] The court approved the request on July 14, 1787.[13]

Peter Bryan Bruin, who had remained in Virginia, at that time was unaware of his father's application for land and decided to present an immigration proposal of his own. He wrote Diego de Gardoqui, the Spanish chargé d'affaires in New York, in July, 1787, outlining an elaborate scheme for the emigration of thousands from the United States to Louisiana. He suggested a five-point plan: first, that lands be granted to immigrants in proportion to the number of persons in each family; second, that all possible assistance be given to aid these people in the hazardous trip to the new country; third, that, because of the multitude of problems in establishing themselves on virgin land, the Spanish should furnish at least one year's provisions for the settlers; fourth, that all males from sixteen to sixty should be supplied with arms and ammunition on their arrival in order to defend themselves against the Indians or other sources of trouble; fifth, that a capital be laid off, fortified, and gar-

---

into Spanish Louisiana," in George P. Hammond, ed., *New Spain and the Anglo-American West: Historical Contributions Presented to Herbert Eugene Bolton* (2 vols., Lancaster, Pa., 1932), I, 230–231; Jack D. L. Holmes, "Livestock in Spanish Natchez," *Journal of Mississippi History*, XXIII (1961), 17–18. In the spring of 1788 when Peter Bruin arrived in West Florida he brought no livestock with him. Lawrence Kinnaird, ed., *Spain in the Mississippi Valley, 1765–1794* (3 vols., Washington, 1946–49), II, 257. Only one horse accompanied the immigrants arriving from Virginia during the first half of 1788, as noted in the "Report of Americans Arriving at Natchez," July 5, 1788, in *ibid.*

[10] An arpent is an old French land measure varying in area, but about .85 acre. Holmes, *Gayoso*, 34, n. 2.

[11] Approval by Miró, Apr. 20, 1787, AHN, *Estado, leg.* 3888.

[12] Miró to the Marqués de Sonora, no. 231, May 1, 1787, AHN, *Estado, leg.* 3888.

[13] The royal order was formally proclaimed by Miró on Oct. 11, 1787. See Kinnaird, "American Penetration into Spanish Louisiana," 231.

risoned at the crown's expense where merchants and tradesmen could carry on their business in security, and the planters and farmers could find refuge in case of attack. He envisioned the settlers used as militiamen if and when circumstances dictated. Peter requested that the plan be treated confidentially, but was so interested in the scheme that he offered to carry it to the royal court if Gardoqui thought it advisable.[14]

Gardoqui's reply was prompt and not at all reassuring. He had been deluged with immigration applications from various parts of the world. He could make no commitment at the time, but promised to be in touch with Peter if something materialized. It was four months before Gardoqui even forwarded the plan to Spain.[15]

In comparing the proposal made by Bryan Bruin with that of his son, one notes two significant differences. Peter mentioned that he was Catholic and that his father's letters had inspired every Roman Catholic who had read them to move to Louisiana. Unlike his father, however, Peter made no accusations about persecution of Catholics, nor did he intimate that religion was the paramount reason for his leaving Virginia. People of that faith in Virginia between 1754 and 1786 probably encountered some degree of displeasure because of their religion, but there is no evidence that the Bruins or any other Catholics living on the Virginia frontier at that time were or were not being persecuted. In Virginia, as in the rest of the southern colonies, all the people were taxed for the support of the Anglican Church, a policy they bitterly resented.[16]

In March, 1787, when Bryan Bruin wrote his letter complaining that Catholics did not enjoy freedom of worship under the "Constitution," the Articles of Confederation were the basis for government and they did not provide for religious freedom.[17] But the whole question of the separation of church and state in Virginia had been seriously discussed and debated there since 1776. In 1779 the Virginia Assembly defeated a

[14] Bruin to Gardoqui, Bath, July 15, 1787. Copies of this letter in English and Spanish are included in Gardoqui to the Count of Floridablanca, Spanish minister of foreign affairs, New York, no. 233, Dec. 6, 1787, AHN, *Estado, leg.* 3893.

[15] Gardoqui to Bruin, New York, Aug. 21, 1787, in Gardoqui to Floridablanca, New York, no. 233, Dec. 6, 1787, AHN, *Estado, leg.* 3893.

[16] J. Franklin Jameson, *The American Revolution Considered as a Social Movement* (Boston, 1963), 84; Merrill Jensen, *The Articles of Confederation* (Madison, 1963), 22. Sister Mary Augustina (Ray), *American Opinion of Roman Catholicism in the Eighteenth Century* (New York, 1936), 158–159, by implication suggests antagonism if not persecution of Virginia Catholics. There is little doubt that Catholics were persecuted in many parts of the United States, but evidence is lacking to determine whether Catholics on the Virginia frontier were or were not being persecuted.

[17] The only place where religion is mentioned in the Articles is an oblique reference in Article 3, which provides for joint action by the states in the event of attack "on account of religion, sovereignty," etc. Jensen, *Articles of Confederation*, 263.

bill providing for religious freedom which had been introduced by Thomas Jefferson. Six years later, on January 16, 1786, Virginia passed virtually the same bill Jefferson had authored earlier. Thus Virginia, five or six months before Bryan Bruin left that state, had enacted a law which declared that no one was compelled to attend or support any church or suffer in any manner because of his religious beliefs. In December, 1786, three months before Bryan Bruin wrote Miró, Jefferson could state that the Virginia law providing for religious toleration had been read throughout Europe, that it had been translated into French and Italian, and that it was appearing in many of the publications there about America.[18] Therefore, it must be concluded that Bryan Bruin's claim that religious persecution was the paramount reason behind the desire of the Virginia Catholics to emigrate to Spanish territory was without foundation. That such a reason would appeal to His Catholic Majesty had obviously occurred to Bruin.[19]

The second major difference between the two Bruin proposals concerned crown financial support. The younger Bruin requested provisions for a year after the immigrants arrived in the province, a supply of arms and ammunition, and the establishment of a capital, all of which would have constituted a large cash expenditure by Spain. No scarcity of impoverished applicants existed and there was little likelihood that the Spanish would have approved Peter's grandiose plan because of the great expense involved. But fortunately for Peter and the other Virginia families who wished to emigrate to Spanish territory, his father's request made no demands on the royal treasury. Therefore, it was the result of his father's petition and not his own that enabled Peter Bryan Bruin and a party of eighty to leave Virginia for Natchez in April, 1788.[20] Approval of Bryan Bruin's request and the departure

[18] Dumas Malone, *Jefferson and His Time* (2 vols., Boston, 1948), I, 274–280; Marie Kimball, *Jefferson: War and Peace, 1776 to 1784* (New York, 1947), 13–14.

[19] Religious orthodoxy had played a significant part in Spanish colonial policy for nearly three centuries. But as a qualification for immigration to Louisiana and the Floridas it was set aside in December, 1788. This unprecedented change in policy, forced upon Spain by the competition for immigrants and its frontier conflict with the United States, demonstrates the importance Spain attached to the development of this region. Whitaker, *The Spanish-American Frontier*, 103.

[20] The pertinent correspondence on Bruin's departure from Virginia includes: Bruin to Gardoqui, Bath, Mar. 1, 1788; Bruin to Gardoqui, Fort Harmer [Harmar], May 9, 1788; Gardoqui to Bruin, New York, Mar. 17, 1788; "Passport for Bruin," New York, Mar. 14, 1788; Gardoqui to the governor of Louisiana, "Letter of Recommendation for Peter Bryan Bruin," Mar. 17, 1788; Gardoqui to Floridablanca, nos. 236, 284, July 25, 1788, all in AHN, *Estado, leg.* 3894. All of these letters are in Spanish. The English originals have not been located. One point needs to be cleared up in regard to Bruin's letter to Gardoqui of Mar. 1, 1788. Invariably this letter has been dated Mar. 10 in the

of his son's party signaled the beginning of Spain's renewed efforts to solve the population problem in Louisiana and West Florida. Under the circumstances, it is surprising that only a few persons have devoted any attention to the Bruins or have attempted to evaluate their role in this crucial period in Spanish colonial history.

Caroline Maude Burson in her biography of Governor Miró placed the cart before the horse in referring to Bryan Bruin. She suggested that he was attracted by the royal order of July, 1787, and that the emigration of Peter and the other families from Virginia followed. Actually, Bruin's petition triggered the establishment of Spanish policy and the royal order was the crown's response to Bruin's request and not the reverse as she concludes.[21] But Burson has not been the only one to mention Bruin's part in this matter.

Lawrence Kinnaird stated that "Bryan Bruin was one of the first colonizers from the United States to arrive at New Orleans with Gardoqui's passport." Bryan Bruin came to Louisiana not as a colonizer, but rather to collect a debt from Collins. His favorable reception in the province and his satisfaction with Spanish justice, coupled with his excellent impression of the country, induced him to apply for permission for his son and others to immigrate and settle there. Furthermore, no evidence has been uncovered to indicate that Bryan Bruin had a passport from Gardoqui when he arrived in New Orleans in 1786.[22] Kinnaird made two other conclusions in regard to Bruin's visit which need closer examination: first, that his mission to the Crescent City took place nearly a year before the arrival of General James Wilkinson, and second, that it antedated the arrival of Pierre d'Argès Wouves in Spain.[23]

Bruin preceded Wilkinson to New Orleans by about a year. However, Bruin's petition had been forwarded to Spain only two months before Wilkinson, the so-called "Tarnished Warrior," reached that city on July 2, 1787. But Bruin's request differed greatly from the proposition Wilkinson laid before Miró. Wilkinson presented a detailed blueprint for immigration and liberalized trade privileges for Kentucky,

---

various English translations. The date was transcribed "Bath, 1º de Marzo de 1788." The Spanish abbreviation for *primero*, the "first," is 1º. Someone incorrectly thought it was 10 and everyone else has followed suit.

21 *The Stewardship of Don Esteban Miró*, 126.

22 Kinnaird, "American Penetration into Spanish Louisiana," 216. The evidence is conclusive that Gardoqui was unaware of Bryan Bruin's visit to New Orleans in 1786. In Peter Bruin's letter to Gardoqui of July 15, 1787, it is quite obvious that he and his father were total strangers to the Spanish official. Bruin to Gardoqui, Bath, July 15, 1787, AHN, *Estado, leg.* 3983.

23 Kinnaird, *Spain in the Mississippi Valley*, II, xxiv.

the region he claimed to represent. He wanted the Spanish to appoint him their commercial agent with control over exports from Kentucky to Louisiana. His plan called for abandoning the highly cherished Spanish policy of keeping the Mississippi closed to American trade.[24] Wilkinson's proposal did not reach Spain until some time after Bruin's request had been approved.

It is also true that Bruin came to Louisiana before d'Argès arrived in Spain in the summer of 1787. But Spanish officials knew of d'Argès's recommendations for a change in colonial policy before Bruin's petition reached Europe. In fact, the Frenchman unintentionally set the stage for approval of Bruin's request. D'Argès reached Paris in the spring of 1787 after having spent three years in Kentucky. He warned the Spanish ambassador, the Count of Aranda (Pedro Pablo de Abarca y Bolea), that Spain must adopt a new policy for its Mississippi Valley possessions if it did not want to lose them. His plan called for strengthening the Spanish provinces and weakening the American West through "the seduction of American settlers and their removal to Spanish soil."[25] His scheme centered on liberal land grants for such immigrants, who should be concentrated at Natchez, one of the more important strategic locations on the river. The plan further provided for opening the Mississippi River to western commerce, but under a 25 percent duty. D'Argès believed that many westerners would move to Spanish territory to take advantage of the land grants and to secure the trade privileges. He convinced Aranda, who wrote the Spanish minister of foreign affairs, the Count of Floridablanca (José Moniño y Redondo), on April 2, 1787, giving the project his enthusiastic support. Floridablanca discussed the plan with the Marquis of Sonora. Therefore, the two most important Spanish officials as far as colonial policy was concerned, the minister of foreign affairs and the minister of the Indies, had d'Argès's immigration scheme under consideration when Bruin's petition with Miró's endorsement arrived.[26]

[24] Arthur Preston Whitaker, "James Wilkinson's First Descent to New Orleans in 1787," *Hispanic American Historical Review*, VIII (1928), 82–97; William R. Shepherd, "Wilkinson and the Beginnings of the Spanish Conspiracy," *American Historical Review*, IX (1904), 490–506 (good on Wilkinson's proposal and the reaction of Miró and Martín Navarro, the intendant); Shepherd, "Papers Bearing on James Wilkinson's Relations with Spain, 1787–1789," *ibid.*, 748–766; Manuel Serrano y Sanz, *El brigadier Jaime Wilkinson y sus tratos con España para la independencia del Kentucky (años 1787 á 1797)* (Madrid, 1915), 1–22; Abraham P. Nasatir, *Spanish War Vessels on the Mississippi, 1792–1796* (New Haven, 1968), 17–20 (a convenient summary).

[25] Nasatir, *Spanish War Vessels on the Mississippi*, 17.

[26] Kinnaird, *Spain in the Mississippi Valley*, II, xxiv; Whitaker, *The Spanish-American Frontier*, 78–81; Holmes, *Gayoso*, 23.

Bruin's request, however, had a distinct advantage over both Wilkinson's and d'Argès's plans. It did not call for a decision on opening the Mississippi River to western trade. In addition, the no-expense-to-the-crown feature of Bryan Bruin's petition no doubt appealed to the economy-minded Bourbon on the Spanish throne, Charles III. Royal approval could be granted Bruin's application for land without any outlay of money and without making a decision on the knotty problem of opening the Mississippi to American commerce. Viewed in that setting, it is easy to see why the Spanish quickly approved Bruin's request, but delayed action on the proposals by Wilkinson and d'Argès.

Kinnaird has concluded that because of the decision in favor of Bruin's project "it became known that lands might be obtained more easily in Spanish territory than in the United States."[27] The policy of free land in the adjacent Spanish colonies brought complaints about the conservative land practices of the United States under the ordinances of 1785 and 1787. Congress even lent a sympathetic ear for a more liberal land policy, but the financial needs of the government quickly ended any tendency in that direction. In May, 1789, Congressman Thomas Scott of Pennsylvania complained "that 7,000 Americans were anxious to emigrate to Spanish territory where they would be welcomed as settlers and vassals of Spain."[28]

During the decade from 1788 to 1797 the population of Spanish Louisiana and West Florida increased by nearly 8,000 persons, or about 19 percent. Two factors were important in bringing these settlers into the area. First was the general liberalization of Spanish immigration policy beginning with the Bruins in 1787–88. Second was the gentleness of Spanish rule. William Dunbar, a prominent Natchez citizen, writing to a friend in Philadelphia in 1790, said that the major attraction of Spanish rule was that there was little or no rule at all for honest citizens. But, as Professor Whitaker has indicated for Louisiana, while the population grew, it did so "far less rapidly than that of the United States." As a barrier against the Americans Louisiana was weaker in 1800 than it had been in 1780.[29] Certainly the same could be said for West Florida.

27 Kinnaird, *Spain in the Mississippi Valley*, II, xxiv.

28 Jack D. L. Holmes, "Notes on the Spanish Fort San Esteban de Tombecbé," *Alabama Review*, XVIII (1965), 281; Roy M. Robbins, *Our Landed Heritage: The Public Domain, 1776–1936* (Lincoln, Neb., 1962), 12–13.

29 Population statistics for the Spanish territories are not accurate. Arthur Preston Whitaker has ably summarized the various sources on population for the area. Based on Whitaker's figures, Louisiana and West Florida had approximately 50,600 inhabitants in 1797. This would mean an increase of 18.74 percent from the 42,611 given by Holmes for 1788. See Whitaker, *The Mississippi Question 1795–1803*, 276, n. 24; Holmes, *Gayoso,*

Thus, Spain's efforts to populate the borderlands of their eastern frontier as a bastion against their northern neighbors proved unsuccessful.

Although the program failed to accomplish its purpose, the Bruins played a seminal part in the new immigration policy. Bryan Bruin's petition was the first to be approved after Spain decided in 1787 to liberalize its program to attract settlers. Peter Bryan Bruin and his party reached Natchez in June, 1788, the first large group of immigrants to arrive as a result of the new policy. But the Bruins' part in the matter has received much less attention and publicity than the proposals of d'Argès and the "scoundrel" Wilkinson. The record has now been partially corrected. Therefore, it is hoped that the Bruins, father and son, will be accorded their proper place in the accounts yet to be written of those times and events.[30]

22. Dunbar's comment was provided by Arthur DeRosier, who is working on the Dunbar biography. DeRosier to Coker, Apr. 9, 1969.

[30] The work on Spanish immigration in the Mississippi Valley by Gilbert C. Din did not appear in print until after the foregoing paper had been written. In the first of two articles, "The Immigration Policy of Governor Esteban Miró in Spanish Louisiana," *Southwestern Historical Quarterly*, LXXIII (Oct., 1969), 155–175, Din emphasizes Miró's role in liberalizing Spanish policy to include non-Catholics, a change which did not affect the Bruins and which came after Bryan Bruin's petition had been approved. In "Proposals and Plans for Colonization in Spanish Louisiana, 1787–1790," *Louisiana History*, XI (Summer, 1970), 197–213, Din summarizes the major immigration proposals including those of the Bruins. He concludes that "the significance of Bruin's arrival in Natchez was that it seemingly confirmed the governor's belief that a deluge of immigrants, hungry for land and seeking a market for their goods, would soon descend upon the province. The trickle of settlers that continued through 1789, however, never reached the proportions that the governor anticipated." *Ibid.*, 204–205. In his third article, "Early Spanish Colonization Efforts in Louisiana," *Louisiana Studies*, XI (Spring, 1972), 31–49, Professor Din estimates that it cost Spain two million *pesos* to settle about 6,000 immigrants in Louisiana between 1776 and 1785. The cost proved too great for the number involved and Spain turned to proposals such as Bryan Bruin's as a far less expensive alternative. Unfortunately, this author has not had the opportunity to read Din's doctoral dissertation (University of Madrid, 1960), "Colonización en la Luisiana española: proyectos de emigración en la Luisiana del siglo XVIII."

Anglo-Spanish Rivalry

on the Louisiana Frontier,

1763-68

JOHN PRESTON MOORE

*F*EW of the statesmen assembled at Paris in February of 1763 for the signing of the Treaty of Peace could have prophesied that the new frontier in North America would be devoid of imminent confrontations. Yet apparently there was less tension in Anglo-Spanish relations for a number of years thereafter than is normally supposed. Among other factors, the explanation may lie in the prudent exercise of the decision-making power by local officials of both nations, guided by the realities of the wilderness and a knowledge of the weaknesses of the respective defense systems. In an understanding of the development of colonial policies the views of on-the-spot agents did carry some weight in European chancelleries.[1] The preservation of peace was in many

[1] While emphasizing the role of "secretaries, undersecretaries, and custom officials," Franklin B. Wickwire in *British Subministers and Colonial America, 1763–1783* (Princeton, 1966), 12, notes that "Colonial governors, colonial agents, merchants, speculators, and hosts of other people were involved with British imperial relations."

In his *Agents and Merchants: British Colonial Policy and the Origins of the American Revolution, 1763–1775* (Lincoln, Neb., 1965), xiii, Jack Sosin suggests what is close to reality in the genesis of both English and Spanish policies during this period: "Seeking to make the interpretation meaningful, historians may have considered British measures as part of 'policy' in the sense of a deliberate comprehensive plan. But this type of rationalizing is, as George Unwin [*Studies in Economic History* (London, 1927), 184] warned some years ago, 'more often an illusion of the scholarly mind than a fact of history.'"

instances due to the discretion of colonial officials. An analysis of Anglo-Spanish relations in this theater between 1763 and 1768 bears out this generalization.

At first glance there were many factors that favored the emergence of provocative incidents. Chief among these were the legacy of national animosities and the peculiar circumstances of life and government on the frontier. The effects of the recent conflict were still being felt in America and Europe. Spain could not forget the ignominy of the capture of Havana and Manila by the British fleet. The Spanish secretary of state, the Marqués de Grimaldi, sensed the precariousness of peace. "What is good still," he wrote the captain general of Cuba, Antonio María Bucareli, in the middle of the summer of 1768, "is that peace is kept and according to reports of conditions in England I flatter myself it may last all this year."[2] A month later to the same official he declared: "Peace continues, and I am confident that we shall have it another year at the least, although, as it hangs from a thread, it cannot be counted upon."[3]

Similarly, British statesmen feared a renewal of the war. To be sure, some viewed the Iberian rival as less dangerous than France. But the Family Compact, unbroken by defeat, posed a threat of future action by the two Bourbon powers. In a communication to General Thomas Gage, commander-in-chief of British forces in America, Sir Henry Conway, secretary of state for the southern colonies, alluded to the new enemy soon to be ensconced in New Orleans: "The Spaniards are, or soon will be, in the actual Possession thereof; who tho' they may not be as dangerous a Neighbour, their Inclination, at least, will probably not be wanting to disturb us; You will, therefor, continue to keep a watchful Eye upon them, as You did before the French."[4] Subsequently, other English leaders echoed suspicious sentiments toward the Spanish.[5]

Mutual recriminations and apprehensions were not the only factors

[2] Grimaldi to Bucareli, San Ildefonso, July 23, 1768, Archivo General de Indias, Seville (hereafter cited as AGI), *Indiferente general, legajo* 1630.

[3] Grimaldi to Bucareli, San Ildefonso, Aug. 27, 1768, *ibid.*

[4] Conway to Gage, St. James, Oct. 24, 1765, *The Correspondence of General Thomas Gage with the Secretaries of State, and with the War Office and the Treasury, 1763–1775,* ed. Clarence E. Carter (2 vols., New Haven, 1931–33), I, 64.

[5] Lord Shelburne similarly distrusted the Spanish. See Shelburne to Gage, Whitehall, Nov. 14, 1767, *ibid.,* I, 54. More sanguine was the Earl of Halifax. Writing to Gage, he was somewhat optimistic over the possible settlement of Indian problems: "Nothing is more likely to give a favorable Turn to Our Indian Affairs than the speedy Cession of Louisiana to Spain. I am glad to acquaint You that there is very great Reason to believe that the Cession will very soon take Place." See Halifax to Gage, St. James, Sept. 8, 1764, *ibid.,* II, 17.

that created possibilities for trouble. Unlike West Florida, the original population remained in the colony. While the Spanish settlers abandoned Mobile and Pensacola for Cuba and other Spanish possessions, the French colonists continued their residence in New Orleans and the vast territory to the west of the Mississippi. The resentful attitude of this latter group was well known to the British.[6] Indirectly, they might strike back through encouragement to Indian disaffection. Adding to the natural unrest in the colony was the extraordinary nature of the new government. During the interval of the first Spanish occupation Louisiana had what appeared to some to be a dual regime. While Charles III claimed the right to rule the region, both Spanish and French officials issued decrees, usually in cooperation though sometimes independently. The uncertainty over the definition of sovereignty was partly responsible for the expulsion of the Spanish governor in October, 1768, and the termination of the initial period of Spanish domination.[7]

To administer these new colonial acquisitions, the Spanish and British governments designated governors, assisted by secretaries and military officers. Since these territories lying in the relatively uninhabited expanse of wilderness had little wealth, their affairs received less attention from Madrid and Whitehall than other more valuable colonies. To Louisiana Charles III appointed Antonio de Ulloa, a naval officer by profession, but at the same time a scientist, author, and administrator. As governor of Huancavelica in Peru, he had sought unsuccessfully to restore the operation of the mercury mines and to end the graft and corruption practiced by the colonial officials and the miners. A man of unusual intelligence and unquestioned probity, he lacked tact in dealing with his subordinates.[8] Nor could the British appointee George Johnstone, also a naval officer, claim outstanding merit in the field of administration. Like his Spanish counterpart, he was unable to establish

[6] In his dispatch to Gage of Oct. 24, 1765, Conway refers to this fact as a source of anxiety: "The Inhabitants [of Louisiana] will, in general, be the same French, who dwelt there before and whose Activity of Spirit demands our strictest Attention." *Ibid.*, I, 64.

[7] John Preston Moore, "Antonio de Ulloa: A Profile of the First Spanish Governor of Louisiana," *Louisiana History*, VIII (Summer, 1967), 203, 204.

[8] There is no full treatment of a man who must rank as one of Spain's outstanding luminaries in the fields of science and letters in the eighteenth century. The most satisfactory brief accounts are to be found in Vicente Rodríguez Casado, *Primeros años de dominación española en la Luisiana* (Madrid, 1942), 51–97; Julio F. Guillén, *Los tenientes de navío Jorge Juan y Santacilia y Antonio de Ulloa y de la Torre-Guiral* (Madrid, 1936); Arthur P. Whitaker, "Antonio de Ulloa," *Hispanic American Historical Review*, XV (May, 1935), 155–194.

a satisfactory government. Disputes with the military authorities, whom he accused of depriving him of prestige and influence, led eventually to his recall and replacement.[9] Yet these governors, exercising initiative and common sense, succeeded in finding solutions to problems that might have led to serious incidents.

To establish a basis for rapprochement, the governors of the two colonies exchanged civilities soon after the arrival of the Spanish representative. Diplomatic protocol, even on the frontier, required mutual dispatch of greetings and, if possible, the sending of representatives to the respective seats of colonial government. Owing to the fact that both men were from the upper class with its devotion to noblesse oblige, this aspect of personal relations received greater attention than might have normally occurred.

The initiative in setting up channels of communication came from the British side. The military commander at Pensacola addressed a note of welcome to Governor Ulloa, which was almost immediately answered.[10] A second letter from the Spanish governor, this time to Johnstone, set forth the basic intentions of Spain in her relations with Great Britain in this part of the Americas. It was his aim to persevere "so that peace and friendship may prevail. . . . In this intelligence," he continued, "Your Excellency may rest content that you will find me prompt to act in any contingency . . . I shall do what is necessary to bring about peace among the savages, who have caused difficulties for the British commander in the Illinois; I hope that henceforth they will offer no further obstacles to the occupation of the territory."[11]

Governor Johnstone's reply to Ulloa of May 3, despite its bombastic language, was one of extreme cordiality: "I shall ever esteem it

[9] The best sketch of the British governor is the one in the *Dictionary of National Biography* (1917), X, 963–965. There are many references to Johnstone in Cecil Johnson, *British West Florida, 1763–1783* (New Haven, 1943), and Clinton Howard, *The British Development of West Florida, 1763–1769* (Berkeley, 1947). None of these is particularly flattering.

[10] This letter, unhappily not extant, involved the Spanish governor in a heated quarrel then in progress between the civil and military aspirants for power in West Florida. Taking umbrage at this slight to his presence in Pensacola, Johnstone complained to the secretary of the Board of Trade in London that this was perhaps part of a deliberate policy by the Spanish "to foment our dispute so that I may be deprived of seizing the first Impression of engaging the French to migrate." A postscript to the letter reflected a different view, crediting Ulloa's mistake to the fact that Lieutenant Colonel Walsh had written to him first. See Johnstone to John Pownal Esq., secretary of the Board of Trade, Pensacola, Apr. 1, 1766, Correspondence of the Governors of West Florida, vol. 574, fols. 698–700, C.O. 5, Public Records Office, London.

[11] Ulloa to Johnstone, New Orleans, Apr. 1, 1766, enclosure in Johnstone's dispatch to the Board of Trade, July 19, 1766, *ibid.*, fol. 17.

as the most engaging Circumstance of my Government, the very elegant Manner in which Your Excellency has been pleased to communicate to me your arrival in Louisiana. There is a Fineza in the whole that obliges me to borrow a Word from Your Language, to express my Sense of it." Taking his cue from Ulloa's reference to Spanish intentions, the governor of West Florida stressed the identical nature of British policy. Peace was essential because of the interdependence of the two colonies: "I am extremely rejoiced to find the Ideas of Your Excellency, respecting the Interest of our Provinces so correspondent to those of Mr Aubry and my own. I am perfectly persuaded, the Prosperity of the one Colony must draw along with it the Prosperity of the other. . . . In a Word, our own Happiness and the Peace of the different Provinces intrusted to our Care, seem to me to depend on a sincere Resolution cordially to unite in mutual good offices, and neither to become the Dupes of the Indians, nor the Indian Traders, who are more savage than them." The letter concluded, however, with a polite warning against trespassing by French traders, which was harmful not only because of a reduction in British commerce but also because of the "Evil Impression which those Savages are liable to receive from the rudest of Mortals."[12] In a separate communication of approximately the same date, Lieutenant Colonel William Taylor notified the Spanish governor of his arrival in Pensacola to assume command of the British forces in the Southern District.[13]

The correspondence between the two governors did not cease with the mere exchange of greetings. Johnstone addressed at least two additional letters to his Spanish counterpart before resigning his position in

[12] Johnstone to Ulloa, Pensacola, May 3, 1766, copy as enclosure in Johnstone's dispatch to the Board of Trade, July 19, 1766, *ibid.*, fols. 25–29. In the expectation that Aubry would soon retire from affairs of government, Johnstone wrote to the French governor to express his appreciation for his friendliness to British subjects and for his wise counsel to the incoming Spanish governor. See Johnstone to Aubry, Pensacola, May 3, 1766, copy as enclosure in Johnstone's dispatch to the Board of Trade, July 19, 1766, *ibid.*, fols. 21, 22.

[13] Ulloa received from Colonel Taylor the personal greeting of General Thomas Gage, commander-in-chief of His Majesty's forces in New York, whose hope it was "to cultivate the most perfect harmony between the two nations." See Taylor to Ulloa, May, 1766, AGI, *Papeles de Cuba*, leg. 109.

Apparently Ulloa had already conveyed to Gage his intention to implement peaceful policies: "And you may rest persuaded, that my wishes are, that Concord, Quietness, and good Harmony may reign, and a happy union Subsist betwixt the Two Nations. It is in this Spirit that I shall contribute everything Conducive thereto, on my part, and promise Myself that Your Excellency corresponds with me, in the same intentions, as I am well Acquainted with the Excellent Qualities of your Nation, and those which your excellency possesses in person. . . ." See Clarence W. Alvord and Clarence E. Carter, eds., *The New Regime, 1765–1767* (Springfield, Ill., 1916), 208, 209.

West Florida. The first, dated June 19, 1766, was devoted mainly to a discussion of the ancient poetry of the Scottish Highlands, a topic believed to be of interest to the eminent scholar and scientist.[14] The second, also dated June 19, announced the dispatch to New Orleans of a prominent citizen of Pensacola, "whom I esteem among the most noteworthy of this colony," to return the courtesy visit made by Ulloa's private secretary. Simultaneously, it underlined once more the imperativeness of "perfect agreement between the Colonies intrusted to our Care."[15]

In a lengthy communication of July 28, 1766, Ulloa acknowledged receipt of the three letters from Johnstone. He reiterated his purpose to preserve friendly relations between the Spanish and the British: "I shall regard it not just as an attention and a courtesy, but as an obligation which rests upon all men, and particularly those who have in their charge powers of government . . . [to] fulfill their Royal Commands which are directed at Peace, by means of harmony between their vassals."[16]

Discounting the customary formalities and the gratuitous niceties of diplomacy, the intercolonial correspondence thus initiated set the tone for future policies for both countries. It is evident that both governors recognized the necessity of peace for the economic development of the region and might act to prevent the occurrence of incidents. Direct communication was to be the instrument for preventive steps. Nor was this recourse to be limited to the two civil chiefs. Messages were exchanged between Governor Ulloa on the one hand and General Gage and Brigadier Frederick Haldimand, commander in West Florida from 1767 to 1773, on the other. The resultant decision cleared the way for action, which in many instances could not be delayed. The procedure might be summed up in the trite formula "Act first and obtain approval later." If a troublesome situation demanded a drastic change in policy or a modification of important regulations, consultation with Whitehall and Madrid was obviously necessary. Ulloa apparently enjoyed more latitude in resolving issues than did the British officials in West Florida. Since the Spanish secretary of state had little real knowledge of the new province, he perforce relied heavily on the extensive reports furnished by his representative. Thus Ulloa's decrees were seldom countermanded

14 Johnstone to Ulloa, Pensacola, June 19, 1766, AGI, *Papeles de Cuba, leg.* 109.

15 Johnstone to Ulloa, Pensacola, June 19, 1766, copy as enclosure in Johnstone's dispatch to the Board of Trade, July 19, 1766, Correspondence of the Governors of West Florida, vol. 575, fol. 37.

16 Ulloa to Johnstone, New Orleans, July 28, 1766, AGI, *Papeles de Cuba, leg.* 109.

or altered. This, of course, does not imply that his pleas for military reinforcements and larger subsidies were immediately filled. While the heads of the two colonial governments on the frontier never met in person, their envoys, usually minor personages, frequently traveled to New Orleans or to Mobile and Pensacola in the settlement of disputes. It is clear that Madrid and Whitehall tacitly recognized the need for delegation of authority to cope with the diverse and serious problems encountered on the frontier.

These questions proved to be numerous. Any one of them might conceivably have provoked grave contention. Ordinarily a source of national controversy, the delimitation of the boundary between West Florida and Louisiana did not create severe tensions. While the framers of the Peace of Paris may have erred in some matters, they succeeded in defining in fairly clear terms the territorial bounds of Louisiana on the lower Mississippi. As Johnstone correctly pointed out to the Spanish governor in his dispatch of May 3, 1766, "The present limits have rendered any Dispute on that subject impossible."[17]

What did arouse mutual apprehension was, however, the adoption of measures for defense in both colonies. Owing to the general run-down condition of Louisiana at the end of the Seven Years' War, Ulloa perceived the need for vigorous steps to make the colony invulnerable to attack. After making an inspection in the spring and early summer of the lower part of the province—the Illinois country was too distant to be included in this preliminary survey—he drew up plans for the protection of the region from possible English aggression. Before putting these into effect he called the attention of the captain general in Havana to the woeful inadequacy of the Spanish defenses: "They [the English] maintain in those places two small armadas which point to the importance that they attach to that frontier, since they had hardly set foot on the soil when frigates were brought in so that close contact could be kept up with Pensacola, Mobile, and Balize; others [vessels] in the anchorage or near the forts at Manchac and, in contrast, on the Spanish side, even the old forts are in ruins and wholly lacking in munitions of war."[18]

Of highest priority was the construction of forts at strategic points along the frontier. As a military engineer with considerable experience in Spain and Peru, Ulloa grasped at once the significance of the control

17 Johnstone to Ulloa, Pensacola, May 3, 1766, copy as enclosure in Johnstone's dispatch to the Board of Trade, July 19, 1766, Correspondence of the Governors of West Florida, vol. 575, fol. 27.

18 Ulloa to Bucareli, New Orleans, May 28, 1766 (Correspondence of Ulloa), Dispatches of the Spanish Governors of Louisiana (11 vols., W.P.A. Survey of Federal Archives in Louisiana, Baton Rouge, 1937–38).

of the mouth of the Mississippi. From September, 1766, to the following spring his major efforts were directed therefore to the building of a fortification on a site called Isla Reina Católica de San Carlos, enabling surveillance of all traffic entering or leaving the river.[19] The scheme of defense for the colony called also for the construction of four additional fortified posts: one across the Bayou Manchac facing the English Fort Bute, a second opposite English-held Natchez, and two at the junction of the Mississippi and Missouri.[20] Minor points throughout the colony would be restored and strengthened. The building of new forts and the renovation of older ones alarmed the members of the English military establishment.

Meantime, the British were energetically undertaking to secure the frontier through the construction of fortifications at vital points and the dispatch of contingents of soldiers to garrison them. Taking advantage of the presence of units at Havana after its capture, the alert British commanders in the Gulf quickly transferred components of several regiments to West Florida. Pensacola and Mobile were occupied by October, 1763.[21] To safeguard the line of communication between the upper Mississippi and Mobile, Governor Johnstone, with the approval of the West Florida Council, enthusiastically recommended the establishment of Fort Bute at the junction of the Iberville River and the Mississippi: "There is no place of so much consequence to this Province as that Settlement, now the Iberville is opened, and which will command the whole Trade of the Mississippi, an Object of the highest Importance."[22] From the beginning, heat, fever, and mosquitoes plagued the workmen, beset also by shortage of provisions and building supplies. It was a matter of months before the blockhouse was completed. In the end nature doomed the Iberville waterway as the link in the design to bypass New Orleans through Lakes Maurepas and Pontchartrain. Like Ulloa's bold plan for a fort at the entrance of the river, the Iberville proved worthless as a counter-move in the opposing strategies.[23] More successful were the British efforts to expand the earthworks and stock-

[19] The problem of terrain proved insurmountable, however, and the location was abandoned later at the orders of General O'Reilly.

[20] Louis Houck, *A History of Missouri, from the Earliest Explorations and Settlements until the Admission of the State into the Union* (3 vols., Chicago, 1908), I, 287–297.

[21] Johnson, *British West Florida*, 8, 9.

[22] Johnstone to Pownall, Pensacola, Feb. 19, 1765, quoted in Howard, *British Development of West Florida*, 30.

[23] To keep the channel clear of mud, tree trunks, and other debris was impossible without great effort and the expenditure of large sums.

ade at "the Natchez," the site of Fort Rosalie, 140 miles above Fort Bute, and the augmentation of defenses at Fort Chartres high up the Mississippi. The movement of troops and supplies to these points at intervals raised the fears of the Spanish and French officials as to the ultimate intentions of the British.

Besides military rivalry, the uncertain attitude of the Indians constituted a potential source of friction between the two colonies. While in general favoring the Spanish as they had the French, the chiefs were not unmindful of playing off one side against the other. Allegiances of the tribes shifted. In addition to the employment of the Indians as allies in time of war, another prize—the lucrative fur trade—was at stake. Bearing these goals in mind, the Spanish governor pursued an undeviating policy of conciliation and friendship with the tribes. Chiefs of the groups residing near New Orleans visited the capital in March and April of 1766. During the late spring of that year on his protracted tour of inspection Ulloa held powwows with the leaders of strong tribes and distributed gifts liberally to the braves. Well coached by the French commandants and traders, the Indians responded in kind to the Spanish gestures of amity. Basically, they evinced less hostility to the Spanish then to the English, for the former did not envisage an extensive colonization that would deprive the natives of their hunting grounds and render game scarce. The general rapport between Spaniard and Indian incited the jealousy of English military authorities and traders.[24] Competition for the favor of the aborigines led to recriminations and accusations which required careful handling by the heads of the two colonial governments. The latent dislike of the French traders for the British enhanced the danger of serious incidents.

Even before the presence of the Spanish in Louisiana, the British government had resolved to revamp its policy toward the Indians along the frontier. Pontiac's rebellion and the spreading influence of the French traders demanded some supervision by Whitehall. Imperial con-

---

[24] The report of a British officer mentions the abundance of gifts as a cause for the display of favoritism by the Indians: "I learn'd from good Authority that the Spanish Governor had brought many sorts of presents for the Indians, & since they had Established two Posts upon the Mississippi received all that came and gave them every sort of thing they would want & since their arrival the late Capt. Rea of the 21st Regimt. who Commanded at the Natchez informed me that the Indians did not seem so attentive to the English as they were before and many of the presents he offer'd them, they rejected with scorn and said they would go to their brothers the Spaniards who gave them so much better presents than we did." See Clarence W. Alvord and Clarence E. Carter, eds., *Trade and Politics, 1767–69, Illinois Historical Collections*, XVI (Springfield, 1921), 115.

trol replaced provincial, with matters of Indian treatment to be in the hands of superintendents, such as John Stuart in the Southern District, who would be directly, though not entirely, responsible to London.[25]

In cooperation with the military authorities on the frontier, the superintendents set up the objectives of general peace through firm control of the tribes east of the Mississippi and a restriction of colonial expansion to the west. Specifically, Stuart sought to realize these aims by protecting Indian lands from claims by settlers, by subtle dealings with tribes known to be unfriendly or neutral, and finally by putting order in the Indian trade.[26] These ideas were embraced in the so-called "Plan of 1764."[27] To Stuart the heart of the "Plan" was control over individual traders through a system of licensing by the superintendent. Supervision was to be supplemented by conferences with influential chieftains and the distribution of gifts. Special groups in the colonies, such as the colonial assemblies and the merchants engaged in the fur trade, opposed the new proposal vehemently.

In 1768 the risks of incidents involving Indian relations were perhaps greater than ever before. Vested interests brought pressure to bear on Lord Shelburne, who authorized the Board of Trade in March of that year to modify its policy by returning control over the trade to the colonial assemblies. The superintendent was to maintain his authority in political affairs with the Indians. While Stuart successfully checked the enmity of the Choctaws, the traders resumed their exploitation of the Indian trade, with the increasing possibility of native resentment.[28] On the Spanish side, the lack of funds from Mexico meant the reduction in supplies and gifts for distribution. In May, 1768, St. Ange, the principal French commandant in the Illinois country, pleaded with Ulloa for the speedy shipment of goods: "They [the Indians] were more liberally provided for during the time of the French. It is no longer a matter of wishing to attract new nations," but of preserving the loyalty of the traditional allies.[29] In these circumstances to avoid Indian forays might be difficult.

Closely linked with the establishment of political ties with the Indians was the conduct of trade. For Louisiana foreign commerce was its

[25] John R. Alden, *John Stuart and the Southern Colonial Frontier: A Study of Indian Relations, War, Trade, and Land Problems in the Southern Wilderness, 1754–1775* (Ann Arbor, 1944), 172.

[26] *Ibid.*, 335.

[27] *Ibid.*, 242.

[28] *Ibid.*, 259–262.

[29] St. Ange to Ulloa, May 18, 1768, AGI, *Audiencia de Santo Domingo*, leg. 2357.

lifeblood. To France the merchants exported furs, receiving in return hardware, clothing, luxuries, and food. Lumber, pitch, and tar were sold to the French West Indies, which in turn supplied the colony with sugar, rum, and other commodities available only from the tropics. From New England the colonists clandestinely secured flour, which could not easily be produced in the warm climate of the south. English merchants, based in Mobile and Pensacola, and on the Mississippi above the Iberville, enlarged the volume of trade through an exchange of staples for pelts with the illegal connivance of officials. In addition, they secretly obtained specie and *palo de Campeche*, or dyewood, through contacts with Spanish vessels bound from Mexico. Smuggling was thus a normal feature of commerce and recognized as such by the citizenry of New Orleans.

Of these commercial activities none was more likely to cause inter-colonial controversy than the Indian trade. French and English traders were bitter rivals for the purchase of furs, for which a rich market existed in northern Europe. Despite the issuance of regulations to the contrary, itinerant merchants of both nations violated territorial bounds to deal with the natives.[30] Trespassing called for arrests and imposition of fines. The British authorities complained of frequent acts of contravention of territorial rights by French traders seeking pelts and hunting game. The sensitivity of the British arose in part from an advantage possessed by their rivals, who were in a position to offer more to the Indians since the prices paid at New Orleans were 10 to 15 percent higher than those received at English ports. In the summer of 1768 General Gage remonstrated vigorously with the Spanish governor against the illegal acts of the French traders.[31] In response Governor Ulloa stated that he had undertaken to prevent their occurrence, "having given most Strict Orders to the Commanders of the different Posts, by no means permit Spanish Subjects to pass to the English, nor to have any Commerce with them, except in particular cases of necessity requiring any to go, and then to have passports directed to the English Commander of the District to which they belong, under Penalty, that if they be found without one, they shall be entirely deprived of the rights of the Nation, and shall be Chastised by the English Chiefs at their Pleasure as the Breakers of the Peace and the Good Harmony that

[30] See Alden, *Stuart*, 172, for the English regulations governing the conduct of traders; Ulloa's ideas concerning commercial regulations with the Indians are contained in his "Instruccion para la expedicion a la parte de Yllinueses, que se le encarga al Capt. Franº. Riu," AGI, *Santo Domingo, leg.* 2357.

[31] See Gage to Hillsborough, New York, Aug. 17, 1768, *Correspondence of Gage*, I, 183.

Subsists between the two Powers."[32] Notwithstanding, violations of this nature persisted to create hazards for the preservation of good relations.

Other aspects of the Indian trade could cause trouble. The sale of firearms and brandy to the natives was a perilous traffic. Unrestricted access to guns put into the hands of the Indians formidable weapons to be used against a foe. Coupled with this was the consumption of brandy with its demoralizing effects. Spanish policy prohibited the sale of brandy to the Indians and limited the purchase of muskets and gunpowder.[33] John Stuart sought through the licensing of British traders to lessen the dangers that could arise from the unrestricted flow of these articles to the aborigines. Enforcement of these regulations was apparently futile.[34] Hence there was the constant possibility of confrontation as a result of Indian raids across the border.

Finally, desertions from the rival garrisons stationed in the wilderness could easily lead to recriminations and incidents. The loneliness of the outposts, the absence of wives or women with whom to consort, poor pay, and bad food created irresistible temptations to "go over the hill." For the Spanish deserters the haven of refuge was Pensacola, Mobile, or a fort on the Mississippi. For the British the usual sanctuary was New Orleans. In a letter to Bucareli in July, 1766, Ulloa emphasized the seriousness of the problem of deserters, "of which we have a great number owing to the opportunity of being so close to the border of the English colony."[35] As early as 1765, prior to the coming of the Spaniards, Major Farmar was disturbed over the number of soldiers who had fled to New Orleans. The situation was so deplorable in 1767 that Ulloa proposed to Haldimand a formal cartel for the mutual return of deserters.[36] Although no definite agreement was worked out, an unofficial arrangement existed permitting the issuance of proclamations

[32] Ulloa to Gage, New Orleans, Aug. 29, 1768, in Alvord and Carter, eds., *Trade and Politics*, 386.

[33] Instruccion para la expedicion a la parte de Yllinueses. . . ."

[34] Alden, *Stuart*, 193, 205–214. With little success, St. Ange endeavored to cut down on the sale of brandy through cooperation with British agents. See St. Ange to Ulloa, June 16, 1766, and Ulloa to St. Ange, New Orleans, July 15, 1766, AGI, *Papeles de Cuba*, leg. 2357.

[35] Ulloa to Bucareli, New Orleans, July 8, 1766, Dispatches of the Spanish Governors of Louisiana. The most notorious example of desertion occurred at the Missouri post of Carlos el Príncipe when Lieutenant Fernando Gómez and about half of the garrison set off down the Mississippi to seek safety at the British fort at Natchez. At Ulloa's appeal General Haldimand ordered the mutineers turned over to the Spanish authorities. See Houck, *History of Missouri*, I, 295.

[36] See Robert R. Rea, "Military Deserters from British West Florida," *Louisiana History*, IX (Summer, 1968), 128.

and visits by officers assigned to such missions.[37] Nevertheless, many British officers readily assumed that the problem reached such dimensions because of the secret encouragement of French and Spanish officers. There were identical views on the other side of the border. In this area of Anglo-Spanish relations, as in many others, the climate for disagreement was highly propitious.

But why was this period from 1763 to 1768 singularly devoid of serious crises or confrontations? Any one of the issues noted above might have led to the exchange of accusatory notes, concentration of troops at strategic points, and even the firing of shots. Yet none of these potentially dangerous questions had such consequences.

The character of the frontier environment and the policies of local officials suggest much of the explanation. Stern realities of existence in the wilderness dictated solutions. Overcoming the hazards of living, of clearing the forest and cultivating the land, and of survival from fever often had priority over purely military and commercial considerations. At the same time the commanders on both sides well understood the inadequacy of the long line of defense along the Gulf and the Mississippi.[38] While the British had numerical supremacy, the Spanish held in New Orleans the key to the communications between Pensacola and the upper reaches of the great river. The construction of forts was not enough. To maintain them with men and supplies was more arduous. The heavy indebtedness of both governments at the end of the Seven Years' War forestalled large expenditures for the protection of an area whose resources were of limited value compared to those of other colonies. Hence Whitehall and Madrid from time to time enjoined their civil and military authorities to observe policies of economy and retrenchment. In the long run it was to the sound interest of merchants engaged in contraband and traders bargaining with the Indians in the hinterland to avoid hostilities as an indispensable condition for prosperity. The adoption of parallel policies, or in a few instances coordination of policies, was an essential element in the relative quiet of the frontier.

To what extent was the absence of provocations due to the foresight

---

[37] *Ibid.*, 133–136.

[38] Haldimand made this plain in a dispatch to Gage in the summer of 1767: "It does not seem that it would benefit the Spaniards ever to undertake anything against us on these banks; perhaps they only foresee what would happen to them at the first war. It is true, however, that our posts on the Mississippi, very badly constructed, perhaps badly situated and dependent on New Orleans for their subsistence, are in a very hazardous position today." See Haldimand to Gage, Pensacola, June 17, 1767, in Alvord and Carter, eds., *The New Regime*, 575.

and moderations of the governors of Louisiana and West Florida? Although neither Ulloa nor Johnstone could be rated a first-class administrator, both men recognized the seriousness of the problems to be solved in establishing viable governments in a wilderness where enforcement of law was frequently nonexistent. Johnstone's successors were likewise cognizant of the common dangers. It must be said to their credit that there were few signs of overreaction. Despite rumors and malicious charges of subordinates, General Gage, certainly no naive observer of events, refused to give credence to reports of the involvement of the Spanish governor in Indian conspiracies against English outposts. "I have never been able to discover that any Intrigues have been carried on with the Indians under the sanction of the French and Spanish Governors; or have I any Reason to Suspect that either Don Ulloa or Mon[r] Aubry have had any Concern in them," he informed Lord Hillsborough in London.[39] These stories, he declared, emanated from the former French officers and traders, who cherished deep resentment and hatred because of their defeat in the war. Nor was there any basis, in his opinion, for the accusation that the Spanish officials deliberately encouraged desertions among English recruits as a means of undermining morale in enemy garrisons.[40] Instead of constant provocations and acts of enmity, one is impressed by the degree of mutual understanding and respect that prevailed. For this détente the attitude of the high officials on both sides of the border had a responsibility.

In the avoidance of dangerous controversies Anglo-Spanish diplomacy in this part of the Americas during the years 1763–68 was a success. That there were minor disputes was inevitable, but none of these attained threatening dimensions. In the resolving of these, decision-making was often local. Spanish and English officials corresponded directly with each other without sanction or interference from Whitehall and Madrid and settled many issues on the realization of the common need to survive on the frontier. Restraining the Indians and curtailing the illegal activities of the traders were essential steps to strengthen colonial administration. Very wisely, Grimaldi approved in the main the decisions of his representative, and to a lesser degree, Shelburne and

[39] Gage to Hillsborough, New York, Feb. 4, 1769, *Correspondence of Gage*, I, 217.
[40] Hillsborough to Gage, Whitehall, June 11, 1768, in Alvord and Carter, eds., *Trade and Politics*, 298. This was also the view of the British captain John Marsh: "And as far as I cou'd learn their desertion was not Encouraged by the French or Spaniards, on the contrary they wou'd be glad they were out of the Country, they are too Idle to work and commit such thefts upon the Inhabitants that many of them have got Public Whipings and if Ill in the streets, are an expence to their Government by taking them into the King's Hospital." See Marsh to Haldimand, Nov. 20, 1767, *ibid.*, 114.

Hillsborough followed suit. It is clear that distinct profit accrued to the extension of authority to those on the scene familiar with conditions. Their counsel contributed to the formation of general policies in the European chancellories. In retrospect, this era was perhaps a brief interlude in the bitter rivalry of Spain and Britain in the colonial world. It was also a period of preparation for competition in the future on a grander scale. Britain's loss of her American colonies precluded the further concession of local power in North America. The shift in focus for Spain, evident during Ulloa's short term of office, proved the substantial value of flexibility in colonial administration, the key to the establishment of a government for Louisiana superior to that devised by France during the first half of the eighteenth century.

Governor Bernardo de Gálvez

and Spanish Espionage

in Pensacola, 1777

———◆◆◆———

ROBERT L. GOLD

*D*URING the last years of the 1770s England and Spain intensified their almost continuous struggle for control of the Mississippi Valley. Eventually, in 1779, the Spanish kingdom entered into the American Revolutionary War against Great Britain in an effort to regain Gibraltar, Minorca, the Floridas, and both banks of the lower Mississippi channel; monopoly over that strategic river had long ago been lost to France in the early eighteenth century and later to British America after the Seven Years' War. The cessation of contraband trade in the Mississippi Valley and the Gulf of Mexico also became a major objective in Spain's military operations against England. Hegemony of the entire Gulf Coast, bordered by Florida, Louisiana, and New Spain, and the exclusion of illicit commerce in the Southeast would certainly be worth a war with Great Britain in the New World.

The Hispanic monarchy historically sought to sustain its power in Middle America by controlling such accesses to the area as the Bahama Channel, the Caribbean, and the Gulf of Mexico. But by 1650 control of those strategic seas was becoming more and more difficult to maintain. As late as the eighteenth century, only the enormous Gulf east of New Spain remained relatively secure as a Spanish sea. After 1763 and the Treaty of Paris, Florida passed under English sovereignty and Spain's precarious hold upon that portal was limited to the Louisiana shoreline west of New Orleans. The Spanish empire in the Indies had lost all its significance and territory east of the Mississippi River. Furthermore, French America no longer existed as a buffer between the British colonies and New Spain. The exclusion of France from the New World mainland left the Spanish forces alone to face their former enemies across the midwestern river and along the Gulf Coast of Mexico. For Spain, the American Revolutionary War therefore provided a major opportunity to remove the English menace from the Mississippi Valley. It would also facilitate the recovery of territory lost as a consequence of the Treaty of 1763. In order once again to guard the Gulf Coast entrance to Mesoamerica and Spanish Cuba, the ministers of Charles III hoped to reconquer East and West Florida, while retaining rule of what was formerly French Louisiana. Repatriation of Florida would re-establish the empire as it had existed prior to 1763 and the seizure of the lower Mississippi Valley would add a very significant territory to Spanish America. If such a conquest could be achieved, all the land approaches to Mexico City might be eventually closed to foreign intrusions and commerce. After 1775, a colonial war with England appeared to be especially advantageous to Spain. Without the presence of French power on the North American continent and with England's involvement in the colonial insurrection, Spanish plans for expansion were reasonable and soon to be realized.[1]

By 1777 Louisiana, under the leadership of Governor Bernardo de Gálvez, seemed ready to begin preparations for the reconquest of Florida. Plans to cross the Mississippi River and penetrate the English provinces appeared in Gálvez's correspondence soon after he assumed office in New Orleans. Following eleven years of Spanish authority (1766–77) and the administrations of three governors, the former French province, surreptitiously ceded to Spain in 1762–63, was apparently capable of confronting the British military position in the Mississippi Valley. The Hispanicization of Louisiana, however, had been a long, difficult, and probably incomplete process when revolution weakened the foreign competition for the Gulf Coast. But by the late 1770s, the Creoles

---

[1] John Walton Caughey, *Bernardo de Gálvez in Louisiana, 1776–1783* (Berkeley, 1934), 1–70 and *passim;* Vera Lee Brown, "Anglo-Spanish Relations in America in the Closing Years of the Colonial Era," *Hispanic American Historical Review*, V (Aug., 1922), 337–344, 369–372; Brown, "Contraband Trade: A Factor in the Decline of Spain's Empire in America," *Hispanic American Historical Review*, VIII (May, 1928), 178–189; Arthur P. Whitaker, "The Commerce of Louisiana and the Floridas at the End of the Eighteenth Century," *Hispanic American Historical Review*, VIII (May, 1928), 191; Zenab Esmat Rashed, *The Peace of Paris, 1763* (Liverpool, 1951), *passim.*

seemed to be reconciled to Spanish rule and apparently supportive of Spain's imperialistic ambitions in the Southeast.[2]

Spanish Louisiana had emerged into existence inauspiciously. At Fontainebleau and Paris, in the winter of 1762–63, the costly territory of Louisiana was willingly transferred to Charles III as compensation for Spanish losses in the Seven Years' War. Spain unenthusiastically accepted the province rather than prolong the expensive conflict waged by the Family Compact powers (France and Spain) against Great Britain. By 1762 the British capture of Cuba, Canada, and the French colonies in Africa, Asia, and the Caribbean had convinced the Bourbon kings of the futility of continuing the struggle. While they negotiated the Peace of Paris with their triumphant opponent, Louisiana secretly became part of the Hispanic empire in America. Despite the loss of Florida and the strategic location of New Orleans and the French Gulf Coast, the government of Charles III waited three years before assuming control of the colony.[3] The Spaniards occupied Louisiana only after their repossession of Cuba and the transfer of the Florida population to other sites in the empire.

With the arrival of Governor Antonio de Ulloa in 1766, anti-Spanish attitudes were soon evident in the province, especially in the capital of New Orleans, where the insurrection of 1768–69 summarily expelled the new official. The severity of the subsequent regime of General Alexandro O'Reilly (1769–70) undoubtedly added other reasons for French resentment. During the governorship of Luis de Unzaga y Amézaga (1769–76), an accord was ultimately achieved between the foreign bureaucracy and the French Creoles despite the failure of all attempts to Hispanicize the Louisiana populace. Franco-Spanish cooperation thus characterized that seven-year administration. In his last year and a half of service, Unzaga was confronted by the colonial rebellion in British America. Recognizing Louisiana's military limitations and exposed po-

---

[2] Caughey, *Bernardo de Gálvez in Louisiana*, 1–57; Charles Gayarré, *History of Louisiana* (4 vols., New York, 1867), II, 131–353, III, 1–112; Kathryn T. Abbey, "Spanish Projects for the Reoccupation of the Floridas during the American Revolution," *Hispanic American Historical Review*, IX (Aug., 1929), 265–285.

[3] Rashed, *The Peace of Paris*, 115–200; Caughey, *Bernardo de Gálvez in Louisiana*, 3–6; Robert L. Gold, *Borderland Empires in Transition: The Triple-Nation Transfer of Florida* (Carbondale, Ill., 1969), 13–19; Arthur S. Aiton, "The Diplomacy of the Louisiana Cession," *American Historical Review*, XXXVI (July, 1931), 701–720; Mildred Stahl Fletcher, "Louisiana as a Factor in French Diplomacy from 1763 to 1800," *Mississippi Valley Historical Review*, XVII (Dec., 1930), 368–369; Louise Phelps Kellogg, "France and the Mississippi Valley: A Résumé," *Mississippi Valley Historical Review*, XVIII (June, 1931), 3–22.

sition to English and rebel forces alike, the governor adopted a neutral policy in the war which his successor wisely continued until 1779. When Bernardo de Gálvez received the appointment to Louisiana, he inherited a relatively stable economy with an improved agrarian production and a pacified French citizenry, many of whom the Spanish colonel recruited for his military campaigns in West Florida. From Unzaga the new governor also inherited a legacy of illegal commerce along the Gulf Coast and in the Mississippi Valley.[4] Spanish control was established in Louisiana, but foreigners freely traded everywhere in the colony.

Historically, the Spanish empire in America and its system of economic exclusivism had continually faced the challenge of contraband trade throughout the colonial period. Before 1763 governors of Spanish Florida also struggled fruitlessly to suppress illicit traffic in the territories and seas bordering the peninsula. Foreign trade, although typically forbidden, actually furnished the presidio of St. Augustine with sufficient provisions to survive some periods of the eighteenth century. Settlement of the Seven Years' War and Spain's assumption of power in Louisiana did not inhibit English traders from conducting their illegal commerce, sometimes insidiously and other times openly, in the Mississippi basin. England's position in Pensacola and Mobile permitted its merchants to be in proximity to New Orleans and the ports on the Spanish side of the river. Because of the Treaty of 1763, British West Florida enjoyed free navigation of the Mississippi River and consequently a substantial portion of the contraband business. Controversy accompanying numerous incidents of smuggling on both sides of the river inevitably affected Anglo-Spanish relations from 1766 to 1779. Ship seizures, imprisonment of seamen, incitement of Indian raids, and asylum for deserters and runaway slaves all contributed to the international discord of the two countries, but illicit trade probably became the *cause célèbre* of conflict between Great Britain and Spain in the Mississippi Valley. Cessation of illegal commerce thus became an im-

---

[4] John Preston Moore, "Antonio de Ulloa: A Profile of the First Spanish Governor of Louisiana," *Louisiana History*, VIII (Summer, 1967), 189–218; Arthur P. Whitaker, "Antonio de Ulloa," *Hispanic American Historical Review*, XV (May, 1935), 155–194; J. E. Winston, "The Cause and Results of the Revolution of 1768 in Louisiana," *Louisiana Historical Quarterly*, XV (Apr., 1932), 181–213; Jack D. L. Holmes, "Some Economic Problems of Spanish Governors of Louisiana," *Hispanic American Historical Review*, XLII (Nov., 1962), 521–543; John G. Clark, "New Orleans: Its First Century of Economic Development," *Louisiana History*, X (Winter, 1969), 43–44; Caughey, *Bernardo de Gálvez in Louisiana*, 1–84; Lawrence Kinnaird, ed., *Spain in the Mississippi Valley, 1765–1794* (3 vols., Washington, 1946–49), I, xv–xxv, 1–236.

mediate priority of Governor Gálvez in the first year of his administration.[5]

On January 1, 1777, Barnardo de Gálvez officially succeeded Unzaga as governor and captain general of Louisiana. An experienced soldier with continental and colonial military service, the new governor came from a Spanish family of considerable influence in the court of Charles III. His father, Matías de Gálvez, later served his king as viceroy of New Spain (1783–84), while his famous uncle, José de Gálvez, Marqués de Sonora, was minister of the Indies from 1772 to 1786. Bernardo's uncle occupied a ministry in the Council of the Indies following six years of extraordinary service in New Spain as visitor general (1765–71). He ultimately became president of the Council of the Indies in 1774. Both Bernardo and his father owed their prestigious positions in America to José de Gálvez, who willingly employed nepotism to promote the careers of his relatives. Indeed, in the late eighteenth century the Gálvez family appeared to be well situated in the colonial government of Charles III. For Bernardo de Gálvez, the governorship of Louisiana would present him with opportunities to advance his own professional ambitions, expand the international power of his colony, and close the lower Mississippi Valley to illegal traffic. He would also wrest West Florida from British rule.[6]

Within the first six months of his new commission, while enforcing trade regulations and seizing English contraband ships, the governor sent a spy across the river to investigate conditions in the Florida colonies. Gálvez wanted to know the state of his neighbor's defenses and the general strength of the garrisons that faced his settlement in Louisiana. His scheme of espionage was authorized by the Council of the Indies. Instructions from Spain in February, November, and December, 1776, urged Unzaga and later Gálvez to collect information concerning

[5] James A. James, "Spanish Influence in the West during the American Revolution," *Mississippi Valley Historical Review*, IV (Sept., 1917), 193–208; Arthur P. Whitaker, *The Spanish-American Frontier: 1783–1795; the Westward Movement and the Spanish Retreat in the Mississippi Valley* (Boston, 1927), 7 and *passim*; Joyce E. Harman, *Trade and Privateering in Spanish Florida, 1732–1763* (Jacksonville, 1969), 40–72; Brown, "Contraband Trade," 187–188; Governor Bernardo de Gálvez to Minister José de Gálvez, New Orleans, Sept. 15, 1777, MSS, AGI 86-6-11. All documents cited as MSS, AGI (Manuscripts, Archivo General de Indias) are included in the Stetson Collection of photostated Spanish colonial records located in the P. K. Yonge Memorial Library of Florida History, Gainesville.

[6] For an enlightening account of José de Gálvez see Herbert I. Priestley, *José de Gálvez, Visitor-General of New Spain, 1765–1771* (Berkeley, 1916); James, "Spanish Influence in the West," 198–208; Holmes, "Some Economic Problems of Spanish Governors," 523–530.

military and civil affairs in British America. Spanish policy-makers were particularly anxious to learn about the progress of the American Revolution and the attitudes of both sides toward Spain. They seemed determined to learn every detail of the conflict in the colonies. José de Gálvez encouraged his governors in Cuba and Louisiana to report all news—even trivia—of events in Canada, the Midwest, and the eastern colonies. *Cédulas* requiring accounts from America recommended colonial officials to control their espionage by means of secrecy and subterfuge. Seeking to acquire additional information, Indian allies, American merchants, and trading vessels were also employed by the Spaniards. The Council of the Indies apparently considered American sources to be more reliable than European spies. By 1778 the viceroyalty of New Spain and the captaincy general of Cuba supported an intelligence system costing 53,000 *pesos* per year. Serving such an organization, the capital of Louisiana became a center for Spanish espionage because of its proximity to the British- and rebel-occupied provinces. News from the north reached New Orleans by riverboat as soon as Spain's "pro-American neutrality" permitted patriots to purchase arms and supplies in the lower Mississippi Valley.[7]

Gálvez's agent, an unnamed but "trusted man," arrived in Pensacola in the summer of 1777. Travelers apparently crossed the river between the British and Spanish ports without interference, but spies from Louisiana pretended to be engaged in diplomacy if challenged during trips to West Florida. Such deceit enabled the governor's "envoy" to enter English territory. His mission included a descriptive survey of the English positions on the east shore of the Mississippi River, scrutiny of the fortifications in the West Florida capital, and, following his return to New Orleans, a report relating the current news of the American Revolution. The assignment was arranged with almost complete secrecy. In order to conceal the clandestine operation from all observers, Governor Gálvez ordered the agent abroad without even the knowledge of subordinates under his command. His treasury officials were likewise ignorant of the mission. Gálvez sustained the espionage by shrewdly paying the costs of the trip from his own personal funds. Later, the crown received requests for remuneration of the money (176 *pesos*, 6 *reales*), which the governor transferred to his informant covertly

7 Kathryn T. Abbey, "Efforts of Spain to Maintain Sources of Information in the British Colonies before 1779," *Mississippi Valley Historical Review*, XV (June, 1928), 56–68; Governor Bernardo de Gálvez to Minister José de Gálvez, New Orleans, Sept., 15, 1777, MSS, AGI 86-6-11; correspondence of Governor Bernardo de Gálvez and Minister José de Gálvez, New Orleans, July 10, Aug. 15, Oct. 13, 1777, MSS, AGI 87-1-6.

through the intermediacy of his private secretary. Several months later, his uncle approved the entire operation and encouraged other similar expeditions.[8]

Although the Spanish agent lacked engineering skills, he provided his superiors with a very detailed study of the Pensacola defenses. He described structural fortifications, including measurements of walls and batteries. An inventory of cannon with specifications of their condition, caliber, and position also appeared in the secret account. Many of the guns, transferred from British frigates, were ineffective following their placement in the fort at Pensacola. More than half of the fifty-eight cannons had been moved to the city without mountings and six or seven of those weapons required extensive reconditioning in England. The garrison also stored a limited supply of ammunition. Seeking to strengthen his colony, Governor Peter Chester (1770–81)[9] requested a warship with seventy-two guns and two frigates, but information gathered in the capital indicated that West Florida would be awarded a thirty-six-gun frigate, an armed sloop, and a reconverted merchant vessel to serve as a naval fleet. In 1777 the military station at Pensacola seemed unprepared for any well-organized assault. The Louisiana spy related that one infantry officer remarked publicly, "If I must fight an enemy at Pensacola, I prefer to lead my troops into combat outside the stockade rather than defend a fortress of such bad construction."[10] Earlier, in 1763, when the English soldiers occupied the Spanish city, they had vehemently criticized their predecessors for the miserable state of the presidio's defenses. Following fourteen years of British administration, the military position of the West Florida capital seemed unchanged.

Bernardo de Gálvez learned from his espionage agent that the West Florida garrisons possessed 850 soldiers. Forty-nine men of that total maintained the defenses of Mobile, while the remainder served the province at Pensacola. Sixty of the troops at the capital were considered

[8] Correspondence of Governor Bernardo de Gálvez and Minister José de Gálvez, New Orleans, July 15, Oct. 13, 1777, MSS, AGI 87-1-6.

[9] For a fine study of the governorship of Peter Chester and the administrative history of British West Florida see Cecil Johnson, *British West Florida, 1763–1783* (New Haven, 1943). The following articles are also informative in the assessment of his eleven years of service in Florida: Kathryn T. Abbey, "Peter Chester's Defense of the Mississippi after the Willing Raid," *Mississippi Valley Historical Review*, XXII (June, 1935), 17–32; James A. Padgett, "The Reply of Peter Chester, Governor of West Florida, to Complaints Made against His Administration," *Louisiana Historical Quarterly*, XXII (Jan., 1939), 31–46.

[10] Correspondence of Governor Bernardo de Gálvez and Minister José de Gálvez, New Orleans, July 10, Oct. 13, 1777, MSS, AGI 87-1-6.

to be "useless for service." According to information from Florida, Governor Chester could not predict when additional reinforcements would be sent since 102 recruits had recently arrived by packetboat from Great Britain. The Spanish emissary expected that situation to change, however, because the British Colonial Office advised its subordinates in America that war was soon anticipated with France and Spain; such news probably startled the Louisiana governor and, perhaps, even his superiors in Spain. Peter Chester therefore received orders from England to fortify Pensacola "sans enconomie."[11]

Regardless of future international relations, England seemed resolved to remain in control of Pensacola. From his informant's report, Gálvez realized the importance of the port city to British colonial policy; because of its strategic and commercial value and its proximity to the Mississippi Valley, the capital of West Florida would be protected and retained "at all costs." Apparently the interior of the province would be expendable in the event of war with the continental powers. Pensacola, however, would be defended with unrelenting determination.[12]

The governor of Louisiana was also informed about Anglo-Indian affairs in West Florida. In an effort to enlist the Chickasaws, Choctaws, and Creeks against the American rebels, the English government in early 1777 convened a congress for those natives at Mobile. Since their arrival in the 1760s, the new occupants of Florida had organized occasional conferences with the major tribes for the establishment of treaties, the exchange of cordiality, and the arrangement of mutually accepted boundaries between the European and native communities. With the help and supervision of special officials from the Office of Indian Affairs, the governors of East and West Florida held several conventions at Mobile, Pensacola, and St. Augustine during the two decades of the British period. In 1777 approximately 25,000 Indians attended the meetings at Mobile. The representatives of the large assembly advised the British spokesmen that their people wished to remain neutral throughout the struggle. Recognizing their apparent reluctance to participate in the war, the Florida negotiators next sought to convince the chiefs of the necessity of obstructing the movement of rebels through their territory. Indian delegates heard stern warnings that the

[11] *Ibid.* Governor Chester later improved the defenses of his province after the winter of 1778, when James Willing and his rebel raiders attacked British stations and communities in the Mississippi Valley. John W. Caughey, "Willing's Expedition down the Mississippi, 1778," *Louisiana Historical Quarterly*, XV (Jan., 1932), 5–36; Abbey; "Chester's Defense of the Mississippi," 17–32.

[12] Correspondence of Governor Bernardo de Gálvez and Minister José de Gálvez, New Orleans, July 10, Oct. 13, 1777, MSS, AGI 87-1-6.

American colonists would usurp their lands and enslave their people if permitted to "put one foot upon their property." The case of the unfortunate Cherokees, who lost their lands and freedom to rebel forces, was cited to the convention as evidence of American avarice and duplicity. Although they listened politely to the harangues of their English hosts, the Indians repeated their policy of neutrality and asserted their intentions to avoid conflict with the colonists. The chiefs were certainly willing, however, to continue receiving gifts from the government of His Britannic Majesty! Subsequently, the confidential agent mentioned another conference where 900 Creeks met with rebel commissioners, and he stated, "Here it is well known that the American flag is flying in seven Creek camps, which comprise almost half their nation."[13] British attempts in Florida to prejudice the Indians against the American patriots had obviously failed.

As a consequence of the surveillance mission in Florida, Governor Gálvez discovered the existence of an English spy organization in New Orleans.[14] Espionage apparently extended to both sides of the river since each of the colonial governments sought knowledge of the other's activities and strength along the Mississippi shores. His man in Pensacola notified him that "news and intelligence" of Spanish Louisiana soon reached Peter Chester by mail. In this manner the authorities across the Mississippi River learned of the preferential treatment accorded to American representatives in Louisiana. Some of Oliver Pollock's negotiations in New Orleans were also known to the British government of West Florida.[15] The Spanish agent presented Gálvez with quite an exposé of the English espionage operation in his province:

> In New Orleans there are some individuals who gather and write to Pensacola all the news and intelligence they can gather relative to the Spanish government. They also correspond concerning the friendly treatment and favors that the Spanish and French governments conceded to the Americans. The powder that

---

[13] *Ibid.*

[14] English spies apparently had been active in Spanish Louisiana since 1773. See Joseph G. Tregle, Jr., "British Spy along the Mississippi: Thomas Hutchins and the Defenses of New Orleans, 1773," *Louisiana History*, VIII (Fall, 1967), 313–329.

[15] For information regarding Oliver Pollock's contribution to the American Revolution see James A. James, "Oliver Pollock, Financier of the Revolution in the West," *Mississippi Valley Historical Review*, XVI (June, 1929), 67–80; James, "Oliver Pollock and the Free Navigation of the Mississippi River," *Mississippi Valley Historical Review*, XIX (Dec., 1932), 331–347; Abbey, "Efforts of Spain to Maintain Sources of Information," 58–64; Caughey, *Bernardo de Gálvez in Louisiana*, 56, 85–86, 98–101, 110–113, 123–124.

went up the Mississippi last fall [1776] is said to have been by permission and consent of Governor Unzaga's administration under the direction of Mr. Pollock, a suspected agent of Congress; Pollock, they say, sent a boat loaded with powder to Philadelphia with the passport of the past governor. So malicious and so antagonistic are these exaggerators of the truth that they never ignore even the most minimal circumstance. . . . Surely, Governor Gálvez must know those who maintain such correspondence since his secret agents seem to be everywhere here in Pensacola.[16]

Bernardo de Gálvez also became aware of foreign attitudes toward his capture and confiscation of eleven ships engaged in contraband trade. The seizures occurred on April 17, 1777, following the interception of three Spanish boats in Lake Ponchartrain. Nine of the vessels appropriated by the Spaniards belonged to British merchants and, following an exchange of accusatory correspondence with Peter Chester and the commander of the Mississippi frigate *Atlanta*, as well as a deputation from Pensacola, the ships and their cargoes were condemned and sold; the Spaniards later secretly released the two American boats taken in the raid.[17] As anticipated, the governor and some of the councilmen proclaimed the Spanish exploit to be a violation of the Treaty of Paris. Other Englishmen explained the ship seizures as retaliation for their own navy's earlier provocations in the Mississippi Valley and Lake Ponchartrain. According to the espionage report from Pensacola:

The opinions of the last confiscations in New Orleans of the English merchandise and vessels are as varied as the prejudices the action has caused. The disposition of those with financial involvement differs too depending upon their personal losses. The governor and some of the councilmen, who seldom disagree with their superior, deceive the people into believing that the act of confiscation was contrary to the trade provisions of the Treaty of Paris. They ignore the sections of the past treaty which outline the rights of His Catholic Majesty to punish those individuals and their accomplices who disembark or attempt to disembark illicit commerce in his dominions. Some other members of the council think

---

[16] Correspondence of Governor Bernardo de Gálvez and Minister José de Gálvez, New Orleans, July 10, Oct. 13, 1777, MSS, AGI 87-1-6.

[17] Governor Bernardo de Gálvez to Minister José de Gálvez, New Orleans, Sept. 15, 1777, MSS, AGI 86-6-11; Caughey, *Bernardo de Gálvez in Louisiana*, 71–77; James, "Spanish Influence in the West," 198–199; Abbey, "Spanish Projects for the Reoccupation of the Floridas," 267–270; John W. Caughey, "Bernardo de Gálvez and the English Smugglers on the Mississippi, 1777," *Hispanic American Historical Review*, XII (Feb., 1932), 46–58.

to the contrary that the confiscations were correct according to law and the current laws with justice and that all actions taken or that should be taken to ask for redemption are vain, absurd, and frivolous. Both parties agree that the confiscation was made in consequence of the recent belligerence of Captain Bardon in the lake.[18]

Gálvez actually employed "English insults to Louisiana property and ships" as a pretext to expropriate the fleet of merchant vessels with their quality cargoes. He later admitted to his uncle that the unwarranted detention and search of Spanish boats in Lake Pontchartrain provided him with the opportunity to order the confiscations of April 17.[19]

One of the most important revelations from West Florida regarded the "probability of war with France and Spain." By the late 1770s, Great Britain seemed certain of a colonial struggle with the Bourbon countries and British subjects in America were advised accordingly. The populace in Pensacola believed in the inevitability of international conflict with the Family Compact countries because of correspondence received from Jamaica. Mail carried in the packetboat from the Caribbean bases predicted the probability of war in view of the massive military preparations in progress under French and Spanish supervision. Reconnaissance reports from English agents in Europe and America presumably supplied such information to the government of George III. The Colonial Office considered the acts of "open aid" and port privileges available to rebel shipping as additional evidence of an impending Franco-Spanish attack in America.[20] For Gálvez and the Council of the Indies in Spain, knowledge of English expectations was obviously invaluable for the formulation of future policy.

The governor also received other information from his emissary describing war events on the eastern seaboard as well as in East Florida. In the spring of 1777, the governor and people of St. Augustine ap-

[18] Captain Bardon commanded a British schooner in Lake Pontchartrain which intercepted and detained three Spanish vessels carrying tar for eventual shipment to Cuba. Correspondence of Governor Bernardo de Gálvez and Minister José de Gálvez, New Orleans, July 10, Oct. 13, 1777, MSS, AGI 87-1-6.

[19] *Ibid.;* Governor Bernardo de Gálvez to Minister José de Gálvez, New Orleans, Sept. 15, 1777, MSS, AGI 86-6-11; Caughey, *Bernardo de Gálvez in Louisiana,* 71–77; Caughey, "Gálvez and the English Smugglers," 46–58.

[20] Correspondence of Governor Bernardo de Gálvez and Minister José de Gálvez, New Orleans, July 10, Oct. 13, 1777, MSS, AGI 87-1-6; Governor Bernardo de Gálvez to Minister José de Gálvez, New Orleans, Apr. 4, May 12, 1777, MSS, AGI 87-1-6; Caughey, *Bernardo de Gálvez in Louisiana,* 85–134; James, "Spanish Influence in the West," 199–202; Abbey, "Spanish Projects for the Reoccupation of the Floridas," 266–272.

parently feared a patriot assault from Georgia and the Carolinas. An invasionary force of 4,000 soldiers was rumored to be marching southward toward the St. John's River valley.[21] Fortunately for those Floridians, the city of St. Augustine never faced a significant attack from the north during the Revolutionary War. Although East Florida appeared better prepared for the possibility of war than West Florida, both provinces required reinforcements, regardless of which enemy—France, Spain, or rebel colonists—the British army ultimately faced in battle.

The Spanish agent returned to New Orleans in early July. His report of reconnaissance and espionage, dated July 10, 1777, was included in the correspondence that Bernardo de Gálvez soon dispatched to the Council of the Indies. A response to his report arrived from Spain during the following fall. In October, the Louisiana governor learned that Charles III seemed very satisfied with the planning and results of his secret mission across the Mississippi River. Other spy operations were therefore ordered by José de Gálvez. "These dispositions have merited the approval of the king and he wants you to use similar methods to assess the activities of the Americans and the English."[22] The progress of the colonial revolution would continue to concern the Spanish government; consequently additional news about the "American advances" was requested from Gálvez.

He also received authorization to establish espionage missions with the same secrecy employed previously. Future reconnaissance expeditions to British West Florida would follow general procedures founded in 1777 with similar success. About a year later, Captain Jacinto Panis, serving as a spy and Spanish plenipotentiary, traveled to Mobile and Pensacola for the purpose of gathering military information for the government of Louisiana. His plans for the capture of Pensacola were subsequently implemented after June, 1779, when Spain declared war against Great Britain.[23] Espionage operations obviously served Spanish interests in Louisiana and the lower Mississippi Valley.

Soon after his installation in the governorship of Spanish Louisiana, Bernardo de Gálvez inaugurated a surreptitious investigation of British West Florida. Obeying the recommendations of his superiors in Spain and recognizing the need to know the state of his neighbor's colony

[21] The St. John's River flows near the present-day port city of Jacksonville. Correspondence of Governor Bernardo de Gálvez and Minister José de Gálvez, New Orleans, July 10, Oct. 13, 1777, MSS, AGI 87-1-6.

[22] *Ibid.*

[23] *Ibid.*; Caughey, *Bernardo de Gálvez in Louisiana*, 141–148; John W. Caughey, "The Panis Mission to Pensacola, 1778," *Hispanic American Historical Review*, X (Nov., 1930), 480–489.

on the other side of the river, the new governor sent a spy to Pensacola to appraise the military garrison, inventory its defenses, and discover all the recent news of the American Revolutionary War. The results of the operation were very rewarding. Gálvez, the Council of the Indies, and, indeed, Charles III of Spain subsequently knew the British situation in West Florida, as well as other vital colonial facts and statistics. In the future, the Spanish monarchy could approach its incipient aggression in the American Revolutionary War with the conviction that Louisiana would not be easily overwhelmed by English colonists in the lower Mississippi Valley. Gálvez certainly held similar convictions after the secret mission of 1777 and the Panis expedition of the following year.

The governor of Louisiana also learned from his intelligence operations that West Florida was vulnerable to seizure by the Spanish army. Because he possessed such accurate descriptions of the British defenses along the Mississippi River and at Pensacola and Mobile, the Spanish governor devised his strategy for an attack on West Florida months before the king issued his declaration of war against Great Britain. Nine weeks after that announcement, Gálvez led across the river a small army which quickly seized Manchac, Baton Rouge, and Natchez. Mobile surrendered to Spanish forces on March 14, 1780, and a year later, on May 10, 1781, Pensacola also succumbed to an invasion from Louisiana. By the spring of 1781, Bernardo de Gálvez had completed the reconquest of West Florida. The impressive victory was the result of careful planning and preparation, the military leadership of the Louisiana governor, and, finally, his effective system of espionage.

More on Pedro Vial
in Upper Louisiana

————◆•◆————

ABRAHAM P. NASATIR

*E*VER since Louis Houck published in 1909 Pedro Vial's diary of his exploratory journey from Santa Fe to St. Louis in 1792,[1] this Frenchman in Spanish employ has been an intriguing but elusive figure in the history of the Spanish Southwest. During many years of research in distant archives and libraries on my lifelong theme of Spain in the upper Mississippi Valley, I found his name recurring frequently, and eventually, with my colleague the late Noel M. Loomis, I was able to bring him from obscurity with the publication in 1967 of our *Pedro Vial and the Roads to Santa Fe*. Though this substantial volume was based on a wealth of documents out of Spanish archives, there were (and still are) blanks in Vial's story. One, at least, of these can now be filled in by the newly recovered diary and accompanying correspondence presented here. By the way of introduction to these papers, I shall recapitulate his earlier activities.[2]

Pedro or Pierre Vial *dit* Manitou was a native of Lyons, France. He was probably born about 1746, but of his early life nothing is known. He seems to have come over to the New World as a young man. There is some evidence that he may have been on the Missouri River before the Revolutionary War, which perhaps has given rise to the widespread notion that he was a Canadian. He first appears on the scene in the

[1] *The Spanish Régime in Missouri* (2 vols., Chicago, 1909), I, 350–358.
[2] The facts of the earlier life of Vial have been summarized from Noel M. Loomis and Abraham P. Nasatir, *Pedro Vial and the Roads to Santa Fe* (Norman, 1967).

Southwest in 1779 when he was living among the Indians in the area of Natchitoches. There he was practicing his trade of gunsmith, repairing the arms of the Indians, and trading with them.

By 1786 Vial had left the Indians and had been chosen to explore routes for the Spanish. In that year he was sent to open a trail from San Antonio to Santa Fe. Accompanied by one man, he was successful in doing so and presently reported to the officials in Santa Fe with his diary and two maps, one of which is still extant. For the next twenty years Vial traveled the wilderness between Santa Fe, San Antonio, Natchitoches, and St. Louis, sometimes being sent on missions to the Comanches. In 1792–93 he opened the route between Santa Fe and St. Louis. It was the speed of his return journey that caused the Spanish authorities to realize the nearness to New Mexico of the United States and the restless Anglo-Americans. He made another trip to Missouri in 1794.

By this time, however, fear of French propaganda and Frenchmen had so possessed Spain that orders were issued for the arrest of all Frenchmen save those who would take an oath of allegiance to the Spanish king. On May 12, 1795, Fernando Chacón, governor of New Mexico, reported to Pedro de Nava, the *comandante general* of the Provincias Internas, that Vial had taken such an oath and had been permitted to remain in New Mexico "in his residence." Though Chacón had some doubts about Vial's trustworthiness, he gave the explorer credit for the good services that he had rendered Spain in New Mexico and Texas and spoke of his good conduct and his aptitude and disposition for whatever he might be employed to do.

Before the order for the arrest of foreigners had been issued in 1795, Vial, on the recommendation of Pedro de Nava, had been sent by Chacón to make a treaty of reconciliation and friendship with the Pawnee Indians on the Missouri River in the summer of this year. Of his activities after his return to Santa Fe we know nothing, but the new Spanish policy may have been the reason for his flight to Missouri in 1797. From Chacón, writing to Nava on November 18, 1797, we learn that Pedro Vial of the French nation, domiciled in New Mexico as an interpreter, had sought a license in May to trap beaver on the Rio Arriba but had deserted to the "Gentile nations" and had passed through the Comanche nation, leaving some debts in Santa Fe for which his property there was seized.

Vial is next heard from two years later in Missouri. A man of this name was listed in 1799 as a resident at Portage des Sioux and in 1801 a Pierre Vial was residing at Florissant, but it seems almost certain to me that our Pedro Vial was engaged for two years or more in mining ventures in the District of Ste. Genevieve near Mine à Breton. The evidence lies in some correspondence of François Vallé, commandant at Ste. Genevieve, with Charles Dehault Delassus, lieutenant governor of Upper Louisiana, at St. Louis. On August 19, 1799, Vallé wrote:

> I received your letter by Moses Austin, who complains that he has received at Mine a Breton bad treatment by the ones named Gachard, Dupont, and Manitou [Vial]; of which I did not know up to this moment and of which I shall inform myself immediately, inasmuch as Jean Bte. Vallé is [has been] at the said mine since last spring, to whom I have confided the subordination which he should take care of. He never sent me any account of the bad treatment that Sr. Austin may have received.
>
> As to the consent and permission which the said Sr. Austin claims to have had from me, they are no other than those that have been accorded to Manitoux and his associate, who have been established at the Mine for two years, and also to Manuel Blanco. As for Dupont and Gachard, they have only been here since this year and they came to smelt the ore of the said Manitoux. According to what I have been informed they constructed a cabin to live in as is practiced by all the other miners and built a smelter. Not having had up to now any choice in the settlement, each person has located himself where he chose in the vast area of the mine. Mr. Austin is said to have obtained a concession from the government of one league of land of superficies at the said Mine a Breton, but I do not know if the said concession can be granted to him in the places occupied by the inhabitant-miners who [have been] exploit[ing] the said mine for the past fifteen to twenty years. That is what I beg you to have made known to me.
>
> According to the copy of the "plan" which the said Austin has just shown me, it includes in the said concession all the old works of the said inhabitant-miners. . . .[3]

In a second letter to his superior six days later, Vallé enclosed one from his brother, militia captain Jean Baptiste Vallé (written from Mine à Breton on August 23), which reaffirms Vial's presence at that place for several years.

> As soon as I received your letter of the 19th of this month, which reached me on the 20th, I summoned Srs. Gachard and Manitoux and questioned them concerning the complaints made

[3] Vallé Letterbook, Archivo General de Indias, Seville, *Papeles de Cuba.*

against them by Sr. Moses Austin to the Lieutenant Governor Don Carlos de Lassuse at St. Louis. These two men assured me of their never having had any difficulties with said Sr. Austin. I then summoned the said Sr. Austin and asked him through the interpreter, Sr. Joseph Pratte, and in the presence of Sr. Fremon de Lauriere, what were the complaints that he had to make against the said Srs. Gachard, Dupont, and Manitoux, and if he had ever received any bad treatment from the said Sieurs, and he responded that he had never had any cause to complain of their conduct toward him, and that he had not made any complaint against them. As regards their establishment, they are on land belonging to the said Manitoux which the latter had purchased from Sr. Henry Paget three years ago and with my consent.[4]

These letters are proof enough that Vial was in the area of Mine à Breton in Missouri very soon after he disappeared from Santa Fe in 1797. His continued presence in the district is indicated by a letter from François Vallé, December 23, 1799, to Louis Rancour enclosing a writ of attachment at the request of J. Robidoux against Pierre Vial *dit* Manitou.[5] Testimony given much later before the U.S. land commissioners regarding confirmation of land grants made by the Spaniards in Missouri also shows that Manitou lived and worked in the area of Mine à Breton in 1799 and 1800. Several witnesses asserted that Manitou and a man named O'Connor had intended to act in partnership with Joseph Pratte both in title and in actual work, a plan, however, which had not worked out.[6]

On July 25, 1800, it is to be noted that François Vallé sent to the lieutenant governor a declaration by Sr. Pierre Vial *dit* Manitou, Labreche and Company of the discovery that they had made, after several months searching, of a lead mine "at a place called La Côte de Cedres, distant about six leagues this side of Mine a Breton and distant from the road to [that place] of one-half a league. This discovery will be very favorable and lucrative to the inhabitants of this post. You will accord them the quantity of land that you may judge agreeable for the discovery which they have made of this mine to exploit the said lead."[7]

One month later Vallé wrote that the report of the mine discovered by Vial and Labreche, "which they are at present exploiting," had been forwarded, and added that "as several persons propose to go there to

[4] *Ibid.*
[5] *Ibid.*
[6] *American State Papers, Public Lands*, III, 593–595.
[7] Vallé Letterbook.

work, they have requested that they be accorded provisionally a quantity of four arpents of land around their work in order to maintain themselves without any difficulty until such time as [they receive] your decision. The environs of the diggings of the said Vial and La Breche may prove to be abundant enough in mineral for any who might wish to settle there."[8]

Several witnesses who testified later in behalf of a concession presented by J. B. Pratte declared that this mine had been discovered about 1800. Joseph Baker, one of the first settlers, said one of the Frenchmen discovered the mine and built a cabin in 1800 and declared that "Manitou, La Brocha, and O'Connor were working there and he [Baker] so informed Pratte," but he did not know when Manitou and his associates left. Another witness stated that he was informed by Manitou in the fall of 1800 that a concession was to be granted and that they and Pratte (the latter coming in August, 1800) were in partnership. William Ally, who for nine years had lived about two and a half miles from that land, also swore that "Manitto" came to work there. John Andrews believed that on April 1, 1801, "Manetto" had informed him that the claimant (Pratte) was to obtain a concession and that he (Manetto) and others were to be in partnership. Several other witnesses declared that "Manetto" and Labreche were working in the area about 1800–1801.[9]

The request of Vial and Labreche for a concession, which Vallé had transmitted to Delassus, was later returned by the lieutenant governor to Vallé, who was told to send it to the intendant, López y Angulo, which was done.[10] What happened to that concession to Vial and Labreche, if indeed the Spanish officials did grant a concession to them, I have not discovered. When the Spanish land grants to the mining areas in Missouri came up for confirmation before the U.S. commissioners, the name of Vial as a concessionaire did not appear; he had long before returned to New Mexico. But one claim for the "Old Mine" concession was submitted by J. B. Pratte and another by John B. Labreche.[11]

How long Vial remained in Missouri is uncertain. He was still there on May 26, 1801, for on that day François Vallé wrote Pierre Vial[12] asking him to make an exact note of all the goods of O'Connor, who had

[8] *Ibid.*

[9] *American State Papers, Public Lands*, III, 593–595.

[10] Vallé Letterbook.

[11] *American State Papers, Public Lands*, III, 593, 603, 607; *Private Lands Claims in Missouri*, House Doc. 59, 24th Cong., 1st Sess., 1835, p. 51.

[12] Vallé Letterbook.

been murdered, presumably by an American named Stone, at Mine à Manitou (according to a letter sent by Vallé to Camille Delassus on May 18, 1801[13]).

At any rate, by June 4, 1803, Pedro Vial was back at Santa Fe. Perhaps word of royal decrees granting amnesty to army deserters and the change of attitude on the part of the Spanish government toward the French or perhaps even the transfer of Louisiana to the French—which was made known in Missouri in 1802—are possible clues to Vial's decision to return to Santa Fe, where he was again taken into service by the Spaniards. Many Comanches were visiting the town and Vial's experience and aid were necessary. Hence he was welcomed back at his old assignment as interpreter and received back pay.

Santa Fe at this moment was the center of activity aroused by fear of encroachment of the British and the Americans, especially of the latter since their acquisition of Louisiana. All movements of American expeditions were watched closely by Spanish officials from the minister in Washington to the viceroy in Mexico, and much correspondence flowed between Spain and its North American possessions. From St. Louis Delassus advised of the appearance of Lewis and Clark there in December, 1803, and suggested that the only course for Spain was to arrest the expedition, "which can hardly avoid passing among the neighboring Indian nations of New Mexico through their forts or villages."[14] He warned Salcedo and Casa Calvo at New Orleans that the Americans claimed that the boundary of the United States approached within thirteen or fourteen leagues of the Rio Grande or Santa Fe and cautioned that the Americans might begin setting up posts for contraband trade into Mexico. Casa Calvo wrote to Ceballos, foreign minister in Spain, about this danger as well as to Salcedo, now in Chihuahua. The latter, to forestall possible blame for inactivity, urgently ordered the governor of New Mexico on May 3, 1804, to dispatch some interpreters and friendly Comanches with instructions to make peace between tribes allied with Spain and to observe the movements of the Lewis and Clark expedition, suggested the use of Vial on the mission, and proposed the arrest of the party of Americans. Salcedo wrote also to Ceballos and hoped that further diplomatic pressure had been exerted by Casa Calvo and by the Spanish minister in Washington.

Chacón organized an expedition led by the experienced Vial, which left Santa Fe on August 1, 1804, accompanied by the interpreter José

---

[13] *Ibid.*

[14] Abraham P. Nasatir, *Before Lewis and Clark: Documents Illustrating the History of the Missouri, 1785–1804* (2 vols., St. Louis, 1952), II, 719–720.

Jarvay (Jarvet) and several Pawnees who were then at the New Mexican capital. At Taos this party was joined by ten white men and ten Indians. By September 3 they had reached the Río Chato (Platte) and were at the village of the Pawnees three days later. They did not find the trail of the Lewis and Clark party but they did meet some twenty Frenchmen from the Illinois who informed Vial that the North Americans had sufficient men and goods and that they had made friends with various Indian tribes, whose chiefs had given up to them Spanish medals and *patentes* in exchange for American *patentes* and flags. Only the Pawnees had refused to ally themselves with the Americans. Vial visited five of their chiefs, among them Caigé and Sartariche. The first named of these, with a detachment of his warriors, escorted the Spanish on their return to Santa Fe on November 5, 1804, where Chacón gave each chief a *patente* of captain, a medal of the king, a good horse, and a gun and balls. The letter reporting this expedition and the diary kept on it are printed below for the first time.

In June, 1805, Pedro Vial was sent to Taos to bring back two Frenchmen, an American carpenter, and two Cuampe chiefs. There was other official work for Vial to do. Salcedo, becoming increasingly concerned over American activities on the Missouri River, wrote to the new governor of New Mexico, Joaquín del Real Alencaster, on September 9 of this year, advising him to take steps immediately to strengthen the friendship with the Pawnees and other Indian nations and to watch the movements of the Lewis and Clark expedition. The allegiance of the Indians was important to Spain, for Spanish interpreters among them could promptly send information to Santa Fe which would enable the province to prepare for eventual emergencies. The Indians might even be induced to attack Lewis and Clark on their return voyage.

Alencaster lost little time in implementing the commandant general's orders. He instructed Vial and Jarvet to head an expedition to the Pawnees and to remain among those Indians with a view of getting them to stop the Americans on their return. Salcedo approved the plan. Alencaster's lengthy instructions to Vial were dated October 13; the expedition departed from Taos on October 24. Vial and Jarvet, however, were not given an opportunity to carry out the objectives of the expedition. They reached the vicinity of the Arkansas River but on November 5 were attacked by a party of about 1,000 Indians, who pillaged two-thirds of their supplies. The assailants were repulsed by the Spanish but Vial and Jarvet, finding their supplies and munitions dangerously depleted, returned to Santa Fe at about the same time that Lewis and Clark reached the mouth of the Columbia River. Other expeditions were sent out to discover the identity of the attackers of Vial and Jarvet without success. In 1806 Vial was again sent on an expedition and again ran into trouble due to desertions.

Now occurs another hiatus in the record of Vial's activities. It may be conjectured that he went once more to Missouri, for in 1808 Meriwether Lewis, then governor of Missouri Territory, issued a license to Vial to hunt on the Missouri River (September 14). Over a year later, in November, 1809, however, we find him once more back in New Mexico collecting his pension and back wages. On October 2, 1814, he signed his will, died shortly thereafter, and was buried in the Church of Ygnacio de los Soldados in Santa Fe.

Pedro Vial, who made the first overland trip from San Antonio to Santa Fe, the first overland trip from Santa Fe to Natchitoches, and the first crossing of the Santa Fe Trail to St. Louis, spent some twenty-six years serving Spain in her losing fight to preserve her New World empire against the driving Anglo-Americans. Noel Loomis and I have resurrected the memory of this unheralded pioneer in the West—guide, trader, hunter, and friend of the Indians. He was not alone among the unsung heroes of that region, but perhaps our efforts to establish his place in history may lead other students to ferret out information from the archives of Spain and Mexico and various localities in the United States about other neglected men who shared in the early exploration and development of this region.

DOCUMENTS

I

Nemesio Salcedo, commandant general of the Internal Provinces of New Spain, to Don Pedro Ceballos, Chihuahua, February 5, 1805. Enclosure no. 7[1]

Gives an account of the results of the expedition sent from New Mexico to reconnoiter as far as the Missouri River; of his having been asked by the Marquis of Casa Calvo to suspend the fulfillment of the royal decree concerning the freedom of the Negroes and of foreigners who may enter the territory of the king; of the *ad interim* resolution that he took and the motives on which he based his decision.

[1] Archivo General de Indias, Seville (hereafter cited as AGI), *Audiencia de Guadalajara, leg.* 398. Some of this information is contained in Salcedo to Viceroy Iturrigaray, Chihuahua, Jan. 23, 1805, Archivo General y Público, Mexico (hereafter cited as AGP), *Provincias Internas,* vol. 200, fols. 308–310. Parts of this letter relating to Vial are translated in Loomis and Nasatir, *Pedro Vial,* 197–198. The parts omitted in that translation refer to Nacogdoches and are similar to the contents of the letter here printed.

Most Excellent Señor,

Upon informing Your Excellency in letter number 4[2] of May 8th of the previous year of the information which the Marqués de Casa Calvo[3] communicated to me in regard to the voyage undertaken by Captain Merri,[4] who was commissioned by the Government of the United States to make discoveries and observations of what was occurring as far as possible up the Missouri river, I also informed Your Excellency of my having ordered that through the Governor of the Province of New Mexico[5] a small expedition be organized which would at the same time be used to ratify the peace and friendship of the tribes of the Panana[6] Indians and also *disimuladamente* to reconnoiter the country as far as the banks of the river mentioned above; and this having been thoroughly verified the Governor himself has just informed me of his return in his official letter together with the diary of which a copy is enclosed in *carpeta* number 1 herewith attached.

[2] Printed in Nasatir, *Before Lewis and Clark*, II, 729–735. See also Casa Calvo to Ceballos, New Orleans, Mar. 30, 1804, *ibid.*, II, 727–729.

[3] Sebastián Calvo de la Puerta y O'Farrill, Marqués de Casa Calvo, was born in Havana about 1754. The O'Farrill family had been established in Havana since 1717. He entered the service as a cadet April 1, 1763; was appointed *capitán vivo de voluntarios de caballería* in 1769, lieutenant colonel *vivo* in 1786, and colonel *vivo* on July 14, 1802. By royal *despacho* of May 20, 1786, he was accorded a Castilian title and became the Marqués de Casa Calvo. He had come to Louisiana with O'Reilly in 1769, was in the expeditions against Mobile and Pensacola in 1780 and 1781, and in the expedition against Providencia. In 1794 he was on the northern frontier of Spanish Santo Domingo, from where he returned to Havana.

Upon the death of Gayoso de Lemos the captain general appointed Casa Calvo governor of Louisiana. Between the death of Gayoso and the arrival of Juan Manuel de Salcedo in 1801, Casa Calvo was acting military governor of Louisiana while the acting civil or political governor was Nicolás María Vidal. After turning over the government of Louisiana to Salcedo, Casa Calvo returned to Havana. By this time Casa Calvo had served in the Spanish forces for thirty-eight years and nine months.

Casa Calvo was commissioned by Charles IV to deliver Louisiana to the French. He was appointed a member of the Commission on Boundaries after the transfer of Louisiana. In 1804–05 he went from New Orleans to Texas to guard Spanish interests there. Suspected by the United States, he was not permitted to remain in New Orleans upon his return. He went to Pensacola and from there to Madrid, where he joined the Bonapartists and was rewarded by promotion to lieutenant general. He held positions under Joseph Bonaparte, but when the latter was driven out of Spain in 1813, Casa Calvo fled to Paris, where he lived out the remaining six years of his life on remittances sent to him by his daughters from Cuba. He died in Paris in May, 1820.

Casa Calvo was a typical bureaucrat, did not like work, and enjoyed company and amusements. He left the government business in Louisiana to Andrés López de Armesto, the secretary of the government.

[4] Meriwether Lewis. This refers to the Lewis and Clark expedition.

[5] Salcedo to the governor of New Mexico, Chihuahua, May 3, 1804, printed in Nasatir, *Before Lewis and Clark*, II, 734–735. See also draft [Casa Calvo] to Ceballos, no. 41, New Orleans, Sept. 15, 1804, printed in Nasatir, *Before Lewis and Clark*, II, 751–752.

[6] Pawnee. See Waldo Wedel, *An Introduction to Pawnee Archaeology, Bulletin 112,* Bureau of American Ethnology (Washington, 1936).

It is evident from the indicated documents that the expedition having advanced as far as the river Chato[7] where the Panana villages are located, he did not get any news concerning Captain Merri, but through some Frenchmen settled in Illinois who at that time were in those remote villages, we were able to find out that the Government of the United States had dispatched another expedition with the objective of reconnoitering the Missouri as far as its origin and to try to attract to their side all the gentile nations that they might find; that they took from all the nearby and better-known nations (that they could) all the medals and patents they had, which had been granted to them by the Spanish Commandants, and, as a recompense, they distributed among them others of the American Republic with its flag; and that only the Panana tribe had refused to accept them and to recognize the said Republic as its ally.

At the same time that all this information reached me, I received an official letter from the Marqués de Casa Calvo,[8] of which a copy is attached in *carpeta* number 2, in which he requested, due to the complaint of the Governor of the Territory of Louisiana, William Claiborne,[9] with respect to the insubordination of the Negroes of Natchitoches, that the enforcement of the Royal Decree of April 14, 1789,[10] be suspended, since it stated that the fugitive Negroes of the foreign colonies should not be sent back to their masters since, by the fact alone of their having entered into the territory of the King, they acquired their liberty in conformance with International Law.[11]

[7] Platte.

[8] Perhaps Casa Calvo to Salcedo and Ugarte, Nov. 10, 1804, AGP, *Provincias Internas*, vol. 200.

[9] Claiborne's letters relating to this matter are printed in *Official Letterbooks of W. C. C. Claiborne*, cited in n. 15 below.

[10] Nemesio Salcedo to Iturrigaray, Chihuahua, Jan. 23, 1805, AGP, *Provincias Internas*, vol. 200, fols. 308–309, says that the royal decree of Apr. 14, 1789, "declared to be free the negro slaves of foreigners who represented themselves in the dominions of His Majesty." The royal decree is in AGI, *Guadalajara*, 104-2-9 (old numbering). Concerning slaves and the Louisiana–Texas frontier problem see J. V. Haggard, "The Neutral Ground between Louisiana and Texas, 1806–1821," *Louisiana Historical Quarterly*, XXVIII (Oct., 1945), 1001–1128 (see pp. 1069–73).

[11] Salcedo wrote the governor of New Mexico from Chihuahua on Sept. 9, 1805: "I likewise warn you that if in doubt as to whether or not one must carry out to its 'puro' and due effect the observance of the Royal Decree of April 14, of '89, which declared that all the Negro slaves of foreign colonies which present themselves in His Majesty's Dominions should be free, consistent with international law; ordered that until [receiving] a new Royal order, there will be detained in any part of the provinces of my command, the Negro slaves of Louisiana who present themselves with the object of enjoying that favor, notwithstanding any supplication which comes from their owners or on the part of the American government, and this step you must bear in mind under the concept that if any Negroes should meet you begging for their liberty you must assign them a place where they may remain confined until their fate is decided, bearing in mind that they may be able to subsist by their labor or industry in the place where you assign them." Archives of Mexico, *Guerra y Marina 1787–1806, expediente* 15, Library of Congress transcript.

When the Governor of Texas sent me by extraordinary express the previously mentioned official letter of the Marqués de Casa Calvo, he did also the same with the letter and documents that the Commandant of the Post of Nacogdoches[12] had given to him as proof of his not having been an instigator of the insubordination of the Negroes, as Governor Claiborne supposed, stating that he had offered them liberty and protection. These papers may be found in *carpeta* number 3, which I also am transmitting to Your Excellency's hands, and from them it was concluded that the said Commandant, informed of the charge against him, declared that such a grave interpretation should not be given to such plain and simpleminded expressions as those spread around to the residents of Louisiana with the only purpose of benefiting them, warning them of the prudent precautions they should observe, and, as a proof,[13] enclosed a letter in which the syndics of Natchitoches[14] thank him for his conduct concerning this matter.[15]

What his attitude [or conduct] was is not stated, but through our knowledge of the antecedents, it may be inferred that those individuals make reference to the case dealt with in *carpeta* number 4, which reduces itself to the fact that the Commandant of Nacogdoches himself and, through his own initiative, without advising his immediate superior, the Governor of Texas, sent out a party of troops to pursue eight Negro slaves who headed toward our border,[16] and that, failing to observe the said Royal Decree and having made them prisoners, he then turned them over to the hands of another party of the militia from Natchitoches who had made a claim for them, in order to restore them to their masters.

Under these circumstances and considering myself as lacking sufficient authority to suspend the fulfillment of the said Royal Decree, persuaded of

[12] Juan de Ugarte was commandant at Nacogdoches.
[13] See Ugarte to Salcedo, Dec. 26, 1804; Salcedo to Iturrigaray, Jan. 23, 1805, AGP, *Provincias Internas*, vol. 200.
[14] Syndics and major of militia to Ugarte, Nov. 14, 1804; Salcedo to governor of Texas, Jan. 23, 1805, AGP, *Provincias Internas*, vol. 200.
[15] For the correspondence relating to this matter see the correspondence of Casa Calvo and Claiborne and relative documents of Turner, etc., printed in Dunbar Rowland, ed., *Official Letterbooks of W. C. C. Claiborne, 1801–1816* (6 vols., Jackson, Miss., 1917), II, 315–316, 319–320, 381–390, III, 5–9, 155–156, 383–386, 392–393.
For the story see I. J. Cox, "The Louisiana–Texas Frontier," *Southwestern Historical Quarterly*, XVII (Oct., 1913), 33–42; C. E. Castañeda, *Our Catholic Heritage in Texas* (7 vols., Austin, 1936–50), V, 250–251, 254, 269, 287, 293–294, 309, 322–323; Mattie Hatcher, *Opening of Texas to Foreign Settlement 1801–1821* (Austin, 1927); Haggard, "The Neutral Ground between Louisiana and Texas."
Correspondence of the commandant of Nacogdoches and the escape of slaves from Natchitoches to Nacogdoches is in AGP, *Provincias Internas*, vol. 200.
[16] See, e.g., Claiborne to Casa Calvo, New Orleans, Oct. 30, 31, 1804; Claiborne to Colonel Butler, New Orleans, Nov. 1, 1804; Edward D. Turner to Claiborne, Natchitoches, Oct. 17, 1804, also Oct. 16, 1804; Claiborne to Turner, New Orleans, Nov. 3, 1804; etc., *Official Letterbooks of W. C. C. Claiborne*, II, 382–390.

how important it is that it be observed, and not having either a war auditor, an assessor, or any other authorized person who could judge this particular matter, I resolved it by the safest principles, giving to the Marqués de Casa Calvo the reply of which a copy is attached in *carpeta* number 5. I told him in it that, in agreement with his own judgment that the complaints of the Governor of Louisiana are apparent although lacking in supporting fact, I could not accede to his request because it violated International Law as well as the Declaration of His Majesty, and also that the importance of the matter persuaded him that it would have been represented to his Government at the very moment when the new territory was acquired from France. In addition, against the new claim which was being made appeared the fact that, in the same case under consideration when Louisiana was a territory of the King, there exists a lack of evidence that the slightest claim might have been made. And finally with respect to the Marqués having pleaded in anticipation, it occurred to the high Ministry, I should decide that the Commandant General appointed to the Eastern Provinces of this kingdom should not appear without bringing with him the Royal decision on this matter; due to these considerations the only thing I could see that seemed to fall within my power was to forewarn the Governor of Texas that Negro slaves of foreigners who might present themselves in any part of the province under his charge be detained until the sovereign decision of the King, or that which in accordance with his particular instructions the said Commandant General might dictate.

The above I have carried out, informing the Governor of Texas of the order, a copy of which is in the same *carpeta* number 5. I warned him that in view of the fact that it was necessary to lend credence to the basic fact [or charge] that the insurrection of the Negroes be attributed to the comments made by the Commandant of Nacogdoches, and that he bring any charges against this official that might result, and that taking the corresponding measures to accredit his ideas and to avoid any other quotations, he should be careful, in consequence, to give me account of whatever may be pertinent.

In order to carry out this decision I took into account not only the previously discussed reasons but also others which, in my estimation, were of considerable weight and seriousness, which led to putting into due effect the mentioned Royal Declaration. These are the facts: that, since this Decree is very much earlier than the treaties of peace, boundaries, and navigation made in 1795,[17] nothing was stated in them [treaties] with regard to this matter; neither do I have any later evidence of anything like this having occurred, and, since the States themselves were anxious for the fulfillment of their own private constitutions, their Government has declared that it cannot prevent its citizens from doing what they please if it is not pro-

[17] Pinckney's Treaty or Treaty of San Lorenzo el Real.

hibited by the law, and there is no existing law that could impede their exterior commerce nor expeditions outside their territory, it has never been willing to participate in the *instancias* which at the request of this General Commandancy have been made through the Spanish Consul in Natches and the Minister of the King in Philadelphia to the effect that appropriate measures be taken in order that Americans stop disturbing the frontiers of Texas and coastal areas of Sonora with frequent expeditions.[18]

I shall add to what I have previously said that in case it is not possible to guard the borders adequately due to their great extent and sparse population, the precise observance of the Royal Decree was one of the best means of defense I considered to have available in order to get the United States to respect the territory in their own interest, continuing at the same time the absolute prohibition of all trade as well as their obtaining horses, which they need so much. Therefore if this consideration is carried out to the point of their being stopped, which this action on our part ought to cause them, far from being harmful to us in the case of the retrocession and the successive sale of Louisiana as is believed by the Marqués de Casa Calvo, I believe it could contribute to facilitate it as long as it is carefully observed.

Besides these ideas, produced by the zeal which I have to fulfill my duties, I have informed the Viceroy of Mexico about the matter,[19] both in order to forewarn him in advance of all those who may be forced to request additional troops, if the problems on the part of Texas increase progressively, as well as with the idea of having him inform me if any reform should be made, and also, that he may tell me whatever he believes best since I only aspire to render the best service to the King as well as the safety and stability of his Dominions.

The relations of which I gave an abstract in the first two paragraphs of this letter show that the United States is not overlooking any means to take away from our alliance the Indian nations that are adjacent to us and that their temptations go as far as reaching unwary Indian villages that are located on the banks of the Chato, all of which belong to the Government of New Mexico, who present themselves in the Capital and receive presents, the well-known perspicacity of Your Excellency will understand the care that is demanded by that remote Province for its preservation (and defense) from the constant intrigues of the said States, which, through such practices as well as their constant reconnaissance in the area, and their ambitious views of extending their territory, do not seem to have any other objective than to facilitate in the future their trade with Asia by obtaining a harbor on

---

[18] On these matters see the works of Cox and Castañeda cited above.

[19] Salcedo to Iturrigaray, Chihuahua, Jan. 23, 1805, AGP, *Provincias Internas*, vol. 200, fols. 308–310.

the South Sea between 40 and 45 degrees of latitude, at which *altura* the Missouri river has its origins, provided they find it navigable.[20]

Your Excellency will please inform all of this to His Majesty for his sovereign intelligence, hoping also that Your Excellency may please let me know the Royal resolution which I will obey.

May God keep Your Excellency many years.

Chihuahua, February 5, 1805

Nemesio Salcedo[21]

TO: Excmo. Sr. Dn. Pedro Ceballos[22]

I I

Fernando Chacón to Nemesio Salcedo, Santa Fe, December 13, 1804, enclosing Vial's diary (copy made at Chihuahua, February 5, 1805)

Señor *Comandante General*—

I am enclosing with this letter to Your Excellency the diary kept by D. Pedro Vial during his voyage to the Chato river, where the pueblos of the Panana and Abajoses[23] people are located, in which no particular mention is made about any discoveries or proofs of those which he was instructed to carry out. Therefore, the only thing I have been able to inquire of the French of St. Louis, Illinois,[24] who have accompanied him on this last occasion, is that the Americans had dispatched an expedition to reconnoiter the Missouri river as far as its origin, with orders to lure to their side all the

[20] On this matter see Loomis and Nasatir, *Pedro Vial.*

[21] Nemesio de Salcedo y Salcedo, general in the royal army, succeeded Pedro Grimarest as *comandante general* of the Provincias Internas about 1804. He had served under Bernardo de Gálvez in America at the siege of Mobile and in Guárico. Previously he had served under O'Reilly in the "Fracasada de Argel." He began his career as a cadet in the Spanish Royal Guards, in which rank he served five years. He served thirteen years as captain of the Regiment of Infantry of Navarre. He returned to Europe in July, 1783, was made lieutenant colonel in 1783, and in 1790 colonel of the Regiment of Infantry of Coruña, although he served in Mexico with the approval of Revillagigedo and Inspector Gorostia, who considered Salcedo talented and zealous. He served as *comandante* of the Provincias Internas until 1813, when he was succeeded by Bonavía. Luis Navarro García, *Las Provincias Internas en el siglo XIX* (Seville, 1965), 1–4.

[22] Pedro Ceballos was born in 1764 and died in 1840. He was minister of state under Charles IV and Ferdinand VII, accompanying them to Bayonne in 1808. He was a favorite of Godoy, who was married to his cousin. He was made Spanish foreign minister, and was also ambassador to Naples and Vienna. He retired to private life in 1820. His merit was below the importance of his office. A Frenchman characterized him as indolent and inert, with stammering and confused discourse. P. C. Brooks, *Diplomacy and the Borderlands* (Berkeley, 1939), 26, n. 8.

[23] Orejones?

[24] See Loomis and Nasatir, *Pedro Vial*, 176–177, 423–426.

gentile nations whom they might meet, that the Americans had called to-gether the most accessible and best-known Indians and had collected the medals and patents which they had been given by the Chiefs of New Orleans, giving them instead some of the American Republic, with flags of the said nation, and that only the Pananas had not wanted to admit them and recognize as their allies any others but the Spaniards; for this reason and in order to further secure the said gentiles in their way of thinking, I gave to the principal of the Panana captains, who arrived recently in this Prov-ince, a medal with the bust of our Sovereign and patent of *capitan agra-ciado,* accompanied with a splendid gift so that he may display it to his own nation and perpetuate them in our friendship.

May God keep Your Excellency many years.

Santa Fe, New Mexico, December 13, 1804

Fernando Chacon[25]

Sr. Don Nemesio Salcedo [signed]
IT IS A COPY: Chihuahua, February 5, 1805
    Bernardo Villamil [rubric]

I I I

Diary of Don Pedro Vial's Visit to the Panana nation, August 1, 1804–November 23, 1804 (certified copy dated Chihuahua, February 5, 1805)

Diary kept by Pedro Vial, commissioned by the governor, Don Fernando Chacón, accompanied by an interpreter, Don José Jarvay,[26] and ten residents and ten Indians from the town of Taos.

[25] Fernando Chacón was appointed governor of New Mexico to succeed Fernando de la Concha. His appointment was dated San Ildefonso, Aug. 13, 1793, and he took possession of the office on July 31, 1794. His successor Alencaster was appointed to relieve him by royal decree of Aug. 25, 1803, while he was still in Spain. It was on Mar. 23, 1805, that Chacón turned over his office to Alencaster. New Mexico Archives no. 1802. Alencaster, in reporting to the Audiencia de Guadalajara, Santa Fe, Mar. 31, 1805, says his royal decree was dated Oct. 3, 1803. AGP, *Provincias Internas,* vol. 204, fols. 288–289, 294–295, 313–314vo. Chacón's appointment is also contained in a draft to Bajamar, Palacio, Aug. 11, 1793, and Alencaster's appointment is in AGI, *Guadalajara,* leg. 300. A *revista* of the New Mexico company showing Chacón still governor in 1804 is in *ibid., leg.* 296.

[26] José Jarvay, Jarvet, Jarbat, Tarbat, Calbert, Chalvert, Chalet—his name is variously spelled—was born in Philadelphia and was a Presbyterian. He came down the Ohio, was at Natchez, and lived among the Taovayas in Texas. He left Philadelphia in 1789 and Pittsburgh in 1794. He was brought by Nava to New Mexico, reaching Santa Fe in 1803. He knew Indian languages and served as interpreter accompanying Vial on several trips. About his activities as interpreter see Loomis and Nasatir, *Pedro Vial.* My former student, Donald A. Nuttall, has some speculations about Jarvet in his unpublished master's thesis "The American Threat to New Mexico 1804–1821" (San Diego State College, 1939). See especially Alencaster to Salcedo, Santa Fe, May 28, Sept. 1, 1805, New Mexico Archives nos. 1838, 1881.

DATE		LEAGUES
August 1	After having received my passport as well as instructions from my Governor, I left from the Village of Santa Fe on the first day of August, [and traveled] until I reached the pueblo of Taos on the third of the present month. . . .	
August 4	The *alcalde* furnished me, by order of the Governor, ten residents of this town and ten Indians and I had a review of arms and called muster roll, and afterward I read to them the orders which I was carrying from my Governor.	
August 7	After having rested until the 7th we left Taos and spent the night at the canyon of	
August 8	San Fernando; we traveled about . . .	4
August 9	Left as the sun rose, traveling through the said canyon until we stopped at Agua Fria. We traveled about . . .	6
August 10	Left in the morning traveling through the Sierra de Taos until we reached the Xayana river. We traveled about . . .	7
August 11	We left in the morning and spent the night at Rio Vermejo, having traveled about . . .	8
August 12	We left in the morning, heading toward the north; we traveled through the plains [*llanura*] until we reached the Ojo de la Sierra, traveling about . . .	8
August 13	We left in the morning in order to reach Palo Flechado, traveling about . . .	7
August 14	We left in the morning traveling by the plains and we stopped around 12 noon in El Charco, where we stayed until the next day, having traveled about . . .	4
August 15	We left in the morning; we entered the canyon of the Casa Colorada, having traveled approximately . . .	8
August 16	We left in the morning and traveled about . . .	1
	Arrived at the Rio de la Anima, which, due to a very heavy rain storm which had fallen the previous night, was quite high and rapid, and we stopped there until the 17th.	
August 17	We left in the morning along the same river. We traveled approximately . . .	5
August 18	We left in the morning, always following the said river toward the north, traveling about . . .	9
August 19	We left in the morning and arrived at the Nampeste [*sic*] river, traveling through the plains the entire day . . .	10

August 20	We left in the morning toward the north, by the plains; we crossed the Rio Negro. We traveled about . . .	8
August 21	We left in the morning toward the northeast. We traveled the whole day not having any water until ten at night, when we arrived at the Rio de los Canzes [Kansas], having traveled about . . .	15
August 22	We left in the morning toward the north through the plains until we reached the Penasco Amarillo river, having traveled about . . .	10
August 23	We left in the morning in the same direction until we arrived at the Rio del Perro con Rabia, which we reached early, having traveled about . . .	6
August 24	We left in the morning, traveling through the plain, spent the night on the plain without water, having traveled about . . .	10
August 25	Left in the morning [and traveled] until we reached a branch of the Rio de los Canzes, having traveled approximately . . .	10
August 26	We left in the morning, following the above-mentioned river until dark, having traveled about . . .	8
August 27	We left in the morning, following the said river until night, traveling about . . .	8
August 28	We followed the river until night, having traveled about . . .	8
August 29	We followed the river and traveled about . . .	8
August 30	We followed the river, having traveled about . . .	8
August 31	We left in the morning; after traveling about two leagues we crossed a plain [*llano*] and arrived at Palo Seco, having traveled about . . .	8
Sept. 1	We did not travel today because a man had remained behind because of his having eaten plums, which hurt his stomach; he was unable to keep up with us. I sent a man to look for him and he came back without being able to find him.	
Sept. 2	I again sent out the same man in search for the man and he found him more dead than alive; the man asked him for water and he took it to him, and he saw many people, all on foot, coming, and he ran away, and came to us saying that many people were coming and that he did not know whether their intentions were good or bad. I immediately sent the Captain of the town of Taos and Don Jose Jarvay, the interpreter, with the flag, to find out what kind	

of people they were, and they met with them. They were the Pananas, who were returning from fighting with the Comanches, lamenting the loss of two of their captains who had been killed by the Comanches.

Sept. 3   We left in the morning in order to reach the Chato river, crossed a plain, having traveled about . . .   10

Sept. 4   We left in the morning, traveling along the Chato river, at full trot, having traveled about . . .   12

Sept. 5   We left in the morning heading north, traveling along the river, having traveled about . . .   12

Sept. 6   We left in the morning and traveled in order to reach the pueblo. Many of their captains came to meet us and we arrived this same day at the pueblo. They gave us a great reception. We traveled about . . .   6

After having arrived in their pueblos, I met about 20 Frenchmen, from whom I learned of the way in which the Americans had received [taken over] the government. They told me that they had many companies, with four carriages [*carruages*] well loaded with effects for all nations of the Missouri river with which they may meet in the interior. Through all the villages which they pass they make big gifts to all of the chiefs and principal people of the pueblos and make them turn in the medals and patents which they possess, given to them by the Spanish Government. I have ordered all of the said chiefs of the country not to return the medals nor the patents, telling them that they do not yet know the Americans but that they will know them in the future. We were the whole day in their town, they took us from house to house, to welcome us, and on the 12th of this month some Indians of the town of Taos scared us because they heard a few shots in the pueblo, believing that the Pananas were killing us, and a frightened mare ran off from the herd and we have not heard news of it since. On the 15th all the captains and all the braves met in a house for a council as well as in order to find out what was the purpose of my arrival. I told them that I was sent by the great Captain Don Fernando Chaco[n] to lead the Pananas who had remained among the Spaniards so that they would not have to come alone, and that the great captain also was sending a long [*largo*]

117

suit and a three-cornered hat, and the rest of the corresponding ornaments that go with the suit. The great Spanish captain was content to have become acquainted with all his Panana nation. Since he [they] had come with Pedro Vial and Jose Jarvay, who speaks the Panana language, they made peace with me. I recommended to them to maintain good relations and be loyal to Captain Caigie [*sic*], who spoke to me of the five who came to make peace with me, and they left well dressed and very happy and I think that insofar as they are concerned they will not give the Spaniards any cause to regret [their decision to make peace]. The great Captain Sarta-riche responded that all the people of the town are contented men, as well as the women and little children, and were happy to see a person of such prestige and well known in the nation, and what a joy, what a pleasure to see the Spanish among us eating together as brothers, and there is no one of us who can say any other thing than that the Span-ish are good. In the Counsel [*Conjelo*] there were two captains of the Panis, which is the same nation and the same language, and two captains of the na-tion of the Otos, who decided that we should leave on the 20th, that the Panis Captain Caigie was com-ing with us together with 11 young men and a Span-ish captive who was living among them. On the 20th we left their pueblo and we took the same road until we reached the mouth of the Rio de la Casa Colorada, where about 100 Comanches met us and fell upon us, not doing any harm to our people nor the Pananas, and they talked with each other and made peace among themselves. And the Pananas consented to go with the Comanches to their *ranch-erías*, and so that no treason should take place, I sent Jose Jarvay and Manuel Archuleta [with them]. About 12 Pananas went with the Comanches, and after three days of traveling, all the Pananas went away at night and the Comanches could only think that they were afraid that the Comanches were bringing them along in order to kill them. The Comanches did not have that intention at all. We came to the Colorado river, we met Spanish people who came from Taos to meet us because I sent someone to request help from the *Alcalde,* because our horses were all in very bad condition and one male horse was left behind. We arrived at Taos on the 29th, where we rested until the 2nd of November and arrived at the Village of Santa Fe in the presence of my Governor on the 5th with Panis Captain Caigie and two braves, who were well clothed, and the *Señor Gobernador* gave the Captain a medal, a horse, and a rifle, gunpowder, and bullets for his journey.

Santa Fe, November 23, 1804

I sign it without any malice.

P. Vial

IT IS A COPY: Chihuahua, February 5, 1805

Bernardo Villamil [rubric]

Philip Nolan's Entry

into Texas in 1800

NOEL M. LOOMIS

$\mathscr{P}$HILIP NOLAN's expeditions into Texas (1791–1800) were made against an international background that gave special significance to his activities and in fact created near panic among Spanish officials by the time he made the last trip. France had ceded Louisiana to Spain in 1762 to keep Louisiana out of the hands of England, and Spain hoped to use Louisiana, bounded then on the west by Texas, the Red River of Natchitoches, the Arkansas, and the Missouri, as a buffer state to protect Santa Fe and northern Mexico from the British. Twenty years later (in 1783), however, the Spaniards had a new nationality to fear—the Americans who had won independence. By the 1790s they also had the French revolutionists in New Orleans, in all of Louisiana, in Charleston, and in Kentucky—to name a few.

A considerable portion of these threats were directed through Upper Louisiana, since the British were in Canada, the Americans were in Kentucky and Tennessee, and the French were trying to work through the restless Americans in Kentucky. Of them all, however, the Americans were the most feared, because, it was said, Americans were ambitious, insubordinate, frugal, and able to travel "200 leagues with no other aids than a sack of cornmeal and flask of powder."[1] Apparently it was true, for Americans probed Louisiana across the Mississippi, along the Missouri, and through Arkansas and Lower Louisiana.

[1] Casa Calvo to Ceballos, New Orleans, July 25, 1804, Archivo General de Indias, Seville (hereafter cited as AGI), *Papeles de Cuba, legajo* 2368.

Also, there were other forms of American threat: at one time President Adams planned to raise an army on the Ohio; George Rogers Clark was involved in a scheme for invading Louisiana; French agents tried to incite Kentuckians to attack; and the Spaniards gave individual Americans permission at various times to go into Louisiana or Texas to settle or to conduct business. All these American threats must have looked to the Spaniards like the thrusts of a many-armed fighter searching for a weak spot.

It was not long before trouble developed between the Kentuckians, who wanted to send their bulky products (wheat, corn, hams, bacon, and whisky, among others) down the river by flatboat to New Orleans for sale or transshipment to Havana or Baltimore, and the Spaniards, who closed the river to navigation. In 1795 this situation was temporarily resolved by the Treaty of San Lorenzo, but there was to be no peace for the Spaniards.

In such an atmosphere did Philip Nolan, the Kentuckian, make his first expedition into Texas in 1791 to capture mustangs. At that time trading between Texas and Louisiana was prohibited, and trading by non-Spaniards was generally prohibited (except that, by a royal order of 1780, cattle could be sent to Louisiana if the governor should request it[2]). However, Philip Nolan got into the good graces of Governor Esteban Rodriguez Miró of Louisiana (then, like Texas, a Spanish province) and obtained a passport; either then or later, Nolan took an oath of loyalty to the Spanish king. He went into Texas as a trader but lost the goods to the Spaniards and lived with Indian tribes for two years; then he began to deal in animal skins and to catch and break wild horses. During that time he became acquainted with Antonio Leal, an Indian trader out of Nacogdoches, and attracted the passionate friendship of Leal's wife, known as Gertrudes de los Santos—a woman twenty years older than Nolan.

In 1794 Nolan finally returned to New Orleans with fifty horses. Miró had been replaced as governor by François Louis Hector, Baron de Carondelet, who gave Nolan another passport, and by June, 1794, Nolan was again in Nacogdoches. He was in Texas for some time then, apparently involved more or less in contrabanding with the connivance of the Texas governor, Manuel Muñoz, and finally returned to New Orleans in January, 1796, with 250 horses.

In July, 1797, after an eighteen-month interval about which there is little information, Nolan was in Texas for what he called the fourth time with another passport from Carondelet and $7,000 worth of goods,

---

[2] Archivo General de la Nación, Mexico (hereafter cited as AGN), *Historia, leg.* 413.

and began a rather long period of probable trading during which he wrote more than one letter to Pedro de Nava, commandant general of the Interior Provinces, to ask permission to stay longer, to go into Nuevo Santander (allegedly for horses), to offer to make a map of Texas, to ask permission to introduce $2,000 worth of goods (to Chihuahua, perhaps?), and to offer a present of a gun (he had started with twelve). At one time he made a map for Carondelet, and promised to make another.

Something had gone on between Nolan and Manuel Gayoso de Lemos, commandant at Natchez, and once Gayoso apparently agreed to enter a contrabanding scheme with Nolan. In March, 1797, Nolan proposed a three-way partnership (to include Muñoz) for sending goods to Texas,[3] and on April 1 Gayoso addressed a long letter to Nolan in which he spoke of "the plan which you have communicated to me, and of which I approve"; in May he said, "I am very glad of the additional good prospect that offers for your future campaign."[4] Whether Gayoso referred to the deal with Muñoz is not specified; however, the enterprise apparently was not carried through.

In this connection, there are two letters whose position is unclear: in March, 1797, Gayoso wrote Nolan a peremptory letter asking about his political interest,[5] and in November Nolan wrote Gayoso a rather indignant letter pretending to straighten him out.[6] The dates are not too clear (and may even be in error), but probably these two letters followed Nolan's meeting with the American surveyor Andrew Ellicott in January of the same year (1797), since Ellicott's arrival in Natchez signaled much trouble and even humiliation for Gayoso in that town, and since Ellicott had been fortified by information furnished by Nolan. If the dates are correct, apparently nothing further came of the letters immediately, though it would seem that they might well have left unpleasant feelings on both sides. By July of that year, Nolan was in Texas.

During his 1797–99 trip to Texas, Nolan said or implied that he had a commission from Carondelet to furnish horses for the Louisiana government,[7] and this statement eventually got him into trouble and caused

---

[3] Nolan to Gayoso, Natchez, Mar. 13 or 14, 1797, photostats in University of Texas Archives, Austin.

[4] Grace King, "The Real Philip Nolan," *Louisiana Historical Society Publications*, X (1918), 98–100.

[5] Gayoso to Nolan, Natchez, Mar. [13?], 1797, AGI, *Papeles de Cuba*, leg. 213.

[6] Nolan to Gayoso, Monday 13th [Nov. 13, 1797], AGI, *Papeles de Cuba*, leg. 188–2. There is obvious confusion in these letters.

[7] The original passport is in the Hermosillo Archives and reads: "The Baron de

Nava to order his expulsion. However, Spanish officials moved slowly (especially Muñoz, who probably was involved in Nolan's trading activities), and Nolan got safely out of Texas.

There is considerable speculation that Gayoso wrote a letter in 1798 or earlier requesting that Nolan be arrested, and that Nolan was saved from arrest by the unexpected death of Governor Muñoz on July 27, 1799, with the order for arrest unopened. However, no such letter of Gayoso has yet been turned up. Gayoso did write the viceroy to mention Nolan's "chameleonic loyalties" in 1798,[8] and Nava wrote to Muñoz on April 30, 1799, telling him to get Nolan out of Texas at once,[9] but there is, so far, no letter of arrest.

While Gayoso was governor of Louisiana, he himself proposed a five-way partnership (to include Nolan and James Wilkinson, commander-in-chief of the U.S. army and long-time friend and employer of Nolan); since Gayoso's last letter on this matter was written in November, 1798, it seems obvious that at that time Gayoso had made no move to bar Nolan from Texas.[10]

The closest approach to an order or request for Nolan's arrest in 1798 seems to be a letter writen to Nava by Miguel de la Grua Tala-manca y Branciforte, the viceroy, on February 12, 1798, saying that he had received a letter from the governor of Louisiana asking to have arrested any foreigner who might appear in Texas, and asking Nava to advise him on Nava's ideas about Nolan.[11] Nava then ordered Nolan's expulsion but not his arrest.

The information about the supposed Gayoso letter of 1797 or 1798

Carondelet, Knight of the Order of St. John, field marshal of the royal armies, governor general, vice-patron of the province of Louisiana and West Florida, and inspector of His Majesty's troops. Agreeable to the order communicated to this governor by the commandant general of the Interior Provinces of New Spain, the field marshal of the royal armies, that there might be made available to this province the horses produced by the province of Texas, I grant free and safe passage to Don Philip Nolan so that with John Murdoch, William Scott, their two Negroes, and four engaged Spaniards, he may pass to that province to buy for this province, conforming strictly to the orders given him upon that matter by the governor of San Antonio of Béxar. I order that the commandants of my jurisdiction—and those who are not, I request—and I charge that they shall not place embarrassment in his going, his stay, or his return, since this is suitable to the service of the king. Given in New Orleans June 17, 1797. The Baron of Carondelet, Andrés López Armesto. It is a copy. Chihuahua, Mar. 20, 1798. Manuel Merino [rubric]."

[8] See Nava to Azanza, Oct. 30, 1798; Nava to Branciforte, Mar. 20, 1798, AGN, *Historia*, leg. 334.

[9] Nava to Muñoz, Apr. 30, 1799, Béxar Archives.

[10] Gayoso to Esteban Minor, Jan. 10, Oct. 23, Nov. 29, 1798, Gayoso Papers, Department of Archives, Louisiana State University, Baton Rouge.

[11] Branciforte to Nava, Mexico, Feb. 12, 1798, very confidential, Hermosillo Archives.

requesting the arrest of Nolan seems to come from a letter from Nolan to Daniel Clark without explanation of the way Nolan had found out about it. Therefore, it may well have been hearsay, or Nolan may have told it for purposes of his own. According to Maurine T. Wilson's unpublished thesis, "Philip Nolan and His Activities in Texas," Daniel Clark said that Nolan was informed of the Gayoso letter by Clark himself.[12]

It was not until June 10, 1799, that Gayoso sent a letter to Nava advising him that there might be war with France, and that in such a case the United States would attack Louisiana and the Interior Provinces; Gayoso urged that Nava not permit any American to reconnoiter Spanish territory and said, "The most dangerous one of all those I know is one Nolan, an astute man, who knew how to win the confidence of my predecessor [Carondelet] and to obtain a passport for San Antonio. . . . I know that this hypocrite has committed sacrileges. . . . It would be advisable to seize this man and send him far away, so well guarded and so secretly that his whereabouts would never again be learned, because I have more than good reason to suspect that he is commissioned by General Wilkinson to make a complete reconnaissance of the country."[13]

The letter of June 10, 1799, is a request for arrest, and the mention of Wilkinson was prompted by Gayoso's own personal (and convivial) acquaintance with Wilkinson and the knowledge that Wilkinson was playing both sides against the middle, and the further knowledge that Nolan and Wilkinson had been close for a long time. Even so, it did not reach Nava until after a "long delay," and he did not issue the order for arrest until August 8, 1800.[14]

Nolan had been ambitious and reckless with others besides Gayoso (especially about his alleged commission to get horses for Louisiana), and had aroused the suspicion of Nava, commandant general of the Interior Provinces, Francisco Rendón, the intendant at Zacatecas, and Miguel José de Azanza, viceroy of Mexico.

Nolan returned to the United States in the latter part of 1799, and so was not arrested (he reached Natchez by November 20, 1799, with 1,000 horses). At that time Gayoso was governor of Louisiana.

By the summer of 1800 Nolan was preparing another (his fifth, by his count) expedition to Texas. He still had horses (1,500, by one account) around Nacogdoches in care of Gertrudes and his hired man,

---

12 (University of Texas, 1932), p. 63, nn. 66, 67.

13 Gayoso to Nava, June 10, 1799, Hermosillo Archives, *tomo* 3, no. 19.

14 Nava to Elguezábal, Aug. 8, 1800, Nacogdoches Archives.

Jesse Cook, and he applied for a passport to return to Texas. Gayoso had unexpectedly died, and the new governor was Sebastián Calvo de la Puerta y O'Farrill, Marquis of Casa Calvo, who liked Americans even less than had Gayoso. He declined to grant the passport, but Nolan went ahead with his preparations and by the end of October had organized a party. José Vidal, the commandant at Concordia, across the river from Natchez, was kept informed by various spies, and went into superior court in Mississippi to charge that Nolan was preparing a filibuster; however, Nolan had friends in Mississippi and the court declined to stop him.[15]

On October 21, 1800, Nolan wrote Jesse Cook a letter from Natchez, saying, among other things: "From the best information I am well convinced that if you do not immediately on rect. of this set out for this place with your horses and as many of mine as you can collect, you and I will both lose all."[16] It is fairly obvious that Nolan knew his days were numbered in Spanish territory—and he certainly made sure of it by something else he said to Cook: "Everyone thinks that I go to catch wild horses, but you know that I have long been tired of wild horses. I expect to return by January." He did not, of course, foresee that the letter would be captured by the Spaniards—as it was at Rapides a few days later.

On October 25 Valentin Layssard, the commandant at Rapides, wrote to Martin Duralde at Opelousas to say: "Just at this moment a resident of this post has arrived from Natchez and tells me in the presence of notable persons of this post that the full intentions of Nolan are to pillage Spanish posts."[17]

Then, on November 1, Vidal wrote to Casa Calvo with the latest news:

> This afternoon Hannah Glasscock returned from Natchitoches with . . . a copy of the letter from Nolan to Cook. . . . Glasscock advises me that the [commandant of Natchitoches] has said to him that already he knew *por allí* the plan of Nolan, which was to post relays between San Antonio and Camargo and there await the trains of gold, which pass through at exactly this time; [he would] capture them and take them to a nation of Indians that speaks by signs, and are always at war against Spain, where Nolan

[15] Joseph Vidal to Casa Calvo, Concordia, Oct. 11, 1800, AGI, *Papeles de Cuba, leg.* 71-A.

[16] Nolan to Jesse Cook at Nacogdoches, Oct. 21, 1800, AGI, *Papeles de Cuba, leg.* 71-A.

[17] Layssard to Duralde, Rapides, Oct. 26, 1800, AGI, *Papeles de Cuba, leg.* 207.

is very well known [the Comanches?]; and to be safe from them [the Indians], he carried much merchandise.

Nolan's expression in his letter to Cook when he told him that he [Cook] knew he was tired of hunting wild horses, and that he made believe that was his plan, makes it easy to see that what the aforementioned commandant told Glasscock is the same as what Nolan intends to do.[18]

As it turned out later, Vidal, at Concordia, was getting news of Nolan from a spy of his own, one Luis Eavans (Evans?),[19] who seems to have kept Vidal pretty well informed. Vidal reported that John Henderson had left Natchez on October 28 "in a pirogue with much merchandise, and that in Avoyelles he ought to take horses that already are there, and from there pass to the post [of Nacogdoches], where he should meet Cook to help him drive the horses that Nolan has in that vicinity. [A Frenchman known as Pierre Longueville and Antonio Leal] intend to come with a great drove of horses for the American territory [in Leal's name]."[20]

It is obvious that all Spanish commandants along Nolan's possible routes were alerted again and again, and most of Nolan's plans were almost common knowledge, except the date of his departure and his route through Texas. His route at first, according to his letter to Cook, was intended to pass a little south of Nacogdoches and go on to the Rio Grande—but whether or not he really intended to go to the Rio Grande is a question. Then, he told Cook, because the news was out he had decided to keep close to the coast, that he knew the country between Opelousas and the Rio Grande and would never be taken there. (Why didn't he stay in Natchez?) However, Nolan changed his plans again and went upriver to Nogales (present Vicksburg), and there crossed the Mississippi and kept to the north (but probably south of the Ouachita), crossing into Texas and going on to the Brazos River at about present Waco. It seems likely that he passed north of Nacogdoches.

At the head of twenty-seven heavily armed men, Nolan was discovered by Carlos Batin, and Vicente Fernández Tejeiro, commandant at Ouachita, immediately sent Batin with a fairly strong party, which located Nolan with "about 30 Americans" and packhorses, each man armed with pistols, saber, and carbine; Nolan himself carried a saber,

---

[18] Vidal to Casa Calvo, Concordia, Nov. 1, 1800, no. 91, AGI, *Papeles de Cuba, leg.* 71-A.

[19] Vidal to Salcedo, Concordia, Aug. 9, 1802, AGI, *Papeles de Cuba, leg.* 77.

[20] Vidal to the commandant of Nacogdoches, Concordia, Nov. 3, 1800, AGI, *Papeles de Cuba, leg.* 71-A.

four pistols, and two carbines, according to Batin. Nolan insulted Batin and dared him to ask for his passport, and sent Tejeiro a letter advising him that he had no passport but that he was going to the north "of your settlement"[21] to avoid embarrassing Tejeiro. In the morning Tejeiro headed a party of eighty men but found Nolan and his men gone; later he discovered that some of Nolan's men had intercepted Tejeiro's courier to Nachitoches but had not found Tejeiro's letter; they had taken the courier's powder and provisions and had broken his carbine.

Tejeiro gives the best possible reason for stopping Nolan when he says that if the expedition should turn out well, "the Americans will acquire knowledge of all the entrances to and exits from the kingdom of Mexico." He also says that Nolan's men said they would return in January[22] as Nolan himself had said.

Vidal sensed more than plunder in Nolan's actions, and he remarked as much to Casa Calvo: "I fear he makes this trip under the influence of others and with the intention of serving the states."[23]

Mordecai Richards, discovering that Nolan had no passport (or getting cold feet), deserted with two other men.

Official letters were flying. Casa Calvo advised Salvador Muro y Salazar, Marquis of Someruelos, captain general at Havana; he said he had gotten information from José de los Santos (a brother of Gertrudes). Commanders at Avoyelles, Rapides, Attakapas, Natchitoches, Nacogdoches, Concordia, Ouachita, and perhaps other posts were advised by the governor and by one another. So far we have not seen Casa Calvo's order for arrest, but on November 18 he told the captain general that he had taken measures to arrest the men of the Nolan party.[24] On December 22 he ordered Nolan's activities arrested.[25]

Spanish forces were alerted from Corcordia and Ouachita to the Rio Grande. Meanwhile, Nolan reached a point near present Waco, Texas, on the Brazos River, and built three log cabins or stockades and holed up there in one of the most inexplicable actions of his eccentric lifetime. He must have been on the Brazos by the time Casa Calvo ordered his

[21] That would throw him pretty far north of Nogales.

[22] Tejeiro to Casa Calvo, Ouachita, Nov. 10, 1800, AGI, *Papeles de Cuba*, leg. 71–A.

[23] Vidal to Casa Calvo, Concordia, Oct. 20, 1800, no. 90, AGI, *Papeles de Cuba*, leg. 71–A.

[24] Casa Calvo to Someruelos, New Orleans, Nov. 18, 1800, no. 26, *reservada*, AGI, *Papeles de Cuba*, leg. 1573. There is another copy in the Archivo General Nacional, Madrid, *leg.* 3901.

[25] Ramón de López y Angulo to the secretary of state, New Orleans, July 13, 1801, no. 63, AGI, *Audiencia de Santo Domingo*, leg. 2617. There is another copy, same writer, same recipient, same date, but different content, in *Papeles de Cuba*, leg. 638.

activities arrested, but behind him were still more troubles—one of them being the desertion of Mordecai Richards and the two other men. Richards had been considered third in command (under David Feró) and was a man who knew the country well, but he became alarmed when he found that Nolan had no passport, deserted, and returned to Natchez, where he sought out Vidal (who lived in Natchez) under cover of night and "with great hesitancy because of fear of reprisals" (and against the wishes of his wife), and told him about their crossing the Mississippi and asked help to pay his bills. He said that Nolan planned to return to Islas Negras and then to Kentucky by the following August or September, when he expected to have a patent from the English minister in Philadelphia, and under that patent he would lead a conquest of Texas or at least a pillaging of Texas. Nolan had said that in two more years he would be rich; that he expected to return to Natchez with his horses and with Gertrudes (and Richards said he thought the presence of Gertrudes would be scandalous). Richards said furthermore that Nolan had taken only three packhorses with merchandise—and that as gifts for the Indians. He also said that Nolan carried mining tools, and that he had said he was going to build an impregnable fort, reconnoiter the mines, catch horses, and run horses to Kentucky.[26] Rather a large order!

Further, he said that Nolan said: "If we succeed in my plan, it will make you of good estate, and your families too, and so that you will have no doubt of the advantages that will result, I hereby promise you by word of mouth—and I will put it in writing—that I will give you [for] each six months a negro when we return from our campaign."[27]

Nolan's projected time of sojourn in Texas is as flexible as his routes, and his objectives are still more so.

Then Richards was put on the Spanish payroll to pursue Nolan, and he suggested that his assignment be to catch Nolan "dead or alive."[28]

Later (in January) Richards seemed to think that Nolan had gone northwest.[29] Tejeiro adds the interesting (and not unexpected) information that horses could not be driven through the Ouachita area in January because of lack of grass. Therefore, Nolan's statements that he was

[26] Vidal to Casa Calvo, Natchez, Dec. 15, 1800, AGI, *Papeles de Cuba*, leg. 152–B; there are long series in *legs.* 72, 137–A, 213 (in French), 2367, and perhaps others.

[27] Casa Calvo to Berenguer, New Orleans, Jan. 2, 1801, AGI, *Papeles de Estado*, leg. 29. (A Negro sold for $300–600.)

[28] Casa Calvo to López y Angulo, New Orleans, Mar. 11, 1801, AGI, *Santo Domingo*, leg. 2617 (enclosed in López y Angulo to Soler, New Orleans, July 13, 1801, *ibid.*).

[29] Tejeiro to Vidal, Jan. 31, 1801, *reservada*, AGI, *Papeles de Cuba*, leg. 72.

not interested in horses and that he expected to be back in January are not incompatible.

Nolan did not go to the Rio Grande; perhaps the interception of his pirogue full of goods stopped that. Nor did he drive horses back to Natchez, because Jesse Cook had already started with a band of horses, accompanied by Pierre Longueville, Antonio Leal, and Gertrudes. They were all arrested and returned to Nacogdoches.

One hundred and fifty miles west of Nacogdoches, Nolan forted up—and stayed forted up for between four and five months. During that time, apparently his principal activity was visiting with Indians—especially Comanches. Perhaps he captured some mustangs, and he certainly traded mustangs from the Indians; at any rate, he and his men seem to have stayed close to their three small forts, for there is no evidence that they were seen near San Antonio or near the Rio Grande. It is rather a pity that they did not go to the Rio Grande, for along that river was one of the greatest mobilizations of Spanish soldiers the northeastern frontier had seen, participated in by the viceroy, the commandant general, the sub-inspector at San Luis Potosí, the governors of Nuevo Santander and Nuevo León, and the commandants at Refugio, Leynosa, Camargo, Mier, Revilla, and Laredo. The practical Spaniards smelled a filibuster in the making and had visions of British and Americans pouring into Texas; so they mobilized against the possibility.[30]

It does not appear, however, that Nolan himself had any idea of doing anything startling except sitting in his three small forts, because when Lieutenant Miguel Francisco Músquiz, with a superior force, found Nolan and his party on March 21, 1801, the men were bearded, ragged, and hungry. There had been no buffalo in that particular season, and Nolan's men were short of powder and lead and had lived for nine days on horsemeat. They had had considerable contact with the Comanches, and had either caught or traded for some 300 horses. Otherwise, they had stayed close to the fort.

Músquiz surrounded the fort and demanded surrender. Nolan elected to fight and was soon killed. A few of the men escaped and the others surrendered.

Músquiz listed the following men who had been with Nolan: Spaniards: Luciano García of Nacogdoches, Vicente Lara of Béxar, Refugio de la Garza of Careyta, Juan Joseph Martínez of Nacogdoches, Lorenzo Ynojosa of Béxar, Joseph Berban of Nacogdoches, and Joseph

[30] See Wilson, "Philip Nolan and His Activities in Texas," 110–127.

de Jesús de los Santos; Anglo-Americans: Simon McCoy of Opelousas and Natchez, Jonas Walters of Virginia, Salomon Cole of Kentucky and Natchez, Ellis P. Bean of South Carolina and Natchez, Joseph Reed of Pennsylvania and Natchez, William Doneley of Pennsylvania and Natchez, Charles Yuin (King?) of Maryland, Steven Richards of Pennsylvania and Natchez (son of Mordecai), Joseph Pierce of North Carolina and Natchez, Thomas Taus (House?) of Virginia and Natchez, Ephraim Blackburn of Maryland and Natchez, David Feró of New York and Natchez, and Juan Bautista (Caesar), a Negro slave of Nolan. Escaped at the time of the report were: Robert Ashley of South Carolinia and Natchez, John Taus (House?) of Virginia and Natchez, Michael Moore of Ireland and Natchez, and Robert (a Negro slave of Nolan) of Maryland and Natchez. Escaped previously were Mordecai Richards, apparently of Natchez, John King, and August (or John) Adams.[31]

Five years later the fate of those still alive and in Spanish hands was decided by the king, and one man, Ephraim Blackburn, was chosen by lot and shot by the Spaniards.[32]

There is still the question of Nolan's very peculiar actions in connection with this fifth expedition. These actions started when, in the face of the active opposition of Vidal, he gathered a party of twenty-seven heavily armed men and went into Texas without a passport, and continued when he was arrogant with Tejeiro. Nolan was not a fool and he was familiar with Spanish customs; so it is conceivable that he wanted to go to Texas so much that he would have tried to bluff or talk his way past Spanish officials on the Rio Grande. But the fact is that he did not try that at all; he went to the Brazos, stopped, and stayed there. He might have shacked up with Gertrudes at Nacogdoches, but Gertrudes was in jail, and it would have seemed most sensible for Nolan to get out of Texas when he found that out. Instead of leaving, however, he stayed in one spot, inviting (or daring) the Spanish army to come after him. Why? He had always used deception and subterfuge before, plus a little bribery and just plain delay. He knew all the answers but he did not use them this time.

On many occasions there are references to his taking goods with him into Texas on this expedition; however, it appears that probably the

31 *Relación* by Músquiz, Nacogdoches, July 17, 1800, AGN, *Historia*, vol. 412.

32 Steven Richards, Mordecai's son, was later released; Ellis P. Bean became a Catholic and fought in the Mexican War of Independence and for quite a while had a Mexican wife in Mexico and an American wife in Texas; Salomon Cole (or Zalmon Cooley) was in Santa Fe when Pike reached there in 1807; Cole, Bean, William Danling [Doneley], and David Feró fought in the Mexican Revolution; Feró was beheaded.

bulk of his trade goods was sequestered in Louisiana. He talked about Camargo and Revilla but did not go there—perhaps because he had no goods to offer. It was said that he was going to pillage, but he did not pillage. It was said that he was going to rob the gold trains, but he made no effort to do so. He was said to have mining tools, but there is no evidence that he used them. It was said that he was after horses, but he said that he was no longer interested in horses. He was expected to make a map, but he does not seem to have made any effort to do so—and this may be more significant than appears at first glance. He defied Tejeiro and intercepted his courier, and he knew that the Spaniards would not accept lightly that kind of treatment.

It is noteworthy that more than once a Spanish official suspected him of invasion, either for the United States or for England. The various circumstances of his actions obviously spelled something other than catching horses or contrabanding to the Spaniards. There is no evidence that he had any expectation of support from either the United States or England—but there is some circumstantial evidence that he might have expected support from James Wilkinson.

Consider the many contradictory references to the length of time he expected to be in Texas—from three months to two years—and consider the various promises he made to his followers. These promises seem to contemplate something more than wild horses.

Consider James Wilkinson for a moment: a consummate conniver, liar, forger, born betrayer. He betrayed General Gates in the Conway Cabal; he betrayed Benedict Arnold's corruption as clothier general and then took Arnold's job; he conspired against General Wayne and succeeded him as commander-in-chief of the U.S. army; he tried to get George Rogers Clark to head an invasion of Louisiana, and then tried to damn Clark for something Clark did not do; he conspired with Aaron Burr to set up an empire in Texas, and then wrote a letter to himself as from Burr and turned that letter over to General Washington; he constantly balanced Governor Miró against the Kentuckians but never let either one go too far because he did not want the situation resolved—his profit was in keeping them balanced; he was always broke and constantly involved in land schemes and lesser schemes—he was on the Spanish payroll for many years and apparently at one time had a promise of land in Louisiana.[33] In short, James Wilkinson was one of the crookedest men in history and one of the greatest opportunists. It seemed to be his particular forte to conspire and then sit back and wait to see which

[33] Wilkinson to Baron, Fort Washington, Sept. 22, 1796, AGI, *Papeles de Cuba, leg.* 2375.

force would triumph before taking a public stand. He was also very clever at covering his tracks on all sides.

In this connection, Félix Trudeau, commandant at Natchitoches, had some interesting remarks to make on April 27, 1801, about a month after Nolan was killed: "I am not persuaded that Nolan's intentions were solely to gather mustangs, that having already resulted [taken place]," and "perhaps those who had promised to join him . . . have not dared to go to see if they could help Nolan."[34]

And consider Nolan's own statement to Samuel P. Moore: "I look forward to the conquest of Mexico by the United States; and I expect my patron and friend, the General, will, in such an event, give me a conspicuous command."[35]

Nolan's defiance of the Spaniards by forting up in Spanish territory does not make sense. His weird actions in staying close for more than four months with no apparent objective other than gathering horses, to the extent that his men were ragged and hungry, are hard to explain. Note, however, that he was in a strategic spot in Texas. He must have been waiting for a purpose—and that purpose may have been to provide a strong point for Wilkinson and an army of Kentuckians, and to provide guidance and knowledge of the country. He did not pillage; he did not rob gold trains; he did not try to mine; he had no goods to trade; and he knew the Spaniards were after him. His reasons for the moment must remain pure speculation, but his position was remarkably like that of Zebulon Montgomery Pike, who in 1807 said that if he should not return by Christmas [of 1806], the general would send 15,000 men up three rivers to rescue him.

But the general did not send men in either case. Perhaps Wilkinson was waiting for the ball to bounce his way; perhaps, when the chips were down, he did not have the courage to move; perhaps he was too devious to move.[36]

At any rate, all this is speculation. The truth about the reason for Nolan's strange actions must remain a mystery until more evidence turns up.

34 Trudeau to Casa Calvo, Apr. 27, 1801, AGI, *Papeles de Cuba*, leg. 72.

35 Deposition of Samuel P. Moore, Mar. 6, 1810, in James Wilkinson, *Memoirs of My Own Times* (3 vols., Philadelphia, 1816), II, app. III.

36 The long history of filibusterers is not one of courage or fortitude. Time after time a filibusterer has had success in his grasp only to fail through inexplicable lack of decisiveness. For example, Raousset de Boulbon in Sonora, 1854; Henry Crabb in Sonora, 1857—among many.

The Role of the City Government
in the Economic Development of New
Orleans: Cabildo and City Council, 1783-1812

———◆◆———

J O H N   G.   C L A R K

𝒮TUDENTS of colonial Latin America have long recognized the role of the city in the settlement process and in the achievement of social and economic stability within the Spanish colonial system. An early student, F. A. Kirkpatrick, in emphasizing the city as the focal point of settlement during the period of conquest, maintained that "as in the Roman Empire, so also in the Spanish Empire, the municipalities were the bricks of which the structure was compacted."[1] More recently an eminent scholar of Spanish America, C. H. Haring, has suggested that municipal organization was more characteristic of the early history of Spanish America than of English America, where there was a greater scattering of people after the initial settlement. Spanish cities in the New World were created as full-fledged municipal organizations from the beginning of the conquest, whereas English cities arose more informally and without a prescribed pattern.[2] Implicit here is the view that the development of the hinterland was more critical to the settlement of English America than the city, while in Spanish America the city was the nuclear agency in establishing Spanish hegemony in Central and South America.

Correctives to this interpretation are offered from various quarters.

[1] F. A. Kirkpatrick, "Municipal Administration in the Spanish Dominions in America," *Transactions of the Royal Historical Society*, 3rd ser., IX (1915), 96.

[2] C. H. Haring, *The Spanish Empire in America* (New York, 1947, 1963), 147–148.

An article by Richard Morse stresses the city in Latin America as an instrument of colonization in that it was the point of departure for the occupation of the soil but simultaneously pointed to the disintegrative pull of the hinterland on the city. Rich lands and natural resources proved more attractive to colonists than did opportunities in the towns and thus retarded city development by stripping the towns of the more enterprising people.[3] A similar competitive struggle for population between town and country in the English colonies is also noted. But the emphasis in recent studies has shifted somewhat from the pull of the hinterland to the impact of generative forces within the towns on the settlement of the back country. Both Carl Bridenbaugh and Richard C. Wade describe the seminal role of towns in the conquest of frontier areas and the subsequent introduction of economic organization.[4]

These scholars all agree that the city was for the most part co-existent with the original settlement, that it propelled individuals into the countryside, that it eventually came to dominate a hinterland by imposing an economic system on it, and that in time the competition of urban units for markets helped knit large regions together economically. In addition, the larger towns were likely to function as administrative centers exercising political control over particular colonies or districts in the name of the royal authority. This latter role was early fastened on the towns as a result of policy and, as Bridenbaugh and Morse point out, the outgoing, metropole orientation of colonial commerce.[5] While the contribution varied from town to town, the major urban centers such as Bogotá, Lima, Mexico City, Boston, New York, or Philadelphia as market towns, religious centers, industrial sites, or political-administrative centers all radiated an economic influence into the countryside that determined in part both the nature and success of local and regional economies.

Within the towns numerous groups channeled their energies and tal-

---

[3] Richard M. Morse, "Some Characteristics of Latin American Urban History," *American Historical Review*, LXVII (Jan., 1962), 325–333.

[4] Carl Bridenbaugh, *Cities in the Wilderness: The First Century of Urban Life in America, 1625–1742* (New York, 1938, 1964); Richard C. Wade, *The Urban Frontier: Pioneer Life in Early Pittsburgh, Cincinnati, Lexington, Louisville, and St. Louis* (Cambridge, Mass., 1959, 1964).

[5] Bridenbaugh, *Cities in the Wilderness*, 30; Morse, "Some Characteristics of Latin American Urban History," 322–323; see also Charles N. Glaab and A. Theodore Brown, *A History of Urban America* (New York, 1967), 3–7. A distinction might be made between a coastal city with an almost built-in commercial orientation and a non-coastal or interior city. The latter should be thought of in its beginnings as a judicial, administrative, and religious center serving the needs of an agrarian or an agro-mining society.

ents into the currents of urban economic life. Unskilled laborers, ped-
dlers, craftsmen and tradesmen, small and large merchants, neighboring
farmers and planters rubbed against one another economically—if not
socially—in striving to make a living and derive maximum individual
benefits from the urban situation. Within this urban milieu on the frontiers of a New World, the jostling for wealth, position, prestige, or even
subsistence and survival made more pressing than even in the Old World
the need for organization, law, and order—for a minimal security of person and property without which there could be no economic growth.

In the larger towns—Lima or Boston—the royal presence was personi-
fied by viceroys and governors. Other agencies of royal authority such
as courts, custom houses, and military establishments also operated, but
the primary task of these bureaucracies was to implement imperial policies and enforce royal law. Such policies and the intentions of the ad-
ministrators, of course, impinged directly upon the citizens and affected
in sundry ways the development of local economies. But at the most
basic level of urban government an entirely distinct institution existed
in the form of the city council or cabildo, which provided necessary
economic services to townsmen and which possessed sufficient influence
or power frequently to negate, divert, or ameliorate the effects of un-
desirable royal policies.

The cabildo has been subjected to more intensive investigation as an
institution of local government than have English—or American—city
councils. Some controversy surrounds the overall role of the cabildo in
the evolution and ultimate dissolution of the Spanish-American empire.
The point of contention seems to revolve around the degree of local
autonomy actually exercised by cabildos at various stages in the colonial
period and the role of these local bodies in the independence movements
of the nineteenth century.[6]

The actual responsibilities of cabildos are described in some detail in
various studies, but it remains quite difficult to obtain any certain estimate of the impact of the cabildos upon the economic growth of the
separate municipalities. John Preston Moore, for example, defines some
of the functions of the cabildo of Lima with precision, writing that "by

---

[6] Most scholars describe the cabildos as losing power from the late sixteenth century
through the third quarter of the eighteenth century and then experiencing a renaissance
with the introduction of the intendancy system into Spanish America in the 1780s and
the breakdown in central control caused by the wars of the French Revolution and
Napoleon. See especially John Lynch, "Intendants and Cabildos in the Viceroyalty of
the Rio de la Plata, 1782–1810," *Hispanic American Historical Review*, XXXV (Aug.,
1955); John Preston Moore, *The Cabildo in Peru under the Bourbons: A Study in the
Decline and Resurgence of Local Government in the Audiencia of Lima, 1700–1824*
(Durham, N.C., 1966).

135

fixing the prices for commodities and the charges for services, the cabildo could exercise a powerful influence over the economy of the municipal district."[7] But the nature of that influence is not demonstrated. By
regulating the local marketplace and intervening in commercial affairs
in the name of the public welfare, was enterprise stimulated or retarded?
Did cabildo efforts to prevent monopolies or forestalling, to guarantee
a just price, and to maintain quality controls induce men to enter the
market, or did a regulated economy result in restricted opportunities for
profit-making and thus discourage entry?[8]

Although it is recognized that the performance of cabildos in minis-
tering to local needs varied from locale to locale, that some possessed
wider powers or were more representative of the community than
others, it may be possible to gain some understanding of the actual economic impact of one cabildo through an investigation of the experience
in New Orleans. This is attempted not in order to explore the nature of
cabildos in general but rather to discover the contribution of a particular
cabildo to the economic growth of a particular city. And while the city
itself was but an outpost within successive far-flung empires, it does
provide a unique opportunity to compare municipal growth under three
separate administrations—French (1715–63), Spanish (1763–1803), and
American. Did the cabildo foster economic growth in New Orleans;
did it build on French precedent; did it influence subsequent American
practice? In short, what role did the municipal government play in the
economic development of the delta town?

New Orleans became an important seaport and a major staple town
between 1783 and 1812. Events occurred far beyond the ability of the
cabildo or council to influence. The American Revolution gave birth to
a power which claimed dominion over half a continent in 1783, exer-

---

[7] Moore, *The Cabildo in Peru*, 66.

[8] Somewhat inflated claims for the cabildo are advanced in Fredrick B. Pike, "Public
Work and Social Welfare in Colonial Spanish American Towns," *The Americas*, XIII
(Apr., 1957), 361–375, in which it is claimed that "in the average Spanish American
colonial town, there was demonstrated a greater solicitude for public work and social
welfare than was typical in the English settlements of North America." The cabildo
was allegedly possessed of a more sensitive social conscience than English colonial city
councils, which were permeated more thoroughly with a laissez-faire attitude. For other
claims see Pike, "The Municipality and the System of Checks and Balances in Spanish
American Colonial Administrations," *ibid.*, XV (Oct., 1958), 139–158. Bridenbaugh,
Cities in the Wilderness, demonstrates the similarity in problems, approach, and methods
of solution between the two bodies and, if anything, the greater success of the English
councils in making urban living tolerable for all classes. See also Sidney I. Pomerantz,
New York, an American City, 1783–1803: A Study of Urban Life (New York, 1938);
and for the Portuguese response, Charles R. Boxer, *Portuguese Society in the Tropics:
The Municipal Councils of Goa, Macao, Bahia, and Luanda, 1510–1800* (Madison, 1965).

cised sovereignty beyond the Mississippi by 1803, and actively set about to people the vast hinterland west of the Appalachians and north of New Orleans. The economic regime of the hinterlands changed radically after 1783 as emigrants from the United States swarmed into both the upper and lower Mississippi Valley. In the upper Valley, farming encroached steadily upon the fur industry, dominant since the coming of the Europeans, and ultimately transformed the area into one of small grain and livestock farms dependent upon the waterways for access to a market and the sea at New Orleans. In the lower Valley, an influx of farmers and planters pressed against the Mississippi from Natchez to the south. Then in the 1790s, cotton replaced tobacco as the major staple north of Baton Rouge while sugar cane replaced indigo from Baton Rouge to the south.

These developments unfolded within the context of a world torn by revolution and war. The French Revolution plunged Europe into a series of wars which sapped the strength of Spain in Europe, weakened her powers of resistance to American penetration in Louisiana, and forced New Orleans into the American sphere of economic influence— all foreshadowing American possession in 1803. During the 1790s, the value of exports from New Orleans probably exceeded $1.5 million annually—three times higher than peak exports during the French period— while the town's population had doubled, reaching 8,000 by 1803. Seven years later, New Orleans was the largest city in the United States south of Baltimore and, with a population of 24,500, the fifth largest city in the United States. Staple exports were valued at $3 million in 1810.

While these developments served the interests of New Orleans—if not those of the Spanish empire—it would be unrealistic to attribute a major causative role to the New Orleans cabildo, for this agency responded to events rather than initiated them. Nonetheless, the cabildo's generally sensible and farsighted response to external events allowed New Orleans to reap maximum benefit from the limited opportunities presented. In this way, the cabildo contributed to the generation of an atmosphere conducive to economic growth.

Governor Alexander O'Reilly, conforming to Spanish custom, established the cabildo in 1768.[9] Provided with a permanent tax-based revenue which it constantly sought to increase, the governing body exercised various responsibilities that expanded as the city grew. As the first bona

[9] Decrees of the King approving the reformation of the new city government for New Orleans by O'Reilly, Aug. 17, 1772, in *Confidential Despatches of Don Bernardo de Gálvez, Fourth Spanish Governor of Louisiana, Sent to His Uncle, Don José de Gálvez, Secretary of State and Ranking Official of the Council of the Indies*, tr. from Spanish transcriptions (W.P.A. Survey of Federal Archives in Louisiana, 1937–38), 7.

fide city government in New Orleans, the cabildo quickly identified with and represented the interests of the municipality in matters which occasionally provoked conflict with royal authority.[10] A few examples, mostly relative to the trade between New Orleans and the United States, will clarify this point.

American trade became essential to New Orleans following the Treaty of Paris of 1783. Indeed, the provisioning of the town depended upon the traffic both from upriver regions and from the Atlantic Coast. New Orleans was open to trade with the French but the latter could not provide the shipping and credits necessary to move Louisiana's staples; the Americans could and did. Nonetheless, the Spanish government attempted at intervals to interdict the American trade both by river and by sea. In 1787, when large stocks of American flour were confiscated, the cabildo, admitting the illegality of the trade, protested to Governor Miró that absolute want would result unless American foodstuffs were received. Miró was aware of this and pointed out to a higher authority that the position of the cabildo was unassailable.[11]

Again, in 1799 and 1800, the Spanish government, in attempting to rescind certain commercial privileges granted to New Orleans in 1797, encountered intense opposition from the cabildo.[12] Seconded by the merchant community of New Orleans, including Americans, the councilmen, through a report of the attorney general, argued that the regulations of 1797 were indispensable to the welfare of the community and that the new orders would cause grave damage to commerce and agriculture. Intendant Morales acknowledged the weight of this reasoning and suspended the implementation of the regulations.[13] A few years later, when Morales suspended the American deposit at New Orleans, the cabildo protested that suspension caused a great scarcity of flour and

[10] The French Superior Council was basically a judicial body, and while located in New Orleans served the entire colony of Louisiana as well as New Orleans. Administratively, then, no distinction was made between the colony and its first city. The cabildo provided the town with a forum and source of power exclusively its own.

[11] Esteban Miró to José de Gálvez, New Orleans, June 10, 1785, Mississippi Provincial Archives, Spanish Dominion, Mississippi State Department of Archives and History, Jackson; cabildo session of Aug. 31, 1787, Records and Deliberations of the Cabildo, bk. III (1784–95), 183–186.

[12] In 1797 the Spanish opened New Orleans to trade with all neutral powers, meaning in practice the United States. These privileges followed upon the implementation of the commercial clauses in Pinckney's Treaty and had the effect of legalizing most phases of American trade with New Orleans.

[13] Cabildo session, Sept. 27, 1799, Cabildo Records, IV (1795–1802), 77–78; report of Attorney General Felix Arnaud, cabildo session, Oct. 25, 1799, *ibid.*, 102; Daniel Clark to James Madison, New Orleans, June 22, 1802, Dispatches from U.S. Consuls in New Orleans, 1798–1807, microcopy T225, roll 1, National Archives.

provisions and obtained a decree from Morales permitting the entry of American foodstuffs from upriver sources.[14]

In such cases as the above, in which the council had no power to act, protests, petitions, and legal briefs formed its arsenal in presenting the community's views to the resident royal officers. These officials, generally desirous of serving both the crown and the community, listened attentively to the cabildo and if at all possible granted its wishes. While the cabildo was not representative of the community in the sense that a locally elected body would have been, its personnel were recruited from among the most prominent Creoles, including town merchants and neighboring planters.[15] It was representative of those who counted in the community and thus endowed with a moral force that required attention.[16]

Moreover, the cabildo treated American merchants—both itinerants and residents—with fairness. This, combined with its recognition of the dependence of New Orleans upon American comestibles, contributed to the evolution of a commercial atmosphere sufficiently attractive to induce numerous American merchants to initiate businesses in the community. Much-needed capital entered the city. Enterprise was stimu-

[14] Cabildo session, Feb. 1, 1803, Cabildo Records, V (1802–03), 45–47.

[15] Among the most common explanations for the diminished effectiveness of colonial cabildos in the eighteenth century are the practice of purchasing offices which frequently became hereditary and, concomitantly, the absence of local elections for places on the councils. See Haring, *The Spanish Empire in America*, 155; Lynch, "Intendants and Cabildos in the Viceroyalty of the Rio de la Plata," 338–339; Moore, *The Cabildo in Peru*, 41–42. In noting the decline of representative institutions in the Indies, Salvador de Madariaga, *The Rise of the Spanish American Empire* (New York, 1965), 77–80, writes that "it is doubtful whether, in the setting of the Indies, the fact that the *regidores* [aldermen] bought their charges made the *cabildo* less representative of local trends, feelings, and interests." De Madariaga is thinking here in terms of psychological representation.

[16] Pike, "The Municipality and the System of Checks and Balances," 139–158, describes the system of intervention and overlapping authority utilized in colonial administration as a brilliant method of checks and balances which served to prevent the rise of an unchecked spirit of local autonomy while not completely stifling an independent municipal life. According to Pike, the cabildos acted as a restraint on higher authorities just as the latter checked the councils. The substance of the article, however, points to overwhelming restraints on local autonomy from several sources, countered or balanced only by the right of appeal enjoyed by the cabildos. Moreover, the term "checks and balances" is confusing, for within the context of Anglo-Saxon institutions, a system of checks and balances generally operates between agencies or institutions which are co-equals constitutionally. Although operating in different spheres, there is sufficient overlap in responsibility and authority for one institution to act as a counter to another. Pike is not writing of agencies of equal status. At the lowest level of government, the cabildo was not really a check or a balance of higher authorities but protected its prerogatives as best it could by appeals to the highest constituted authority, the crown. It remained the prerogative of the crown to grant or deny such protection.

139

lated. New merchants moved to town. In short, capital formation and the augmentation of entrepreneurial skills proceeded at a much brisker pace than would have been the case had the cabildo acted antagonistically toward American economic involvement in the city. By 1803 enough capital and managerial talent were present to support the organization of insurance, improvement, and banking corporations.

In other areas the cabildo operated with a greater autonomy from outside control. Repair and construction of bridges, roads, and levees; regulation of the port of New Orleans; the establishment of city lighting, sanitation, police, and fire-prevention services; regulation of the local food market including the awarding of supply contracts—all were properly within the cognizance of the cabildo.[17]

Of these duties, none was more difficult or more pressing than the regulation of the marketplace. The root of this problem was the need to guarantee an adequate and edible food supply for the populace at a price equitable to producer, processor, and consumer. Acting fully within the tradition of paternalistic municipal government, the cabildo intervened directly to set prices, inspect for quality, assure the use of standard weights and measures, and prevent recurrent food shortages from benefiting private monopolists and forestallers at the expense of the public welfare. Private interests employed various tactics to circumvent the regulatory authority of the public agency. Conflict between the public welfare and private interests continued into the American period. Ultimately, municipal governments throughout the United States lost much of their power to intervene so directly in the marketplace, but in Louisiana the tradition of regulation endured longer than in many areas of the United States. During the Spanish period, regulatory powers were persistently utilized by the city with some success.

Government in New Orleans did not solve the problem of food supply, which was eventually resolved by the movement of farmers into the upper Mississippi Valley. Time and again, as in the French period, the city suffered serious food shortages which compelled the cabildo to move into the market, purchase foodstuffs, and oversee distribution, as in 1772, 1779, 1781, 1788, 1792, 1794, and later. The cabildo requisitioned flour from merchants, distributed it to the city's bakers, and then administered the sale of bread to the populace. In 1796, in an effort to stretch existing supplies of flour and rice, the councilmen supervised experiments in which mixtures of rice and flour were baked into bread

---

[17] Colonial cities throughout the western hemisphere dealt with similar problems; see Bridenbaugh, *Cities in the Wilderness, passim;* Boxer, *Portuguese Society in the Tropics, passim;* and for Lima, Moore, *The Cabildo in Peru, passim.*

until an edible combination was finally hit upon. In both 1800 and 1803, the cabildo, fearing further shortages, formally and successfully requested that the intendant forbid rice exports.[18]

City authorities tried to ascertain the precise quantity of flour baked into bread since the bakers paid a tax on each barrel. This revenue, along with a tax on butchers, supported the street-lighting system. At the same time, the cabildo regulated the price, weight, and quality of bread and meat offered to the public at retail. There was obviously need for such regulation. One English merchant confided with obvious satisfaction to some associates that he had managed by a strategem to conceal some "excessively rotten" flour from the cabildo, whose subcommittees periodically stormed through the warehouses seeking out and dumping spoiled flour and meat into the river.[19]

Various systems were also tried to obtain an adequate meat supply for the city. Between 1770 and 1789 the cabildo granted a monopoly of the meat market to an individual after receiving competitive bids. Then, in 1789, the cabildo ended the contract system and established a free meat market by allowing livestock raisers to sell their herds on their own terms to the city's butchers. The city retained a tax on each head sold and fixed the retail price of meat. The new policy stimulated the growth of the cattle industry in the prairie regions of Attakapas and Opelousas and increased the supply of fresh meat available to the city while requiring additional butchers to distribute the meats. In general, the introduction of a free market assured the city of an adequate supply of meat at moderate prices as well as guaranteed the city a revenue of over 4,000 *piastres* annually from the tax on butchers.[20]

No brief is presented for the total success of such measures. As the

[18] Cabildo session, Sept. 18, 1772, Cabildo Records, I (1769–79), 106; session, Oct. 1, 1779, *ibid.*, II (1779–84), 3; session, Aug. 17, 1781, *ibid.*, 68–70; session, Oct. 10, 1794, *ibid.*, III (1784–95), 160–162; session, Oct., 1796, *ibid.*, IV (1795–1802), 155–159; session, Dec. 16, 1796, *ibid.*, 165; session, Mar. 11, 1796, *ibid.*, IV (1795–1802), 99; session, Apr. 18, 1800, *ibid.*, 165; Account of Rice Purchases by the City, Sept. 30, 1796 [untitled manuscript], New Orleans Municipal Records, Department of Archives, Louisiana State University, Baton Rouge.

[19] John Fitzpatrick to McGillivray & Struthers, New Orleans, Sept. 2, 1796, John Fitzpatrick Letterbooks (3 vols., 1768–1800), I, New York Public Library; Proclamation Fixing Prices, New Orleans, Sept. 7, 1769, in Lawrence Kinnaird, ed., *Spain in the Mississippi Valley, 1765–1794* (3 vols., Washington, 1946–49), I, 93; cabildo session, Oct. 30, 1772, Cabildo Records, I (1769–79), 108; session, Mar. 5, 1773, *ibid.*, 121–122; session, Mar. 3, 1775, *ibid.*, 210; session, June 20, 1777, *ibid.*, 266; session, June 22, 1792, *ibid.*, IV (1784–95), 6; sessions, Apr. 19–May 17, 1793, *ibid.*, 61–66.

[20] Cabildo session, Aug. 2, 1771, *ibid.*, I (1769–79), 68; session, Aug. 3, 1781, II (1779–84), 67–68; session, Sept. 4, 1789, III (1784–95), 74; Tax Collected on Meat, 1795, and Account Regarding the Distribution of Meat, Jan. 21, 1799, New Orleans Municipal Records.

Americans took over, bakers were still mixing bad with good flour, spoiled meat was still a problem, and the tavern owners were in collusion to fix the price of wines purchased at public sales. Nonetheless, successive city governments recognized the existence of such practices and sought to eliminate or control them through the application of methods derived from the medieval city. Such concepts as the fair price, a reasonable profit, consumer access to the marketplace, purity in products, accurate weights and measures, and prohibitions against engrossment were all applied in the name of the public welfare.

Among other civic responsibilities of the cabildo, the maintenance, improvement, and construction of public works were the most critical and, unlike the regulation of the market, involved the outlay of considerable sums of public moneys. As in most cities, budgetary considerations compelled the municipality to formulate projects on a somewhat smaller scale and perhaps less rapidly than the legitimate needs of the city demanded.[21] Thus visitors and residents alike complained about the disrepair of the streets and levees, the lack of street lights, inefficient drainage and sanitation systems, inadequate police and fire protection, and similar deficiencies.

Spain was reasonably liberal in committing funds from its own sources to finance public improvements in New Orleans, and Spanish colonial officials were permissive in allowing the city to broaden its tax base.[22]

[21] Pike, "Public Work and Social Welfare in Colonial Spanish American Towns," 369–372, defines the responsibilities of cabildos in this area but says little about accomplishments; Haring, *The Spanish Empire in America*, 159, writes of the generally wretched physical conditions found in Spanish colonial cities; Moore, *The Cabildo in Peru*, 82–84, notes that revenue problems made it difficult for the cabildo of Lima to pursue an energetic program of public works; similar problems confronted the Portuguese city councils [*cámaras*] treated in Boxer, *Portuguese Society in the Tropics*, *passim*; the English colonial towns investigated by Bridenbaugh, *Cities in the Wilderness*, *passim*, concentrated their efforts on the maintenance and improvement of port facilities and supporting road systems. Professor Bridenbaugh points out that many public works, especially docks and wharves and bridges, were initially built with private capital. This was apparently a more common practice in the English towns than in the Spanish. In the latter, however, a certain lavishness in public buildings was made possible through capital provided by the church and crown. In general, it appears that a town like Lima contained a larger number of magnificent buildings and private residences than Boston but that the roads, sanitation system, and market facilities of Boston were superior to those in Lima.

[22] O'Reilly's political settlement assured the city government of a permanent annual revenue derived from an anchorage tax (of French inception), a tax on tafia (a rum-like commodity), and taxes on taverns, rooming houses, butchers, bakers, and billiard halls. At intervals thereafter licenses were required for the operation of certain businesses, and fees charged by various officials went for the salaries of civil servants. O'Reilly to Arriaga, New Orleans, Dec. 10, 1769, in Kinnaird, ed., *Spain in the Mississippi Valley*, I, 134; Decrees of the King approving the reformation of the new city

While a gap always existed between the quality and variety of services offered to and services demanded by the public, the cabildo did purchase fire-fighting equipment in 1788, erect street lights in 1794, organize a night watch or city patrol, and make major disbursements each year to repair roads, bridges, and levees and to drain and fill low areas in the city. These jobs were let on bids to local contractors, who frequently subcontracted with others for the actual work.[23] In this way, public funds were pumped back into the local economy, particularly for port operations, while employment opportunities were created for local residents.[24]

Effective political institutions that are not revolutionary in nature are normally compatible with the total social environment. In doing the expected they avoid deviating radically from the commonly accepted behavioral norms of the community. Under Spanish rule, the cabildo of New Orleans was such an institution. It applied paternalistic solutions to problems which had traditionally been resolved by government intervention. Councilmen sought—as councilmen in other Spanish cities sought—to maintain their prerogatives against threats from any source. In one confrontation with Governor Gálvez, stemming from the cabildo's opposition to certain of his economic policies, the loyalty of the cabildo was impugned. In another, with Governor Salcedo over the right of the cabildo to a larger box in the theater, several councilmen were arrested. Both were cases in which the cabildo asserted its self-identity and its identity with the larger community.[25] Challenge and

---

government for New Orleans by O'Reilly, Aug. 17, 1772, *Despatches of Gálvez*, 7; Partial Balance of the City Treasurer for the Year 1776, and Balance Presented to the Cabildo by the City Treasurer for the Year 1780, New Orleans, 1780, New Orleans Municipal Records; cabildo session, Jan. 25, 1793, Cabildo Records, III (1783–95), 46; Berquin-Duvallon, *Travels in Louisiana and the Floridas, in the Year 1802, Giving a Correct Picture of Those Countries*, tr. from the French by John Davis (New York, 1806), 35.

[23] Cabildo session, July 3, 1789, Cabildo Records, III (1784–95), 69; session, Apr. 25, 1794, *ibid.*, 128; bills and receipts of the cabildo, 1770, 1779, 1786, 1796, New Orleans Municipal Records; Caroline Maude Burson, *The Stewardship of Don Esteban Miró, 1782–1792* (New Orleans, 1940), 267–271.

[24] The port handled an increasing number of both river and ocean-going vessels with fair efficiency during the decade prior to the Louisiana Purchase. In 1786, 124 vessels entered the river, compared to 181 in 1801 and 256 in 1802. In 1802, two-thirds of the entering tonnage was American. See John G. Clark, *New Orleans, 1718–1812: An Economic History* (Baton Rouge, 1970), 228.

[25] Gálvez to José de Gálvez, New Orleans, Mar. 2, 1779, *Despatches of Gálvez*, 60; cabildo session, Nov. 9, 1781, Cabildo Records, II (1779–84), 85–89; session, Jan. 15, 1802, *ibid.*, IV (1795–1802), 154–155; session, Jan. 20, 1802, *ibid.*, 161; session, Feb. 5, 1802, *ibid.*, 168; session, July 19, 1802, *ibid.*, V (1802–03), 1–3. Moore, *The Cabildo in*

response were well within the conventional limits of action of the historic cabildo. Cabildos knew their place, were sensitive to the outer limits of their authority, and strove to secure the one and achieve the other. The body that succeeded the cabildo in New Orleans had no such certain knowledge of its place or its duties.

Probably no other institution in Louisiana suffered a greater buffeting during the first decade of American control than the city council. The council inherited all the powers and responsibilities of the cabildo, and its duties were further defined by "An Act to Incorporate the City of New Orleans" passed by the territorial legislature in 1805.[26] Its basic tasks, while not radically different from those of the cabildo, were complicated by the need to define relationships with other political bodies exercising some degree of authority in New Orleans. Chief among them was the government of the United States, but hardly less significant were the territorial and parish governments. Concurrently, the city fathers were confronted with the need to formulate relationships with private or quasi-public corporations operating in the city under charters granted by the territorial and, after 1812, state governments.[27] These aggregates of private capital occasionally acted with disregard for the public welfare, precipitating a clash with its guardian, the city council.

Critical to the evolution of the city council were the economically liberating promises and consequences of American sovereignty. While the Spanish had acted leniently toward Louisiana in formulating economic policy, the regulation of economic and political affairs in New Orleans was a fact of life. Relative to the past, American sovereignty meant a free economy in New Orleans and the territory, making possible not only the chartering of private corporations but also stimulating bakers, butchers, and others to attack the regulatory powers traditionally exercised by the city government. Between assaults by the butchers,

---

Peru, 103–105, relates the story of a famous actress in Lima who converted one of the three boxes claimed by the cabildo into a dressing room and the cabildo's successful challenge to this affront to its dignity.

26 The act provided for the election of fourteen aldermen presided over by the recorder and a mayor, appointed by the territorial governor, who held a limited veto over council enactments. *Acts Passed at the First Session of the Legislative Council of the Territory of Orleans . . . in New Orleans . . . [1804]* (n.p., n.d.), 46–64.

27 Between 1804 and 1812, eight chartered corporations operated in New Orleans, including the New Orleans branch of the First Bank of the United States. Among the others were three banks (the Bank of Louisiana, chartered in 1804; the Bank of Orleans, 1811; and the Louisiana Planters Bank, 1811); the New Orleans Insurance Company (1805); the New Orleans Navigation Company (1805); the New Orleans Water Company (1811); and the Mississippi Steamboat Navigation Company (1812).

the parish, the state, and the federal government, the city government was an institution besieged during its first decade of life.

The city waged a losing battle against the principle of free enterprise. Between 1803 and 1816, butchers, bakers, and other tradesmen challenged the taxing and regulatory powers of the council with success, culminating in 1813 when the state legislature prohibited the city from taxing flour and in 1816 when an act prohibited the city from fixing the sale price of any goods whatever.[28] An important tax on imported rum and tafia, opposed by tavern owners and importers, was voided by the federal courts, and the anchorage tax was threatened on at least two occasions by congressional action.[29] Essential sources of revenue were lost at just the time population and territorial expansion intensified service demands on the city and at a time when embargoes and finally war caused grave economic dislocation in the community.[30]

No less frustrating to the council, which had to maintain roads, bridges, and levees, administer the port, and provide security to the community on a revenue base that was constantly narrowed, was the need to formulate a viable working relationship between the municipality and certain of the private corporations located in the city. A confrontation between the public welfare and the dynamic of the profit motive pitted council against corporation with predictable results.

Complicating the issue was the composition of the city council during the formative period of the relationships.[31] While seats in both the

[28] *Louisiana Gazette* (New Orleans), June 4, 1810; *Louisiana Gazette and New Orleans Advertiser*, Oct. 13, 1812; city council session, Sept. 3, 1809, New Orleans City Council, Proceedings of Council Meetings, 1809–10, II, no. 2, 108; session, Nov. 2, 1812, *ibid.*, 1812–14, II, no. 3, 263; session, Dec. 5, 1812, *ibid.*, no. 4, 9–10; session, Apr. 10, 1813, *ibid.*, 62–63; session, June 16, 1813, *ibid.*, 84; "An Act Repealing in part the sixth section of the act incorporating the city of New Orleans, and for other purposes, March 28, 1813," *Acts Passed* . . . [*1812–13*] (n.p., n.d.), 246–248; "An Act to regulate the price of baking each and every barrel of flour in the city of New Orleans, December 14, 1814," *Acts Passed* . . . [*1814*] (New Orleans, 1815), 10–12; "An Act to amend the act entitled 'An Act to incorporate the city of New Orleans' and . . . [another act], March 14, 1816," *Acts Passed* . . . [*1816*] (New Orleans, 1816), 92.

[29] Council session, May 22, 1805, City Council Proceedings, 1805–06, I, no. 2, 33–35; session, Mar. 26, 1806, *ibid.*, 1806–07, I, no. 3, 30; session, Jan. 26, 1807, *ibid.*, 151; session, July 6, 1807, *ibid.*, 1807–08, II, no. 1, 4; session, Nov. 19, 1808, *ibid.*, 303; session, Dec. 21, 1811, *ibid.*, 1811–12, II, no. 3, 126–127; session, Dec. 23, 1812, *ibid.*, no. 4, 16; session, Jan. 15, 1814, *ibid.*, 176; *Louisiana Gazette*, Apr. 28, 1807.

[30] In 1811 the police department budget equaled the total city budget of 1804. Council session, Sept. 29, 1804, City Council Proceedings, 1803–05, I, no. 1, 189–192; session, Feb. 6, 1811, *ibid.*, 1811–12, II, no. 3, 7.

[31] Another problem for the council, which came to view itself as the arbiter between public and private interests, was the fact that the corporations owed their legal existence

cabildo and the council were held mostly by merchants, the presence of private corporations in New Orleans added a new dimension to both the makeup of the municipal government after 1803 and the intensity of pressure from the private economic sector to which the council was subjected. An analysis of seventy-seven councilmen who served at least one year between 1805 and 1814 inclusive reveals that twenty-eight held directorships in one or more of the private corporations during those years and that twenty-three of the twenty-eight held those positions while serving on the city council.[32] These twenty-three men filled 31 percent of all the corporate positions during the ten years. Three of the corporations were in an especially favorable position to exert influence in the municipal government: the Bank of Louisiana, the New Orleans Insurance Company, and the New Orleans Navigation Company. Of these, the navigation company did actually exercise its power.[33]

Between 1806 and 1810, twenty-one men served on the board of the New Orleans Navigation Company, of whom thirteen served at least one year on the council, twelve serving concurrently.[34] During those years, acrimony and suspicion divided the two agencies into warring camps. Company construction on the Bayou St. John and the Caronde-

---

to the territorial or state legislature and were thus protected from attacks by the city save through the courts. As it turned out, it was the city that was assaulted through the court system.

[32] It is believed that the figure of seventy-seven includes most, if not all, of the incumbents during this period. Data for the following discussion were derived from such a number of sources that citation would be too cumbersome. In chap. 16 of my manuscipt on the economic history of New Orleans, tables are included which reveal the various corporate positions held by individual councilmen-directors. The water company and the steamboat company were excluded from the calculations, leaving six corporations. For a more detailed analysis of the corporate elite see John G. Clark, "The Business Elite of New Orleans before 1815," *Papers of the Sixteenth Business History Conference*, ed. Charles J. Kennedy (Lincoln, Neb., 1969), 94–103.

[33] Between 1805 and 1817, thirty-one men served as directors of the Bank of Louisiana for at least one year, of whom seventeen were councilmen with fourteen serving concurrently. During the same period, twenty-one men served as directors of the insurance company with ten sitting at least one year on the city council and seven holding both positions concurrently. While a potential for influence certainly existed, there is no evidence that either corporation exerted any pressure on the council in favor of a particular policy.

[34] The corporation was chartered in 1805 to provide a system of navigable waters from Attakapas and Opelousas to the Mississippi and to open up water communication between Lake Pontchartrain and the Mississippi. Cost factors quickly determined that the latter objective become the sole concern of the company, and the state legislature restricted the company to its privileges in New Orleans in laws passed in 1809 and 1814. The charter and supplementary legislation are printed in *Acts Passed . . . [1805]*, 430; ibid. *[1809]*, 56; ibid. *[1814]*, 46.

let Canal interfered with the city sewerage system, and the company challenged the historic right of the city to collect certain tolls on the canal. In both controversies, the city came out second best. In the latter, the company went to court and a series of decisions voided the tax power in question.[35] The great sewerage debate commenced in 1806 and occurred intermittently through 1810. In that year, a company offer to construct new drainage ditches at its expense was rejected as inadequate by the council. A resolution to that effect was passed 8 to 1. In December, 1810, the company proposed another solution. This followed a city election in which five company directors won seats on the council. A settlement favorable to the company passed by a vote of 5 to 4.[36]

According to one boomer, the age ushered in by American possession heralded the transformation of New Orleans into "the new Alexandria of America." Waiving the question of the preciseness of the comparison, it cannot be doubted that New Orleans entered a period of unsurpassed growth and prosperity, especially after 1815. But for the municipality, the experience was unsettling. New Orleans and its hinterlands were placed under one sovereignty by the Louisiana Purchase and yet several "sovereign" bodies exercised authority in the community. The lowering and removal of economic barriers; the establishment of representative, not to be confused with democratic, government; the application of U.S. laws and procedures such as the appellate court system and jury trials; the arrival of the Fourth Estate in force—all these developments fostered the birth of a host of interests and provided forums from which they struck out on their own behalf. Members of the New Orleans Typographical Society enjoyed a good brew at the Eagle Tavern while promoting their interests. New Orleans' mechanics lashed out at the Louisiana Senate for its failure to incorporate a mechanics' benevolent society. Shipbuilders in front of the meat market ignored city orders to move. Saloon owners and food handlers hired lawyers to dispute city authority. The navigation company blocked the sewers and packed the council while the United States compelled the city to relocate its ferry.

Unlike the cabildo, the city council experienced great frustration in searching for its proper role and sphere of authority. Indeed, the net

---

[35] *Le Télégraphe* (New Orleans), 1 février 1804; *Louisiana Gazette*, Oct. 30, 1807, Aug. 27, 1810; council session, July 12, 1809, City Council Proceedings, 1809–10, II, no. 2, 80–84; session, Jan. 20, 1810, *ibid.*, 139–141; session, Feb. 17, 1810, *ibid.*, 152; session, Apr. 27, 1811, *ibid.*, 1811–12, II, no. 3, 39; session, Aug. 21, 1813, *ibid.*, 1812–14, II, no. 4, 127–128; session, Sept. 28, 1813, *ibid.*, 146; session, Jan. 29, 1814, *ibid.*, 181–182.

[36] Council session, Aug. 13, 1806, *ibid.*, 1806–07, I, no. 3, 102; sessions, Mar. 3, 12, 24, 1810, *ibid.*, 1809–10, II, no. 2, 160–166; session, Apr. 7, 1810, *ibid.*, 171–172; sessions, May 30, June 6, 13, 1810, *ibid.*, 189–199; sessions, Dec. 19, 26, 1810, *ibid.*, 254–257; session, Feb. 23, 1811, *ibid.*, 1811–12, II, no. 3, 11; sessions, May 11, 18, 29, 1811, *ibid.*, 44–49.

result of the transition from cabildo to American council was the weakening of the municipal government of New Orleans. Events leading up to American belligerency in 1812 worsened an already precarious position. Political and economic freedom and the expansion of opportunity created difficulties as well as benefits. Spanish officials could solve problems arbitrarily, without recourse to public opinion. While the Spanish governors were generally sensitive to the economic needs of the city, they did not have to be. Local Spanish officials could and did take independent action, knowing that a reprimand was months away. Both governors and cabildo operated within a universe that was not only familiar but unimperiled by unknowns. The corporation of New Orleans enjoyed no such luxury.

Larger sovereignties pressed against the city at all times, while smaller interests resisted its authority and rural groups resented its economic power. New Orleans, serving an ever-expanding hinterland and fragmented into a random collection of organized and unorganized interests, learned in the first decade of American rule that it could not unilaterally define its economic role. The community had still to learn the secret of binding into a stable whole its diverse and swirling atomistic parts. Such an alchemy still remained undiscovered when Louisiana left the Union in January, 1861.

Spanish Regulation of Taverns
and the Liquor Trade
in the Mississippi Valley

———•◦•———

JACK D. L. HOLMES

*T*HERE is a small tavern in Seville, Spain, where the following sign appears:

> IS THERE SOMETHING BETTER THAN WINE?
>
> The act of drinking is an art that only races of ancient lineage possess. When one makes use of wine moderately, as with all precious things, it is health and medicine, it increases muscular power, it exalts the sexual drive, it stimulates the nervous and psychical system, it renders eloquence easy, it leads to benevolence, to good fellowship, to forgiveness, and to heroism.
>
> Wine exalts fantasy, makes the memory lucid, increases happiness, alleviates pain, destroys melancholy, reconciles dreams, comforts old age, aids convalescence, and gives that sense of euphoria by which life runs smoothly, tranquilly, and lightly.[1]

Given the Spanish propensity for imbibing wine, it is not surprising that certain patterns of drinking and control were brought to the Mississippi Valley during the Spanish domination (1766–1803). Regulation of the consumption of alcoholic beverages apparently is as old as man's interest in drinking, for the famous Hammurapi Code dating back to

[1] Sign in the "Bodega Puenta," Seville, copied by writer in 1962.

about 1670 B.C. provided the death penalty for wine-sellers who adulter-ated their products or who charged excessive prices. Convicted felons were barred from those ancient taverns.[2] In colonial English America tavern keepers were warned against selling to minors, servants, or sailors, while a New York ordinance prohibited shuffleboards and bowling al-leys in their taverns.[3]

In Louisiana the pattern of liquor regulation was first established dur-ing the French dominion. One of the earliest taverns was located at Mobile between 1706 and 1712. Operated by Jean Baptiste LeMoyne, Sieur de Bienville, the tavern sold wine at $200 a cask until Antoine Crozat's agents lowered the price to $64.[4] French laws governing the distribution of liquor forbade its sale to Negro slaves or Indians, set hours for the taverns, and established fair price schedules.[5] In 1746 Gov-ernor Pierre Rigaud, Marquis of Vaudreuil, issued an ordinance fixing the number of licensed taverns in New Orleans and establishing regula-tions governing the sale of liquor.[6] One of the last measures passed by the French Superior Council in May, 1766, governed "les cabaretiers."[7]

During the Spanish domination of Louisiana and the Floridas the government sought to control the importation and consumption of liquor in various ways. In the laws, edicts, and decrees governing tav-erns, the Spanish theory and practice can be noted.

SPANISH LICENSING OF TAVERNS

The authority of the government to license the sale of liquor in the Spanish colonies was recognized in Spanish law, as it was in regulations passed by other colonial powers.[8] The famous *Recopilación de las leyes*

---

[2] Cyrus H. Gordon, *Hammurapi's Code, Quaint or Forward-Looking?* (New York, 1957), 9–10.

[3] Oscar Theodore Barck, Jr., and Hugh Talmage Lefler, *Colonial America* (New York, 1958), 358–359.

[4] N. M. Miller Surrey, *The Commerce of Louisiana during the French Régime, 1699–1763* (New York, 1916), 273.

[5] *Ibid.*, 274.

[6] Henry P. Dart, "Cabarets of New Orleans in the French Period," *Louisiana His-torical Quarterly*, XIX (July, 1936), 582–583. See also police regulations by Vaudreuil and Rouvillière, New Orleans, Feb. 18, 1751, in Charles E. A. Gayarré, *History of Louisiana* (4th ed., 4 vols., New York, 1903), II, 361–363.

[7] Regulation "de la Police," New Orleans, May, 1766, Archivo General de Indias, Seville (hereafter cited as AGI), *Papeles de Cuba, legajo* 187–A.

[8] For example, see Sidney and Beatrice Webb, *The History of Liquor Licensing in England, Principally from 1700 to 1830* (London, 1903); Leonard S. Blakey, *The Sale of Liquor in the South* (New York, 1912).

de los reinos de las Indias and the Ordinances for the Intendancy of New Spain contain rules for licensing *pulperías*, or, as they were called in Louisiana, *cabarets*. By royal decree of February 5, 1730, the intendants were granted the power to fix the number of taverns and to collect license fees every six months. The license fees were usually set at between $30 and $40 a year. It was stated that the government opposed monopolies in supplying the people with such "necessities" as wine, bread, oil, and vinegar.[9]

One of the first measures passed by Alexander O'Reilly when he established Spanish power and dominion over Louisiana in 1769 was a decree governing the number of taverns in New Orleans because of the disorders originating therein.[10] On October 8, 1769, he issued a comprehensive set of regulations for tavern keepers, innkeepers, billiard parlor proprietors, and the master lemonade seller.[11] O'Reilly provided for six inns, twelve taverns, six billiard parlors, and one lemonade shop. License fees varied, but tavern keepers were expected to pay 200 *livres* or $40 per year on a quarterly basis, and O'Reilly expected the city would be assured of $840 per year from this source of revenue.[12]

In 1775 Pedro Moris appeared before the New Orleans cabildo asking for the post of lessee for the tavern licenses. He was required to post a bond of $6,600, pay an annual fee of $840 to the city, draw up a list of all taverns within a distance of three-fourths of a league from New Orleans, report unlicensed taverns to the government, and donate $100 annually to the charity hospital.[13] Apparently Moris expected to make a profit on his investment, and he persuaded the cabildo to increase the number of taverns from thirteen to twenty-four.[14]

The tavern license fee varied from an annual cost of $23 in 1771[15] to

[9] Francisco Rendón to Francisco Luis Héctor, Baron de Carondelet, New Orleans, Apr. 15, 1795, AGI, *Papeles de Cuba*, leg. 31, citing the *Recopilación*, ley 12, título 8, *libro* 4, and the Ordinances for the Intendancy of New Spain (Dec. 4, 1786), arts. 160, 161.

[10] Jack D. L. Holmes, "O'Reilly's Regulations on Booze, Boarding Houses, and Billiards," *Louisiana History*, VI (Summer, 1965), 294. The decree is in the collection of the Louisiana State Museum, New Orleans. See Douglas McMurtrie, *Early Printing in New Orleans, 1764–1810, with a Bibliography of the Issues of the Louisiana Press* (New Orleans, 1929), 91.

[11] Holmes, "O'Reilly's Regulations," 293–300.

[12] Alexander O'Reilly to Bailio Fr. Don Julián de Arriaga, no. 16, New Orleans, Dec. 10, 1769, in Lawrence Kinnaird, ed., *Spain in the Mississippi Valley, 1765–1794* (3 vols., Washington, 1946–49), I, 134.

[13] New Orleans Cabildo Minutes, Oct. 27, Dec. 1, 1775, New Orleans Public Library Archives.

[14] *Ibid.*, Dec. 1, 1775.

[15] List of tavern keepers, New Orleans, Jan. 4, Sept. 1, 1771, AGI, *Papeles de Cuba*, leg. 110.

$30 in 1786[16] and $40 by 1794.[17] By way of contrast, under the American government in 1816, the tavern license cost $60 plus a $2.50 issuing fee.[18]

The number of taverns varied considerably and a perusal of the records indicates a large turnover in the persons who paid for the privilege of selling liquor in New Orleans. The number varied from thirteen in 1775 to ninety-four in 1789, and the revenues from tavern licenses varied from $360 in 1777 to $1,996.31 in 1789.[19]

Free Blacks and Mulattoes were allowed to operate taverns in New Orleans and four names appear in the records. Of the 280 persons who held licenses from 1770 to 1796, twenty-five were women, including eight widows.[20] Apparently there was a waiting list, and when Diego de Alva surrendered his tavern license on December 21, 1770, Simon Lorenzo was granted that tavern's number and paid the license fee for the balance of the year.[21]

Although Bourbon Street today is famous throughout the world for the number and variety of its taverns and bars, during the Spanish period only two taverns were listed on that street in 1791, while on the river side of Front Street (now Decatur) there were twenty-six taverns.[22]

Collecting license fees in New Orleans was not always easy. When tavern keepers left with the militia on the Baton Rouge campaign in 1779, they declined to pay their license fees, leaving the city with a deficit of $1,200.[23] City steward Luis Boisdore reported in 1781 that there was considerable trouble in collecting the license fees.[24] Soldiers from the Louisiana battalion stationed in New Orleans frequently ran their own taverns and, when the licenses came due, switched taverns with each other to avoid paying. Because they came under the *fuero militar*, which exempted them from ordinary civil justice, they were able to avoid being called into court on the matter.[25]

[16] Report of Francisco Blache, 1786, New Orleans Municipal Papers, box 1 (1770–1806), Tulane University Archives, New Orleans.

[17] Report of Blache, 1794, *ibid.*; see app. 3.

[18] License to sell liquor, 1816, MS, Kuntz Collection, Tulane University Archives.

[19] See app. 3.

[20] See app. 2.

[21] List of tavern keepers, New Orleans, Jan. 4, Sept. 1, 1771, AGI, *Papeles de Cuba*, *leg.* 110; New Orleans Municipal Records, folder 1 (duties for 1772), Louisiana State University Archives, Baton Rouge.

[22] New Orleans Census, Nov. 6, 1791, New Orleans Public Library Archives.

[23] New Orleans Cabildo Minutes, May 26, 1780.

[24] *Ibid.*, Feb. 24, 1781.

[25] *Ibid.*, Oct. 27, 1780.

O'Reilly had forbidden anyone to operate a tavern without a government license posted on the tavern door beside a sign giving the proprietors' names. Topers could be served liquor in the taverns, but the only food they could eat with their beverages was restricted to bread, butter, cheese, oysters, salad, sausages, and radishes. Taverns could serve wine, brandy, and rum, but no beer, cider, bottled liqueurs, or syrups. On the other hand, thirsty boarders at the New Orleans inns could buy wine and liquor only with their meals or if consumed off the premises. Billiard parlors could serve beer and cider but not wine, brandy, or rum.[26]

Anyone failing to abide by the rules established by O'Reilly and subsequent governors faced the loss of his license and the closing of his tavern. Juan Puche, who ran a tavern on Front Street as early as 1787, continually violated the rules, and the cabildo suspended his license at the end of 1792, replacing him with another tavern keeper.[27]

Thus the Spanish government licensed taverns for two reasons: to raise revenue and to curtail disturbances which might occur from the proliferation of unauthorized and unsupervised taverns. Those tavern keepers who violated any of the regulations established were often fined, and these fines put to good use. Antonio de Ulloa, Louisiana's first Spanish governor, forbade anyone to carry liquor up the Mississippi River for the purpose of selling, trading, or giving it away subject to a fine of $25 per quarter-cask, one half being given to the commandant of the post who had captured the guilty party, and one half devoted to orphans and hospitals of the settlement.[28] Esteban Miró, governor general of Louisiana, provided that $20 fines levied on tavern keepers guilty of a variety of violations would go to a fund for chamber and justice expenses.[29] Informers in Upper Louisiana who reported persons selling forbidden liquor were granted one-third of the $100 fine, while the balance was placed "at the discretion of the government."[30]

A number of uses for tavern licensing taxes appear in the records. O'Reilly intended for the New Orleans fees to be placed in the police fund of the city.[31] In 1795 the intendant of Louisiana, Francisco Ren-

---

[26] Holmes, "O'Reilly's Regulations," 294–299.

[27] New Orleans Cabildo Minutes, Jan. 25, 1793.

[28] Ulloa's regulations (New Orleans?), Mar. 14, 1767, in Louis Houck, ed., *The Spanish Régime in Missouri* (2 vols., Chicago, 1909), I, 15.

[29] Miró's *Bando de buen gobierno*, New Orleans, June 1, 1786, in New Orleans Cabildo Minutes.

[30] Art. 12, Proposed Trade Regulations for Spanish Illinois, St. Louis, Oct. 15, 1793, in Kinnaird, ed., *Spain in the Mississippi Valley*, III, 195.

[31] Holmes, "O'Reilly's Regulations," 295–296, 298.

dón, claimed that he had the power to license additional taverns himself and consign the fees for the treasury department.[32] While license fees from six taverns during the French period were used to aid the city's poor,[33] in 1797 the cabildo decreed that tavern taxes were to be used to support the San Carlos Charity Hospital.[34] Justice Francisco Pascalis de la Barre wanted to create six new taverns in 1794, the proceeds from which would pay two or three additional constables for the city.[35]

In 1792 Governor General Carondelet decreed that the *cabareteros* of Louisiana and West Florida should pay a tax of 50 cents a month to be used for repairing the piers and wharves of the provinces.[36] In New Madrid, the annual license fee was used for public works.[37] In 1794 a man named Miguel bid $52 for a tavern license for the purpose of building a jail,[38] and the following year the fees collected from Jean Baptiste Olive, Edward Robertson, and Charles Guilbault went to the same fund.[39] Those operating taverns and gaming tables at Opelousas paid a fee which went for the building of a jail also.[40] Miró authorized two taverns in the Pointe Coupee settlements, the revenues from which were devoted to such public works as a jail and repair of the government buildings.[41] At Valenzuela Andrés de Vega bid $100 for the privilege of running the post's only tavern, and this money was set aside for the parish church there.[42] The $700 collected at the post of San Carlos of Missouri in Upper Louisiana was supposed to go for the support of the

[32] Rendón to Carondelet, New Orleans, Apr. 15, 1795, AGI, *Papeles de Cuba, leg.* 31.

[33] Gayarré, *Louisiana, French Domination,* II, 361–363.

[34] New Orleans Cabildo Minutes, Oct. 20, 1797.

[35] Letter of de la Barre, New Orleans, June 13, 1794, inserted in New Orleans Cabildo Minutes, June 27, 1794.

[36] Manuel de Lanzós to Francisco Belêtre, no. 29, Mobile, Aug. 8, 1792, letterbook in AGI, *Papeles de Cuba, leg.* 224–A.

[37] Carondelet to Tomás Portell, New Orleans, July 30, 1793, Mississippi State Provincial Archives, Spanish Dominion, V, 8, Mississippi State Department of Archives and History, Jackson.

[38] Carondelet to Portell, New Orleans, Aug. 5, 1795, AGI, *Papeles de Cuba, leg.* 22.

[39] General order of Carlos Dehault Delassus, New Madrid, n.d., in Frederic L. Billon, comp., *Annals of St. Louis in Its Early Days under the French and Spanish Dominations* (St. Louis, 1886), 333–334. Another New Madrid tavern keeper licensed on Aug. 24, 1795, was Jacob Myers, who bid $60 for the franchise at a Fort Celeste auction. Louis Houck, *A History of Missouri, from the Earliest Explorations and Settlements until the Admission of the State into the Union* (3 vols., Chicago, 1908), II, 274–275.

[40] Carondelet to Martin Duralde, New Orleans, Oct. 1, 1795, AGI, *Papeles de Cuba, leg.* 22.

[41] [Miró] to Valentin LeBlanc, New Orleans, Sept. 4, 1789, draft, AGI, *Papeles de Cuba, leg.* 134–B.

[42] Anselmo Blanchard to [Miró], Valenzuela, Dec. 27, 1782, AGI, *Papeles de Cuba, leg.* 159.

parish church there, but Father Diego Maxwell reported to Governor General Manuel Gayoso de Lemos that Zenon Trudeau, the lieutenant governor at St. Louis, had decided to give the money to the poor.[43] At Pensacola the thirteen tavern keepers who each paid $30 a year for licenses saw that money go to build an embarcadero with a wharf.[44] At Natchitoches half of the proceeds from the "trucks" gaming tables supported the militia drummer,[45] while two wine-sellers paid $80 a year to subsidize the salaries of two constables.[46]

The Spanish government also attempted to use its licensing power in a regulatory manner to prevent abuses generally associated with taverns in Louisiana. Brandy-sellers at Natchitoches paid £400 each year to keep the wine shops there closed.[47] In Upper Louisiana unlicensed tavern keepers who sold liquor were fined $2 and imprisoned for three days for the first offense; $50 and fifteen days for the second; and expulsion under guard to New Orleans for the third.[48]

In 1804 a settler complained to Governor Vicente Folch y Juan of West Florida that five unauthorized taverns were operating on the Tickfau River and its tributaries above Lake Pontchartrain, to the "great dissatisfaction of many quiet subjects," because they were the meeting places of deserters, thieves, wandering vagabonds, and Indians.[49] Governor Folch issued a regulation reiterating the ban on unlicensed taverns, providing a fine of $25 and confiscation of the liquor for the first offense; a $50 fine and confiscation for the second; and a $100 fine and expulsion from the province for a subsequent violation.[50]

At the post of San Fernando de las Barrancas on the Chickasaw Bluffs (Memphis, Tennessee), tavern keepers who failed to obey the regulations were punished for the first offense with eight days' imprisonment;

[43] Luis [Peñalver y Cárdenas], Obispo [bishop], to Gayoso, New Orleans, Feb. 16, 1798, AGI, *Papeles de Cuba*, leg. 2365.

[44] Juan Buenaventura Morales to the secretary of state and treasury (Eugenio Llaguno y Amirola), no. 331, New Orleans, Oct. 15, 1799, AGI, *Audiencia de Santo Domingo*, leg. 2638.

[45] Athanase de Mézières to Luis de Unzaga y Amézaga, no. 402, Natchitoches, Feb. 16, 1776, in Herbert Eugene Bolton, ed., *Athanase de Mézières and the Louisiana–Texas Frontier, 1768–1780* (2 vols., Cleveland, 1914), II, 121.

[46] Mézières to Unzaga, Natchitoches, Feb. 28, Mar. 14, 1771, *ibid.*, I, 241, 243.

[47] Mézières to Unzaga, no. 402, Feb. 16, 1776, *ibid.*, II, 121.

[48] General order of Carlos Dehault Delassus, in Billon, comp., *Annals of St. Louis*, 333.

[49] T. Hutchins to the governor of West Florida (Folch), New Orleans, Aug. 12, 1804, AGI, *Papeles de Cuba*, leg. 59.

[50] "Regulations" issued by Folch, Baton Rouge, Oct. 30, 1804, AGI, *Papeles de Cuba*, leg. 2368.

for the second, one month; and for the third, the loss of the liquor in their taverns, one month in prison, and permanent expulsion from the post.[51]

One of the primary duties of the tavern keeper was to maintain order within his establishment. Settlers at Opelousas were divided in their opinions regarding the tavern which the commandant, Louis Pellerin, had established within a short distance of the parish church, and Father Valentin appealed to acting French governor Charles Philippe Aubry to close the tavern in 1766. Other settlers insisted that there had been no disorders in the tavern and asked for its re-establishment the following year.[52]

O'Reilly's 1769 regulation required tavern keepers to report all disputes and rows immediately to the nearest police officer and to seek aid from the guard in arresting those guilty of provoking disputes. Criminals, vagabonds, and prostitutes were barred from frequenting the taverns. Swearing and blasphemy were forbidden.[53] At Natchez, the twelve tavern keepers agreed to report to the nearest guard any disturbances within their establishment,[54] but a brawl broke out between Charles King and Edward Carrigan at James Riley's tavern after an episode of name-calling.[55] At San Fernando de las Barrancas, Gayoso decreed that the "tavern" would serve people standing outside, but would not permit anyone to enter in order to "avoid the results of gathering at similar spots."[56] Tavern keepers in Upper Louisiana were also ordered to inform the nearest police officer so as to arrest the guilty culprits and maintain order.[57]

Spanish officials attempted to control taverns by fixing their locations and selecting those to whom the franchise would be given. For the convenience of the patrons, Miró decreed that the two taverns at Pointe Coupee be located at public places serving the settlements which stretched along the river for twenty-six miles. He recommended they

---

[51] Jack D. L. Holmes, "The First Laws of Memphis: Instructions for the Commandant of San Fernando de las Barrancas, 1795," *West Tennessee Historical Society Papers,* XV (1961), 104.

[52] Petition of Opelousas settlers to Aubry, New Orleans, Sept. 25, 1767, fragment, AGI, *Papeles de Cuba,* leg. 198.

[53] Holmes, "O'Reilly's Regulations," 298.

[54] Agreement of Natchez tavern keepers, Natchez, June 26, 1792, Natchez Chancery Court Records (7 vols., translations), vol. D, 109.

[55] King *vs.* Carrigan, Sept. 6, 1796, *ibid.,* vol. E, 227.

[56] Holmes, "The First Laws of Memphis," 104.

[57] General order of Carlos Dehault Delassus, in Billon, comp., *Annals of St. Louis,* 333–334.

be located near the plantations of "honorable settlers," who would report any violations of the rules of good behavior.[58]

In the provinces, tavern licenses were offered at public auction to persons of good character.[59] If a person who had operated a tavern decided to give up his license, someone else could bid for it, but this sometimes caused problems. At Valenzuela Miguel Homs (Holmes?) kept the tavern in 1781, but apparently gave up his license because he could not collect debts from those to whom he had extended credit. Andrés de Vega bid $100 for the franchise, which was granted to him by Commandant Anselmo Blanchard, but in the meantime Homs had obtained from Governor General Miró an extension of his franchise, thus providing two taverns for the post, which was restricted to one. Blanchard asked that Miró approve Vega's license and cancel that of Homs.[60]

At San Fernando de las Barrancas, Commandant Elías Beauregard selected the sole tavern keeper from among those of good reputation, but there seems to have been no license fee collected.[61] Because settlers at New Madrid resented the tavern franchises, Carondelet authorized Commandant Tomás Portell to allow all persons to buy and sell at retail and wholesale, but provided that only the licensed taverns might sell liquor at retail. Licenses for the tavern were sold at public auction on an annual basis.[62]

Occasionally tavern licenses were granted to help out a worthy, but poor, settler. Agustín Richard, the ferryboatman at Placaminas below New Orleans, asked Governor General Gayoso for a license to run a cabaret. Gayoso extended provisional permission while he sought the views of the commandant and suggested that some taverns might be closed if they were not obeying the laws set forth and replaced by others whose proprietors would follow instructions.[63]

Illicit pawnbroking occurred frequently at the taverns. At Natchitoches, where Indians and Negroes brought stolen horses and clothing to the taverns in exchange for liquor, the situation was acute, and the

[58] Miró to Valentin LeBlanc, New Orleans, Sept. 4, 1789, draft, AGI, *Papeles de Cuba, leg.* 134–B.

[59] *Ibid.*

[60] Anselmo Blanchard to [Miró], Valenzuela, Dec. 27, 1782, AGI, *Papeles de Cuba, leg.* 195.

[61] Holmes, "The First Laws of Memphis," 104.

[62] Carondelet to Portell, New Orleans, July 30, 1793, Mississippi Provincial Archives, Spanish Dominion, V, 7–9. Miró also forbade liquor shippers to sell their goods at retail, preferring that alcohol be vended exclusively by licensed tavern keepers. [Miró] to Valentin LeBlanc, Sept. 4, 1789, AGI, *Papeles de Cuba, leg.* 134–B.

[63] [Gayoso] to Lauretat Sigur, New Orleans, Mar. 12, 1798, AGI, *Papeles de Cuba, leg.* 251–A.

commandant reported that even the troops at the presidio of Los Adaes on the Texas frontier engaged in the illegal practice.[64] James Ross and John Olaverry operated taverns at Natchez, where stolen goods frequently changed hands for the price of a few drinks.[65]

Because gambling at taverns frequently resulted in disputes, Gayoso forbade such games as dice in the Natchez taverns.[66] Hours of opening and closing were also set to avoid trouble. O'Reilly had decreed that taverns were not to sell liquor on feast days or Sundays, or during High Mass or Vespers, when the Sacrament was blessed. Taverns in New Orleans were to close at 8 P.M.[67] Miró reiterated these restrictions in 1786.[68] At Natchez the hours for closing were 8 P.M. in winter and 9 P.M. in summer, but they could open at sunrise.[69] At San Fernando de las Barrancas the tavern was ordered closed during working hours.[70] Jacob Myers agreed to close his New Madrid tavern on holidays and Sundays and after tattoo in the evenings.[71] When Gayoso became governor general at New Orleans, he ordered taverns and billiard parlors closed at the hour of tattoo but made an exception by permitting wicket openings at the taverns through which liquor might be sold to "sick persons" at "unseasonable hours." As in earlier decrees, taverns were to be closed on Sundays and feast days until after High Mass, and workers were forbidden to enter taverns until after working hours.[72] These restrictions had little effect, however, due to the prevalence of crooked police, who, for a little palm-greasing, would allow the New Orleans taverns to remain open at all hours of the day and night.[73] Dr. Paul Alliot commented in 1803 that New Orleans policemen collected enough graft in this fashion to enable them to retire in a short time.[74]

[64] Mézières to Unzaga, no. 87, Natchitoches, Mar. 14, 1771, in Bolton, ed., *Athanase de Mézières*, I, 243.

[65] Jack D. L. Holmes, *Gayoso: the Life of a Spanish Governor in the Mississippi Valley, 1789–1799* (Baton Rouge, 1965), 112.

[66] Agreement of Natchez tavern keepers, vol. D, 108.

[67] Holmes, "O'Reilly's Regulations," 296–297.

[68] Miró's *Bando de buen gobierno*.

[69] Agreement of Natchez tavern keepers, vol. D, 108–109. On Natchez taverns see Holmes, *Gayoso*, 112.

[70] Holmes, "The First Laws of Memphis," 104.

[71] Bond of Jacob Myers, New Madrid, Aug. 24, 1795, in Houck, *A History of Missouri*, II, 274–275.

[72] Gayoso's *Bando de buen gobierno*, New Orleans, Jan. 1, 1798, Louisiana Collection, Bancroft Library, Berkeley; photostat in MS Collection, New York Public Library.

[73] Berquin-Duvallon, *Vue de la colonie espagnole du Mississipi, ou des provinces de Louisiane et Floride Occidentale* (Paris, 1803), 187.

[74] Quoted in James Alexander Robertson, ed., *Louisiana under the Rule of Spain, France, and the United States, 1785–1807* (2 vols., Cleveland, 1911), I, 79.

Other abuses at the taverns included serving adulterated liquors and cheating on the weights and measures. O'Reilly forbade the sale of adulterated liquors or sour or stale wines under any pretext and ordered such beverages confiscated and thrown in the streets.[75] At the post of San Carlos de Barrancas, three leagues from Pensacola, it was the common practice to sell adulterated liquor to the troops in violation of the laws, and there it involved the adjutant Josef Noriega.[76] The city of New Orleans examined annually the weights and measures used, and if tavern keepers were discovered selling unmeasured liquor in bottles, the beverages would be confiscated and thrown into the street.[77]

SPANISH RESTRICTIONS ON SALES

There were laws established which forbade the sale or exchange of liquor for three classes of people in Spanish Louisiana: Negroes, military personnel, and Indians. O'Reilly forbade the sale of liquor to Mulattoes, Mulattresses, Negroes, and Negresses who lacked written permission from their masters or mistresses, subject to a fine of $20 and eight days in jail for the first offense.[78] Miró repeated the prohibition in 1786,[79] after he had already forbidden coasters to sell liquor to Negro slaves along the Mississippi River.[80] The New Orleans cabildo in 1784[81] and Governor General Gayoso in 1798[82] condemned the practice of selling liquor to Negro slaves, but they were as unsuccessful as the French had been after issuing a similar ban as early as 1717.[83] The practice was forbidden throughout Louisiana at such widely scattered posts as New Madrid[84] and Natchez.[85]

Various restrictions were placed on the sale of liquor to military personnel. A custom in French Louisiana allowed the daily issue of brandy

[75] Holmes, "O'Reilly's Regulations," 297.

[76] Folch to the Conde de Santa Clara, Pensacola, Aug. 18, 1798, AGI, *Papeles de Cuba*, leg. 154-A; Gayoso to Santa Clara, no. 18, confidential, New Orleans, Oct. 3, 1798, AGI, *Papeles de Cuba*, legs. 154-A, 1502-B.

[77] Holmes, "O'Reilly's Regulations," 297.

[78] *Ibid.*

[79] Miró's *Bando de buen gobierno*.

[80] Miró's regulation, New Orleans, Oct. 14, 1785, AGI, *Papeles de Cuba*, leg. 3. This has been translated in Kinnaird, ed., *Spain in the Mississippi Valley*, II, 150–151.

[81] New Orleans Cabildo Minutes, Apr. 30, 1784.

[82] Gayoso's *Bando de buen gobierno*.

[83] Surrey, *The Commerce of Louisiana*, 273.

[84] Billon, comp., *Annals of St. Louis*, 333–334; Houck, *A History of Missouri*, II, 274–275.

[85] Agreement of Natchez tavern keepers, vol. D, 109.

rations to troops and sailors, but Antonio de Ulloa attempted to halt the custom when an expedition left for Upper Louisiana in 1767. He claimed such a practice resulted in "intoxication and disorder" and ordered the *filet*, as it was called, stopped. He did permit those who were "habituated" to alcohol to buy their own, however.[86] Gayoso forbade the sale of liquor to sailors on the Mississippi squadron of galleys and gunboats on the grounds that they were issued a daily *filet* with their meals, thus indicating that Ulloa's prohibition was not followed by subsequent governors, but Gayoso was opposed to a special tavern ashore for the sailors because, leaving their ships and becoming intoxicated, they would fail in their duty.[87] Yet the sailors finally did get their own tavern at San Fernando de las Barrancas the following year.[88]

As can be noted from earlier remarks, a number of soldiers from the New Orleans battalion operated taverns in New Orleans,[89] but such practice was officially discouraged. At San Fernando de las Barrancas, non-working soldiers were entitled to buy a quantity of liquor not to exceed one-third of their monthly salary. Working soldiers could buy a maximum of two flasks of brandy or its equivalent each month, compared to the three flasks of brandy authorized for sale to civilian workers "in consideration that they habitually need more and that they enjoy greater wages than the soldier." If a tavern keeper at the post sold a greater amount to a soldier on credit, the latter was not obliged to pay his debts.[90]

Tavern keepers were warned not to extend credit to soldiers or sailors at New Madrid.[91] At Fort San Phelipe de Placaminas below New Orleans, tavern keepers who extended credit to soldiers or accepted items in pawn faced the loss of the items, their money, and a $10 fine.[92]

Of all the restrictions placed on sales of liquor, the most confusing regarded the distribution to Indians. Here Spain followed a difficult policy of continuing the French practice of supplying the natives with

[86] Ulloa's regulation of Mar. 14, 1767, in Houck, ed., *The Spanish Régime in Missouri*, I, 3.

[87] Holmes, "The First Laws of Memphis," 104.

[88] Jack D. L. Holmes, "Fort Ferdinand of the Bluffs, Life on the Spanish–American Frontier, 1795–1797," *West Tennessee Historical Society Papers*, XIII (1959), 47, citing Manuel García to Gayoso, San Fernando de las Barrancas, Aug. 24, 1796, AGI, *Papeles de Cuba, leg.* 48.

[89] New Orleans Cabildo Minutes, Oct. 27, 1780.

[90] Holmes, "The First Laws of Memphis," 104.

[91] Houck, *A History of Missouri*, II, 274–275.

[92] Pedro Favrot to Carlos Howard, no. 44, Fort San Phelipe de Placaminas, Jan. 18, 1799, "The Favrot Papers" (12 vols., W.P.A. Louisiana Historical Records Survey, New Orleans, 1940–63), IV, 79.

liquor, to which they had become accustomed, while at the same time forbidding traders and tavern keepers to sell any alcoholic beverages to the Indians. While Antonio de Ulloa recognized that the one thing most desired by the Indians in Upper Louisiana was brandy, he ordered that none be distributed to them. Commandants who discovered illegal brandy being shipped northward were to confiscate it and pour it into the river, thus causing the first water pollution in the Mississippi Valley![93]

The French had banned the sale of liquor to Indians in 1717,[94] and the Spaniards followed suit: O'Reilly in 1769;[95] Miró in 1786;[96] Gayoso in 1798.[97] As for the commandants of the Louisiana posts, they, too, issued various decrees against selling liquor to the Indians: Coulon de Villièrs at Natchitoches,[98] Francisco Cruzat at St. Louis,[99] Carlos Dehault Delassus at New Madrid,[100] Louis DeBlanc at Natchitoches,[101] Vicente Folch at Baton Rouge,[102] Gayoso de Lemos at Nogales,[103] to mention just a few.

Pedro Piernas, lieutenant governor of Upper Louisiana, had reported in 1769 that "if the Brandy trade were vigorously forbidden them, one could do with them whatever he pleased. But with the abuse of that trade," he added, "the Indians are found to be importunate, insolent, and perhaps murderous, because of the intoxication to which they are inclined. . . ."[104] Captain Philip Pittman, an English officer, observed at about the same time that the "immoderate use of spirituous liquors" had virtually decimated the Tunicas.[105]

[93] Houck, ed., *The Spanish Régime in Missouri*, I, 11, 15.

[94] Surrey, *The Commerce of Louisiana*, 273.

[95] Holmes, "O'Reilly's Regulations," 297.

[96] Miró's *Bando de buen gobierno*.

[97] Gayoso's *Bando de buen gobierno*.

[98] Coulon de Villièrs's proclamation, Natchitoches, Nov. 29, 1767, MS, Natchitoches Parish Records; microfilm copy in Northwestern State College Library, Natchitoches.

[99] Cruzat's ordinance, St. Louis, Oct. 7, 1780, in Houck, ed., *The Spanish Régime in Missouri*, I, 240.

[100] Billon, comp., *Annals of St. Louis*, 333–334.

[101] Louis DeBlanc to Carondelet, no. 29, Natchitoches, Sept. 4, 1794, AGI, *Papeles de Cuba, leg. 30*.

[102] Folch's printed "Regulations to be Observed by the Syndics and Alcaldes of the Jurisdiction of Baton Rouge," Baton Rouge, Oct. 30, 1804, AGI, *Papeles de Cuba, leg.* 2368.

[103] Gayoso's instructions to the commandant of Nogales (Elías Beauregard), Nogales, Apr. 1, 1791, AGI, *Papeles de Cuba*, in Mississippi Provincial Archives, Spanish Dominion, III, 503–520.

[104] Piernas's description of Spanish Illinois, New Orleans, Oct. 31, 1769, in Houck, ed., *The Spanish Régime in Missouri*, I, 72.

[105] Captain Philip Pittman, *The Present State of European Settlements on the Mississippi, with a Geographical Description of That River* (London, 1770), 35.

The Indians obviously made spectacles of themselves when drunk. Not all of the incidents were as harmless as that described at New Orleans in 1799:

> Outside of the gate we saw a large circular shade for drying and manufacturing bricks, under which were upwards of fifty Indians of both sexes, chiefly intoxicated, singing, drinking, rolling in the dirt, and upon the whole exhibiting a scene very disgustful. We soon came to another company of ten men sitting in the middle of the road, all intoxicated, amongst them was one standing, with a bottle of rum in his hand, whose contents he alternately administered to the rest, first by shaking the bottle and then pouring part of its contents into their mouths.[106]

One wild night affair among Indians at the Avoyelles post resulted in the death of a brave, but the other members of the tribe were so drunk they couldn't give testimony regarding the incident.[107] At Nogales a drunken Indian killed another, and the following day the dead Indian's kinfolk used a shotgun to atone for the death, thus retaining their "honor."[108] When Bentura Orueta gave brandy and whiskey to a group of Abenaqui Indians near Fort Carlos III in 1787, the result was a near riot between the Abenaqui and Arkansas tribes.[109] A Cherokee and Choctaw had a drunken fight at Natchez resulting in a black eye and a dead horse.[110] Drunken Choctaws, supplied by the pro-Spanish trader Turner Brashears, broke up a conference with American commissioners at Muscle Shoals in 1792.[111] At Mobile the Alibamons raided farms, stole horses, and killed slaves due to the influence of liquor, according to Indian commissioner Juan de la Villebeuvre, but he reluctantly asked for more liquor to keep the natives content![112]

---

[106] Anonymous narrative, 1799, in Fortescue Cuming, *Sketches of a Tour to the Western Country* . . . , vol. IV, *Early Western Travels, 1748–1846*, ed. Reuben Gold Thwaites (Cleveland, 1904), 365. Cf. Carondelet to Gayoso, New Orleans, Mar. 18, 1795, transcript in the Spanish Papers, North Carolina Department of Archives and History, Raleigh.

[107] Corinne L. Saucier, *History of Avoyelles Parish, Louisiana* (New Orleans, 1943), 19.

[108] Gayoso to Miró, no. 102, Natchez, May 16, 1791, AGI, *Papeles de Cuba*, leg. 41.

[109] Report of Vallière, San Carlos, May 19, 1787, in Kinnaird, ed., *Spain in the Mississippi Valley*, II, 203–208.

[110] Holmes, *Gayoso*, 157.

[111] Governor William Blount to the secretary of war (Henry Knox), Knoxville, Sept. 20, 1792, in Clarence E. Carter, ed., *Territory South of the River Ohio, 1790–1796*, vol. IV, *Territorial Papers of the United States* (Washington, 1936), 172–174.

[112] Juan de la Villebeuvre to Carondelet, Boukfouka, July 22, 1794, in Kinnaird, ed., *Spain in the Mississippi Valley*, III, 328.

Villebeuvre wrote that the Choctaws had become so addicted to the rot-gut, raw rum that they would go to the Americans to get it if Spain failed to keep them supplied.[113] He was probably correct, for two months later the Americans delivered 100 gallons of whiskey to the Chickasaws they were trying to win to their side.[114] Although Governor General Miró had discouraged the distribution of liquor to the Indians,[115] he reluctantly agreed to supply tafia to those chiefs and warriors he was courting for defensive alliances against the expansion of the United States.

His successor, the Baron de Carondelet, saw nothing wrong in yielding to the pleas of the Indians for a little tafia for "medicinal purposes."[116] Although traders were forbidden to give liquor to Upper Louisiana Indians,[117] in 1787 Francisco Cruzat reported he had given them 1,400 jugs of tafia and 14 casks of liquor.[118] At San Fernando de las Barrancas, where distribution of liquor to the Indians by the tavern or local soldiers was forbidden,[119] Chickasaws received annual presents from the Spanish government which consisted of 660 pots of tafia valued at 81 cents a pot.[120] Indians pleaded with Gayoso for brandy, wine, and tafia.[121] At Natchez Choctaw Indians received gifts of liquor from the commandant, Carlos de Grand Pré.[122] Governor Gayoso, who personally preferred not to give them liquor, was forced to provide barrels of tafia for leading Choctaw chiefs in 1792,[123] and when he was governor general of Louisiana, he ordered the shipment of ten barrels of spirits

[113] Juan de la Villebeuvre to Carondelet, Boukfouka, Feb. 4, 1793, AGI, *Papeles de Cuba, leg.* 208. This is translated in Duvon C. and Roberta Corbitt, eds., "Papers from the Spanish Archives Relating to Tennessee and the Old Southwest, 1783–1800," *East Tennessee Historical Society Publications,* no. 29 (1957), 149.

[114] War Department, Apr. 27, 1793, "Correspondence of General James Robertson," *American Historical Magazine,* II (Oct., 1897), 363.

[115] Miró's *Bando de buen gobierno;* Miró to Alexander McGillivray, New Orleans, July 12, 1784, AGI, *Papeles de Cuba, leg.* 2360.

[116] Carondelet to Gayoso, New Orleans, Feb. 21, 1792, AGI, *Papeles de Cuba, leg.* 18.

[117] Carlos Dehault Delassus to [Gayoso], "Expenses of New Bourbon," 1797–98, tr. into Spanish by Pedro Derbigny, New Orleans, Aug. 9, 1798, AGI, *Papeles de Cuba, leg.* 215–A.

[118] Francisco Cruzat's list of presents for the Indians, St. Louis, Nov. 27, 1787, in Houck, ed., *The Spanish Régime in Missouri,* I, 268.

[119] Holmes, "The First Laws of Memphis," 104.

[120] Gregorio LaRosa to Carondelet, no. 49, Natchez, Aug. 13, 1795, AGI, *Papeles de Cuba, leg.* 32.

[121] Payamataha to Gayoso ("Abacan"?), Aug. 20, 1793, AGI, *Papeles de Cuba, leg.* 215–A.

[122] Carlos de Grand Pré to Martín Navarro, Natchez, Dec. 1, 1781, AGI, *Papeles de Cuba, leg.* 590.

[123] Holmes, *Gayoso,* 157; Gayoso's list of presents, Natchez, Sept. 4, 1792, AGI, *Papeles de Cuba, leg.* 160–A.

for Upper Louisiana.[124] In the final analysis, it was the Spaniards' policy to provide moderate amounts of liquor at special occasions or designated times for the Indians, but they tried to discourage private traders or tavern keepers from adding to the problem.

Official Spanish policy discouraged intoxication, but, except for rare occasions, laws urged moderation rather than abstinence. Liquor was forbidden altogether along the Upper Missouri by agreement of the stockholders in the Missouri Trading Company.[125] Governor Gayoso was a great believer in banquet diplomacy, and when Colonel John Pope visited the Walnut Hills in 1791 he was regaled with "delicious Nuts and excellent Wines."[126] Gayoso considered that the moderate use of wine and other beverages was conducive to good health along the frontier.[127] Another visitor to Spanish Louisiana, Samuel S. Forman, was treated by Commandant Pierre Foucher to the hospitality of the New Madrid post, which included "an elegant dinner in the Spanish style, and plenty of good wine and liquors," including numerous toasts "to the health of the ladies."[128] A visitor to New Orleans remarked that the settlers were moderate in their use of wine, but that northern visitors preferred their grog, a "poison in this climate."[129] The same visitor commented that wine was served at breakfast, dinner, and supper without limit.[130]

Intoxication seemed to prevail at all levels and among all classes of society. Among the troops stationed in Louisiana and West Florida, the immoderate use of alcohol was notorious. Colonel John Pope wrote that the "inordinate use of Ardent Spirits and bad Wine" contributed to the poor health of the soldiers.[131] "The abominable vice of drunkenness" became so serious at the Nogales post that Gayoso was forced to warn the commandant that if he failed to check it, he would be severely repri-

[124] Gayoso to Morales, New Orleans, Mar. 5, 1798, enclosed in Morales to Príncipe de la Paz (Manuel de Godoy), no. 6, New Orleans, Apr. 30, 1798, Archivo Histórico Nacional, Madrid, *Estado, leg.* 3902.

[125] Art. 12 of proposed trade regulations for Spanish Illinois, St. Louis, Oct. 15, 1793, in Kinnaird, ed., *Spain in the Mississippi Valley*, III, 195.

[126] John Pope, *A Tour through the Southern and Western Territories of the United States of North-America; the Spanish Dominions on the River Mississippi, and the Floridas; the Countries of the Creek Nations; and Many Uninhabited Parts* (Richmond, 1792, New York, 1888), 29.

[127] Holmes, "The First Laws of Memphis," 101.

[128] Samuel S. Forman, *Narrative of a Journey down the Ohio and Mississippi in 1789–90* (Cincinnati, 1888), 49.

[129] William Johnson's journal, quoted in Arthur P. Whitaker, *The Mississippi Question 1795–1803* (New York, 1934), 44.

[130] *Ibid.*

[131] Pope, *Tour*, 44.

manded and punished.[132] Elías Beauregard, the commandant, was well known for his own affection for the bottle.[133]

It was the custom on the river to give three daily *filets* of "liquor breaks," a custom known to some as "smoking the pipe." Gayoso maintained this policy, which Governor Ulloa had attempted to curtail, but he hoped this would be an example of moderate use of liquor which would not lead to drunkenness.[134] Carondelet found that the commandant of Upper Louisiana's military detachments paid the men in brandy because of the lack of specie, and he ordered Lieutenant Governor Trudeau to stop the practice.[135]

Still, drunken soldiers were the rule rather than the exception. Stephen Minor claimed that he feared to call out the militia because the men were usually drunk.[136] When Captain Josef Portillo from the second battalion of the Louisiana infantry regiment complained of suffering from a "fever," Diego de Vega wryly commented that it was probably a "calentura de aguardiente"—rum fever![137] Zenon Trudeau cited the prevalence of inebriation in Upper Louisiana in 1798,[138] and at the end of the Spanish regime, an officer wrote that so prevalent was drunkenness among the soldiers that they were whipped on bare backs daily for the "vice."[139] Nor were the Spanish soldiers on the frontier the only ones guilty of tippling too much. Andrew Ellicott disgustedly wrote that the American commander of troops at Natchez was subject to "frequent and outrageous fits of intoxication."[140] Recognizing the danger of such behavior, Governor Winthrop Sargent recommended that no liquor be distributed to American troops in Natchez.[141]

If the troops drank too much, so did the settlers. Zenon Trudeau wrote in 1798 about "passive idleness which gave them over to the tast-

---

[132] Gayoso to Beauregard, Natchez, July 16, 1794, AGI, *Papeles de Cuba, leg.* 42.

[133] Holmes, *Gayoso*, 232.

[134] Gayoso to Beauregard, Natchez, Mar. 22, 1791, AGI, *Papeles de Cuba, leg.* 41.

[135] Carondelet to Zenon Trudeau, New Orleans, Oct. 19, 1795, AGI, *Papeles de Cuba, leg.* 22.

[136] Minor to Gayoso, Natchez, Nov. 29, 1797, AGI, *Papeles de Cuba, leg.* 2371.

[137] Vega to Arturo O'Neill, San Marcos de Apalache, Sept. 11, 1788, AGI, *Papeles de Cuba, leg.* 184–A.

[138] Report of Zenon Trudeau, St. Louis, Jan. 15, 1798, in Houck, ed., *The Spanish Régime in Missouri*, II, 251.

[139] Report of Ignacio Fernández de Velasco on the state of Louisiana and West Florida, Aranjuez, May 12, 1806, Archivo del Servicio Histórico Militar, Madrid, *leg.* 5–1–9–15.

[140] Andrew Ellicott to the secretary of state (Timothy Pickering), Natchez, Apr. 1, 1798, Southern Boundary, U.S. and Spain, RG 76, vol. II, National Archives.

[141] James R. Jacobs, *Tarnished Warrior, Major-General James Wilkinson* (New York, 1938), 177.

ing of spiritous liquors and drunkenness, a taste fatal to all the villages, and which has caused the total ruin in these new settlements of the greater part of the best families, upon which was placed the hope of the prosperity of this country."[142] Francisco Bouligny observed a similar problem at Natchez: "Every time that an inhabitant comes to present his complaint to the commandant he passes the entire day in the town of Natchez where it is the custom, particularly of the common people, to deliver themselves up to drink with the greatest excess. This gives rise to disputes and fights, which occasion great injuries and inspire in the vicious ones a greater desire to come to town in order to become intoxicated than does the importance of the complaint that they have to present."[143]

Governor Gayoso, who once decreed that workers who reported absent because of drunkenness would lose their wages for that day and be charged the value of the rations issued to them,[144] was forced to fire his own overseer for habitual drunkenness.[145]

Professional men also succumbed to the lure of "demon rum." Dr. Alexander Skirving of Baton Rouge ordered such large quantities of rum in 1799 that he began to vomit—he drank himself to death.[146] The American surgeon stationed at Fort Stoddard on the Spanish-American frontier in 1799 fell on a bottle of rum which he carried in his pocket and died as a result.[147]

Not even the clergy were immune to overindulgence. Irish priests in Natchez were particularly known as convivial topers. Father Malone was well liked by everyone but had a weakness for the bottle, particularly on St. Patrick's Day. Father Gregorio White was so drunk on one occasion that he could not baptize an infant who was in danger of dying. He was finally removed because he "was abandoned to the excessive habit of drink."[148] The priest of Galveztown dismissed the

---

[142] Report of Trudeau, St. Louis, Jan. 15, 1798, in Houck, ed., *The Spanish Régime in Missouri*, II, 251.

[143] Bouligny to Miró, Fort Panmure de Natchez, Aug. 8, 1785, in Kinnaird, ed., *Spain in the Mississippi Valley*, II, 138, 141.

[144] Holmes, "The First Laws of Memphis," 95–96.

[145] Gayoso to Peggy Watts Gayoso, New Orleans, Oct. 18, 1797, MS owned by Mrs. C. Grenes Cole, Houma, La.

[146] Spanish West Florida Records (18 vols., W.P.A. Louisiana Historical Records Survey, Baton Rouge, 1939), III, 87.

[147] Bartholomew Schaumburgh to Thomas Cushing, Fort Stoddart [*sic*], Dec. 1, 1799, in Jack D. L. Holmes, ed., "Fort Stoddard in 1799: Seven Letters of Captain Bartholomew Schaumburgh," *Alabama Historical Quarterly*, XXVI, nos. 3–4 (Fall and Winter, 1964), 252.

[148] Jack D. L. Holmes, "Irish Priests in Spanish Natchez," *Journal of Mississippi History*, XXIX (Aug., 1967), 173–174.

sacristan of that parish for a similar reason.[149] Ellicott claimed that a Baptist preacher named "Hannah" had become drunk, had proceeded to preach to the Irish Catholics of Natchez, had been thrashed, and, when arrested, had provoked a two-week revolt against Spanish rule.[150] Actually, the man referred to was Barton Hannon, a shoemaker by trade and a Baptist only by faith. But Ellicott was right in saying he was drunk—so much so that he couldn't remember at his trial what he had done![151]

SPANISH REGULATION OF THE LIQUOR TRADE

Two motives determined the regulations passed concerning the liquor trade to Spanish Louisiana: revenue and protection. On February 22, 1770, Alexander O'Reilly imposed a tax or tariff on imports of rum at $1 a barrel or $2 a pipe.[152] This product usually came from the West Indies and found a ready market in New Orleans. Cuban rum bound for the Crescent City paid an export tax at Havana of $2 a pipe in addition to the tariff imposed by O'Reilly.[153]

By checking the records it is possible to note the quantity of this product which was imported at New Orleans.[154] Between 1778 and 1798 the annual shipment varied and the revenues ranged from $369 to $3,082.86. O'Reilly had expected an assured annual income from this source of $500.[155]

In the Spanish period authorities allowed a deduction of 10 percent for waste,[156] a policy carried on by the American government, which

[149] Luis, Obispo, to Manuel Gayoso de Lemos, New Orleans, Mar. 27, 1799, AGI, *Papeles de Cuba, leg.* 102.

[150] Andrew Ellicott, *The Journal of Andrew Ellicott* (Philadelphia, 1814, Chicago, 1962), 100.

[151] The trial of Hannon is in AGI, *Papeles de Cuba, leg.* 163–A. On this episode see Jack D. L. Holmes, ed., *Documentos inéditos para la historia de la Luisiana, 1792–1810* (Madrid, 1963), 318.

[152] O'Reilly's decree, New Orleans, Feb. 22, 1770, New Orleans Cabildo Minutes; copy in Kuntz Collection.

[153] Royal decree of Aug. 17, 1772, cited in Ruth Ameda King, "Social and Economic Life in Spanish Louisiana, 1763-1783" (Ph.D. dissertation, University of Illinois, 1931), 165.

[154] See app. 4.

[155] *Ibid.;* O'Reilly to Arriaga, no. 16, New Orleans, Dec. 10, 1769, in Kinnaird, ed., *Spain in the Mississippi Valley,* I, 134.

[156] Henry P. Dart and Laura L. Porteous, eds., "Account of the Credit and Debit of the Funds of the City of New Orleans for the Year 1789," *Louisiana Historical Quarterly,* XIX (July, 1936), 585.

charged the same tariff rate.[157] Shippers noted that a cargo of tafia from Santo Domingo on arrival at New Orleans had shrunk considerably. A 1771 shipment, for example, started out with 130 *bariques* consisting of 65 pipes or 7,800 gallons of tafia, but on arrival at New Orleans, what with leakage and consumption during the voyage, only 120 arrived at the city and, after paying duties, only 100 were put up for sale.[158] It was natural to find that importers sought to avoid paying the duties.

Felix de Materre imported fifty-six barrels of tafia in 1785 but failed to pay the duties of $7, and the treasurer of New Orleans demanded that he be forced to make restitution.[159] Most shippers had the privilege of making their own declarations regarding the cargoes, and the cabildo sought to prevent fraud by appointing one of the city coopers to act as inspector for unloading, inspection, and taxing of the incoming tafia.[160] Still, abuses continued, and in 1795, of the 809 pipes entering New Orleans, only 603 were taxed, the balance having been declared "leakage."[161]

The following year the cabildo considered the claims for exemption from paying duties by such shippers bringing Jamaica-refined rum into the city. Simon Tevenot, who brought a cargo from Charleston to New Orleans, insisted he need pay only the tariff on his Havana rum, but that rum from other ports was exempt. Samuel Moore claimed his fourteen barrels of Jamaica rum brought aboard the *Alfredo* were also exempt. The cabildo answered these claims by decreeing that all rum, whether refined or not, coming to New Orleans from any port in the Americas, was subject to the usual $2-a-pipe duty.[162]

The intendant, Martín Navarro, had suggested that all liquor imports would be taxed at the rate of 8 percent of the selling price.[163] Taxes were levied on shipments of French Bordeaux and brandy, which, after the commercial decree of January 22, 1782, were allowed to enter Louisiana.[164] On August 24, 1796, an extensive tariff list for Louisiana was issued by the intendant, Juan Buenaventura Morales.[165] In 1798, how-

---

[157] Proclamation of Mayor James Mather, New Orleans, Mar. 24, 1807, Kuntz Collection.

[158] Report of Feb. 6, 1771, New Orleans Municipal Records.

[159] Report of Francisco Blache, New Orleans, Jan. 29, 1785, *ibid.*

[160] New Orleans Cabildo Minutes, Jan. 25, 1793.

[161] *Ibid.*, Aug. 29, 1795; Carondelet to Rendón, New Orleans, Sept. 28, 1795, AGI, *Papeles de Cuba*, leg. 32.

[162] New Orleans Cabildo Minutes, May 13, 1796.

[163] Reflections of Martín Navarro, *c.* 1780–84, in Robertson, ed., *Louisiana*, I, 255.

[164] Hugo de Pedesclaux to Martín Navarro, Burdeos [Bordeaux], Aug. 16, 1787, AGI, *Papeles de Cuba*, leg. 550.

[165] Morales, "Tariff," New Orleans, Aug. 24, 1796, AGI, *Papeles de Cuba*, leg. 184–A; see app. 5.

ever, the cabildo asked the crown to determine whether duties would be collected on quantity alone or whether the quality and selling price should be taken into consideration in fixing the internal revenue taxes.[166]

Americans migrating as settlers to Louisiana were forbidden to bring brandy with them,[167] but apparently this prohibition was not strictly adhered to. In 1792 there arrived at Natchez 728 *potes* of brandy in several barrels valued at $595.[168] Peach brandy was popular, and Robert R. Livingston claimed that Louisianians would prefer that to the best French brandy.[169]

Smuggling was a constant problem, and rum, wine, and brandy were among the products most frequently involved. A royal decree of October 20, 1792, provided that, when no actual culprit was involved in liquor confiscated in this illegal smuggling, the intendant could order the commandant to make an inventory of the goods, place a tax or tariff fee thereon, and then sell the goods at public auction. In 1797 seven *toneles* or *bocoes* of rum were seized at Mobile from the schooner *Havanera* because they were not included in the manifest of the cargo. After being valued, they were said to be worth $1.25 a gallon, and on April 22, 1797, an auction was held at Mobile during which the 743 gallons of rum were sold at a price of $918.50. The government realized a commission of one-sixth of the sale price on this English rum.[170]

Governor General Miró, who was charged with smuggling in his *residencia*, admitted that occasionally ships carrying Louisiana lumber to Havana returned with two or three hidden barrels of Bordeaux wine, but that the total amount of all smuggled goods never exceeded $6,000 a year.[171] Throughout the Spanish period the government officials sought, usually without success, to eliminate smuggling, but the Gulf Coast was too extensive to check the abuse completely.

After rum or tafia, the most important import was wine. At first the Louisiana settlers refused to drink the Spanish *riojas* which were sent to replace French Bordeaux, Burgundies, and clarets. Indeed, one of the

[166] New Orleans Cabildo Minutes, May 18, 1798.

[167] Charles E. A. Gayarré, *History of Louisiana: The Spanish Domination* (New York, 1854), 185.

[168] Statement of Francisco Candel (*guarda-almacén* of Natchez), Natchez, May 16, 1792, AGI, *Papeles de Cuba, leg.* 1446.

[169] Memoir of R. R. Livingston to Secretary of State James Madison, Paris, Aug. 10, 1802, in U.S. Congress, *State Papers and Correspondence Bearing upon the Purchase of the Territory of Louisiana* (Washington, 1903), 43–44.

[170] Carondelet to Pedro Olivier, New Orleans, Feb. 7, 1797, AGI, *Papeles de Cuba, leg.* 24; Morales to Pedro Varela y Ulloa, no. 161, New Orleans, Oct. 16, 1797, Archivo Histórico Nacional, Madrid, *Estado, leg.* 3902.

[171] Miró to Campo de Alange, Madrid, Aug. 11, 1792, Museo Naval, Madrid, MS, vol. 569, fols. 108–164; printed in Holmes, ed., *Documentos inéditos*, 33.

alleged causes for the revolt of 1768 was said to be the "inferior" Spanish wines.[172] The San Sebastian firm of Larralde sent a ship in 1777 with ninety-eight casks of *rioja*, but it did not find a market in New Orleans, "for when the colonists tasted it, they manifested as much repugnance for it as if they had taken an emetic." The merchant declined to continue his efforts to market the Spanish wines in Louisiana as a result.[173] Intendant Martín Navarro agreed that the Spanish wine did not travel well and that the New Orleans tipplers would not have taken it "as a gift."[174]

The royal decree of March 23, 1768, had forbidden the importation of foreign wines into Louisiana,[175] however, and within a few years ships were bearing shipments from Cataluña and other Spanish regions to Louisiana. Apparently the forty-four cargoes of wines brought between 1773 and 1775 found some sort of market in New Orleans.[176]

Another royal decree of January 22, 1782, allowed French wines to enter Louisiana subject to duty, and the *Joven Josef* brought Bordeaux and brandy to New Orleans in 1787.[177] Spain's minister of the exchequer, Diego de Gardoqui, urged that Spanish merchants send such fine-quality *riojas* as those of Manuel Quintano to Louisiana because they closely resembled the Bordeaux wines in sweetness, color, and lightness.[178] New York ships occasionally carried wine to New Orleans,[179] and during 1798 the lack of wine in New Orleans had been remedied by a number of shipments,[180] notwithstanding the rise in price on Bordeaux wines during the undeclared naval war of 1798 from $40 to $100 a cask.[181] During 1798 Bordeaux and white wines arrived at Mobile, Pensacola, and St. Marks, in addition to New Orleans.[182]

The price of wine varied, of course, with the quality, supply, demand, and other factors. Gregorio Vergel, a tavern keeper at Baton Rouge,

---

172 King, "Social and Economic Life," 139, citing Louisiana General Correspondence, 1769, vol. XLIX, Louisiana Historical Society MSS, New Orleans.

173 Arthur P. Whitaker, ed., *Documents Relating to the Commercial Policy of Spain in the Floridas, with Incidental Reference to Louisiana* (Deland, Fla., 1931), 7.

174 Reflections of Navarro, in Robertson, ed., *Louisiana*, I, 256.

175 Royal decree of Mar. 23, 1768, cited in King, "Social and Economic Life," 159.

176 Royal decree, Aug. 17, 1772, *ibid.*, 165; see also *ibid.*, 139.

177 Pedesclaux to Navarro, Bordeaux, Aug. 16, 1787, AGI, *Papeles de Cuba, leg.* 550.

178 Whitaker, ed., *Documents Relating to Commercial Policy*, 121.

179 Gayoso to Stephen Minor, New Orleans, Sept. 6, 1798, Gayoso Papers, Louisiana State University Archives.

180 Gayoso to Minor, New Orleans, Sept. 6, 19, 1798, Gayoso Papers; Gayoso to Peggy Watts Gayoso, New Orleans, Aug. 22, 1797, MS owned by Mrs. C. Grenes Cole.

181 Robertson, ed., *Louisiana*, I, 170.

182 Whitaker, ed., *Documents Relating to Commercial Policy*, 256, 257.

reported white wine sold at $1 a bottle.[183] At the estate sale of Gayoso in 1799, however, three bottles of white wine brought only $1.50.[184] At Natchez in 1792, 112 bottles of wine sold for an average price of 50 cents a bottle.[185] The same price prevailed with the sale of 3,000 bottles of wine at the death of Gilberto de St. Maxent.[186] During 1777 the average price for wine was 10 cents a bottle.[187]

Wine-drinking habits were noted by Dr. Alliot and C. C. Robin. Dr. Alliot commented:

> The great exports of wine which ship furnishers send to Louisiana, make that product very cheap. The captains and merchants sell very little of it in their stores. It is only those who can not pay cash for it who buy it of them. All wines are exposed at public sale. Some days it is sold for only eighteen or twenty piastres per barrel. Since the tavern-keepers only make their purchases at public sale, it happens that when they are all assembled at the market place, they agree among themselves that when any piece is fixed at a certain price by them, however little or much it be, the barrel will never be sold at a higher figure.[188]

Robin wrote:

> . . . Wines of different types are brought in, principally those of Madeira, Málaga and especially those of Bordeaux and the coasts.
>
> The English drink the Madeira and the Spaniards the Málaga, but the French, being the most numerous, insure that the greatest consumption is of French wines. Besides, the Spaniards have adopted our ways and also taken up drinking them and their greater abundance is more conducive to habitual use. It is hardly possible to ascertain the wholesale price of wine because it is so variable, but the consumption of French wines is so great that their abundance never lowers the price for long. One can always make a reasonable profit out of wine.[189]

Considering these comments, it is curious that Robert R. Livingston

---

[183] Deposition of Gregorio Vergel, Baton Rouge, Aug. 6, 1799, Spanish West Florida Records, III, 109–110.

[184] *Causa mortuoria* of Gayoso, 1799, AGI, *Papeles de Cuba*, leg. 169.

[185] Statement of Francisco Candel, Natchez, May 16, 1792, AGI, *Papeles de Cuba*, leg. 1446.

[186] Caroline Maude Burson, *The Stewardship of Don Esteban Miró, 1782–1792* (New Orleans, 1940), 241.

[187] King, "Social and Economic Life," 140–141.

[188] Quoted in Robertson, ed., *Louisiana*, I, 79.

[189] C. C. Robin, *Voyage to Louisiana, 1803–1805*, ed. Stuart O. Landry, Jr. (New Orleans, 1966), 43.

could write that French wines would not be pleasant to "the palates or the purses of the inhabitants" of Louisiana![190]

Brandy was not as popular as other liquor because of its cost. Robin wrote that "if the price of brandy were lower, the people would become accustomed to it and would prefer it," but that tafia and rum were more popular in Louisiana.[191] In 1777 French brandy sold for $4 a cask,[192] but by 1796 the tariff had driven the price much higher.

Whiskey—sometimes known as "Monongahelie," "bald face," "bust head," or "the stranger"—was not as popular in New Orleans as along the vast Mississippi Valley frontier. The price of whiskey in the west varied from 50 cents to $1 a gallon, although in 1794 during General Anthony Wayne's campaign against the northwestern Indians a keg containing ten gallons sold for $80![193] The tariff on whiskey imported into Louisiana was 31 cents a gallon.[194]

Although Athanase de Mézières, lieutenant governor at Natchitoches, had suggested that Louisiana rye be used to "manufacture whiskey which is used in Flanders and Holland,"[195] it was the United States which produced that product rather than Louisiana. A center of the industry was Knoxville, where Abraham Sittler and John Taylor advertised copper stills with "broad bottom, wide neck, large cap, and free access for the vapour into condensation, with my patent worm of copper, covered or lined with pewter."[196] During 1794 over 500 gallons of whiskey were shipped from these western settlements to Natchez and then reshipped to New Orleans.[197] With the repeal of the whiskey tax in 1797, trade between the Kentucky and Tennessee settlements and New Orleans increased.[198]

On occasion, the importation of whiskey presented problems to Louisiana commanders. Elías Beauregard, commandant of Nogales, kept more than one gallon of the whiskey coming downriver, and when Spain decided to evacuate that post, Gayoso humorously commented,

---

[190] Memoir of Livingston, Aug. 10, 1802, *State Papers and Correspondence*, 43–44.

[191] Robin, *Voyage to Louisiana*, 43.

[192] King, "Social and Economic Life," 142.

[193] "Daily Journal of Wayne's Campaign, from July 28th to November 2d, 1794, Including an Account of the Memorable Battle of 20th August," *American Pioneer*, I (Sept., 1842), 354; Gilbert Imlay, *Topographical Description of the Western Territory of North America* . . . (3rd ed., London, 1797), 545.

[194] Morales, "Tariff," Aug. 24, 1796, AGI, *Papeles de Cuba, leg.* 184–A.

[195] Athanase de Mézières to Unzaga, no. 200, Natchitoches, Feb. 1, 1771, AGI, *Papeles de Cuba, leg.* 110; translated in Bolton, ed., *Athanase de Mézières*, I, 147.

[196] Knoxville *Gazette*, Aug. 1, Sept. 14, 1796.

[197] Minter Wood, "Life in New Orleans in the Spanish Period," *Louisiana Historical Quarterly*, XXII (July, 1939), 669.

[198] Knoxville *Gazette*, May 1, 1797.

"I dare say that the wisky Beauregard has at the Hills will offer greater difficulties to dislodge than the King's effects. . . ."[199] When Joseph Calvet brought eleven barrels of Kentucky whiskey to Natchez, they were confiscated by Grand Pré and placed in the royal storehouse pending the decision on their disposition from Governor General Miró. Years later Calvet was still asking that his whiskey be returned to him or that he receive payment for its value.[200]

Gin was not overly popular, but bottles of Holland and Island gin sold at 20 and 30 cents respectively.[201] At Baton Rouge the price of a bottle of gin in 1799 had risen to $1.[202]

Cherry liqueur was sold at auction in 1799;[203] thirty bottles of absinth sold in 1777 for only $17.[204] Anisette and cider were also sold at varying times.

Beer was another popular beverage in Spanish Louisiana. In 1771 Athanase de Mézières had urged that the government support the manufacture of malt liquors and vinegar and the brewing of ale, which was already being produced at Natchitoches. He claimed that valuable foreign exchange would be saved if Louisiana produced its own malt products.[205] In 1782 Marcos Olivares bought thirty-one barrels of beer at New Orleans for $530.[206] Francis Baily noted that the porter was drunk at New Orleans in 1797.[207] At the sale of Gayoso's estate, fifty-five bottles of beer were valued at $20.56.[208]

Spaniards enjoy a wine punch called *sangría*, which features red wine, sugar, fruits, water, and ice. Baily thought the punch mixed with claret and water was weak,[209] and in 1775 it had been outlawed in New Orleans taverns.[210]

Domestic trade accounted for some of the liquor supply in Spanish

[199] Gayoso to Minor, New Orleans, Mar. 2, 1798, Gayoso Papers.

[200] Petition of Joseph Calvet, New Orleans, Mar. 23, 1793, AGI, *Papeles de Cuba,* leg. 206.

[201] King, "Social and Economic Life," 142.

[202] Deposition of Gregorio Vergel, Baton Rouge, Aug. 6, 1799, Spanish West Florida Papers, III, 109–110.

[203] Gayoso's *causa mortuoria.*

[204] King, "Social and Economic Life," 140–141.

[205] Athanase de Mézières to Unzaga, no. 200, Natchitoches, Feb. 1, 1771, AGI, *Papeles de Cuba,* leg. 110; translated in Bolton, ed., *Athanase de Mézières,* I, 147.

[206] Laura L. Porteous, tr., "Index to Spanish Judicial Records," *Louisiana Historical Quarterly,* XIX (Jan., 1936), 242–251.

[207] Francis Baily, *Journal of a Tour in Unsettled Parts of North America in 1796 and 1797* (London, 1856), 310.

[208] Gayoso's *causa mortuoria.*

[209] Baily, *Journal,* 310.

[210] New Orleans Cabildo Minutes, Oct. 27, 1775.

Louisiana. James Rose carried a barge laden with rum, wine, and liquor from New Orleans to Natchez in July, 1793.[211] But domestic production was also an important source. Two Spaniards named Méndez and Solís experimented with the first tafia produced in Louisiana.[212] The cabildo was not sure whether to tax this tafia, which was so important in supplying the Indian trade, and asked the crown for its opinion in 1798.[213] In 1799 a traveler brought a 1,500-gallon still to Mr. Delongua, who distilled tafia near New Orleans.[214] By the end of the Spanish dominion twelve distilleries turned out huge quantities of tafia near the Crescent City and it was estimated that one Parisian arpent of 185 square feet could produce an average of 1,200 pounds of sugar and 50 gallons of tafia. Predictions were that Louisiana could produce, along its river plantations alone, 25,000 hogsheads of sugar and 12,000 puncheons of tafia.[215]

CONCLUSION

Spain, as France before her, attempted to solve the liquor question by licensing taverns and restricting the sale of alcoholic beverages. Violations of the regulations were a commonplace occurrence. Although tariffs were levied on incoming liquor, smuggling and other subterfuges denied Spanish officials the money they should have received. Efforts to prevent overindulgence were generally not successful, and Louisiana under Spanish domination would have applauded another ancient Spanish slogan: "Hermano, bebe, que la vida es breve"—"Brother, drink, for life is short."[216]

SOURCES

"Licenses pour detail de Boissons et liqueurs par pinte et au dessus a $60 par an et deux piastres et demie d'expedition." 1816. MS, Kuntz Collection, Tulane University Archives, New Orleans.

List of individuals who have permission to have taverns, inns, and billiard parlors, and their license fees for 1771. New Orleans, Jan. 4, 1771. Archivo General de Indias, Seville, *Papeles de Cuba, legajo* 110.

[211] Statement of James Hillen, Natchez, Aug. 6, 1793, in May Wilson McBee, ed., *The Natchez Court Records, 1767–1805* (Greenwood, Miss., 1953), 151.

[212] Gayarré, *Louisiana, Spanish Domination,* 347.

[213] New Orleans Cabildo Minutes, May 18, 1798.

[214] Anonymous narrative, 1799, in Cuming, *Sketches of a Tour,* 364.

[215] Jack D. L. Holmes, ed., "Louisiana in 1795: The Earliest Extant Issue of the *Moniteur de la Louisiane,*" *Louisiana History,* VII (Spring, 1966), 148n.

[216] Sign in the Spanish restaurant "Bilbao," Miami, Fla., Aug. 2, 1969.

List of individuals who have to pay the city treasurer the amounts assigned to each one for tavern licenses through the end of August, at the rate of 115 *libras*. New Orleans, Sept. 1, 1771. Archivo General de Indias, Seville, *Papeles de Cuba, legajo* 110.

New Orleans Census for 1791. New Orleans, Nov. 6, 1791. New Orleans Public Library Archives.

New Orleans Cabildo Minutes, 1769–1803. New Orleans Public Library Archives.

New Orleans Municipal Papers. Tulane University Archives.

New Orleans Municipal Records, 1778–99. Louisiana State University Archives, Baton Rouge.

Paxton, John Adems, ed. *The New Orleans Directory and Register*. New Orleans, 1822.

APPENDIX 1. EQUIVALENTS
OF LIQUID MEASURES

Ancre. 23 *potes*, when filled with brandy (Surrey, *The Commerce of Louisiana*, 274).

Barrel. .14 of a *pipa* (7.1 barrels equals 1 *pipa*). In Florida, 25 gallons of four small wine bottles each content, or 32½ gallons (260 English pounds or 10⅓ Spanish *arrobas*) (Holmes, "José del Río Cosa," *Tequesta*, XXVI [1966], 51–52). One barrel contained 46 *potes* of tar (Adolph B. Benson, ed., *The America of 1750, Peter Kalm's Travels in North America, The English Version of 1770* [2 vols., New York, 1937], II, 492).

Barrica. ½ of a *pipa*. A cask containing 60 gallons (Mariano Velázquez de la Cadena *et al.*, eds., *A New Pronouncing Dictionary of the Spanish and English Languages* [Chicago, 1943], 81). *Barrica la velte*: 2 gallons (1796 tariff, AGI, *Papeles de Cuba*, leg. 184-A). A *barrica* of tafia was one-half a *pipa* or 60 gallons (1786 New Orleans Municipal Papers, box 1). A *barrica* contained 110 *potes* (Gregorio LaRosa to Carondelet, no. 49, Natchez, Aug. 13, 1795, AGI, *Papeles de Cuba*, leg. 32).

Barril. Of vinegar, it contained 5 gallons (1796 tariff, AGI, *Papeles de Cuba*, leg. 184-A). A *barril* of turpentine or tar at St. Augustine, 1787, had 32½ gallons (260 English pounds or 8 Spanish *arrobas*) (Holmes, "José del Río Cosa," 52). Another equivalent was that one *barril* contained 10⅓ *arrobas* or 25 gallons (*ibid.*).

Boco (*bocoes*). Identical with *tonel* (*toneles*), which varied in quantity as indicated in confiscations at Mobile and Pensacola in 1797: from 93, 102, 104, 108, 110, 112, and 114 gallons, or an average of slightly more than 106 gallons per *boco* (see *expediente* in Morales to Pedro Varela y Ulloa, no. 161, New Orleans, Oct. 16, 1797, Archivo Histórico Nacional, Madrid, *Estado*, leg. 3902).

Boucaut. The same as *boco. See also* Hogshead.

Galon. 4 small wine bottles or 8 English (and Spanish) pounds (Holmes, "José del Río Cosa," 51–52).

Hogshead. Generally used interchangeably with *boucaut* or *boco.* By Superior Council decree of May 7, 1728, a hogshead of red wine contained 110 *potes;* of white wine, 100 *potes;* and of brandy, 150 *potes* (Surrey, *The commerce of Louisiana,* 274). A hogshead in Louisiana during the Spanish period was equal to one-half a *pipa.*

Pipa. A cask used for wine of varying quantities. The *pipa* or pipe of the Canary Islands consisted of 480 liters or 120 gallons for wine, while the *pipa* of export was 450 liters or 100 gallons (Andrés de Lorenzo Cáceres, *Malvasía y Falstaff* [La Laguna, Spain, 1941], 24). About 1600 the *pipa* was fixed by the Casa de Contratación of Seville at 27.5 *arrobas* or 975 liters (François Chevalier, "Les cargaison des flottes de la Nouvelle Espagne vers 1600," *Revista de Indias* [Madrid], IV [1944], 224). In 1962 this writer learned at the Spanish winery of Pedro Domecq in Jerez de la Frontera that their *pipas* of sherry for export contained 500 liters. Wine from Madeira imported by England in the same year was contained in *pipas* of two hogsheads each or 105 gallons each (May, 1962, issue of the *New Yorker*). Madeira *pipas* imported by Louisiana in 1796 varied from 105 to 108 gallons each (tariff, AGI, *Papeles de Cuba, leg.* 184-A). At New Orleans the *aguardiente pipa* contained 7.1 barrels each. The *pipa* also included 2 *barricas* or 4 *quartas* (1786 tariffs, New Orleans Municipal Records).

Percheon. See Puncheon.

Pote (Pot). French measure equivalent to 2 liters French measure (Benson, *Peter Kalm's Travels,* II, 492n).

Puncheon. Called *poinçon* by the French, it was a large cask of varying size, often of 70 gallons. It was used in Daniel Clark, Jr.'s "Description of Louisiana" (*Annals of Congress,* 8th Cong., 2nd Sess., 1804–05, p. 1515).

Quart. French measure equal to .905 liters (Benson, *Peter Kalm's Travels,* II, 492n). 50 *potes* per quart of red or white wine (Surrey, *The Commerce of Louisiana,* 274).

Quarta. Spanish measure equal to one-fourth a *pipa* or 30 gallons (tariff, AGI, *Papeles de Cuba, leg.* 184-A; 1794 New Orleans Municipal Papers, box 1).

APPENDIX 2. NEW ORLEANS
TAVERN KEEPERS

Adam, Widow, 1771
Aguiar, Antonio, 1786
Aguiar, Francisco, 1786, 1788
Aguiar, Josef, 1786

Aguilera, Marcos, 1786
Agustin, Estevan, 1786, 1787, 1788, 1794, 1796
Alemand, Antonio. *See* Armand

Alonso, Eugenio, 1788
Alva, Diego de, 1771
Alvarez, Pedro, 1788
Anselmo, Joseph, 1791
Antonio, Bartholomé, 1786
Armand, Antonio, 1771
Arrlico (?), Juaquín, 1788
Arse (Arce), Francisco, 1788
Austen, Agustín, 1788
Aydeman, Juan, 1791
Badia, Ignacio, 1796
Badia, Jaime, 1788
Bahy, Ventura, 1791
Balentino, Josef, 1788
Balles, Joseph, 1791
Balsamo, Angelo, 1788
Barba, Andrés, 1786, 1788
Barba, Mateo, 1791
Bardely, Domingo, 1791
Barflau, Ignacio, 1791
Barrios, Diego de, 1786, 1788
Basinet, Juan Batista, 1791, 1794, 1796
Baxea, Simon, 1787
Baya, Pedro, 1786
Beloso, Estevan, 1796
Beltran, Thomas, 1786, 1787, 1788, 1794, 1796
Benites, Juan, 1786, 1794, 1796
Benseau, Ignacio, 1788
Bentura, Alberto. See Ventura
Bentura, Christobal, 1788
Bernard, Luis, 1794
Bichet, Francisco, 1791, 1794, 1796
Blanco, Vicente, 1788, 1791
Bolier (Boliu), Josef, 1788, 1794
Bonite (Bonitte), Santiago, 1771
Bosquez (Bosque), Sevastian, 1788, 1791
Boudean, Juan, 1788
Bouffard, Lorian, 1822
Boute, Josef, 1788
Brasillet, Juan, 1788
Braza, Domingo Hernández, 1786
Briu, Antonio, 1771

Brunet, Juan, 1771
Bruson (Brosones), Bernardo, 1788, 1791
Buch, Diana, 1771
Cadello, Francisco Juan, 1794, 1796
Callas, Francisco, 1788
Campos, Josef, 1786
Canola, Estevan, 1786, 1787
Carlota (Mulata), 1786
Carpentera, Widow, 1771
Casaberg, Juan Luis, 1794
Casanoba, Antonio, 1791
Casas, Joaquín, 1786, 1787
Casas, Narciso, 1791, 1794, 1796
Caya, Francisco, 1786
Chapenet (Charpenet), Juan, 1771
Charpentier, Pedro, 1771
Charpi, Juan, 1786
Charrlo, Madame, 1788
Chaval, Maria Theresa, 1794, 1796
Chavot (Chabot), Claudio, 1791
Chevert, Simon, 1771
Chico. See Manuel, Josef
Chiloque, Bernardo, 1786
Cofy, Antonio, 1788
Comba, Luis, 1788
Coroalles (?), Domingo, 1788
Crespo, Josef, 1794, 1796
Crosiño, Manuel, 1788
Dabadia, Juan, 1786
Daniel, Santiago, 1786
Dauphin, Widow, 1771
Deforge, 1787
Delate, Luis, 1794, 1796
Delate, Mariana, 1786
Delcampo, Pedro, 1771
Derneville, Carlota, 1794, 1796
Diaz, Manuel, 1791
Diaz, Pedro, 1794
Doriole, Luis, 1794
Dubreuil (Dubreville), Juan, 1791, 1794, 1796
Dubuisson, Guillermo, 1771
Duchêne, Luis, 1771, 1786
Duclos, 1771

Mañan, Pedro, 1786

Manuel, Josef ("Chico"), 1786 (2), 1787, 1788

Manuel, Widow, 1771

Marcany, Estevan, 1791

Marchal, Pedro, 1791

Marguete (Marquete?), Felix, 1788

Maria Theresa (Mulata), 1786

Maró, 1786

Martínez, Antonio, 1788

Martínez, Francisco, 1786, 1788, 1791

Martínez, Narciso, 1786

Mas, Sebastian, 1786, 1788

Maya, Damian, 1788

Mayola, Pedro, 1786

Mayoron, Juan Bautista, 1791

Melo, Pedro, 1794

Memingre (Meningre?), Antonio, 1786, 1794

Mena, Francisco, 1788

Meninger, Gorge (Jorge?) Antonio, 1771

Meninger, José, 1791

Mercenario, Francisco, 1791

Merida, Nicholas Hernández, 1794

Metzinger, Henrique, 1771

Metzinger, Madame, 1771

Millet, Isidoro, 1771

Mioton (Miotou?), Widow, 1771

Miranda, Joseph, 1791

Molina, Francisco, 1786

Monget, Juan, 1786

Montanel, Pedro, 1794

Monton, Josef, 1788

Morales, Antonio, 1786, 1787, 1791

Moreno, Josef, 1786

Moton, Andrés, 1786

Normand, Joseph, 1771

Nova, Juan Bautista, 1796

Olivier, Bautista, 1786

Padrol, Antonio, 1788

Padrol, Joseph, 1791

Padrot (Padrol?), Jorge, 1788

Paillet, Guillermo, 1771

Paillet, Juan, 1771, 1786

Pasqual (Pascal), Carlos, 1788, 1791, 1794, 1796

Peche, Urban (Urbain), 1771

Pérez, Antonio, 1786

Petrino, Marios (Marcos?), 1788

Plaser, Josef, 1788

Pollo, Juan, 1788, 1794, 1796

Pontes, Benito, 1788

Porta, Pablo, 1791

Poteins, Roze (Rose?), 1791

Potens, Juan Bautista, 1794

Pratz, Joseph, 1771

Prudhomme, Widow, 1771

Puche, Blas, 1788

Puche, Juan, 1787, 1788, 1791, 1792

Puche, Urbain. *See* Peche

Queler, Juan, 1791

Renau, Bartolomé, 1788

Revelo, Antonio, 1771

Reynaud, 1786

Reyne, Josef, 1786

Ricardy, Nicolas, 1791

Richelieu, Widow, 1771

Rivas, Francisco, 1791, 1796

Rivero, Josef, 1788, 1794

Robiquet, Juan Bautista, 1771

Roch, Juan Baptista, 1791

Roich, Francisco, 1796

Roich, Pedro, 1796

Roque, Andrés Manuel, 1786

Roque, Lorenzo, 1786, 1787, 1788, 1791

Ros, Angelo, 1788

Rosignol, Noel, 1794, 1796

Saint Jean (San Juan), 1786, 1788

Sala, Delmas, 1791

Salvador, Felix, 1794, 1796

Sánchez, Josef, 1786

Santana, Pedro, 1788

Sargo, Juan, 1788

Sarpy, Juan, 1788

Sarpy, Juan Baptista, 1791

Savio, Juan Bautista, 1786

Serguza, Antonio, 1786

Sicard, Felix, 1771
Solis, Manuel, 1771
Suarez, Antonio, 1791
Talladas, Zenon, 1786, 1788
Taulon, Francisco, 1787, 1788
Terriere, Claudio, 1771
Tio, Joseph, 1791
Tio, Marcos, 1786, 1787, 1788, 1791
Treine, José, 1787
Tremoulet, Bernardo, 1786, 1791
Triguer, Enriquez, 1788
Tusana, Josef, 1794, 1796
Valentino. *See* Balentino
Valles. *See* Balles
Ventura, Alberto, 1791. *See also* Bentura

Versalles, Juan, 1786, 1787
Vierte, Francisco, 1788
Vila, Francisco, 1791
Vilavo, Thomas, 1794, 1796
Villaró (Villaré?), Ventura, 1786
Ville, Lazaro, 1794, 1796
Ville, Lorenzo, 1771
Viola, Juan, 1788
Wilkoc (Wilkox?), Georg (George), 1791
Wizcuich, Antonio, 1786
Ylas, Isidro, 1788
Yles (Ylas?), Juan, 1788
Zerezola, Juan Domingo, 1786

APPENDIX 3. TAVERN REVENUES FOR NEW ORLEANS[1]

Year	Number	License Fee / Year	Tavern Revenue	Total with Inns
1771	35–40	$23.00	$ 920.00	
1772	–	–	–	$ 880.00
1775	13		840.00	
1776	24	–	–	
1777	16	22.50	360.00	680.00
1778	17			902.50
1782	–			1,210.75
1786	75	30.00	1,847.75	
1787	73	30.00	1,843.75	
1788	83	–	1,912.25	
1789	94	30.00	1,996.31	
1791	67	–	–	
1794	–	40.00	1,449.00	2,146.00
1795	36	40.00	1,450.00	
1796	37	40.00	1,480.00 est.	
1798	–	40.00	1,917.56	2,917.56
1816	42	62.50		

[1] Lists, New Orleans, Jan. 4, Sept. 1, 1771, AGI, *Papeles de Cuba, leg.* 110; treasurer reports, New Orleans, 1772–98, New Orleans Municipal Records and New Orleans Municipal Papers; Henry P. Dart and Laura L. Porteous, "Account of the Credit and Debit of the Funds of the City of New Orleans for the Year 1789," *Louisiana Historical Quarterly*, XIX (July, 1936), 586–589; New Orleans Census, Nov. 6, 1791, New Orleans Public Library Archives; "Licenses pour detail de Boissons et liqueurs . . . ," 1816, Kuntz Collection; 1795 revenues, Miscellaneous Spanish Documents, I, 26–28, New Orleans Public Library Archives.

APPENDIX 4. DUTIES COLLECTED ON IMPORTS OF RUM AT NEW ORLEANS[1]

Year	Quantity	Rate	Revenue
1778	177 pipes	$2.00 / pipe	$ 369.00
	45 barrels	.27 / barrel	
1782	605 pipes	2.00 / pipe	1,210.75
	2 barrels		
1786	—	—	2,344.00
1787	—	—	1,558.00
1788	763 pipes	2.00 / pipe	1,526.00
1789	905 pipes	2.00 / pipe	1,810.00
1794	804 pipes	2.00 / pipe	1,608.00
	1 quart		
1797	1,557 pipes	2.00 / pipe	3,082.86
1798	—	2.00 / pipe	2,972.75

[1] New Orleans Municipal Papers, box 1 (1770–1806); Dart and Porteous, "Account of the Credit and Debit," 585; Juan de Castanedo's report, New Orleans, Dec. 31, 1797, Miscellaneous Spanish Documents, I, 41–51.

APPENDIX 5. TARIFF ON LIQUOR IMPORTS FOR LOUISIANA[1]

Type of Liquor	Container & Size	Duty in Reales
Brandy	Dozen bottles	16
Bordeaux brandy	Small barrels (*barrilitos*)	18
Provençal brandy	Small barrels	12
Bordeaux brandy	*Barricas la velte* or 2 gallons	8
Provençal brandy	Same	5
Rum (*aguardiente de caña*)	*Barricas*	80
Whiskey	Gallon	3
Cherry brandy	Dozen bottles	16
Anís	Quintal	40
Anisette (fine)	Basket of two flasks	12
Anisette (ordinary)	Basket of two flasks	8
Kirsch	Dozen bottles	32
Liqueurs	Bottle	4
Liqueurs of Provençal and like quality	Dozen flasks	5
Red Burgundy wine	*Barrica*	400
White Burgundy	Same	180
Red Burgundy	Dozen bottles	48

[1] Juan Buenaventura Morales, "Tariff," New Orleans, Aug. 24, 1796, AGI, *Papeles de Cuba*, leg. 184–A.

Type of Liquor	Container & Size	Duty in Reales
White Burgundy	Dozen bottles	18
Champagne	Dozen bottles	60
Chipre wine	Dozen bottles	32
Condui wine	Dozen bottles	24
Madeira wine	*Pipa* of 108 gallons	880
White or red wine from Cataluña, Valencia, & Aragón	*Arroba*	4
White or red wine from Málaga, Jerez, & rest of Andalucía	*Arroba*	10
White or red wine from Andalucía	Dozen bottles	16
Wine from Malvasia	Dozen bottles	24
Wine from Frontignan	Dozen bottles	20
Muscatel wine	Dozen small flasks (*frasquitos*)	8
New red wine from Bordeaux & Cahors	*Barrica*	12
Old red wine from the same	*Barrica*	200
Old red wine from the same	Dozen bottles	20
White Bordeaux wine	*Barrica*	80
White Bordeaux wine	Dozen bottles	12
Provençal wine, usually called Coastal, Languedoc, and Rochelle	*Barrica*	64
The same	Dozen bottles	12
Red wine from the Cape of Good Hope	Dozen bottles	60
White wine from the Cape of Good Hope	Dozen bottles	40
Moselle & Ringau wines	Dozen bottles	12
Naples & Portuguese wines	*Pipa*	200
Corcega wines	*Pipa*	150
Canary Island wines, called *vidueño*	*Pipa* of 120 gallons	720
Dry wine from Canary Islands	*Pipa* of 120 gallons	320

NOTE: To determine net weight from gross weight, deduct 70 pounds for the *barrica* and 25 pounds for the *barril*.

Almonester: Philanthropist and Builder in New Orleans

SAMUEL WILSON, JR.

$\mathcal{I}$N the floor of the St. Louis Cathedral of New Orleans in front of the old altar of St. Francis of Assisi (now dedicated to St. Joseph) is embedded a marble slab covering the burial place of the city's first notable philanthropist, a Spaniard whose benefactions have left an indelible imprint on the city of his adoption. The Spanish inscription upon the present slab, a replacement of the original, which was removed to the Cabildo many years ago, broken and indecipherable, may be translated as follows:

Here lie the remains
of
Dn. Andrés Almonester y Roxas
Native of Mairena
In the Kingdom of Andalusia
Died in the City of New Orleans
The 26 of April of 1798
At the age of 73 years.
Knight of the Royal and Distinguished Spanish
Order of Carlos III.
Colonel of the Militia of this Plaza
Alderman and Royal Ensign of this Cabildo
Founder of the Lepers' Hospital
Founder and donor of this holy Cathedral Church.
Founder of the Royal Hospital of San Carlos and of its church.
Founder of the church of the Convent of the Ursuline Nuns.

Founder of the Classes for the Education of young children
and founder of the house for the Clergy
All which he has erected at his
Expense in this City

Requiescat in Pace.

Each of the institutions listed here as being founded by him received through his generosity a new building, each a building of some architectural importance that did much to enhance the appearance of the city. Almonester is thus remembered as the foremost builder of his day, although there is little evidence to indicate that he was an actual building contractor. He seems to have been rather a builder in the larger sense, as instigator, donor, and financier of great building projects.

Almonester was extremely proud of his family name and of the titles and honors conferred upon him. So obviously did he seek his recognition that his true motives of piety and charity were often questioned by jealous contemporaries. Almost in the last year of his life he had recorded in the archives of the Cabildo a certificate concerning his illustrious family name and coat of arms. It reveals that the family had had its "primitive manorial home . . . in the Province of Leon in the ancient hermitage called *San Pedro de Cabatuerta*, where the family is known by its coat of arms . . . in the border of which is inscribed the following motto: *A Pesar de Todos Venceremos Godos.*"[1] Almonester's great-grandfather and an uncle were also named Don Andrés, a popular name in the family since the year 1212, when their ancestors in Vizcaya participated in a great naval victory on the feast of St. Andrew. This distinguished son was born at Mairena del Alcor in the province of Seville in Andalusia, Spain, about the year 1725, the son of Don Miguel Joseph Almonester and Doña María Juana de Estrada y Roxas, both Andalusians. In his native land Almonester married Doña María Martínez, by whom he had a son who died at birth. In his will he states that "we both came on equal terms to that marriage, without fortune or dowry."[2]

It was probably after the death of his wife that Almonester decided to come to Louisiana, the former French province that Louis XV had given to Spain by the Treaty of Fontainebleau in 1762.[3] Don Antonio

[1] Cabildo Minutes (translations), bk. IV, no. 3, p. 5, July 21, 1797, New Orleans Public Library (hereafter cited as NOPL).

[2] Henry P. Dart, ed., "Almonester's Will," *Louisiana Historical Quarterly* (hereafter *LHQ*), VI (Jan., 1923), 21.

[3] Charles Gayarré, *History of Louisiana: The French Domination* (New York, 1854), 111.

de Ulloa did not arrive as Louisiana's first Spanish governor until March, 1766, and having no troop support, did not even attempt to set up a new government.[4] Eventually some of the leading French citizens, including members of the Superior Council, plotted a revolt and drove Ulloa from the colony. Charles III of Spain then dispatched Don Alexandro O'Reilly with sufficient troops to suppress the rebellion, bringing its leaders to trial, execution, or prison, and to establish Spanish rule firmly. He arrived in New Orleans on August 18, 1769.[5] The Superior Council was abolished and a Spanish cabildo was installed.[6] The French language was replaced with Spanish for official documents except in remote country areas, and Louisiana became truly a Spanish colony peopled by Frenchmen with merely a handful of Spanish officials. Among these latter arrived Don Andrés Almonester y Roxas.

Almonester first appeared before the members of the Illustrious Cabildo on March 16, 1770,[7] at a meeting held in the residence of the governor, the old French colonial capitol at the corner of Toulouse and Levee streets. The new home of the cabildo was then under construction adjacent to the parish church facing the Plaza de Armas, under a contract signed by O'Reilly on December 11, 1769, with the local French builder François Hery, called Duplanty.[8] At this meeting of the cabildo "a Royal Edict from His Majesty was read by me [J. B. Garic], the present Secretary, dated August 11, 1765, at San Ildefonso, in which His Majesty honors Don Andrés Almonester y Roxas with the position of Secretary for all His Kingdom, and at the same time I read the appointment as Public Secretary for War in charge of the Royal Treasury, made in favor of the said Don Andrés, dated March 12th of this year by the said Governor-General [Luis de Unzaga y Amézaga]." Unzaga had been appointed to succeed O'Reilly as governor. In acknowledging Almonester's appointment and in respect to the king, the members of the cabildo enacted a curious ceremony, "taking the Royal Edict in their hands and placing it upon their heads."[9] Such a ceremony was repeated whenever a document signed by the king was received by the cabildo. With the royal appointment went "the amount of 500 *pesos* per year with the privileges, power and exemptions bestowed upon the said appointment."

[4] *Ibid.*, 132.

[5] Cabildo Minutes, I, 1, Aug. 18, 1769.

[6] François Xavier Martin, *History of Louisiana* (2 vols., New Orleans, 1829), II, 10.

[7] Cabildo Minutes, I, 22, Mar. 16, 1770.

[8] Louisiana Miscellaneous Documents, 1599, Manuscripts Division, Library of Congress; *LHQ*, VI, 521.

[9] Cabildo Minutes, I, 22, Mar. 16, 1770.

This appointment seems to have been the beginning of Almonester's fortune in Louisiana. It was in effect an appointment as notary public, an important position in the colony under both French and Spanish rule. After the reading of the edict, Almonester made his entrance into the assembly room and was sworn into office by the cabildo. Royal confirmation of his commission was issued by the king at El Pardo on March 11, 1773.[10] Almonester succeeded José Fernández, whose notarial records cover the period between August 18, 1768, and March 8, 1770. Almonester's begin with a slave sale dated March 20, 1770, and end May 28, 1782;[11] on May 31, 1782, he resigned as "Notary Public of War and Royal Treasury" and the office passed to Rafael Perdomo.[12]

O'Reilly, during the period of his administration, decided to dispose of public lands within the city which were no longer in use. The site of the old governor's residence, two squares of ground bounded by Levee (Decatur), Bienville, Royal, and Iberville, he gave to Hery, contractor of the first Cabildo building, in part payment of his contract. He gave the lots formerly occupied by the barracks, on either side of the Plaza de Armas, and other vacant lots to the cabildo, or sold them to individuals in its name on a perpetual ground-rent basis. Most of the purchasers were members of the cabildo, some of whom quickly sold them while others built houses. One of the first such sales was made of a 70½-foot lot on the St. Ann Street side of the Plaza to Francisco Simars de Bellile, sold by O'Reilly for the cabildo on January 23, 1771,[13] later acquired by Almonester. Almonester, however, was not among the original purchasers, but as his fortunes improved he began to buy up this valuable real estate until eventually he had obtained all the land on the two sides of the square, property now occupied by the Pontalba buildings, built in 1849–50 by his daughter Micaëla, Baroness de Pontalba. Almonester's purchases of the Plaza properties extended over a period from 1774 to 1782[14] or later, and by the latter year were probably all occupied by new houses. On August 31, 1778, he leased part of his large house at the corner of Levee and St. Peter to Pedro Buygas, an area composed of "a salon, a hall, and a room beneath the staircase that serves as a winecellar."[15] Rents from his extensive real estate holdings eventually made him one of the wealthiest men in the

10 *Ibid.*, 185, May 13, 1774.
11 Records of Almonester, New Orleans Notarial Archives (hereafter NONA).
12 Cabildo Minutes, II, 128, May 31, 1782.
13 Records of J. B. Garic, Jan. 23, 1771, NONA.
14 *Ibid.*, V, 1; VI, 1; VIII, 119.
15 *Ibid.*, X, 400; Gayarré, *History of Louisiana: The Spanish Domination* (New York, 1854), 35.

colony. The houses he built on his own properties introduced him to the problems of construction in Louisiana, although no records have been found of building contracts or other data concerning these, his first buildings. This, of course, may indicate that he was himself the contractor for them.

THE LEPERS' HOSPITAL

The first of the major philanthropic building projects undertaken by Almonester, commemorated on his tombstone, was the Lepers' Hospital. Leprosy seems to have first appeared in the colony soon after the arrival of the first Acadian exiles in 1765.[16] One of the accusations brought against Spain's first Louisiana governor, Ulloa, in 1768 was of "removing leprous children from the town to the inhospitable settlement at the mouth of the river."[17] On July 14, 1780, a report was made to the cabildo that a Negro in the house of a Madame Wels, recently arrived from Mobile, seemed, according to Dr. Robert Dow, to be afflicted with leprosy. Orders were given that if this was found to be true, legal steps should be taken to have him isolated.[18] No further mention is made of lepers in the cabildo records until nearly five years later.

At its meeting of April 22, 1785, a letter addressed to the cabildo two days earlier by Almonester was read, "offering a house to lodge the lepers."[19] In this letter Almonester informed the members that he had constructed a hospital for lepers composed of four separate sections, "large enough to house many white families and other separate quarters for negroes." This structure had been erected at his expense in the rear of his plantation near the city, "a distance of about two gunshots—bounded by the lands of Joseph Cultia on one side and on the other by a canal which he has constructed for the bathing of sick people, which will serve as boundary to said hospital, which he graciously offers to your Lordships so that the lepers may be kept together, of whom there are large numbers, so the public may perpetually enjoy this. Therefore from now on and for all time, I will donate in form according to law and renounce all rights that I have or may have to the said buildings and lands which I have donated within the referred-to boundaries."

[16] C13A, VI, 21, Archives Nationales, Paris (hereafter AN); *LHQ*, XXII, 679.
[17] George W. Cable, *Social Statistics of Cities: Southern States, New Orleans, Louisiana* (Washington, 1881), 224.
[18] Cabildo Minutes, II, 33, July 15, 1780.
[19] Cabildo Minutes, III, 49, Apr. 22, 1785.

The cabildo immediately appointed two of its members "to visit said location and in the presence of the Secretary have it measured by the surveyor and have said land and building appraised by experts and take possession of same in the name of this illustrious Council, and file all documents in the archives of the Cabildo." The act of donation of this property to the city is dated April 20, 1785.[20] When Almonester's daughter, after his death, married Joseph Xavier Celestín de Pontalba in 1811, she gave him in the marriage contract the remainder of this large plantation on Bayou Road.[21]

In 1813, after Pontalba and his bride had taken up residence in France, he had the plantation resurveyed by Bartolomé Lafon, subdivided it into 90-foot-wide strips, and sold it at auction. A copy of this survey, listing the purchasers of the various tracts, was made by Joseph Pilié.[22] The survey shows a "site with an area of 2,500 toises claimed by the Corporation of New Orleans," and also shows the boundary canal. No buildings are shown, indicating that the Lepers' Hospital had by that time disappeared.

Paul Alliot, who claimed to be a physician, expelled from New Orleans by the Spanish authorities in March, 1803, in his reflections on Louisiana addressed to Thomas Jefferson in April, 1804, mentioned the Lepers' Hospital and the area in which it was located as follows: ". . . it is absolutely necessary for the traveler who desires to have a perfect knowledge of Louisiana to retrace his steps to New Orleans, and to go out by the gate of the Bayou. A hundred paces from that gate he will find some country houses, several tile and brick yards, a large hospice for lepers, distant about three hundred paces from the main road leading to the small port of the Grand Bayou [Bayou St. John], which is about three quarters of a league from the city."[23]

Governor Miró, on August 10, 1790, addressed a letter to Antonio Porlier regarding Almonester's charitable works and his expectations of royal honor; he hoped "to obtain this from the piety of the King for having constructed [a chapel for the nuns] and a leper hospital on his own land, which he gave at a proper distance from the city. The latter had such a good effect that, since the death of the five lepers who were caught, no others have been seen in the province."[24]

[20] Spanish Documents, bk. 4083, City Council, no. 101, fol. 196, NOPL.

[21] Acts of Pedro Pedesclaux, LXIII, 448, Oct. 22, 1811, NONA.

[22] Plan Book 15, fol. 1, NONA.

[23] James Alexander Robertson, *Louisiana under the Rule of Spain, France, and the United States, 1785–1807* (2 vols., Cleveland, 1911), I, 97.

[24] Lawrence Kinnaird, ed., *Spain in the Mississippi Valley, 1765–1794* (3 vols., Washington, 1946–49), II, 373.

The site of the Lepers' Hospital was indeed a remote and dreaded one that came to be called "la terre des lépereux" or "lepers' land,"[25] a place seldom seen or visited by any except the inmates and those who cared for them. The plantation perhaps included the four-arpent plantation on Bayou Road that Almonester purchased from Joseph Chalon in 1781.[26] The total width of the tract along Bayou Road was 1,082 feet at the time of the subdivision and sale in 1812, with the site of the hospital having a width of 310 feet, an approximately square tract lying back from Bayou Road about 1,000 feet, with a 30-foot access roadway designated "Hospital Road" leading to it.

The Leper's Hospital ceased to function soon after Alliot's visit, the building was destroyed by fire, and the city advertised the land for lease, probably as pasture. On April 7, 1808, the following advertisement was placed in the local newspaper, the *Moniteur de la Louisiane*:

Mayoralty of New Orleans

Thursday, 21 current, at noon, there will be proceeded with, in the office of the Mayoralty, the adjudication to the highest offerer and last bidder, at lease for rent for the space of one year, of the dependant land of the old Lepers Hospital, situated on the road to Bayou St. John. One can address himself to the said office in order to see the plan of the said land, and to learn the conditions of the Lease.

This 7 April 1808

James Mather, Mayor.[27]

This leasing of the land by the city probably continued until 1833, when the plague that year carried off nearly a thousand people in September alone. Another cemetery was urgently needed, and the council, at a special meeting, authorized the opening for burials of Almonester's land on "Leprous Road."[28] This change of use from that intended by the donor brought a strong reaction from his daughter and heir, who filed suit in the Third District Court in order to recover possession of the property. This court ruled in her favor, but when the city took the case to the Supreme Court of Louisiana, the judgment was reversed.

The account of this case in the records of the Supreme Court gives an interesting summary of the history of the Lepers' Hospital:

[25] Gayarré, *Louisiana, Spanish Domination*, 167.
[26] Acts of L. Mazange, May 7, 1781, NONA.
[27] *Moniteur de la Louisiane*, Apr. 17, 1808, no. 813, p. 3, col. 1.
[28] Leonard V. Huber and Samuel Wilson, Jr., *The St. Louis Cemeteries of New Orleans* (New Orleans, 1963), 28.

On the 20th of April, 1785, Don André Almonaster y Roxas [*sic*], the father of the plaintiff, made to the *Ayuntamiento* [government] of the city of New Orleans, a donation [for a lepers' hospital]. The donation was accepted unconditionally, and the *Ayuntamiento* proceeded to take possession of the property, and to apply it to the use contemplated by the donor. Up to 1805, lepers were admitted in the hospital. After that period it was abandoned, and became the refuge of Indians, who, after some years, set fire to it and burned it down. The ground then ceased to be used for any purpose, till 1833, when the city council passed an ordinance converting it into a cemetery. This change of destination gave rise to the present controversy.

. . . After this suit had been pending some years, the parties to it entered into a written agreement by which the property was to be sold, and its proceeds deposited in bank, subject to the final decision of the court. The property was accordingly sold, and the only question now presented is, to which of the parties the proceeds of the sale belong.[29]

The ordinance referred to was passed by the city council at a special session on September 25, 1833, and was entitled "An Ordinance to provide for a temporary place of interment." The ordinance stated that "pending the purchase of a lot more suitable and of larger dimensions, the Mayor . . . is hereby authorized to cause to be enclosed and used as a burying ground, the lot given to the Corporation of New Orleans in 1785 by Don André Almonester and situated at the place called Leprous Road." A paid guardian was to be appointed and a fee for persons of all religious denominations was to be $3 for each corpse. Thereafter none but tomb burials were to be permitted in the old Catholic cemetery, St. Louis No. 1.

The court, in rendering its decision in favor of the city, cited several other cases regarding donations and legacies and, in regard to the Lepers' Hospital, stated: "If there were still persons afflicted with leprosy when the hospital ceased to be kept up, the city could no longer compel them to resort to it; and as it is not shown that any applied for admission, we must presume that the purpose of the donation failed. . . . Unless the right of return, in case of the inexecution of the mode, charge or condition, be expressly stipulated in the act, these donations are irrevocable. . . ."[30]

---

[29] Merrit M. Robinson, *Reports of Cases Argued and Determined in the Supreme Court of Louisiana* (12 vols., New Orleans, 1849), III, 660.

[30] *Ibid.*, 663.

The judgment was quoted in most of the local newspapers without comment in their then lengthy court columns.[31] Unfortunately the records and testimony of the case in the third district court have not been located, nor has any description been found of the building that Almonester built for the hospital. It was probably a simple house of brick-between-posts construction, elevated on brick piers or walls, with galleries, in the characteristic Louisiana plantation-house style of the day. It perhaps somewhat resembled the house known as "Madame John's Legacy" built just three years later, in 1788,[32] when an earlier house on the site had been destroyed, along with most of New Orleans, in the great conflagration of that year.

THE CHARITY HOSPITAL

Perhaps the most ancient institutions in New Orleans are the Ursuline Convent and the Charity Hospital; both were to be recipients of the benefactions of Almonester. For both he erected substantial and important buildings.

The Charity Hospital had its beginnings when a sailor, Jean Louis, wrote his will on November 16, 1735, leaving the residue of his estate, after bequests to the church, the poor, and the orphans, "to be devoted to the founding of a free hospital for the poor and needy sick."[33] He died on January 21, 1736, and on May 10 of that year the old house of the Kolly concession, that had been occupied by the Ursuline nuns from the time of their arrival in 1727 until the completion of their first convent in 1734, was purchased with the bequest.[34] The house, which stood at the corner of Chartres and Bienville streets, was repaired by the contractor Joseph Villars Dubreuil, who added a brick ward, 25 by 45 feet, and 14 feet high.[35]

Some years later, in 1743, a new site was obtained consisting of a 300-foot-wide tract of land on Rampart Street at the end of Toulouse, extending back about 600 feet toward the swamps in the rear of the town. A new building, known as the Hospital of St. John, was build under the supervision of Father Charles de Rambervilliers, Capuchin

[31] New Orleans *Weekly Delta*, Dec. 4, 1848, p. 3, col. 4; New Orleans *Daily Cresent*, Nov. 27, 1848, p. 1, col. 3; New Orleans *Daily Picayune*, Nov. 29, 1848, p. 2, col. 6.

[32] Acts of Pedro Pedesclaux, II, 427, Apr. 1, 1788.

[33] *LHQ*, V, 275; III, 555.

[34] *LHQ*, IV, 361; XXIX, 597; III, 558.

[35] Contract for building the Charity Hospital, doc. 5740, June 10, 1736, Cabildo Archives, Louisiana State Museum, New Orleans (hereafter LSM); *LHQ*, III, 557.

superior and pastor of the parish church.[36] The hospital was blessed on March 9, 1752, by the Jesuit superior, Father Michel Baudoin, at the invitation of the then Capuchin superior, Father Dagobert de Longuory.[37] The old hospital building at Chartres and Bienville was rented to the Capuchin priests of the parish church,[38] probably when their rectory or presbytère next to the church was rebuilt in 1744. Meanwhile the French colonial authorities decided in 1760 to construct fortifications around the city, the palisade of which cut across the lands of the hospital. At their meeting on August 20, 1764, the directors decided to petition the acting governor, d'Abbadie, to grant them another site to replace the one taken for the fortifications.[39] The hospital apparently remained in the same building and some additional land inside the fortifications was given to it to compensate for the area lost outside them. In 1769 extensive repairs were made to the building and the old Chartres Street house was at first leased and then sold to Andrés Chiloque.[40]

In 1779 the city was struck by a severe hurricane that virtually destroyed the Charity Hospital,[41] and in 1780 two more hurricanes completed its ruin. A kitchen and storehouse, however, had remained standing after the first hurricane; in these a provisional hospital of six beds was established.[42] On September 14, 1781, a memorandum was presented to the cabildo "by the Attorney General in which he relates the miserable condition of the poor, with no mitigation or assistance in their sickness and needs, owing to the misfortunes suffered by the hospital in which they were gathered, cured, and cared for, which was destroyed by consecutive hurricanes."[43] It was then decided to "take the necessary steps toward rebuilding same, for the assistance of the poor unfortunate subjects of His Majesty, which they need on account of their sickness."[44] Nothing was accomplished because of problems relating to the hospital funds, and on February 15, 1782, a report was made to Don Bernardo de Gálvez, the governor, that the destruction of other buildings, the rents

[36] Documents relating to the Charity Hospital, 1735–94 (typed abstracts and translations), 13 (Oct. 1, 1764), LSM.

[37] Gayarré, *Louisiana, French Domination*, 81.

[38] Documents relating to the Charity Hospital, 6 (Jan. 15, 1769), 13 (July 2, 1769).

[39] *Ibid.*, 4.

[40] *Ibid.*, 7.

[41] Roger Baudier, *The Catholic Church in Louisiana* (New Orleans, 1939), 199.

[42] John Duffy, ed., *The Rudolph Matas History of Medicine in Louisiana* (2 vols., Baton Rouge, 1958), I, 250.

[43] Cabildo Minutes, II, 75, Sept. 14, 1781.

[44] *Ibid.*, 76.

from which had supported the hospital, "makes its reconstruction impossible, leaving the miserable sick in a deplorable condition, to die in the streets, or in any corner, deprived of all assistance and help."[45] The cabildo also noted "the high and angry . . . spirit of the citizens who observe that no steps have been taken to remedy and help the lamentable condition of those affected."

The hospital administrator Don Andrés López de Armesto, who had been originally the director of the Spanish school, complained that his many other official duties made it impossible for him to "give the proper attention to alleviate the condition of the poor sick, which, perhaps, with zeal and charity someone else, in time, might procure for them."

In reply to the cabildo's representations, a letter was received on December 13, 1782, that Gálvez, although absent from the colony, wrote on August 18, 1782. In it he stated that he regarded the hospital as a particular concern of the governor's office and the captaincy general, and said therefore that "under this date I am ordering the acting Governor [Don Esteban Miró] . . . to put into operation all necessary steps that he deems useful in order to have it repaired and re-established to its former condition."[46] Then ensued a controversy between the cabildo and the governor over the question of jurisdiction, Miró asserting his authority jointly with the church authority despite customs that had prevailed under French colonial rule.

It was thus to Miró and the parish priest that Almonester, late in 1782, made the offer to rebuild the hospital at his own expense. With their permission he took over the site of the old hospital and all the materials salvageable from the wrecked buildings. The cabildo, feeling its authority usurped, doubted Almonester's motives, and although not wishing to "dissuade the giver to such pious works . . . [and] without trying to penetrate secret intentions," questioned the way in which "disposition [was] made of all materials of the ruins of the primitive hospital for rebuilding it, obstructing the extension of a street of this city."[47] This latter reference was to the blocking of Toulouse Street by the new hospital building.

Miró replied to these complaints in a lengthy letter addressed to the cabildo on March 20, 1783:

> Since the hurricane in August, 1780, which caused suffering in this province and left the hospital building in ruins and the in-

45 Ibid., 28, Feb. 15, 1782.
46 *Ibid.*, 152, Dec. 13, 1782.
47 *Ibid.*, 156.

habitants of this capital in misery, unable to rebuild the same with alms, being left in a deplorable state until the end of last year, when Don Andrés Almonester presented himself and offered to rebuild it at his expense, constructing it much larger and with more solid materials than before. He immediately began its reconstruction with the consent of the Ecclesiastical Judge [Father Cirilo of Barcelona, pastor] as well as mine, being allowed to use the materials belonging to said hospital. This is but very little help toward the heavy expenses he has to meet in the undertaking, which is worthy of praise and admiration.

In what condition would the poor of the city have been if some pious citizen had not offered to rebuild the hospital, even adding extra room. I see in this citizen's action nothing else but his wish of doing a pious deed, being a benefactor deserving the most praise. . . . This unforseen gift . . . might not take effect if I would adhere to Your Lordships' pretensions, which in substance means to force this citizen to present himself to Your Lordships for permission to execute his philanthropic gift.[48]

Miró then referred to the cabildo's objection to the location of the new building, practically on the axis of Toulouse Street. The land in question was part of the land dedicated for the city fortifications and therefore under the jurisdiction of the governor. To have left the prolongation of the street vacant would have necessitated "the demolition of the storehouse and kitchen which at present exist,"[49] which would have deprived the deserving poor of any assistance at all. Otherwise it would not have been possible, as proposed by Almonester, "to build the house and chapel larger than they were before."

The cabildo's chief reason for objecting to the new building seems to have been Almonester's claim to the patronship of the hospital, a privilege in which the cabildo and the clergy had formerly shared.[50] Apparently only the king could grant such honors and privileges, and this he eventually did, by a royal decree issued on April 23, 1793, stating that Almonester should enjoy this patronship in the king's name and should be entitled to the use of the royal tribune or seat of honor in the hospital chapel. This decree was published in Madrid in 1793 together with a lengthy "Constitution for the new Charity Hospital, constructed at the expense of Don Andrés de Almonester y Roxas, Colonel of the Militia

---

48 *Ibid.*, 173, Apr. 11, 1783.

49 *Ibid.*, 174.

50 Stella O'Conner, "The Charity Hospital of Louisiana at New Orleans," *LHQ,* XXXI (Jan., 1948), 21.

of the city of New Orleans, in the Province of Louisiana, and Perpetual Alderman of the same, approved by His Majesty."

In this printed document, a copy of which is in the John Carter Brown Library at Providence, Rhode Island, is the fullest description of the new hospital, the name of which Almonester changed from St. John to St. Charles, in honor of the Spanish monarch Charles III. Work was begun under Almonester's direction early in 1783 and completed in 1786 at a cost of over 100,000 *pesos*. The new building was entirely of brick construction whereas the old one had been only of wood, probably brick between posts, a common French colonial type of construction.

John Pope, in his journal published in 1792, mentions that the hospital chapel was still under construction at the time of his visit to New Orleans: "The hospital is situated at the western edge of the city where nothing interrupts its ventilation from the east, south and north; but unfortunately, as if intended to banish cheerfulness from its mansions, the priests have laid off a burial ground, which is enclosed on one side by the front wall of the building. The chapel is in a ruinous state and will not be repaired.—A new one is erecting, to which all the internal decorations of the old will be transferred."[51]

The Charity Hospital, when it was moved to its location at the end of Toulouse Street in 1743, was placed directly facing the old cemetery, which had been established at about the time the city was laid out in the 1720s in the square bounded by Toulouse, St. Peter, Rampart, and Burgundy. When a new cemetery was established in 1788, it was located about a block beyond Rampart Street between Conti and St. Louis, "in the rear of the Charity Hospital about 40 yards from the garden."[52] This is now St. Louis Cemetery No. 1, more than a block away from the site of the Charity Hospital. Pope must therefore have referred to the old cemetery, which had existed long before the Charity Hospital was founded.

The hospital contained a church 52 feet long, a sacristy of 20 feet, a chapel of 24 feet, four wards for beds, the first of 80 feet, the second of 60, the third of 40, and the fourth of 20, with two rooms, one of 24 feet for the Hospitaler and the other of 20 for the pharmacy. A vestibule at the opposite side from the church served as entrance to the hospital. The chapel was placed under the invocation of the Virgin of Consolation and the wards were dedicated to St. Joseph, St. Matthew, St.

---

[51] John Pope, *A Tour through the Southern and Western Territories of the United States of North-America; the Spanish Dominions on the River Mississippi, and the Floridas* . . . (Richmond, 1792), 39.

[52] Huber and Wilson, *The St. Louis Cemeteries*, 8.

Bernard, and St. James. These descriptions were as set forth in Almonester's petition to the king dated May 1, 1784.[53]

To support the hospital, Almonester offered to give a 50-arpent dairy farm known as La Metairie, probably located on the bayou of that name beyond Bayou St. John and extending back to Lake Pontchartrain. Milk from the dairy was sold in the city and would also supply the hospital. He also offered a 22-arpent plantation on Bayou St. John with a quantity of lime for sale and quantities of timber. The farm could supply the hospital with vegetables, chickens, and milk. Another plantation just beyond the city gate on Bayou Road, adjacent to the land he gave for the Lepers' Hospital, was also offered by Almonester, with the brickyard that had been established there by the Company of the Indies in 1725 and granted to Charles de Morand in 1731.[54] In addition Almonester proposed to build fifteen houses, each 25 feet wide and 36 feet deep, including a 6-foot gallery, each on a lot 30 by 120 feet. The rent from these houses would be used for the maintainance of the hospital. Until they were constructed Almonester offered to bear these maintainance costs himself, mortgaging his houses facing the Plaza de Armas.

Finally he offered the revenues from the six stores that occupied the ground floor of his own residence at the corner of Levee and St. Peter streets next to the Government House. Each of these stores was described in Almonester's petition to the king dated November 20, 1786.[55] The following day a group of leading citizens was appointed with the approval of Governor Miró to carry out the intent of Almonester's offer, including Father Antonio de Sedella, the pastor, and Don Martín Navarro, the intendant.

On November 25, 1786, this board met with the governor and Almonester in the Government House.[56] The several proposals that the donor had made for the support of the hospital were discussed and all but the last rejected for various reasons. It was agreed that the rent of the stores on the Plaza would produce about 1,500 *pesos* annually and this was accepted. Almonester also offered to donate several slaves for the use of the hospital, one of whom "could take care of the vegetable gardens that Don Almonester has fenced in alongside of the hospital for the good of the inmates."[57] He also repaired five houses that had been donated to the hospital through the years. It was specified that the pa-

---

[53] "Constitution and By-laws for the New Charity Hospital, Constructed at the Expense of D. Andrés de Almonester y Roxas" (translation), 3, LSM.

[54] C13A, XIII, 82, AN.

[55] "Constitution and By-laws for the New Charity Hospital," 6.

[56] *Ibid.*, 7.

[57] *Ibid.*, 8.

tronship of the hospital, at his death, would be inherited by his nephews, sons of his sisters, since at the time Almonester had no children of his own.

When he died in 1798 Almonester had become a father, and his daughter Micaëla inherited the patronship, exercised for her by her mother. This continued until September 22, 1809, when the entire hospital was destroyed by a disastrous fire.[58] In a letter of September 27 following, Mayor James Mather reported:

> The disaster that occurred at the Charity Hospital . . . is especially to be deplored through the loss of three individuals whom it was impossible to save from the fire, the progress of which was already considerable when the alarm was given. The City Hall served as a refuge in the first moment to about thirty of the sick, who were transported there during the night. . . . The sole [volunteer fire] company from the Faubourg St. Mary showed on this occasion that subordination, that intelligence without which zeal is always fruitless. The other companies . . . almost refused to serve when the destruction of the entire city might have been the result of their defection. . . . Only the calm of this night saved us from a more terrible conflagration. . . .[59]

The mayor proposed that a paid fire department be set up and that a sentinel be stationed "on the terrace roof of the church in order to sound the alarm in case of fire," a precaution that the church wardens had previously opposed. He also asked, "Does the burning of the hospital put an end to the patronship [of Almonester's heirs]? If not, then should not the patron rebuild the building or should not the City Council be the proper body to assume these rights and obligations?"

As a result of long negotiations, Almonester's daughter, Micaëla, assisted by her mother, now the widow of Jean Baptiste Castillon, agreed, on March 9, 1811,

> that considering that the patronship of the Charity Hospital of this city which she has inherited from the late Don Andrés Almonester y Roxas, her father, has ceased to be an honorific title, and that the prerogatives which were attached to it as a just recompense for the considerable expenses which her late father made to found this establishment, are found in great part abolished by the changes that have affected the Government of this country; considering besides that the burning of the Charity Hospital and of

[58] O'Conner, "The Charity Hospital," 35.
[59] MS letter in the collection of Samuel Wilson, Jr.

its church have entirely altered the state of things . . . [she does] renounce the rights that had been assured to her by the foundation Charter of the said Hospital granted to her late father by the King of Spain in the year 1793.[60]

Micaëla Almonester also renounced her rights to the house where she and her mother lived at the corner of Levee and St. Peter streets, facing the Plaza de Armas, and also any claims on materials salvageable from the ruins of the old hospital. The city council took over the patron's prerogatives and the same day sold its rights to the house on the Plaza de Armas back to Madame Castillon for $20,000.[61] On April 18, 1811, she contracted with the builders Gurlie and Guillot to demolish the house and erect a new one in accordance with the plans of Lacarrière Latour and Hyacinthe Laclotte, architects, at a cost of $62,000.[62] The city then took over a square of ground on Canal Street between Baronne and Dryades and erected a new hospital under a contract with the young architect Henry S. Latrobe. This building served as the Charity Hospital until a new one was built on the present Tulane Avenue site in 1834, at which time the old hospital was remodeled into a state capitol building. Thus an end came to an important phase in the history of the Charity Hospital, an institution with which Almonester's name will always be associated, though all physical reminders of his generosity disappeared in the great fire that destroyed his splendid hospital building in 1809.

No plans or sketches of the Hospital of St. Charles have been found and few descriptions of it have survived. Its location and form appear on Pilié's map of August 18, 1808,[63] which shows that one of the wings, probably the one containing the chapel, was located almost on the axis of Toulouse Street, terminating the vista from the river and the Government House. A map of the city in 1793 contained in the journals of Mathias James O'Conway[64] also indicates the hospital but erroneously shows it outside the fortifications. It does, however, clearly indicate an H-shaped plan with a suggestion of an elevation, gabled ends to each of the two wings, and a pedimented central bay with a small circular attic window above an entrance doorway. The architect of the building is unknown but it may have been Gilberto Guillemard, who was in Louisiana

---

[60] Acts of S. Quinones, XIII, 80, Mar. 9, 1811, NONA.

[61] *Ibid.*, 83.

[62] Acts of M. de Armas, Apr. 18, 1811, NONA.

[63] MS map, Tulane University Library, New Orleans.

[64] Laurence F. Flick, "Mathias James O'Conway," *Records of the American Catholic Historical Society of Philadelphia*, X (Sept., 1899), 285.

at the time, having participated in Gálvez's campaigns against Manchac and Baton Rouge in 1779. Dr. John Sibley mentioned the hospital briefly in his journal on September 21, 1802: "Visited the hospital; tis a large old building in form of an H. Did not go through it. . . ."[65]

Major Amos Stoddard, in his *Sketches . . . of Louisiana*, mentions that "the Charity Hospital stands on the westerly or back part of the city. Poor Spanish subjects and sometimes strangers, (provided they paid half a dollar per day) were admitted into this asylum. Those entirely destitute were admitted gratis. They had medicine, sustenance, and other aid afforded them."[66]

One of the most interesting events to occur in the chapel of the Charity Hospital was the solemn funeral services held in commemoration of the death of the Spanish king Charles III, in whose honor the hospital had been named. He died on December 14, 1788, but the news was not received by the New Orleans cabildo until April 4, 1789. It was then decided

to observe it with the greatest solemnity and propriety possible in the small church of the hospital which was not destroyed by the flames of the last disastrous fire, in which a sepulchral monument will be erected in proportion to its small capacity, the bier draped in mourning. . . . At 9 o'clock on the 22 day of [April, 1789] . . . the Illustrious Council forming in a body presided over by Don Esteban Miró . . . Governor . . . preceded by their mace bearers, all dressed in strict mourning . . . proceeded from the Government House . . . to the church of the Charity Hospital . . . in the center of which was placed a majestic sepulchral bier comprised of five steps in proportion to the height of the church, on top of which was placed a sepulchral urn covered with bright red velvet in the form of a royal mantle. The head pillow was made of the same material, both with gold braid, with edges and tassels of the same. Resting on it was a septre and gilt crown adorned with bright and beautiful enamel which resembled precious stones, with a good arrangement of the magnificent insignias of the King and medals of distinguished Royal Orders. All this was adorned by a beautiful canopy, which, forming a colorful crowning, descended from the top in four arched festoons with beautiful ornaments. This embraced the four corners of the monument, all of which was draped in mourning like the main chapel, the contour of the altar,

[65] G. P. Whittington, "Dr. John Sibley of Natchitoches, 1751–1837," *LHQ*, X (Oct., 1927), 479.

[66] Amos Stoddard, *Sketches Historical and Descriptive of Louisiana* (Philadelphia, 1812), 199.

its furnishings and pulpit adorned with sixty Royal Coats of Arms placed in symmetrical harmony, all illuminated by a large number of torches and candles placed in large torch holders and candlesticks, the large number of lights giving splendor to the mournful display.[67]

Almonester must have been highly gratified to see this splendid display of royal pomp and ceremony in his chapel. The cost of the entire affair amounted to 1,216 *pesos*, 5 *reales*, and it is not unlikely that Almonester, then junior judge in the Illustrious Cabildo, had had an active part in planning and carrying out the royal obsequies. A few days later the trappings of mourning were temporarily laid aside for the joyous ceremonies of formally proclaiming the new king, Charles IV. The religious rites connected with these ceremonies were not held in the hospital chapel but within the parochial church, which had probably been temporarily established in the hastily repaired *corps de garde* of the royal jail, for the cornerstones for the new church to replace the burned one had only been laid on February 14, 1789, and the building was not to be completed until December, 1794.[68]

THE URSULINE CHAPEL

The first building erected by the Company of the Indies in New Orleans for the Ursuline nuns, who arrived in 1727 under contract with the company, was a large three-story, half-timber structure into which the nuns moved in 1734. Occupying part of the ground floor was a chapel which opened into the adjacent royal military hospital, enabling the sick to follow the chapel services from their beds. The first convent building rapidly deteriorated, and in 1745 a new brick structure to replace it was designed by the architect-engineer Ignace François Broutin. In his designs Broutin included a separate building for the chapel, enclosing a forecourt on the river side of the new convent and occupying part of the site of the old convent, in the same location as the original chapel so it could continue to serve both the convent and the hospital.[69] Due to lack of funds only the convent proper, the building that still stands at 1114 Chartres Street, could be built, and the old convent was left stand-

---

[67] Cabildo Minutes, III, no. 2, p. 55, Apr. 4, 1789.

[68] Leonard V. Huber and Samuel Wilson, Jr., *The Basilica on Jackson Square* (New Orleans, 1965), 14–15.

[69] Samuel Wilson, Jr., "An Architectural History of the Royal Hospital and the Ursuline Convent of New Orleans," *LHQ*, XXIX (July, 1946), 602.

ing, the original chapel probably still continuing in use. The old structure was eventually demolished, but when Louisiana was transferred from France to Spain, the inventory made in 1766 by representatives of the two countries listed on the grounds of the Ursuline Convent "a building serving as chapel for the nuns as well as for the hospital."[70] Either the original chapel from the first convent was still standing or it had been rebuilt as proposed by Broutin in 1745. When Don Alexandro O'Reilly arrived in August, 1769, to take full possession for Spain and suppress the revolution of some of the French leaders, the Ursulines recorded in their annals that "their small bell added its very modest voice to that of the parish church to proclaim their new lord . . . and prayed in their poor chapel and begged the God of armies to appease the just anger of the new-comers. . . ."[71] When the leaders of the revolution were executed, the annals continue, "the discharges of the executioners shook the windows of the Ursuline chapel, where the relatives of the victims had taken refuge."[72] The chapel belfry had been rebuilt in 1766 by the contractor, Gilbert Antoine de St. Maxent.[73]

The "poor chapel" was probably closed off from the hospital when the Ursulines gave up the care of that military facility in 1770 soon after O'Reilly's arrival.[74] Perhaps the part of the chapel containing the sanctuary was moved to the corner of Ursulines and Levee (Decatur) streets, for a survey of the property made by Gilberto Guillemard in April, 1793, shows a small square structure in this location designated "C. Ancient Church."[75] This relocation of the chapel may have been the result of a request to the king from the mother superior asking that a brick wall be constructed to separate the convent from the hospital and that the chapel be repaired since it was in a very dilapidated condition.[76] The wall was authorized in 1785 and built as shown on Guillemard's plan of 1793.

The chapel, or "Ancient Church," only about 30 feet square, must have been painfully inadequate for the needs of the convent. This situation, coming to Almonester's notice, prompted him to offer to build an entirely new church adjacent to the main convent, the building of 1745. On September 8, 1785, Almonester petitioned the king for the

[70] C13A, XLVI, 47, AN.
[71] "Deliberations du Conseil," Ursuline Annals, II, 31, Ursuline Convent Archives.
[72] Ibid., 34.
[73] Louisiana Miscellaneous Documents, 1579.
[74] Jane Frances Heany, O.S.U., "A Century of Pioneering: A History of the Ursuline Nuns in New Orleans (1727–1827)" (Ph.D. dissertation, St. Louis University, 1949), 294.
[75] Wilson, "An Architectural History," 647.
[76] Heany, "A Century of Pioneering," 294.

right to build this church and to dedicate it to Our Lady of Consolation, whose feast was celebrated annually on September 8, the birthday or feast of the Nativity of the Blessed Virgin Mary.[77] Work on the construction of the church must have begun soon after, and it was completed and blessed on March 19, 1787.[78]

At a meeting of the Ursuline community on August 23, 1787, the annals record: "The Mother Superior proposed on behalf of M. Don André, to change the title of the Blessed Virgin which we have, to that of Our Lady of Consolation, but that the feast and dedication would still be on the day of the Nativity of the Blessed Virgin. The whole community consented in recognition of the charity that this Gentleman has had in building our church at his expense, and it was decided to make a general communion for him on the feast of St. André and a three-nocturn office at his death, with a sung high mass."[79]

The Ursuline annals also record that it was the noted Père Antoine, Father Antonio de Sedella, who obtained the generous gift of a new chapel for the Ursulines from Almonester.[80]

As is the case with all of Almonester's earlier buildings, no record has been found of the chapel's architect or builder. Somewhat similar sketches of the chapel appear in early nineteenth-century New Orleans guide books. Norman's of 1845, practically quoting Gibson's of 1838 verbatim, describes the building as follows:

The Chapel of the Ursulines

An edifice strongly characteristic of our city, and well calculated to cause reflection on the many and sudden changes of dynasty to which New Orleans has been subjected. This building of a quaint old style of architecture, was erected, according to a Spanish inscription on a marble tablet in the middle of the facade, in 1787, during the reign of Carlos III, (Don Esteban Miró being governor of the province) by Don André Almonaster y Roxas. It is exceedingly plain and unpretending in its exterior, and chiefly interesting from its associations, and extremely antiquated appearance.[81]

An earlier engraved view of the chapel from the garden side appears as one of the marginal sketches of Jacques Tanesse's plan of New Or-

[77] *Ibid.*, 198.
[78] *Ibid.*, 297.
[79] "Deliberations du Conseil," I, 65.
[80] *Ibid.*, 67.
[81] B. M. Norman, *New Orleans and Environs* (New Orleans, 1845), 98.

leans published in 1817.[82] Here is shown a curious connection from the second floor of the convent into the attic of the chapel, probably a later addition permitting the nuns to go directly from the convent building to the chapel choir loft without going outside. No other connection was possible, as the chapel appears from Guillemard's map of 1793, and other later maps, to have been attached to the convent only at the corner. The Tanesse sketch and remaining evidence at the site indicate that a colonnade once extended along the garden side of the chapel. If further archaeological investigation verifies this, it will be included in the contemplated restoration project being planned by the Crescent City Convent Corporation.

As had been the case when Almonester built the church of the Charity Hospital, he requested and was granted the special privileges of the church's patron. This brought on a conflict between Almonester and the new governor, François Louis Hector, Baron de Carondelet, who had succeeded Almonester's friend Miró in 1791.[83] As patron of the church, Almonester was given a seat in the sanctuary at the left of the governor general, the official royal vice-patron. Father Theodoro Henríquez, who had been appointed auxiliary vicar general in February, 1792, questioned the arrangement that Almonester had enjoyed since 1787 and ordered that it be discontinued.[84] When Father Patrick Walsh was appointed administrator of the newly created Diocese of New Orleans in 1793, he directed that the seat and its privileges be restored on orders from the king, the following official record being drawn up by the notary Esteban de Quinones:

> I have just received a royal order, signed at San Ildefonse, the 14 August of the present year [1794] by His Majesty . . . addressed to Don Andrés Almonester . . . relative to a seat that he has in the church of the convent of the Ursulines. His Majesty orders that, Sunday the twenty-first of this month, at the High Mass celebrated at eight-thirty, at which the Baron de Carondelet, Governor-General of this Province and Royal Vice-Patron, will assist, the aforementioned Don Almonester be given possession of his seat. This seat should be placed on the Epistle side, outside the sanctuary. It should consist of a seat covered with a cushion but without a priedieu. To this seat are attached all the privileges, the

[82] Samuel Wilson, Jr., *The Vieux Carré, New Orleans: Its Plan, Its Growth, Its Architecture* (New Orleans, 1968), 71.

[83] Gayarré, *Louisiana, Spanish Domination*, 312.

[84] Heany, "A Century of Pioneering," 279.

incense, the kiss of peace, and the candle, in the same way as it is observed for the Governor-General.[85]

Father Walsh, however, defended Father Henríquez's action, since, according to the laws of the Indies,

> churches here have the King (may God keep him) as patron, and without his special permission, no one can enjoy the privileges of patron . . . [thus] Don Andrés had no right to the use of the said seat or privileges . . . [though] I have nothing against the enjoyment of the rights of honor and privileges that Don Andrés claims, for it is true that he built the said church at his own expense. This is a good work in the eyes of God, for the temple is very becoming and an appropriate place for the celebration of the divine office. Formerly the religious had only an old cabin that was separated from the convent by a large courtyard which the nuns had to cross in all kinds of weather.[86]

It must have greatly pleased Almonester to have the king honor him with the privileges of patron, not only of the Ursuline chapel but also of the chapel that he built at the Charity Hospital and later of the cathedral he built some years later.[87] These ceremonial honors meant much in those days, and in a colonial town like New Orleans, even the governor and other public officials were piqued if any of the prescribed honors due them were omitted.

Even after Almonester's death his heirs sought to keep the privileged seat in the Ursuline chapel. His widow's second husband, Jean Baptiste Castillon, in a letter to the Ursulines' superior, Sister St. Xavier Farjon, on May 24, 1805, wrote: "In my capacity of spouse and attorney of the widow and daughter of the late M. Almonester y Roxas who built your education classrooms and your church where this Monarch fixed for him a place of honor . . . I must ask you: why this last Holy Week you did not ask to whom they should give the key of the tabernacle as you formerly did, an office as much assigned to M. Almonester as to his widow before her marriage?"[88]

The mother superior replied that the seat had never been refused but that the ceremony of confiding the key of the tabernacle was not observed in churches of the United States but only of Spain.

The Ursuline chapel had served briefly as the parish church when

85 *Ibid.*, 302.
86 *Ibid.*
87 Cabildo Minutes, IV, no. 2, 62.
88 MS, Pontalba Family Papers, Mont l'Evêque, France; restricted microfilm copy in Tulane University Library.

the temporary church, established in the repaired *corps de garde* after the fire of 1788, was again destroyed in the fire of December 8, 1794.[89] Here the Ursulines and the women of New Orleans prayed before the statue of Our Lady of Prompt Succor for Andrew Jackson's victory in the Battle of New Orleans in 1815.[90] When the nuns moved to their new convent below the city in 1824 the chapel became the church of the bishop, to whom the Ursulines gave their old convent as a residence.[91]

Among early travelers visiting New Orleans who described the chapel was Christian Schultz, who said in his book published in 1810: "The chapel of the convent of the Ursuline nuns is small but very neat within, being chiefly calculated for the accommodation of the sisterhood. Public service is performed here regularly. The nuns are separated from the audience by a partition of lattice work, through which they may barely be distinguished."[92]

During the years following the Louisiana Purchase, the church in New Orleans was split by disputes between the Spanish pastor of the cathedral, Père Antoine, and Father Walsh, acting as vicar general.[93] When Father Walsh died on August 22, 1806, his body was buried beneath the floor of the Ursuline chapel, where it was discovered during renovations in 1920 and quietly re-interred in St. Louis Cathedral beside his old enemy Père Antoine.[94] During the regime of Bishop Joseph Rosati in 1828 the old chapel, which had become known as the "Bishop's Church," was enlarged to a length of 114 feet and a width of 85.[95] With the building of a new church for the bishop in 1845 at the opposite end of the old convent, now St. Mary's Italian Church, the old chapel was abandoned.

A newspaper writer visiting the abandoned chapel in 1866 referred to it erroneously as "the first religious edifice that was built in this city or State," and described it as follows:

> . . . the principal object of interest about the grounds is the old chapel. . . . Religious service is now performed in a church of

[89] C. M. Chambon, *In and Around the Old St. Louis Cathedral of New Orleans* (New Orleans, 1908), 40.

[90] Henry C. Semple, S.J., *The Ursulines in New Orleans and Our Lady of Prompt Succor* (New York, 1925), 73.

[91] Wilson, "An Architectural History," 637.

[92] Christian Schultz, *Travels on an Inland Voyage—Performed in the Years 1807 and 1808* (New York, 1810), 193.

[93] Baudier, *The Catholic Church*, 258.

[94] *Morning Tribune* (New Orleans), Mar. 24, 1921, p. 1, col. 6.

[95] Wilson, "An Architectural History," 640.

more modern origin, and indeed all of the wood work of the chapel's interior is in a state of ruin. The flooring has almost entirely rotted away; one or two pews hint at its former use, and the general aspect of the interior reminds the observer of Hood's "Haunted House." Some portion of the altar is still remaining, and singularly enough, a fine painting of the Virgin, just above, is but little injured by time. Otherwise the walls of the building are in good preservation, and we were pleased to learn that a plan is thought and talked of . . . to restore the chapel to the uses of religion.[96]

The chapel was never restored, and in 1870 its roof was removed and its walls apparently used as the first story of a three-story seminary that was then erected on the site. This building, St. Mary's School, now abandoned, still stands. It will be demolished and the original remaining walls of the old chapel reused for the contemplated restoration of the building as part of the complete restoration of this splendid group of historic structures.

THE URSULINE CLASSROOMS

Among many benefactions mentioned on his tombstone, Almonester is listed as "Founder of the Classes for . . . young children." This is probably the least known of all his charitable works and just what or where these classes were is somewhat uncertain. As a matter of fact, there were probably two separate classroom buildings. One he erected for the Ursuline nuns on the grounds of their convent; this is to what the tombstone inscription is generally believed to refer. This may have been a small building facing the levee near the corner of Ursulines Street adjacent to the "Ancient Church" which stood on that corner of the convent grounds. The location of these and the other convent buildings are shown on a plan dated April 10, 1793, drawn by Gilberto Guillemard, copied and translated by the city surveyor, Joseph Pilié, on January 1, 1821.[97] On this plan, the small structure, about 25 by 50 feet, is marked "B. Externs or School-Room" and was probably entered through the entrance way to the convent from Levee (Decatur) Street, marked "A" on the plan. A royal order, dated August 14, 1794, at San Ildefonso mentions that Almonester had built the Ursulines "classrooms

[96] *Ibid.*, 641.
[97] *Ibid.*, 646–647.

for the students in brick."[98] In an account published in 1825, Almonester is said to have built for the Ursulines "the church, the choir, and the school for the externs." Almonester's schoolhouse is also said to have been a three-room brick building; he is at the same time credited with having made extensive repairs to the convent.[99]

No pictures or descriptions of this small classroom building are known to exist, nor has even the date of its construction been determined. Major Amos Stoddard, in his *Sketches* published in 1812, described the convent and mentioned the schoolhouse: "Near to the main building and on the street stands an old schoolhouse where the female children of the citizens appear at certain fixed hours to be gratuitously instructed in writing, reading and arithmetic."[100]

The schoolhouse was probably demolished after the Ursulines moved from their old convent on Chartres Street to their new location farther down the river. In 1830–31 the row of houses facing Decatur Street between Ursulines and Gov. Nicholls Street was built for the nuns by the architect-builders Gurlie and Guillot, and the site of the old schoolhouse is still covered by those buildings.[101]

THE SPANISH SCHOOL

On July 17, 1771, a letter was addressed from Madrid to Louisiana's Spanish governor, Don Luis de Unzaga, stating that the king desired "to establish schools and arrange for masters to teach them . . . in order that the Christian doctrine, elementary education and grammar be taught . . . and an opportunity be provided to acquire the knowledge and use of the Spanish language."[102] As a result, in 1772 the Spanish authorities established a public school in New Orleans under the direction of Don Manuel Andrés López de Armesto with teachers of Spanish grammar, Latin, reading, and writing.[103] This Spanish school was never too well accepted by the French population of the city, and according to Governor Esteban Miró, writing in 1788, "no pupil ever presented himself for the Latin class; a few came to be taught reading and writing only; these never exceeded thirty, and frequently dwindled down to six.

[98] Cabildo Minutes, IV, no. 2, 60.
[99] Heany, "A Century of Pioneering," 298.
[100] Stoddard, *Sketches*, 155.
[101] Wilson, "An Architectural History," 631.
[102] Montes Wood, "Life in New Orleans in the Spanish Period," *LHQ*, XXII (July, 1939), 682.
[103] Henry E. Chambers, *A History of Louisiana* (3 vols., Chicago, 1925), I, 314.

For this reason, the three teachers taught nothing beyond the rudiments."[104]

No location or description of the schoolhouse in which these classes were held has been found, but it was probably not too distant from the Plaza de Armas beyond Chartres Street, for it was destroyed in the conflagration of March 21, 1788, which burned the Cabildo, the parish church and presbytère, and a great number of other structures. Perhaps the site was the same one on Royal Street on which it was re-established after the fire.

Following the conflagration, Almonester "offered as a substitute, free of charge, and as long as it should be wanted, a small edifice containing a room thirteen feet in length by twelve in width, which would suffice for the present, because, since the occurrence of the fire, many families had retired into the country, so that the number of pupils had, by that event, been reduced from twenty-three to twelve."[105] Again, the location of this temporary schoolroom is unknown, but it was possibly in one of Almonester's buildings facing the sides of the Plaza de Armas that had escaped the fire.

The Spanish school was re-established in a new plastered-brick, tile-roofed, one-story building located at what is now 919 Royal Street, below Dumaine. This house was no doubt the one built as a result of Miró's proposal for "the construction of a more respectable schoolhouse, the cost of which he estimates at $6000."[106] It is not known whether or not Almonester had anything to do with the construction of this building, which was typical of the smaller structures being built during the Spanish colonial period in New Orleans. Old photographs[107] show it with gable ends and a fairly steep pitched roof covered with round Spanish tiles, the ridge parallel to the street. Along the left side of the house was apparently a carriage way, entered from Royal Street through a large, arched gateway. There were indications in the roof that this may have been an addition to the house after it had become a private residence. There were four other square-headed openings across the front, one of which was converted into a shop window. Across the facade was a typical plastered-brick cornice, above which a canopy or fixed awning, supported on projecting iron bars, extended over the sidewalk. In the front slope of the roof were two chimneys, a smaller one above the inner wall of the carriage way, probably a later addition,

[104] Gayarré, *Louisiana, Spanish Domination*, 205.
[105] *Ibid.*
[106] *Ibid.*
[107] Vieux Carré survey, square 57, Tulane University Library.

and a larger original one that served fireplaces in the two front rooms of the house. This suggests that the plan was typical of the period: four nearly square rooms, two in the front and two in the rear, each pair with a double fireplace served by a single chimney. Generally, behind the rear two rooms was a recessed porch or gallery with a small anteroom or *cabinet* at each end.

When Don Luis Peñalver y Cárdenas arrived as first bishop in New Orleans in 1795, the Spanish school was still in operation, and he made note of it in his dispatch of November 1 of that year, reporting that "the Spanish school, which has been established here at the expense of the crown, is kept as it ought to be. . . . Excellent results are obtained from the Convent of the Ursulines in which a good many girls are educated. . . . As to what the boys are taught in the Spanish school, it is soon forgotten . . . they leave the school when still very young, and return to the houses of their parents mostly situated in the country, where they hear neither the name of God nor of King, but daily witness the corrupt morals of their parents."[108]

Spain returned Louisiana to France in 1803, and twenty days later, on December 20, France transferred the vast territory to the United States. A few days later, the French battalion chief of engineers, Joseph Vinache, with his assistants and appraisers, together with his Spanish counterpart, Lieutenant Colonel Don Gilberto Guillemard, with his assistants and appraisers, made an inspection, inventory, and appraisal of all the royal buildings in New Orleans, including the Spanish school, which they described as follows:

Estimate of the Spanish School[109]

This house, well built, is in very good state, having 50 feet of facade, 45 of depth by 13 feet 6″ of height, its walls having 2 feet of thickness. It is divided by two partitions in its interior, forming 4 chambers with fireplaces and 4 large pilasters to support the roof, plus a kitchen constructed in wood with a large fireplace.

A well in the yard, having 10 feet of depth by three of diameter and well lined with bricks.

The general total of the survey [*toisé*] of this building including its roofing in tile is carried at 48 *toises* ½, fixed at 80 *piastres* per cubic *toise*, makes in French money the sum of ——   19,400 ″ ″
 Framing and Woodwork

The framing of this house is generally good, the woodwork is in the best state. The whole has been estimated, with its sash and

[108] Gayarré, *Louisiana, Spanish Domination*, 378.
[109] C¹³A, LIII, 149, AN.

doors and the kitchen, at the sum of —— 2,463 6 "
    Iron Work
    The total of the iron work, heavy iron as well as all the hard-
ware, at the sum of —— 315 " "

After the transfer of Louisiana to the United States, Colonel Constant Freeman arrived in New Orleans early in June, 1804, and Governor William C. C. Claiborne reported to the secretary of war that since New Orleans was an expensive city in which to live, he had "put the Colonel in possession of a public building, and the charge of house rent being saved, perhaps with economy, he may be enabled to live on his pay."[110] The public building referred to was the Spanish school on Royal Street. About a year later Dominick A. Hall, being appointed federal district judge, sought a suitable building in which to hold his court, and on June 1, 1805, wrote to Claiborne that "I know of no building belonging to the United States in this city proper for those purposes, but that at present occupied by the Commandant of the Troops."[111]

Colonel Freeman had previously been informed by Claiborne that his house was desired for court use, being told that "the civil officers may, of right, claim a preference in the occupation of public buildings not attached to the barracks."[112] This controversy continued for some time, Colonel Freeman protesting that "when I arrived in this city from South Carolina, the quarters I now occupy were used as a hospital or barracks for Spanish soldiers. Your Excellency had them removed and delivered to me the house. I came into it with reluctance for it was dirty and required great labor to put it into decent condition, and now that I have made it a comfortable dwelling I have not the smallest predilection for it, and I would remove from it with greater pleasure than I moved into it, if I were furnished with other quarters. . . . There are no rooms unoccupied in the Barracks—there is not any house at my control—where shall I move?"[113]

Claiborne replied that the colonel, when being first put in possession of the house, "was told that the building had formerly been occupied as a Public School House." The controversy was taken to the secretary of war, the secretary of state, and the president, Thomas Jefferson. Claiborne informed him on October 23, 1805, that "the Public School Room should remain . . . for the use of the Court . . . [and] the commis-

[110] Dunbar Rowland, ed., *Official Letterbooks of W. C. C. Claiborne, 1801–1816* (6 vols., Jackson, Miss., 1917), II, 199.
[111] *Ibid.*, III, 60.
[112] *Ibid.*, 56.
[113] *Ibid.*, 62.

sioners for settling land claims, who are to convene in this city, may also be accommodated in the School House . . . [but] I feel extremely solicitous that the School House should early be appropriated to the object for which it was originally intended. . . . This is a brick building and well calculated for a public school."[114]

Judge Hall's court soon thereafter moved into the house, and remained for a number of years, although the mayor of the city had written to Jefferson as early as 1808 that the building had been "built at the time [of Spanish domination], at the expense of the government, to establish there a public school, which the city needs no less to-day than then, because it is devoid of any public use of this kind."[115] As late as 1820, when plans were being made by the architect Benjamin Buisson for a new custom house, the council passed a resolution stating that "the building in which at present the U.S. District Court at New Orleans is sitting, was built by the Spanish Government to establish a public school, and Congress is requested to restore it to its original destination as soon as the new building which must be constructed for the use of the said court is completed."[116]

Meanwhile, some important events had occurred in the old Spanish school. As early as November 20, 1805, the recently organized congregation of Christ Church, the first Protestant church in New Orleans, adopted the following resolution: "That a commiteee be appointed to petition His Excellency William C. C. Claiborne for the use of the house, at present occupied by Col. Freeman for the purpose of public worship."[117]

Although Governor Claiborne agreed that this should be done as soon as the house was vacated by Colonel Freeman, it is doubtful if services were held for a long period, if at all, in the old schoolhouse. However, the church may have used it at times during the period of the court occupancy, for the *Louisiana Courier* on June 30, 1809, announced: "REMOVAL: Dr. Cyprien Gros has the honor to inform the public that he now resides in Royal street, next door to the Protestant church, formerly the Spanish school."

In 1815 the old Spanish school again came into prominence, for it was here that Judge Hall summoned Andrew Jackson to his court after the Battle of New Orleans and imposed a fine of $1,000 for his continued imposition of martial law. The grateful people of New Orleans promptly

114 *Ibid.*, 209, 211.
115 Records of the City Council, Jan. 16, 1808, p. 108, NOPL.
116 *Ibid.*, Feb. 5, 1820, p. 209.
117 Records of the Wardens and Vestry of Christ Church, New Orleans, 17.

paid the fine.[118] Judge Hall had again set the civil and judicial authority above the military.

The old schoolhouse never reverted to its original use. Instead, after it ceased to be used as a court, the federal government ordered it sold in 1826.[119] It passed into private ownership, Louis Daquin being the purchaser.[120] By 1876 it had become a mineral water manufactory, and in 1880 Henry Pfeiffer purchased it,[121] demolishing it in 1888 "to erect a two story brick building to be used for a store and residence."[122]

THE ST. LOUIS CATHEDRAL

Almonester's last three major building projects left the greatest impact on the visual appearance of New Orleans and became his most enduring monuments. These were the St. Louis Cathedral, the Presbytère, and the Cabildo, three impressive public structures facing the Plaza de Armas, the public square, that caused the noted Anglo-American architect Benjamin Henry Latrobe to say in 1819: "New Orleans has at first sight a very imposing appearance beyond any other city in the United States, in which I have yet been."[123]

The great conflagration of March 21, 1788, destroyed the buildings that had stood on these three sites. Immediate rebuilding of each of them was an urgent necessity but no funds were available either from church or state. It was only through the generosity of Almonester that their reconstruction in larger and finer form became possible. The first of these projects to be started was the parish church of St. Louis, which before its completion was to become the Cathedral of the Diocese of Louisiana when that area was separated from the Diocese of Havana by papal decree on April 25, 1793. The architect selected by Almonester to design this important building was Don Gilberto Guillemard, a native of Longuy in the kingdom of France,[124] where he was born about the year 1747. He entered the service of Spain in January, 1770, as a cadet and served for a few years before being sent to Louisiana. He dis-

---

118 Gayarré, *History of Louisiana: The American Domination* (New York, 1867), 625.

119 *Louisiana Courier*, Oct. 8, 1826, p. 4, col. 4.

120 Acts of Felix de Armas, VII, 285, Mar. 6, 1827, NONA.

121 Acts of J. Meunier, Aug. 6, 1888, NONA.

122 *The Daily States* (New Orleans), Oct. 8, 1888, p. 2, col. 2.

123 Samuel Wilson, Jr., ed., *Impressions Respecting New Orleans, by Benjamin Henry Boneval Latrobe* (New York, 1951), 18.

124 Marriage Register II, act 186, June 1, 1787, St. Louis Cathedral Archives (hereafter SLCA).

tinguished himself in the campaigns of the Spanish governor Don Bernardo de Gálvez against the British at Manchac, Baton Rouge, Mobile, and Pensacola in 1779–80.[125] He was a nephew of Doña Isabel de la Roche, his mother's sister, wife of the noted Gilbert Antoine de St. Maxent,[126] one of whose daughters was the wife of Governor Unzaga and another the wife of Governor Bernardo de Gálvez, later viceroy of Mexico.[127] Guillemard in 1786 held the rank of captain of infantry and town aide-major at New Orleans, "charged by commission of the government with the functions of Engineer and surveyor in this province."[128] In 1790 he drew plans for a church at Natchez as well as for several other buildings in that area for Governor Miró.[129] He was undoubtedly the most qualified architect in New Orleans at the time, and with his distinguished military career and family connections, it is not surprising that Almonester selected him to design the new parish church and rectory that he offered to rebuild at his own expense.

Almonester's offer was made soon after the fire, for in a letter to Don Antonio Porlier dated August 10, 1790, Miró reported "that a junta was held on March 22, 1788, as a result of the terrible fire in this city. . . . It was stated [in the report of these proceedings sent April 1, 1788] . . . that Don Andrés Almonester had promised to construct a new parish church of brick and wood, as large or larger than the one destroyed, and near by, a house suitable for lodging the Reverend Father Vicar, the priest's assistants and the chief sacristan."[130] Apparently nothing was done for almost a year, for at a meeting of the cabildo on February 13, 1789, the following was recorded:

> Don Andrés Almonester y Roxas, ordinary Junior Judge of the city and its jurisdiction for His Majesty, made known his desire of beginning construction of the parochial church as he had offered and called upon this Illustrious Council to fix the day for placing the four cornerstones and at the same time to appoint two commissioners to place two of them. The first two will be placed by the Governor [Miró] and the Reverend Father Vicar [Père Antoine de Sedella?]. In consequence it was agreed that the said stones be

---

[125] "Dispatches of the Spanish Governors of Louisiana-el Baron de Carondelet" (translations), V, 310, LSM; Archivo General de Indias, Seville, *Papeles de Cuba, leg.* 1443, fol. 730.

[126] *Ibid.*, XIII, bk. 3, 16, Nov. 9, 1784; AGI, *leg.* 1394, fol. 71.

[127] James Julian Coleman, Jr., *Gilbert Antoine de St. Maxent* (New Orleans, 1968), 53.

[128] Spanish Documents, box 45, doc. 1073-3, no. 14, LSM.

[129] Acts of R. Perdomo, XV, 162, Mar. 30, 1790, NONA.

[130] Kinnaird, ed., *Spain in the Mississippi Valley*, II, 372.

placed tomorrow the 14th inst.; Don Joseph de Ortega, Senior Judge, and Don Carlos de Reggio were unanimously appointed for this ceremony.[131]

At the time of this formal ceremony the plans of the new church had not even been drawn, for Almonester had evidently made his offer to rebuild the church and rectory contingent upon the king's conferring upon him a title of Castile. When this royal honor was not forthcoming, Almonester's fervor seemed to cool and no work was done on the proposed new church.

Months passed and by the end of the summer the populace began to show signs of impatience and to urge that some action be taken. At the cabildo's meeting on October 2, 1789, the attorney general, Don Valentin Robert Avart, presented a statement

> relative to the considerable inconveniences the public suffers, having been disappointed by the promises made by Don Andrés Almonester, actual Junior Judge, after the fire and at the public gathering of the most notable people of this city. He made this statement at the said meeting, motivated by the inexplicable suffering to the health of those who are obliged to go to the poor ruined church that serves as a parish church. It is very small and uncomfortable in the wretched rainy weather. The people who attend are compelled to be tightly packed or to suffer outside in bad weather, resulting in negligence and laxity in attending the Divine Services. . . .[132]

If Almonester had indeed changed his mind about rebuilding the church, the cabildo agreed that it would then appeal to the king to provide for the building "as he usually does under similar circumstances as Protector of all the Indies." The inhabitants also expressed a desire to contribute if the king could not provide the requisite funds. In consequence, a letter was written to Almonester, to which he replied on November 6, 1789, in an apparently unconvincing way. Again the matter was brought up at the meeting of the cabildo on December 12, 1789, with a long discussion

> relative to ascertaining the intentions of Don Andrés Almonester y Roxas regarding the reconstruction of the parish church he had promised. Due to the urgency of the said work, to better conditions for those coming to worship God and for the comfort of

[131] Cabildo Minutes, III, no. 2, 50.
[132] *Ibid.*, 76.

the inhabitants . . . to obviate new delays and eliminate all evasive
answers, it was unanimously decided to . . . have the annual Commissioners send a simple message to the said Don Andrés for the
sole purpose of asking him to kindly state plainly whether he has
decided to reconstruct the said Parish Church or not, so that in
view of his final answer, in case of an unexpected refusal, other
suitable steps might be taken to achieve this holy objective.[133]

The following day, December 12, 1789, Almonester gave his answer
to the cabildo through its two representatives, de Reggio and de la
Barre, who reported at the session of January 15, 1790, that they had
been informed by Almonester that "he promises that he will start the
work of repairing [rebuilding] the church on the first of the coming
month."[134]

In Miró's letter to Porlier of August 10, 1790, previously quoted, the
governor recalls that in his letter of June 3, 1789, he had reported that
"Almonester laid the first brick of the parish church according to the
plan I have submitted." The plan he referred to is unknown, but in a
later decree, issued by King Charles IV on May 7, 1798, it is stated that
"Don Andrés offered to have it [the parochial church] rebuilt in accordance with the plan drawn in the year 1791 by Sergeant-Major
Don Gilberto Guillemard, who at that time was acting Engineer."[135]

It is possible that the date for the plan, 1791, is not accurate, for on
February 22, 1790, Almonester had already signed a contract with the
master mason Joseph Duguet "to conduct the works of the parochial
church that is being rebuilt by the Señor Don Andrés . . . [Duguet
agreeing] that he will put on the said work three hired workmen and
one laborer. . . ."[136] None of Guillemard's plans for the church have
been found. There is, however, a plan drawn by Carlos Trudeau, dated
June 12, 1801, entitled "Geometrical Plan of the Parochial Church of
the City of New Orleans."[137] This plan shows a building with massive
brick walls additionally strengthened by exterior buttresses. In front,
facing the square, are two hexagonal bell towers with three entrance
doors between them, the central entrance being embellished by double
columns against the wall on each side. Within, the church is divided into
a nave and side aisles by rows of columns forming colonnades of five

[133] *Ibid.*, 87.

[134] *Ibid.*, 91.

[135] "Proceedings Instituted by Doctor Don Luis Peñalver y Cárdenas, Illustrious
Diocesan Bishop, against Doña Luisa Delaronde, Widow Almonester" (translation), doc.
3777, p. 12, LSM.

[136] Acts of Pedro Pedesclaux, IX, 134.

[137] Baptismal Register I (photostat plans bound in back), SLCA.

bays each. The sanctuary is beyond this and in the rear is a narrow room, probably for use as a sacristy.

Miró's account of the construction of the church given in his letter to Porlier, dated April 10, 1790, cited above, is perhaps the best source of information on this important project. He mentions that since the 1788 fire many people were not attending mass due to the inconvenience and crowded conditions of the temporary churches. At first, services were held in Almonester's chapel at the Charity Hospital, but this was too small and too far from the center of town. Then arrangements were made "to have the Holy Sacrifice celebrated in a gallery of the Government House and at other places in the city." Finally a temporary church was set up in the restored old French *corps de garde*, now part of the Cabildo building, which, said Miró, "has been adorned with great propriety." This served as the parish church until December 8, 1794, when it was again destroyed by fire and the church was moved to Almonester's chapel at the Ursuline Convent.

Miró had apparently encouraged Almonester in his quest for titles and honors, but added in his letter that even though "there was no hope of the success of the petition of Don Andrés Almonester for a title of Castile, under which condition he had promised to build a new church at his own expense, he requests that he be allotted twelve thousand *pesos* of the property which belonged to this mission. He proposes to construct a parish church and rectory with this assistance and with the timbers promised him by some citizens, also using the bricks from the wall of the old cemetery. . . ."[138]

After laying the first brick, according to Miró, Almonester continued the work: "He had the remaining ruins demolished, the refuse cleared away, the site enclosed, and prepared to begin the actual work. He did so on March 15, this year [1789], pursuing it with such vigor that at the present time the wall has reached a height of six feet above ground all around, with a thickness of five feet and the columns of the nave fifteen in height. If he continues, it may be expected that three years from now, as the work cannot be carried on in the cold season, it will be entirely completed and the divine services may be held in it."

Miró then continued, explaining that Almonester's petition for a title was not a condition for his undertaking the rebuilding of the church and rectory, but he hoped such honors would be forthcoming as a result of his other philanthropic works such as the Lepers' Hospital, the Charity Hospital, and the Ursuline chapel. These works, said Miró, were "calculated without exaggeration at the sum of 112,868 *pesos*,

[138] Kinnaird, ed., *Spain in the Mississippi Valley*, II, 371.

7 ½ *reales*," besides disbursements for the maintenance of the buildings and the poor hospital patients. Almonester was not unmindful, however, of his title hopes, and Miró continues:

> I have known his fervor to abate at times and I have seen it re-
> vive when his attorney informed him that the matter of his title
> was discussed in the council, and on another occasion when the
> *Contaduria General* made a favorable report. This vacillation re-
> sulted in his suspending the work after laying the first brick, re-
> moving the ruins of the old church and clearing the ground.
> Whereupon the *Ayuntamiento* [cabildo] wished to reprimand him
> strongly, but I, having prevented this indiscretion, which would
> have exasperated him, convinced him in such a manner by assisting
> in his re-election as *Alcalde* this year, which I know he desired in
> order to gain merit, that he again took up the work with great
> vigor. He promised me that he would continue it to completion,
> despite the flood which caused a break in the river levee on his
> lands, entailing the loss of his harvest, washing away his fences and
> destroying a large brick kiln, which cannot be rebuilt for another
> month when the waters recede. For this reason he was on the point
> of suspending the work, but on my giving him the bricks of the
> walls of the old cemetery, as they are to be replaced by stakes, he
> is using them to continue the works. For this assistance, which
> saves him less than 200 pesos, I beg your Excellency to secure the
> approval of His Majesty.
>
> I do not know how the Reverend Auxiliary Bishop can imagine
> that the church and rectory could be constructed for twelve thou-
> sand pesos, even with the donation of the timbers which he says
> have been promised to him by some citizens. I know that they will
> not amount to one thousand pesos, as they are very cheap now be-
> cause the lack of market which was experienced caused a fall of
> price.
>
> The cost of the church being built by Don Andrés is estimated
> at 72,350 pesos and 7 reales at the least, and I shall not be sur-
> prised if it costs him much more. . . . If he had contented him-
> self with building the church entirely of wood, instead of brick as
> he is now doing, he could have constructed both [church and
> rectory] for less than seventy thousand pesos.[139]

In the meantime Almonester had given up his petition for a title of Castile and instead requested the post of colonel for the local militia battalion, which he received on February 10, 1791.[140] In his military

[139] *Ibid.*, 374.
[140] Jack D. L. Holmes, *Honor and Fidelity* (Birmingham, 1965), 163.

service sheet, dated December 31, 1797, when he had reached the age of sixty-eight, it is stated that he was of robust health and "of inestimable usefulness because of his philanthropic spirit, supposed valor, good application—capacity and conduct." He had also attained a higher position in the cabildo, for on the resignation of Don Carlos de Reggio as royal ensign and perpetual commissioner, Almonester purchased this rank in the customary manner. On March 18, 1790, Governor Miró issued the royal commission,[141] and Almonester was sworn into the new position in the cabildo which he was to retain for the remainder of his life.

As Almonester had hoped and expected, his liberality in rebuilding the church was brought to the attention of the Spanish king, Charles IV, whose decree of May 7, 1798, points out that Almonester had seen to it that "the work of reconstruction was performed with the required solidity, having added to the beauty of the Church's interior various decorations such as sculptures, paintings, a well-made marble floor, windows with glazed sashes, bells and other accessories necessary to the splendor of a church which was to serve as a Cathedral. In this work he spent not only the estimated cost, which was set at 72,350 *pesos, 7 reales*, but also an additional 25,635 *pesos*, 2½ *reales*, so that when the said church was left in servicable condition, he had spent a grand total of 98,988 *pesos*, 1½ *reales*. . . ."[142]

When the parish church of New Orleans was elevated to the rank of a cathedral upon the creation of the new Diocese of Louisiana in 1793, Almonester had quickly changed his plans and added the embellishments mentioned above by the king, as well as a gallery on each side of the nave with a fine choir balustrade and the high altar. His health was beginning to fail and he feared he might not live to see the completion of the cathedral that was intended to be his most important monument as well as his tomb. On August 20, 1794, Almonester drew up his will before the notary Carlos Ximenes. In it he included references to the new church, and indicated that he had, before his marriage to Louise de la Ronde, set aside a sum of 400,000 *pesos* for his philanthropic works, from which fund the cost of the church was being paid. His will states:

> 8] I declare, that of the fund of four hundred thousand pesos which I have said that I had before my second marriage, for the pious works mentioned, one of which is the parish church of San Luis in this city, some money remains at my disposal, wherefore I

141 Cabildo Minutes, III, no. 2, 100.
142 "Proceedings against Widow Almonester," 12.

order and it is my will that the said church shall be finished with the said remainder and in consideration of its not being sufficient to finish the whole, [let them finish] the iron screen-work belonging to the large sanctuary [*Capilla*], the sacristy and the side chapel, the pulpit in Roman style, the stalls for the lower choir, the high altar in Roman style, and the screen-work toward the galleries.

9] I declare, that the gallery which I have built in the said church in front of the sanctuary, over the principal door of the latter, I have reserved for myself and my family, and I have solicited and petition should be made to His Majesty to obtain the assignment [approval] of this; and hoping that the King (whom God preserve) may be pleased to grant it, I order, and it is my wish that this privilege and favor which I hope for may descend to my successors.[143]

By the end of the year 1794 the new cathedral was nearing completion. On December 8 it almost met disaster, for on that day the city was struck by a second conflagration. Starting on Royal Street between St. Louis and Toulouse, the fire spread rapidly over many of the structures that had been rebuilt since the fire of 1788. The flames leaped across St. Peter Street and again destroyed the *corps de garde*, which was being used as the parish church, severely damaged the prisons in its rear, and destroyed the small fire-engine house that had been built on the site of the old Cabildo, across Orleans Alley from the new cathedral. At this point, almost as if by a miracle, the wind shifted, and the fire reversed itself and spread in the opposite direction, cutting a swath of destruction as far as the city fortifications, along present Canal Street. The new cathedral was saved and hastily completed in time for the Christmas services that year.[144]

An account of the dedication was recorded at the time by Father Joaquín de Portillo:

In the year of our Lord 1794, in the twentieth of the Pontificate of our Holy Father, Pope Pius VI, and in the seventh year of the reign of His Catholic Majesty, Don Carlos IV, Don Luis Peñalver y Cárdenas being elected first bishop of the newly erected See of Louisiana; Baron de Carondelet, Brigadier General of the Royal Army, being governor of this city and province, on the 23rd day of the month of December, the new St. Louis parochial church of this city was blessed.

[143] *LHQ*, IV, 21.
[144] Huber and Wilson, *The Basilica*, 467, 629.

219

This parochial church, which became the Cathedral church since the erection of Louisiana into a diocese distinct from that of Havana, owes it existence to the piety and zeal of Don Andrés Almonester y Roxas, a native of the city of Mayrena del Alcor, kingdom of Sevilla, in Spain, a knight of the illustrious Order of Carlos III, colonel of the militia of New Orleans and perpetual Regidor of the Supreme Court.

This knight, so commendable for his eminent piety, is almost without an equal; the three churches of this city in which are offered prayer and sacrifice to our Lord are monuments of his devotion and piety. At his own expense he built the Chapel of the Ursuline Convent, a school for young girls, the Charity Hospital and its chapel, and also donated ground to serve as a site for a lepers' home.

These works alone would suffice to make his name illustrious, and gain for him the esteem and friendship of all his fellow-citizens. Yet, he did more. A fire having destroyed the parochial church on the 21st of March, 1788, the grief of the people made him conceive the vast project, worthy of his great heart, of rebuilding this sanctuary at his own expense. The edifice was begun in March, 1789, and in spite of a thousand obstacles, Almonester succeeded within five years in giving it the perfection, grandeur, solidity and beauty which we now admire.

Finally, the parish being unable, for want of funds, to decorate the interior in a manner worthy of a cathedral, he took upon himself the necessary expense of building a gallery on each side of the nave and providing a beautiful balustrade for the choir, together with a main altar on which the workmen were still engaged when another terrible fire broke out on the 8th of December and destroyed the temporary chapel. The Blessed Sacrament was carried to the chapel of the Ursulines and the ornamentation of the main altar hastily completed to receive our Lord so that the people might with more facility assist at the offices of the Church.

The new edifice was blessed on the day and in the year before mentioned, in the presence of the ecclesiastical and civil authorities of this city. At the opening of the ceremony, our illustrious benefactor presented the keys of the church to the Governor, who then handed them over to me. Immediately afterwards, Don Patricio Walsh, an Irish priest, chaplain of the Royal Hospital, Foreign Vicar, Ecclesiastical Judge of the Province for the Bishop of Havana (the Bishop of Louisiana having not yet taken possession), blessed the church. The Holy Sacrifice of the Mass followed the blessing, and these magnificent ceremonies filled with joy the hearts of all the faithful.

The next day, December 24, the clergy assembled in the monastery of the Ursulines, to which the Blessed Sacrament had been carried after the fire of December 8. The Governor, with all the notable personages of the city, also met therein; a procession was formed and the Blessed Sacrament carried with the greatest solemnity to the new church, in which I sang the first Mass and preached the first sermon.

After the benediction of the Blessed Sacrament, the ceremony was closed by the chanting of the *Te Deum* for the greater glory of God, and this was followed by loud salutes of artillery. It is then but just that the people and the ministers of the church should render perpetual gratitude to their illustrious and noble benefactor, Don Andrés Almonester y Roxas, and it is to prevent his works from falling into oblivion that I mention his name here "Ad perpetuam rei memoriam."

Don Joaquín de Portillo   December 30, 1794[145]

Almonester's friend Miró was succeeded as governor of Louisiana by François Louis Hector, Baron de Carondelet, who took the oath of office in the presence of the cabildo on December 31, 1791. It was he who by law enjoyed the privileges of vice-patron royal in the cathedral, an honor coveted by Almonester. The donor was, however, awarded a seat of honor by the bishop and the privilege of burial in the cathedral, these honors being conferred by the Spanish king in his above-mentioned decree of May 7, 1798:

in consideration of the fact that the laws forbid that Don Andrés Almonester y Roxas be granted the patronage of the Cathedral Church as he petitioned, therefore, I have resolved that said Don Andrés may hold the right to the seat granted him by the Reverend Bishop in the Choir of the said Church, and also that he be assigned a chapel, outside of the main one, to serve as his tomb with an inscribed flat stone placed on the exterior of the chapel proclaiming his generosity, piety, and liberality in the reconstruction of the Cathedral Church as well as in the works of the Hospital, the school of the Ursulines, and others, in which he has spent very large sums, and for all of which he has merited my Royal gratitude, as well as that he be so informed in my Royal name, and also that his deeds shall be borne in mind in the event he may ask for any other particular grace that may not be in conflict with the laws, resting assured that my Royal will, always benevolent toward my loyal subjects, shall be prompted to grant it.[146]

[145] Chambon, *In and Around the Old St. Louis Cathedral*, 39.
[146] "Proceedings against Widow Almonester," 15.

221

In previous decrees dated August 14, 1794, and May 4, 1795, which Almonester presented to the cabildo at its session of November 6, 1795, the king had made most flattering references to Almonester's generosity and deplored local court actions against him and apparent local opposition and animosity toward him. The king also admonished Governor Carondelet to "distinguish, assist and attend in a very special way, the said Almonester in everything he might justly require, without giving him cause to complain, for he has endeared himself to my Royal Person . . . as a subject whose actions have so well distinguished him by donating a large part of his wealth for the construction of the cathedral. . . ."[147] As a reward for Almonester's "inspiring zeal . . . in the construction of the parish church of New Orleans, built and decorated at your expense," the king on March 30, 1795, told Almonester that he had "seen fit . . . to grant you the use and as your property, a special pew erected on the inside of the said church and over the principal entrance. . . ." The special pew was to bring about a controversy in later years when his daughter Micaëla, Baroness Pontalba, directed her agent, N. B. LeBreton, to write the church wardens on April 3, 1832, "to reclaim from you her tribune which is located in the cathedral church, facing the chapel, and to which she has the right of full ownership."[148] By that time, however, under the American democracy, such royal privileges had lost their meaning.

Almonester was evidently not on the same good terms with Carondelet as he had been with Miró and felt that the new governor did not appreciate his charitable works, but saw only his selfish aims of honors and patronage. In a letter to Miró written on April 26, 1792, Joseph Xavier Delfau de Pontalba said:

> . . . we dined at Almonester's, who regrets you from the depths of his heart. He told me frankly that he would never find anyone to rejoice in the good that befalls others as much as you. He is entirely disgusted with being beneficent. Under your reign it was a joy to him, for you knew how to appreciate it, but now he intends to be selfish. He has abandoned the church. He has not laid a brick on it since your departure, and he added that before he takes up the work again they will have time to render an account to the court. He laid it aside to enjoy the patronage of the hospital and of the nuns. The Baron [de Carondelet] told him that the King's approbation was necessary. He [Almonester] pretends that the approval the King gave for the work is sufficient. . . . He supposes

[147] Cabildo Minutes, IV, no. 1, 60–63.
[148] Miscellaneous Cathedral MSS, SLCA.

that when he produces the inventory of the goods of the hospital, they will ask for remittal of the revenues with which he has endowed it. His intention is to answer that as the King's approval is necessary for the patronage, he also demands it for the endowment.

If force is brought to bear to compel him to turn it over, he will give in under protest and declare that he renounces the continuation of the church. . . . He is inconsolably awaiting the outcome and is being tormented in his old age.[149]

Governor Carondelet himself was one of those who had reported local feelings against Almonester during the course of construction of the cathedral. In a letter to Captain General Las Casas of Cuba, dated August 20, 1792, Carondelet wrote:

The said Colonel Don Andrés Almonester, having enriched himself in this colony while exercising the office of notary public, undertook the erection of several public works, which to his efforts were highly useful, such as the Charity Hospital, which was destroyed by the last hurricane that struck this city, and which he reconstructed. He built the chapel of the Ursuline Nuns, and at present the parochial church, which is well advanced.

It seems as if these proofs of patriotism should have won for Don Andrés Almonester the good will of all the citizens, but it has turned out all to the contrary. The opposition that they have shown him, has arrived to such a degree, that they would sooner stop attending Mass than enter the church he is constructing. I believe that a great part of this hatred is due to the fact that almost the entire city was destroyed four years ago by a very fierce and disastrous fire, and that many unfortunates, finding themselves without shelter, turned to Don Andrés in order to rent some of the houses belonging to him, which had escaped being destroyed by the fire, and because of this he suddenly raised the rent of his clients. He took advantage of the unfortunate public in order to increase his capital. In the meanwhile he vacated the command of the militia battalion serving in this city.

After I had made His Majesty acquainted in regard to the expenses Don Andrés Almonester had been put to in favor of the public welfare, he (His Majesty) deigned to promote him to the rank of colonel and in command of the militia. This news caused the greatest consternation among the populace, due to the aforementioned reasons. . . .[150]

---

149 Pontalba Miscellaneous Correspondence (translations), letter 6, LSM.

150 "Dispatches of the Spanish Governors," II, 12; AGI, *Papeles de Cuba, leg.* 1441, no. 179.

Almonester lived for several years after the completion of the great church and enjoyed the privileges of his tribune of honor. He also had the distinction of being invested there with the royal order of Charles III on September 8, 1796. His neighbor, Pontalba, commented as follows: "He was enveloped in the great mantle of the Order and his train was carried by three lackeys in red. An immense crowd followed him as he went in state from the cathedral to his dwelling. . . ." Pontalba, referring to Almonester as "the famous Knight of Charles III," added: "That poor man is never satisfied. As soon as he gets one thing he strives for another. Now his mind is full with the title of Brigadier and he can talk of nothing else."[151]

When Don Andrés wrote his will in 1794 he left specific instructions regarding his burial, stating that "my body I commit to the earth . . . and order that on my dying, it be dressed with my military insignia and given burial in the parish church of San Luis in this city, built at my expense, in such place as may be designated by my executors." When he had finished writing the will, however, he changed this provision in a gesture of humility, stating "that it was his desire that he should be buried in the cemetery or ground consecrated to the burial of the faithful, for on further reflection he has decided it thus, as deeming it fit, and that it not be done in the church as he had resolved."[152] Thus it was that at his death his body was buried in the parish cemetery, from whence it was later removed by order of the king and buried in the cathedral,[153] where it still rests.

Almonester's cathedral, being the central element in the composition facing the public square, never failed to attract the attention of visitors. Francis Baily, an Englishman visiting New Orleans in 1797, said merely that "the church is a plain brick building of the Ionic order and is fitted up within in nearly the same style that all Roman Catholic chapels are. It no farther attracts the attention than as being the best edifice in the place."[154]

Thomas Ashe, visiting in 1806, was apparently more impressed:

> The religion is Roman Catholic: that is, the religion of the French and Spanish is Catholic: as for the Americans, they have none. They disregard the Sabbath entirely; or if they go to the Catholic Church, there not being any other, they go as to a specta-

---

[151] Grace King, *Creole Families of New Orleans* (New York, 1921), 98.

[152] Dart, ed., "Almonester's Will," 28.

[153] Funeral Records, 1793–1803, no. 314, Apr. 26, 1798; no. 642, Nov. 11, 1799, SLCA.

[154] Francis Baily, *Journal of a Tour in Unsettled Parts of North America in 1796 and 1797* (London, 1856), 299.

cle, where fine women are to be seen, and where fine music is to be heard!

The Catholic church, as well as the town-house, the jail, and the palace of the priests, were all built by the once celebrated merchant Don Andrés, on condition that he should be made a noble of Spain. He lived to expend two millions of dollars on these and other public works, but he died before the ambitious honors were lavished on him; and his wife has the mortification still to be called Madame André.

The church is a very large structure, built of brick, and plastered and painted in front, to give it the appearance of marble.

The altar is magnificent for the western world, and is adorned with paintings and sculpture of considerable taste.—Queen Esther, fainting away in the presence of Ahasueras, is fine; for though she is lost to sense, and in a swoon, her majesty and beauty still remain. She is dressed in her royal robes, and as she sinks, she leans to the right side, and is supported by one of the ladies who attend her; they are six in number, elegantly dressed, and handsome.—There is another lady and a youth, who do their utmost to keep the Queen from falling. Her neck is bare, and her arms hang motionless; and her body is as weak and helpless as if the soul had left it; the retiring of the blood, the falling of the muscles, and the natural and graceful manner in which she dies away, are expressed with the greatest skill and propriety. The King seems surprized, and rises from his throne with his sceptre in his hand, as giving his assistance. The persons that attend upon the King, both by their actions and countenances, appear to be under the same concern. Haman, who is the cause of this distress, stands in the presence chamber wearing a gold collar, behind the throne and appears to be affected, and to share in the calamity. There stands a spirited figure of an officer, in rich armour, with one of the ensigns of war in his hand; his attention seems to be taken up with what passes. At a distance are other soldiers that belong to the guard. There is a youth also near the throne, dressed in scarlet, with a white shock dog in his arms, which has a very good effect.

In the sacristy there are several relics, among which there is a thorn of our Savior's crown, tinged with his blood; a cloth of Santa Veronica, enriched with his image, and a cross of Indian workmanship, said to have been found on the banks of the river Noir, on the very spot where the famous Ferdinand de Soto ended his discoveries and his life, and where his remains now lie buried. The priest who exhibited the altar and the relics, appeared much displeased with the little belief afforded them by the Americans, and informed the bishops of Cuba and Mexico to forward all the pictures and relics from the churches of Louisiana to New Spain, where the honours of belief and admiration, in anxious solicitude await them.[155]

Fortescue Cuming, visiting New Orleans a year or so later, says that he went "to the Roman church; found it elegantly ornamented and upon the whole to exceed my most sanguine expectations."[156]

In 1819–20 the architect Benjamin H. Latrobe designed and built a central tower on the cathedral to contain the town clock, making a rather careful elevation drawing of the building at it was in 1819, and remarking that the building was "extremely discolored and looks venerable beyond its years which are only 25." This tower was one of Latrobe's last projects, for he died in New Orleans of yellow fever on September 3, 1820.[157]

Various proposals were made in the 1830s for remodeling and enlarging the cathedral, but nothing was done until 1849 after the mansard roofs had been added to the Cabildo and the Presbytère. Then the building, except for a part of the front wall, was demolished and rebuilt in its present form as designed by the French architect J. N. B. de Pouilly.[158] The historian Charles Gayarré was outraged that Almonester's cathedral should be so completely destroyed: "Although the monumental and venerable relic of the past was pulled down in 1850 in the wantonness of vandalism to make room for the upstart production of bad taste, yet the stone which covered the mortal remains of the pious founder of the destroyed temple has at least been respected."[159]

Although practically nothing recognizable of Almonester's building remains in the present St. Louis Cathedral, the basilica on Jackson Square will always be associated with its benefactor, who lies buried beneath its floor.

THE PRESBYTÈRE

After the terrible Good Friday fire, March 21, 1788, Almonester offered to rebuild the church rectory or presbytère at the same time that he offered to rebuild the parish church. This first generous gesture was made the day after the fire, when a special meeting or junta was held,

[155] Thomas Ashe, *Travels in America* (London, 1808), 336.

[156] Fortescue Cuming, *Sketches of a Tour to the Western Country . . .* , vol. IV, *Early Western Travels, 1748–1846*, ed. Reuben Gold Thwaites (Cleveland, 1904), 364.

[157] Huber and Wilson, *The Basilica*, 20.

[158] *Ibid.*, 27.

[159] Gayarré, *Louisiana, Spanish Domination*, 271.

the proceedings of which were reported by Governor Miró in a letter of April 1, 1788.[160] On March 15, 1789, when the cornerstones of the new church were laid, no mention was made of beginning construction of the rectory on the adjacent site, where the Capuchin clergy of New Orleans had resided since the beginnings of the colony.

The first simple frame structure, built at the corner of Chartres and St. Ann streets, matched the *corps de garde* at the St. Peter Street corner on the other side of the church facing the public square. Both were designed by Adrien de Pauger, the French military engineer who had laid out the plan of New Orleans in March of 1721 and designated the site for these buildings. Built at the expense of the Company of the Indies, construction of the first Presbytère was begun late in 1723 or early 1724 and completed during the following year, 1725. By 1738 it was almost in ruins,[161] but because of the Chickasaw wars, nothing was done to rebuild it until 1744. It was then decided to build a new structure, to be financed by a tax upon the parishioners as well as upon the clergy and religious.[162] A new two-story brick building was then built, and on July 8, 1753, a payment was made by the church wardens "to the Sr. Dubreuil on account of what is due him by the parish for the Presbytère building."[163] Jonathas Darby, writing about this time, stated that "the house of the two Capuchins [next to the church] . . . is a fine two story brick building."[164] Darby was for several years the church treasurer.

Either the new Presbytère was left in an unfinished state or it rapidly deteriorated, for when the British captain Philip Pittman visited New Orleans about 1765, he wrote: "The Capuchins are the curates of New Orleans; on the left hand side of the church, they had a very handsome and commodious brick house, which is totally destroyed and gone to ruin; they now live on their plantation and in a hired house in town."[165]

The "hired house in town" was one rented from the Charity Hospital for Father Dagobert for 800 *livres* per year, according to the church's financial records of 1769.[166] The plantation was probably the one known as "La Metairie," a large tract along both sides of Bayou Me-

[160] Kinnaird, ed., *Spain in the Mississippi Valley*, II, 372.

[161] *LHQ*, VI, 138.

[162] CF[3], 243, fol. 18, AN.

[163] Financial Records, I, 35, SLCA.

[164] Conrad M. Widman, S.J., "Some Southern Cities (in the U.S.) about 1750," *Records of the American Catholic Historical Society of Philadelphia*, X (June, 1899), 203.

[165] Philip Pittman, *The Present State of the European Settlements on the Mississippi* (London, 1770; Cleveland, 1906), 42.

[166] Financial Records, I, 115.

tairie, extending in the rear to Lake Pontchartrain. It was eventually purchased from the Capuchins by Almonester on August 2, 1784, and sold off in smaller portions in subsequent years. The late historian Roger Baudier stated that "when O'Reilly arrived in the city [in 1769] and noted the ruined presbytère he ordered a new house built. The work was undertaken by Monsieur Durel, whose work was accepted and payment approved by Gálvez in 1777."[167] Whether this was an entirely new building or an extensive renovation of the earlier French colonial structure is unknown, but the building must have been in a fairly good state of repair when it was destroyed in the fire of 1788.

Although Almonester's offer to rebuild the Presbytère was apparently first made the day after the fire, nothing was done for several years. In Miró's letter of April 1, 1788, to Don Antonio Valdéz, the governor stated that Almonester had promised to construct a new church, "and near by, a house suitable for lodging the reverend father Vicar, the priest's assistants and the chief sacristan." In his letter to Don Antonio Porlier of August 10, 1790, in which he referred to his earlier letter to Valdéz, Miró stated, regarding Almonester's promises, that

> it has been long since I have heard him say anything to indicate that he intended to fulfill the second part of his promise, that is, to build the rectory; but I have not lost hope that he will do so if he suffers no decline in income, which consists principally in rents from houses. Your Excellency will please inform me as to whether or not I should compel him to do so if he refuses, in view of the formality with which he made the promise. . . . The rectory needed to lodge the *religiosos* serving this parish, and where the reverend Bishop planned to live as before, was built with the aid of a gift from the citizens here generally; but as they were badly hit by the fire which destroyed it, I fear that, in case Almonester does not rebuild it and the Reverend Bishop should solicit another gift from the parishioners, it would be very small. I hope that His Majesty will order that the balance be paid from the funds of the mission, which amount to three thousand and eighty five pesos, six reales, with the provision that the cost of said rectory shall not exceed eighty thousand pesos.[168]

It was not until 1791 that a plan for rebuilding the church was drawn by Gilberto Guillemard,[169] although the cornerstones had been laid

---

167 Baudier, *The Catholic Church*, 194.
168 Kinnaird, ed., *Spain in the Mississippi Valley*, II, 374.
169 "Proceedings against Widow Almonester," 12.

two years before. It is probable that Guillemard at the same time drew up plans for rebuilding the Presbytère. When Almonester offered, on January 16, 1795, to rebuild the Cabildo, he specified that he would use "the same plan he will use in reconstructing the priests' house or presbytère."[170]

Guillemard probably made use of the walls of the old Presbytère that stood after the fire of 1788 as he later made use of the surviving walls of the old *corps de garde* in designing the Cabildo. The old Presbytère, as shown in "A View of New Orleans Taken from the Opposite Side of the Mississippi—1765," somewhat resembled the old Ursuline Convent down Chartres Street, a two-story building with pedimented central bay facing the Plaza. The roof, however, appears to have been lower-pitched, with gable ends rather than the steep French-hipped roof of the Ursuline Convent. Like the convent, its windows were segmental-headed, as may still be seen in the front wall of the Presbytère where the stucco has been removed.

The building had eight openings across the front and no central entrance. An old undated plan from the Spanish archives shows a narrow passage running through the building marked "No. 7 Corridor which goes to the parlor," a room the size of two of the other rear rooms. A broad gallery is indicated across the front of the building, but none in the rear. Stairways at each end of this front gallery led to the second story; there was no interior stair. The drawing is rather crude, and the exterior walls are shown only by a single line without any indication of exterior openings or gallery supports. There are two floor plans, identical except for a stairway indication. Each has a list of ten numbers indicating room uses, chimneys, walls, doors, etc. Each bears the following notation: "Note: the house is 103 feet long and 30 wide, the back rooms 14 feet square and the front ones 14 wide and 16 deep, having the same length as before. It should have two floors, the lower one of 10 feet and the upper one of 15 feet. It is understood that two rooms downstairs and two above, upstairs, will belong to the rector and his assistants for the kitchen and dispensary, and the parlor may be added by the rector for holding audiences as confessor."

These plans, which may or may not be the work of Guillemard, may be an early study for rebuilding the Presbytère; they are in many ways similar to another, more carefully drawn plan dated June 12, 1801, signed by Carlos Trudeau. In this later plan the narrow central corridor is omitted and the two center rooms are combined into one. The cross wall dividing front and rear rooms is also omitted except for a small

[170] Cabildo Minutes, III, no. 2, 85.

229

segment intersecting the partition walls, usually where chimneys had been indicated on the earlier plan. This Trudeau plan also shows the arcaded galleries in front and rear, as they exist today except that the engaged columns on the four center piers of the front are not shown. This drawing is entitled "Geometrical Plan of the Presbytère, work erected as far as the crown of the first cornice."[171] To the left, "part of the parochial church" is shown and notes show the "front to the Plaza de Armas," the "front to the patio," the "front to St. Ann street," and the "alley by which to go out to Orleans street."

From these plans it would appear that Guillemard had designed a new facade, the familiar arcaded and pedimented one that still stands, and made use of the old walls of the earlier building with their existing doorways. It will be noted that these old openings do not relate to the arches of the new arcade. It was apparently not until the Presbytère was finally completed in 1813, long after Almonester's death, that the present monumental entrance and flanking arched doorways were installed and the earlier openings bricked up.

Almonester seems to have done but little work on the Presbytère until after the completion of the cathedral at the end of the year 1794. Even then progress was slow, and on July 21, 1797, the cabildo records refer to the fact that Almonester "at the present time is building the priests' house made of brick and lime, the first floor being already finished." Work on the Cabildo was progressing more rapidly, but it too was far from completion. The cabildo records for its meeting of November 10, 1797, again mention that both buildings were designed by Gilberto Guillemard, who at this time pointed out "that he made a plan for the construction of the new Cabildo building and that he is at the present time, directing its construction . . . and he requests that certain compensation be assigned to him. . . ." This was agreed to by the cabildo, but one member, Don Juan de Castanedo, the city treasurer, argued that Almonester should pay these fees since the Cabildo "is to be built on the same plan as the presbytère . . . the engineer who made the plan should not be paid with city funds. . . ."[172]

Almonester did not live to see the completion of either the Presbytère or the Cabildo. He had been in failing health for some time, and on August 20, 1794, had drawn up his will before the notary Carlos Ximenes, a document which he could not sign "because the impediment of the right hand in which his infirmity consists, did not permit him to

171 Baptismal Register I.
172 Cabildo Minutes, IV, no. 3, 85.

do so."[173] Although Almonester lived nearly four years more, witnessing the completion and dedication of his cathedral, work on the Presbytère never progressed above the first floor cornice line. In his will he made no provisions for completing it and in fact made no mention of it or the Cabildo, nor of his two infant daughters, who were born after he had written the 1794 will, to which he apparently added no codicils.

After his death on April 25, 1798, his widow, Louise de la Ronde, whom he had married on March 20, 1787, refused to carry on the work of finishing the Presbytère, claiming that her husband had already depleted his fortune excessively by his charitable works and that anything that remained should be for the benefit of his daughters, Micaëla, who was born on November 6, 1795, and Andrea Antonia, born on October 17, 1797.[174] The former became the celebrated Baroness Pontalba, whose 1850 buildings still flank Jackson Square, but the latter died in infancy.

As a result of the widow's refusal, Bishop Luis Peñalver y Cárdenas filed a suit against her before the Spanish governor Manuel Gayoso de Lemos on March 29, 1799.[175] The bishop had first petitioned the governor to order the completion of the building in a letter of March 11, 1799:

> Under date of September 16th, of last year, Your Lordship tells me, among other things, that after completion of the Cabildo building you will take care that the Rectory of this City be finished, by the late Colonel of the Militia Don Andrés Almonester, as you consider his successors obliged to do this according to the promise made to that effect by the said Colonel to His Majesty, which promise is known to his widow.
>
> As the coming season is the most suitable for the performance of that kind of work and the largest number of unfinished architectural details on the Cabildo building are not in charge of the Colonel's successors, it seems to be the proper time to resume the work, for as time goes by I recognize with increasing certainty the need there is for the proceeds from said building as a source of income to defray the expenses necessary to the maintenance and repair of the church, without which it would go to ruin.[176]

On March 14 following, the governor sent a copy of the bishop's letter to the Widow Almonester so that the "said widow be informed of

[173] *LHQ*, VI, 28.
[174] Funeral Records, Marriage Register, and Baptismal Register for dates cited.
[175] "Proceedings against Widow Almonester," 1.
[176] *Ibid.*

231

the contents thereof, in order that without any delay, she may comply with the obligation contracted by her late husband."[177] The widow immediately replied, asking to be exonerated from any responsibility for completing the Presbytère, pointing out that the inventory of her late husband's estate did not amount to a third of the sum he had spent in charitable works, "which he undertook at a time when he did not expect to have any successors, for it may be assumed reasonably enough that if he had had any at that time he would not have undertaken such expensive works or at least he would have greatly limited his generosity in order to leave his family in a more comfortable position." She then requested the governor "to please grant my petition, or, if denied, to submit this case to the supreme consideration of His Majesty, for him to render His Royal decision."

In accordance with the court's request, she then submitted various proofs of her claims including copies of the baptismal records of her daughters. She also pointed out that to complete the Presbytère would amount to at least 40,000 *pesos*, and added that "it is not presumable that our Most Pious Sovereign would wish or even permit that this new enormous burden be imposed on the two little daughters of one of his subjects, who, with such generous patriotism, spent the largest part of his fortune for the sake of both Majesties."[178]

This celebrated court case contains innumerable documents of great interest, including royal orders of the king, a summary of the inventory of Almonester's estate, the appraisal made by Gilberto Guillemard and Bartolomé Lafon of the work done so far on the Presbytère, and also an estimate that these same two architects made of the work still to be done to complete the building. Included in this latter estimate were three rows of bricks for the flat or terrace roof of the building, thirteen ornamental iron railings for the upper arches of the front and side facades, and nine wood balustrades for the upper arches of the rear gallery. It was estimated that the amount needed to complete the rectory in accordance with the original plan would be 33,327 *pesos*, 7 *reales*, which, added to the 20,935 *pesos* 1 *reale* value of the work already done, would make a grand total of 54,263 *pesos*. The appraisal was dated June 16, 1799.[179]

The bishop and clergy became increasingly impatient at the delay in resuming the work, but the litigation dragged on through the summer. Madame Almonester requested that an appraisal also be made of the Cabildo building, which was likewise in an unfinished condition at Al-

---

[177] *Ibid.*, 2.
[178] *Ibid.*, 5.
[179] *Ibid.*, 32.

monester's death. His estate, however, was to be reimbursed by the city for the cost of this work. She pointed out that "the enormous cost of [the Cabildo building] may as well be considered as a frozen asset for it does not even yield any interest nor can it be expected to be repaid in many years."[180] Meanwhile Governor Gayoso, who had been acting as judge in the proceedings, died on July 18, 1799, to be succeeded as governor and judge by the Marqués de Casa Calvo.

The litigation continued, the bishop's attorney pointing out that the estimate made by Guillemard and Lafon for completing the rectory was excessive. In a petition dated November 16, 1799, Juan de Dios Valdéz protested:

> Without doubting the competency of the appraisers, I must say that they included several structural parts which are of a purely ornamental nature, such as the sculptural work of the facade, the decorative ironwork, the flat ceilings and the cornices, as well as others that are not necessary, such as the quarry stone flooring and several very costly items such as the staircases and the covering of the roof with three different layers of bricks, which would require a very heavy framework. This is now in disuse because of its little durability, tile being substituted at half the cost besides its far greater longevity.[181]

He also proposed other economies, saying that it is "unwise to attempt the performance of a work such as the one in question, with all the pomposity suggested by the appraisers. It would suffice that it be completed with the necessary solidity and propriety." He also pointed out that Almonester had, on January 14, 1796, after the birth of his first daughter, renewed his offer to rebuild the Presbytère. In her reply to the arguments, Madame Almonester revealed that she and her husband had not always agreed on such matters:

> . . . in renewing such promise, my husband was moved by two factors: one, the honest purpose of not breaking his word, and the other a spiteful feeling he harbored against me because of certain domestic disagreements, some of which grew out of my just opposition to his excessive spending, he having set his mind upon squandering our entire estate. . . . It is therefore quite understandable that if, during our married life, I opposed my husband's enormous outlays, out of which serious differences arose between

180 *Ibid.*, 38.
181 *Ibid.*, 51.

us, I should now after his death endeavor to discontinue such outlays. Nothing else proves more conclusively my difference of
opinion on such expenditures than the fact that I never intervened
in the planning of the work in question, nor in any other way. . . .[182]

Madame Almonester became more vehement in her opposition as the
proceedings continued, all of which were conducted in Spanish. She had
apparently approved some statements that she had not understood, ob-
serving that "I would never have consented to such statements had I had
any knowledge of the Spanish language, with which, as it is publicly
known, I am not acquainted." She also pointed out to the opposing
churchmen that apparently "God did not will it to be finished by the
devout benefactor who undertook it." She then appealed to the new
governor to submit the matter to the Spanish king. The governor,
however, on February 1, 1800, decreed that in spite of her objections, Madame Almonester was obliged to complete the building as had been promised by her late husband. The lady was not one to give up the struggle
easily; new petitions were filed, legal opinions quoted, and civil and
canon laws cited. The records of the case were finally sent to Spain for
consideration by the king and the Royal and Supreme Council of the
Indies. On June 17, 1801, the king, Charles IV, sent his decree to the
Louisiana governor, reminding him that "by Royal Decree of July 14,
1800, I directed you not to molest nor for the time being compel Doña
Luisa de la Ronde, widow of Don Andrés de Almonester, or her children to complete the works left unfinished by her said husband." In conclusion the king declared that "I have resolved to declare the estate of
Almonester and his family free of the aforesaid obligation, as this is my
will—I the King."[183]

Thus the work on the Presbytère was not resumed. A temporary roof
was put over the unfinished structure and the rooms rented out as stores.
In 1803 the artist Boqueta de Woiseri sketched the Plaza de Armas and
showed the Presbytère as a one-story building. It remained in this incomplete condition until 1813, when the church wardens contracted
with the architect-builders Claude Gurlie and Joseph Guillot, whose specifications for its completion, dated July 1, 1813, are preserved in the St.
Louis Cathedral Archives. The building was never used for its intended
purpose as a rectory but continued to be rented out as stores and apart-
ments. Some of the rooms were eventually rented as court rooms, and in
1834 the entire building was leased by the Orleans Parish Police Jury as

182 *Ibid.*, 55.
183 *Ibid.*, 114.

a courthouse. In 1853 the city bought the building, which by that time had had several additions including the present mansard roof, built in 1847.[184] It continued in use as a courthouse until the courthouse at Royal and Conti streets was built in 1911. The Presbytère then became part of the Louisiana State Museum, which still occupies this historic building so ambitiously begun by Almonester.

THE CABILDO

The cabildo was the name applied to the governing body of most Spanish-American cities and to the one instituted by the Spanish governor Don Alexandro O'Reilly in 1769, after he abolished the rebellious New Orleans Superior Council that had governed the city since its founding.[185] He then had a new building constructed to house the cabildo[186] on the site of the front part of the prison that the French had built in 1730 adjacent to the parish church. In 1750–53 they also built a large *corps de garde* or police station, adjacent to the prison, at the corner of Chartres and St. Peter streets.[187] In the great fire of March 21, 1788, O'Reilly's Cabildo building, of brick-between-posts construction, was totally destroyed, as were the roof and other wooden parts of the *corps de garde*. Most of its massive brick walls, however, remained standing. A new roof was soon erected and the building repaired and put to use as a temporary church[188] until a new one could be built on the old site.

Following the fire, the cabildo for a time held its sessions in the Government House (at Toulouse and Decatur streets). This was, however, contrary to the laws of the Indies, so the cabildo sought suitable rooms that might be rented as a meeting place until its building could be rebuilt. Rooms in the upper story of Almonester's own large residence at the corner of St. Peter and Levee (Decatur), overlooking the Plaza de Armas, were finally selected[189] and used until the new Cabildo was finished in 1799. Rents were paid annually to Almonester and, after his death, to his widow.[190]

Nothing was done about rebuilding the Cabildo for several years, as

[184] Acts of Joseph Couvillier, XLVII, 247, July 12, 1847, NONA.
[185] Gayarré, *Louisiana, Spanish Domination*, 3.
[186] Louisiana Miscellaneous Documents, 1599–1602; *LHQ*, VI, 521.
[187] *Ibid.*, 1086.
[188] Kinnaird, ed., *Spain in the Mississippi Valley*, II, 372.
[189] Cabildo Minutes, II, 155, Oct. 21, 1791; 161, Dec. 2, 1791.
[190] MS rent receipts in the collection of Samuel Wilson, Jr.

no funds were available in the city treasury and none were forthcoming from the king, as this was considered a city project—a city hall, not a royal property. Meanwhile the temporary church, in the old, repaired *corps de garde*, was destroyed in the second great fire that occurred on December 8, 1794, again leaving only its heavy brick walls standing. Fortunately the new cathedral that Almonester was building adjacent to the old Cabildo site escaped the 1794 conflagration and, a little over two weeks later, was dedicated. The completion of this, his major project, left Almonester free to continue the work on the Presbytère on the lower side of the church. To be certain that the Cabildo would be built in a style compatible with Guillemard's design that he had adopted for the new Presbytère, Almonester decided that he should also build the new Cabildo. If no funds were available he would provide the funds himself as a loan to the city.

Thus it was that at the session held in Almonester's residence on January 16, 1795, when the problems of rebuilding the Cabildo were discussed by its members, "Don Andrés Almonester y Roxas generously promised that he would reconstruct the Cabildo building following the same plan he is using in constructing the Presbytère. At the time the building shall have been completed, it shall be appraised and its value will be paid out of city funds, in installments, without detriment to the City Treasury nor causing delays in making other payments to which this office must attend. The commissioners, grateful for such a generous offer, accepted it, duly thanking Don Andrés Almonester y Roxas and they agreed to let this gentleman proceed to reconstruct it under the terms he has proposed, giving him sufficient authority to carry it out."[191]

Guillemard, who had designed the Presbytère and the cathedral and probably most of Almonester's other buildings as well, prepared plans for the new Cabildo and spent much of his time in supervising its construction. It was soon decided that the new building would occupy not only the site of the old one destroyed in 1788 but also should include the old *corps de garde* that had been so severely damaged by both fires. Governor Carondelet pointed out to the members of the cabildo that in accepting Almonester's offer they had failed to inform him that

> the said Cabildo should extend to the corner of the Plaza [to St. Peter Street] including 41 feet front by 60 feet in depth belonging to His Majesty and assigned to quarter the main troops, leaving the lower floor of this building for the same purpose, constructing

191 Cabildo Minutes, II, 191.

236

therein the rooms that might be required for the officer and soldiers of the guard, the upper floor remaining for the use of the Cabildo forever.

For this purpose, all the ruins and bricks remaining on the grounds would be left for Don Andrés and 2,000 *pesos* besides would be delivered to him from the Royal Treasury. The Intendant with whom His Excellency held a conference about this matter, gave his consent, finding the proposition profitable to the Royal interests. It would otherwise be necessary to construct another building in the same place at His Majesty's expense for the use of the said guard. . . .[192]

The 2,000 *pesos* were given to Almonester to cover the costs of repairing the *corps de garde* for the king's account. The brick walls were restored and the windows and doors replaced. Entirely new construction was required on the site of the old Cabildo, and the two units were then combined by the great arcaded galleries that Guillemard designed for the facades of both the Presbytère and the Cabildo. The spacing of the five casement windows on the St. Peter Street side of the *corps de garde* dictated the spacing of the windows of the council chamber or *sala capitular* above, the great room intended for the meetings of the cabildo.

No plans or specifications for the Cabildo have been found, though several of Guillemard's plans for repairs and additions to the prisons in the rear exist in the city archives. Few references were made to it in known contemporary documents during the four-year period of its construction. Work had, however, been started by December 4, 1795, for on that date the cabildo "agreed that the hangman could not continue living in the place where he now resides as it is the place where Don Andrés Almonester has started to build the *Casas Capitulares*."[193]

While waiting for the completion of the new building, the cabildo continued to hold its sessions in the rooms it had rented in Almonester's residence. Each year he received the annual rental of 240 *pesos* on December 31 from Don Juan de Castanedo, the city treasurer, for which Almonester gave a signed receipt. Aside from this rent and the 2,000 *pesos* given him from the royal treasury, Almonester was given no payments during his lifetime for the work and expense he incurred in building the new Cabildo. Actually the intendant's action in advancing the initial 2,000 *pesos* was not officially approved until he received a royal

[192] *Ibid.*, IV, no. 1, 58, Nov. 6, 1795.
[193] *Ibid.*, 72.

order from the Spanish court dated June 8, 1796, signed by Diego de Gardoqui and addressed to the intendant of Louisiana in acknowledgment of his letter of January 30, nearly six months before.[194]

In his letter to Spain explaining the terms of his agreement with Almonester for building the *corps de garde* as part of the new Cabildo, the intendant, Francisco Rendón, said:

> Most Excellent Sir:
> In the conflagration of the 8 of December of the past year 1794, the flames consumed the royal prison of this capital and the principal *corps de garde* contiguous to it, that occupied a lot belonging to His Majesty of 41 feet of front by 60 of depth. The city government ordered the rebuilding of the most necessary cells for the security of the prisoners, and I equipped one at small cost for the guard. Meanwhile, determined to replace the ruins, but having discussed in the Cabildo the rebuilding of the *Casa Capitular* that formerly stood next to the same lot on which the *corps de garde* was situated, Colonel of Militia Don Andrés Almonester offered to take charge of its construction under the same plan as the presbytère that occupied the other side of the church, with the idea of unifying the front of the Plaza, which in truth would beautify it, for they would form two wings to the temple that has just been finished and used for the first time.
> The Governor, Baron de Carondelet, thought it suitable to the interests of the King that the said Don Andrés Almonester should take charge of building the principal (*corps de garde*), uniting the lots, aligning the building to the same front as the one on the other side. He in fact made this proposition to him, which the said Almonester accepted (always ready to sacrifice a great part of his magnificent fortune in public works, as he did at his own expense for the Cathedral, Church of the Nuns, Charity Hospital, and the said Casa Curial [Presbytère]), with the sole condition that there be ceded to him, the brick ruins which are standing on the lot, and two thousand *pesos* that he believes must be spent to buy the requisite materials for the walls and partitions of the said *corps de garde*, taking it upon himself to finally deliver it in all its extent without the King having to make any other expenditure.[195]

The intendant concluded his account of his arrangements with Almonester by pointing out that, after careful study, he was convinced that to build an entirely new and separate building for the *corps de garde* would cost the royal treasury from 4,000 to 5,000 *pesos* besides

---

[194] *Ibid.*, no. 3, 188, Dec. 7, 1798.
[195] Miscellaneous Spanish Documents, fol. 369, NOPL.

the annual maintenance costs. By taking advantage of Almonester's offer, a larger and better finished building would be obtained by the king and most of the expenses for repairs would be borne by the cabildo, as the upper part of the building, including its roof, would be the property of the city.

Thus the Cabildo was built and financed almost entirely by Almonester. Although he was not always well liked by his contemporaries, including no doubt some of his fellow members of the cabildo, Almonester's generosity in the donation of public works to the city and his paying for the construction of the new Cabildo as the work progressed could not but be acknowledged and recognized. Thus at its session on July 21, 1797, the cabildo commended him for his public-spiritedness. After listing the various buildings he had built at his own expense, they mentioned that only for the Cabildo would he ever expect any repayment. The progress of the work, the generous terms of his agreement, and their gratitude were then explained as follows:

> Perhaps by the early part of next year the Cabildo building will be completed in brick from top to bottom. No doubt its cost will be over 30,000 *pesos* . . . [for which] the city is only to make partial payments from what is left in the City Treasury after its annual expenses have been covered, to be applied to its appraised value after the said building is completed. This benefit is considered a great favor, for the cash on hand in the city treasury is usually pledged for public outlays, and if there should be a balance left, it is not of a considerable amount. The results therefore will be that several years will elapse before this amount can be paid, the actual benefit at the present time being in favor of this city and none in favor of the benefactor. . . . Without his liberality we could not have a Cabildo building in this city without having to implore His Majesty's mercy in order to obtain some means for this purpose. As it seems to the Commissioners that the city is anxious to express to the said benefactor how grateful we are, in an honorable and creditable manner for said buildings, which is the only thing his modesty would accept, the Commissioners agreed that with city funds, a portrait of the said Don Andrés be made and placed in the chambers of the Cabildo, with the proper inscription concerning his deeds and liberality.[196]

A life-size portrait of Almonester with such an inscription was painted, but dated 1796, a year before the resolution was passed. It is be-

[196] Cabildo Minutes, IV, no. 3, 3, July 21, 1797.

lieved to be the work of José de Salazar y Mendoza, a native of Mérida, in Yucatan, Mexico, who is referred to by a contemporary in New Orleans, the Irishman Mathias James O'Conway, as "the celebrated, self-taught, portrait painter."[197] Perhaps Salazar painted a duplicate of the 1796 work, or possibly the cabildo purchased an already completed portrait to hang in its council chamber.

At the same meeting of the cabildo at which the portrait of Almonester was authorized, Don Andrés presented a document "in which he requests their Lordships to please order that the enclosed certificate be recorded and filed in order that it be returned to him, together with the coat of arms and blazon concerning his illustrious family's name so that he may make use of them and be shown the honors and preeminences he is entitled to as a nobleman and famous Knight."

The coat of arms, which was duly recorded, appears in one corner of the Almonester portrait, now owned by the St. Louis Cathedral. In it he appears with a rather pompous air, ready to be shown the honors he so coveted, the insignia of the royal order of Charles III prominently displayed on the lapel of his coat. On a cartouche in another corner of the portrait is the "inscription concerning his deeds and liberality." This inscription is almost exactly the same as the epitaph on his tombstone in the St. Louis Cathedral.

Almonester's health had begun to fail several years before, as indicated by the writing of his will in 1794. It was after this, however, that he undertook the construction of the Cabildo, and he continued to play an active part in the affairs of the city and to attend to his duties as the perpetual commissioner and royal ensign of the cabildo, which duties included the inspection of the frequent repairs and improvements to the royal prison behind his new Cabildo building. But he was not destined to live to see the completion of his last and perhaps most important building project. On April 20, 1798, he attended his last meeting of the cabildo, which was still holding its sessions in his residence. Five days later, on April 25, 1798, he died. He was buried the following day in the parish cemetery behind his Charity Hospital building in accordance with the desire expressed in his will.[198] Later his body was transferred to his tomb in the cathedral.

Don Manuel Gayoso de Lemos, who had succeeded Carondelet as governor, suggested that if it was agreeable to Almonester's widow, the work on the Cabildo should be carried on under the direction of its

[197] O'Conway Journals, American Catholic Historical Society of Philadelphia Archives, St. Charles Borromeo Seminary, Overbrook, Pa.
[198] Funeral Records, no. 314, Apr. 26, 1798.

architect Guillemard. An appraisal of the work on the new building was ordered to be made by two experts representing the cabildo and two representing the Widow Almonester in order to determine the amount due his estate for the project. Hilaire Boutté and Godefroy Dujarreau, prominent architect-builders, were appointed by the cabildo. Not until October did Madame Almonester appoint Nicolás de Finiels and Bartolomé Lafon to represent her in the appraisal, which was to be made in the presence of Guillemard.[199]

Meanwhile, on December 3, 1798, Madame Almonester had asked to be relieved of the obligation of completing her husband's project, stating to the governor "that my present condition, by virtue of various occupations, does not permit me to continue to supervise the completion of the Cabildo, and as there are a few small items to be finished, as the ceiling and staircase, requests your Lordships to please accept my withdrawal from continuing it, leaving the said building in its present unfinished condition. . . ."[200]

This withdrawal was agreed to by the cabildo, the building was finished entirely under Guillemard's direction, and the debt due Almonester's estate was paid off within a few years. The building was substantially completed and the first session held in the new *sala capitular* on May 10, 1799. On December 30, 1799, Louise de la Ronde, Widow Almonester, gave a receipt to the city treasurer for four months' rent "of rooms of my property that served as a council chamber [*capitulares*], at the rate of twenty *pesos* per month, from the first of January until the end of April, when the Cabildo moved to one of the rooms of the new *Casa Capitular*. . . ."[201]

The appraisers eventually completed their work, with Hilaire Boutté being replaced by Carlos Trudeau. They had spent more than five months and fifty-two sessions at the task, "sometimes from sunrise until midnight,"[202] for which they were offered in compensation by the cabildo only "eleven *reales* for each session, a price lower than the wages allowed a day laborer."[203] A fee of 22 *reales* for each session was recommended by Guillemard on June 3, 1803, but as late as August 10, 1804, at least one of the appraisers, Dujarreau, was still attempting to obtain "a payment due for a very long time" from the cabildo's successors, the mayor and aldermen of the American city of New Orleans.[204]

[199] Cabildo Minutes, IV, no. 4, 99, Oct. 8, 1799.
[200] *Ibid.*, no. 3, 182, Dec. 3, 1799.
[201] MS in the collection of Samuel Wilson, Jr.
[202] American Documents, 1804–14 (4077), no. 482, Nov. 20, 1802, LSM.
[203] *Ibid.*, Feb. 28, 1803.
[204] *Ibid.*, Aug. 10, 1804.

The cabildo's accounts with the Widow Almonester were also finally settled. The appraised value of the building had amounted to 32,348 *pesos, 6 reales.* On August 19, 1803, she petitioned the cabildo for "the balance due her for the final payment of the *Casas Capitulares.*" It was pointed out by the city treasurer that up to that date she had received a total of 27,500 *pesos,* plus Guillemard's fee of 500 *pesos* for directing the work, leaving a balance due her of 4,348 *pesos, 6 reales.* This amount was ordered to be paid.[205] Thus when the colony was transferred on November 30, 1803, from Spain to France, the cost of the cabildo had been fully repaid to Almonester's estate.

When Laussat took possession for France he remarked that practically no new buildings had been built in New Orleans since France gave up the colony in 1762. He mentioned that "a rich Spaniard, however (Don Andrés Almonester), has constructed in masonry, a charity hospital, a city hall, and a church. His Catholic Majesty recompensed him for it by worthy honors."[206] In another report Laussat again referred to the Cabildo or city hall: "What has been designated under the title of royal prison is really the city hall. On the ground floor there is a large *corps de garde* with the prisons in the rear and linked to this building. This is the most remarkable edifice in the city. It was constructed at the expense of a rich individual, the King contributing but a sorry sum in spite of the accessory use made of some parts for prisons and *corps de garde.* It is so especially affected to the local authorities that it does not seem just in any case for the price of it to revert to France."[207]

Thus it was that the title to the entire Cabildo as well as the prison and *corps de garde* was given to the city of New Orleans, even though parts of it had been built at the king's expense and would normally have passed to the ownership of the French government, to be transferred with the other royal properties to the United States. Almonester's great building continued to serve as the city hall until 1853, when the three municipalities that constituted the city at that time were consolidated. The city hall was then established in the newly completed Second Municipality Hall on Lafayette Square,[208] now known as Gallier Hall in honor of its architect, James Gallier. The Cabildo has recently (1969) been restored by the Louisiana State Museum, the *sala capitular* looking

205 Cabildo Minutes, V, no. 1, 93, Aug. 19, 1803.
206 C13A, LI, 84, AN.
207 C13A, LIII, 73, AN.
208 Leonard V. Huber and Samuel Wilson, Jr., *The Cabildo on Jackson Square* (New Orleans, 1970).

now as it probably did when the historic transfer of Louisiana Territory from France to the United States was signed in it on December 20, 1803. Almonester's portrait will again hang on the wall of this historic room for which it was ordered to be painted in 1797.

CONCLUSION

When Almonester died on April 25, 1798, he was buried in the parish cemetery near the Charity Hospital as he had requested in his will. In the 1794 will he had at first specified that he be buried in the new cathedral, but changed this before signing the will to interment in the cemetery. So thus he was buried on April 26, 1798. This change of burial place appears to have been a gesture of humility on Almonester's part, but it may also have had something to do with obtaining the king's approval for such a church burial. In a decree dated at Aranjuez, February 17, 1799, the king said that

> owing to the late arrival of the Royal Decree of May 7 last (1798), whereby Almonester was granted the privilege of selecting a chapel (excepting the main one) in the Cathedral, to serve as his tomb, he (the King) feared that Almonester had been buried some other place. He asked that if this were so, the Reverend Bishop of that Province be ordered to communicate with Almonester's widow and, together with her, to select a chapel to which Almonester's remains might be transferred and that the said Bishop, jointly with the Friar Antonio de Sedella, Priest of the Cathedral of that city, inform me of the entire proceedings through private channels. . . .[209]

The royal decree of May 7, 1798, which of course had not been written before Almonester's death, did not arrive until long after his burial in the cemetery. His widow, however, presented a copy of it to the court on April 24, 1799, in the litigation with Bishop Peñalver over the completing of the Presbytère. In that decree the king had referred to Almonester's many generous gifts to the city, for which he

> has spent large sums of moneys for the benefit of the church and the state in the construction and endowment of the Royal Charity Hospital as well as in the construction of the buildings for school

[209] "Proceedings against Widow Almonester," 42.

243

girls, which works, according to the information given by the authorities of that province, represented an expenditure of more than one hundred thousand *pesos* . . . and also bearing in mind the information which, in compliance with the Royal Decree of April 18, 1796, was furnished by the Reverend Bishop in the following month of August and by the Governor on July 31, 1797, upholding and corroborating all the statements set forth by the said Don Andrés, which showed him as a public benefactor, as in the instance of the reconstruction of the City Council (Cabildo) buildings which show actual proofs of his generous liberality and honesty of purpose. . . . I have resolved that the said Don Andrés may hold the right to the seat granted him by the Reverend Bishop in the choir of the said church and also that he be assigned a chapel outside of the main one to serve as his tomb, with an inscribed flat stone placed on the exterior of the chapel proclaiming his generosity, piety, and liberality in the reconstruction of the cathedral church . . . for all of which he has merited my Royal Gratitude.[210]

Thus it was by royal decree of the king of Spain, Charles IV, that Almonester's remains were removed from the cemetery and ceremoniously buried in the cathedral. This event was recorded in the church archives as follows:

Translation and interment of the bones of the Señor Don Andrés Almonester y Roxas, which have been buried at the foot of the marble step of the altar of the Most Holy Virgin of the Rosary of this Holy Cathedral Church.

By order of His Catholic Majesty, the Señor Don Carlos IV (whom God guard) and at the solicitation of the most Illustrious Señor Diocesan, Don Luis Peñalver y Cárdenas, worthy first Bishop of this Province of Louisiana and the Floridas, was disinterred from the common cemetery of the faithful, the body of the notable benefactor of this Holy Cathedral Church of New Orleans, Don Andrés Almonester y Roxas, founder of the three churches which there are in the said city, which works of his piety are not only useful to religion, but likewise to humanity. A native of Mairena del Alcor, Province of Andalusia in Spain, Archbishopric of Seville: died the twenty-fifth of April of the year just passed of ninety-eight, and to-day eleventh of November of ninety-nine, with the assistance of the mentioned Illustrious Prelate and all his clergy,

210 *Ibid.,* 12–15.

was given honorable sepulture, with all possible funeral pomp, to the memorable bones of the aforesaid deceased; and in evidence of which, I sign

Fr. Antonio de Sedella
curate of the sacristy[211]

It is interesting to note that Almonester was buried in front of the altar of the Virgin, which has always been the one to the left when facing the main altar. On April 9, 1802, the body of his four-year-old daughter Andrea Antonia was buried in front of the same altar, "at the side of the bones of her father."[212] The bodies of father and daughter have not remained undisturbed, for on May 16, 1849, during the rebuilding of the cathedral, they, with the remains of other notables, were removed from the crypts beneath the church and returned to the cemetery, where they remained until the new cathedral had been completed.[213] It is possible that at that time Almonester's tomb was placed on the other side of the sanctuary rather than in its former location.

In spite of the many public honors that were paid to Almonester in life and in death, he evidently left behind a number of bitter enemies who did much to tarnish his name and reputation. Perhaps they were persons whom he had bested in business transactions, or who were envious of his wealth and honors. Perhaps they were only annoyed at his pompous and probably sometimes arrogant attitude. Such ideas are reflected in some of the letters of Pontalba and in Carondelet's remarks regarding Almonester's construction of the parish church and the opposition of the citizens toward him for having raised the rents of his buildings after the fire of 1788.

In any event, quite a few visitors to New Orleans eagerly picked up, repeated, and no doubt elaborated on the derogatory remarks they had heard about the city's great benefactor, in written and published works. Perhaps the worst of these was that published by John Pope at Richmond in 1792, six years before Almonester's death. Pope apparently understood little of the French-Spanish Catholic town he had visited or of its Latin love of ceremony, processions, and pageantry. He made the following remarks concerning Almonester, undoubtedly based on tales he had picked up from local gossips:

Don Andrea, a Catalan, arrived in New Orleans about Twenty Years ago:

[211] Funeral Records, 1793–1803, no. 642.
[212] *Ibid.*, no. 910.
[213] Huber and Wilson, *The Basilica*, 36.

"Propt on a Staff, deform'd with Age and Care,
"And hung with Rags that flutter'd in the Air."

For ten Years past he hath been the richest Subject in Louisiana or either of the Floridas. About three Years since, he got disgusted with his Lady, against whom he prayed and obtained a Divorce *a Vinculo Matrimonii*, and a Dispensation from the Archbishop of Toledo, Primate of Spain and great Chancellor of Castile, for an incestuous Marriage with her younger Sister. To procure an Indulgence of this Kind, required a considerable Largess from the Coffers of the old Mammomist. He is now erecting to the Glory of God, and in Atonement of his Rascalities a superb Church and Hospital. No Doubt when these shall be completed, but that he will be reminded by the Priests, who will know how to excite the Passions of Hope and Fear; that some other expiatory Acts remain, and which he is indispensably bound to perform, under no less Penalty than of having his Soul everlastingly damned in the liquid Flames of Hell-fire. To soothe his Vanity, his Name and Pious Deeds, will be ensculptured over the Front Doors and other Parts of the Buildings.

"Who builds a Church to God, and not to Fame,
"Will never mark the Marble with his Name."

POPE.[214]

The story of the divorce seems to be completely without foundation. Almonester's first wife had died before he left Spain[215] and he had remained a widower until his marriage to the twenty-nine-year-old Louise de la Ronde in 1787.[216] Four years before this second marriage, he had purchased a fine house and presented it to his intended bride "that she might have an establishment."[217] The act of donation is dated May 3, 1783.[218]

An anonymous "Memoir of Spanish Louisiana 1796–1802," attributed to James Pitot, who became the first elected mayor of New Orleans after the Louisiana Purchase, does not mention Almonester by name but declares that New Orleans "still owes to the French the greatest part of the Royal or public buildings . . . and if it has a church, a town hall, a charity hospital, it owes these honorable establishments to the super-

---

214 Pope, *A Tour*, 39.
215 Stanley Clisby Arthur and George Campbell Huchet de Kernion, *Old Families of New Orleans* (New Orleans, 1931), 27.
216 Marriage Register II, act 179, Mar. 20, 1787.
217 *LHQ*, VI, 24.
218 Acts of L. Mazange, VII, 412.

stition of an enriched Spaniard who assured himself by this means of blessings and of honors. . . ."[219]

The American major Amos Stoddard, in his memoirs published in 1812, had evidently also heard unflattering remarks concerning Almonester and attributes his generosity in public and religious works to motives other than simple piety and charity: "The church belonging to the convent is small and was the gift of a gentleman who died a few years ago at New Orleans. He was in early life a notary and, by various speculations amassed an imense property and failed at last to leave an unspotted name behind him. He likewise built the cathedral church and charity hospital and endeavored by acts of beneficence near the end of his days, to atone for the errors of his youth."[220]

Almonester's true motives and feelings can never be known, but his good works as evidenced in his buildings speak for him. Although only the Cabildo and the Presbytère remain substantially as he conceived them, his buildings around the Plaza de Armas and those added by his daughter, the Baroness de Pontalba, established the center of the Vieux Carré of New Orleans as one of the most notable civic centers in America. His contributions to the St. Louis Cathedral, the Ursuline Convent, and the Charity Hospital will always be remembered and cause his name to be held in respect and gratitude by these ancient New Orleans institutions.

[219] From a copy of an unpublished manuscript furnished the author by Réné J. Le Gardeur, Jr., and Henry C. Pitot. See John Francis McDermott, ed., *Frenchmen and French Ways in the Mississippi Valley* (Urbana, Ill., 1969), 73.

[220] Stoddard, *Sketches*, 155.

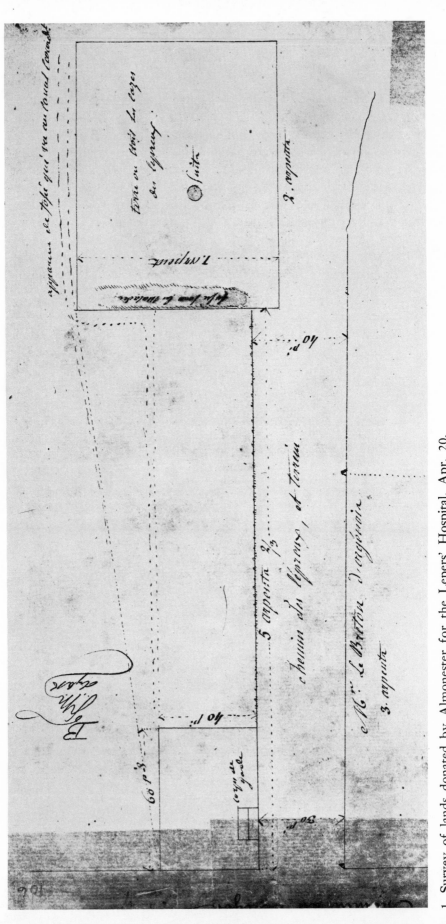

1. Survey of lands donated by Almonester for the Lepers' Hospital, Apr. 20, 1785. New Orleans Public Library.

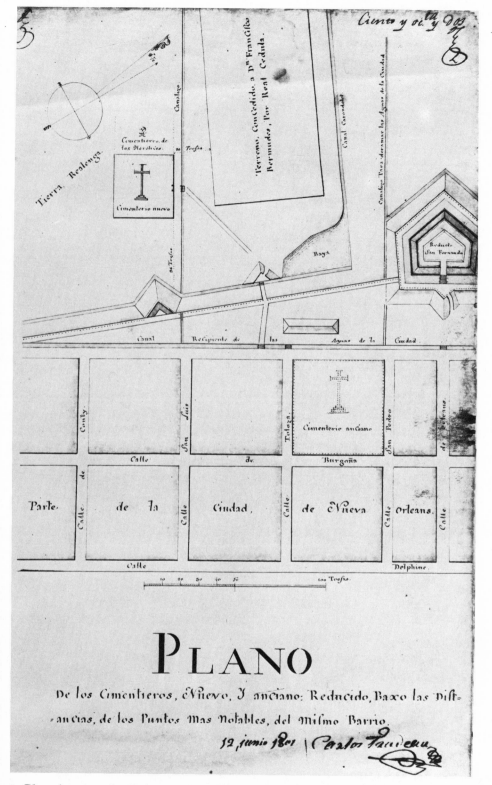

2. Plan showing the location of the Charity Hospital of St. Charles, at the end of Toulouse Street opposite the old cemetery, by Carlos Trudeau, June 12, 1801. St. Louis Cathedral Archives.

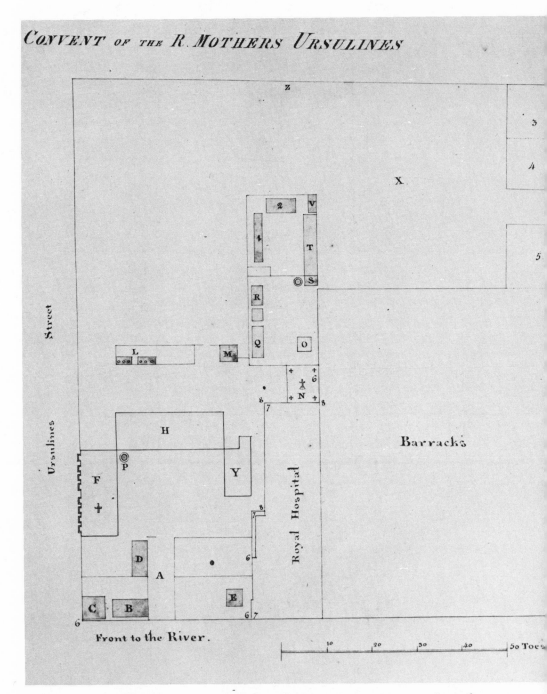

3. Plan of the Ursuline Convent by Gilberto Guillemard, Apr. 10, 1793 (copy by Joseph Pilié, Jan. 1, 1821), showing "B. Externs or School-Room, C. Ancient Church, F. Church and Choir and 8.8 Walls, built at the expense of his Majesty in the year 1789." Ursuline Convent Archives.

4. The Spanish school on Royal Street, demolished in 1888, from an old photograph, *c.* 1885. Wilson Collection.

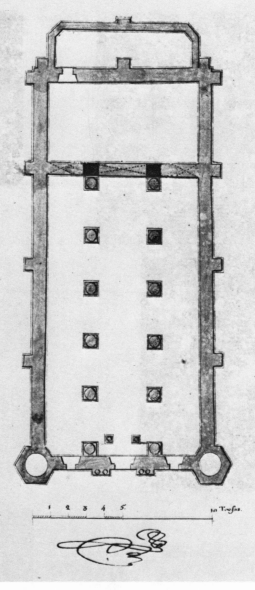

PLANO GEOMETº

De la Iglesia Parrochial De la Ciudad de Nueva Orleans.
19 junio 1801 *Carlos Trudeau*

5. Plan of St. Louis Cathedral as built by Almonester. Drawing dated June 12, 1801, by Carlos Trudeau. St. Louis Cathedral Archives.

6. St. Louis Cathedral with the Cabildo and Presbytère, *c.* 1840, lithograph by A. Lion. The central tower was added to the cathedral by B. H. Latrobe, architect, in 1820. Richard Koch Collection.

7. The Plaza de Armas in 1803, by J. S. Boqueta de Woiseri, showing the Cabildo, St. Louis Cathedral, and unfinished Presbytère, with Almonester's buildings flinking the plaza. Louisiana State Museum.

8. Portrait of Don Andrés Almonester y Roxas, attributed to José de Salazar, dated 1796. St. Louis Cathedral Archives (Delgado Museum photo).

9. The chapel of the Ursuline Convent as built by Almonester in 1787, from Norman's *New Orleans and Environs*, 1845.

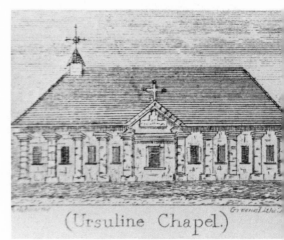

(Ursuline Chapel.)

10. Detail from "A View of New Orleans taken from the Opposite Side of the Mississippi—1765" showing the church of St. Louis with the old Presbytère on the right and the French prison on the left. Louisiana State Museum.

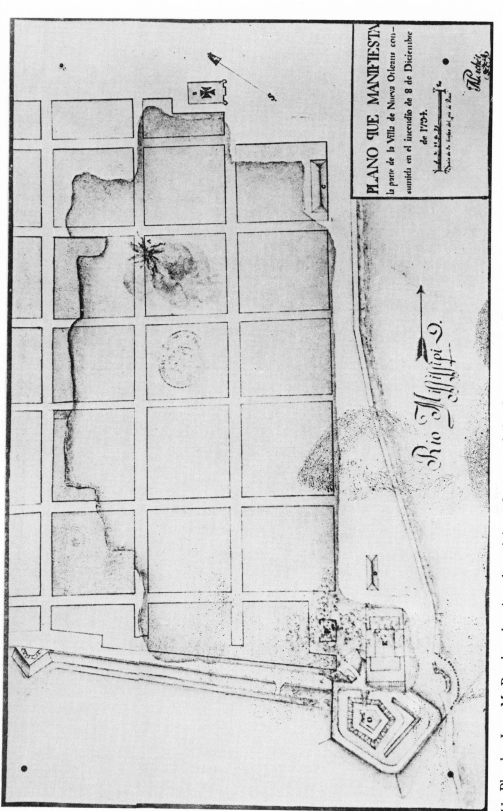

PLANO QUE MANIFESTA
la parte de la Villa de Nueva Orleans con—
sumida en el incendio de 8 de Diciembre
de 1794.

Rio Missisipi.

11. Plan by Juan M. Perchet showing the origin and extent of the fire of Dec. 8, 1794. Archivo General de Indias.

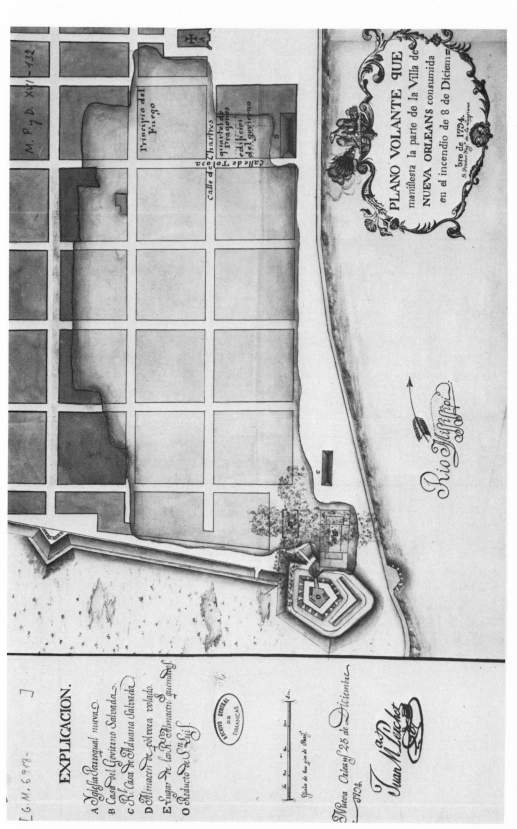

11A. Plan showing the part of the city of New Orleans consumed in the conflagration of Dec. 8, 1794, by Perchet, engineer of Louisiana. Archivo General de

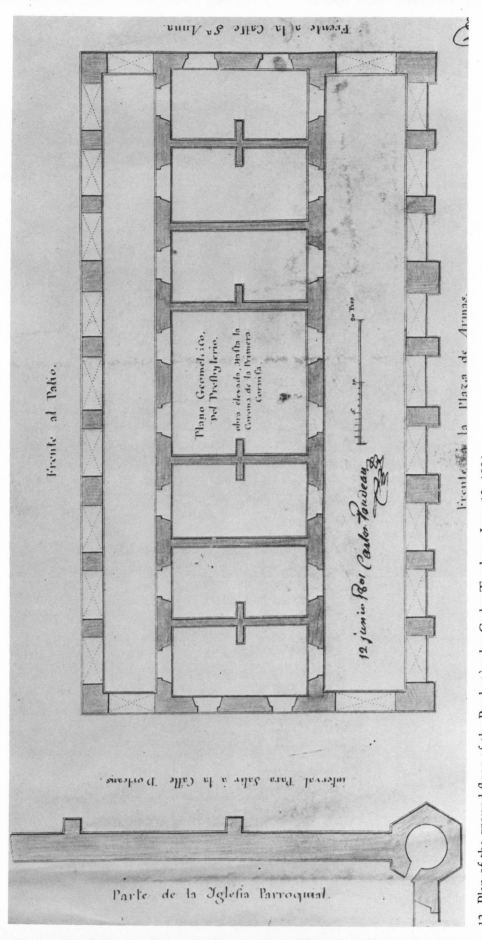

Frente a la Calle S.ᵃ Anna.

Frente al Patio.

Plano Geometrico, del Presbyterio.

obra elevada, hasta la Corona de la Primera Cornisa.

12 junio 1801 Carlos Trudeau

Frente a la Plaza de Armas.

intervalo Para Salir a la Calle D'orleans.

Parte de la Iglesia Parroquial.

12. Plan of the ground floor of the Presbytère by Carlos Trudeau, June 12, 1801.
St. Louis Cathedral Archives.

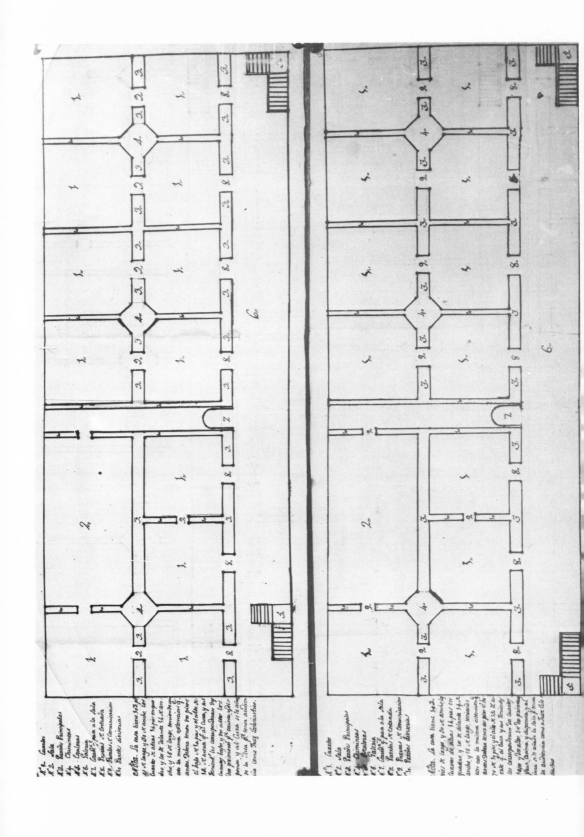

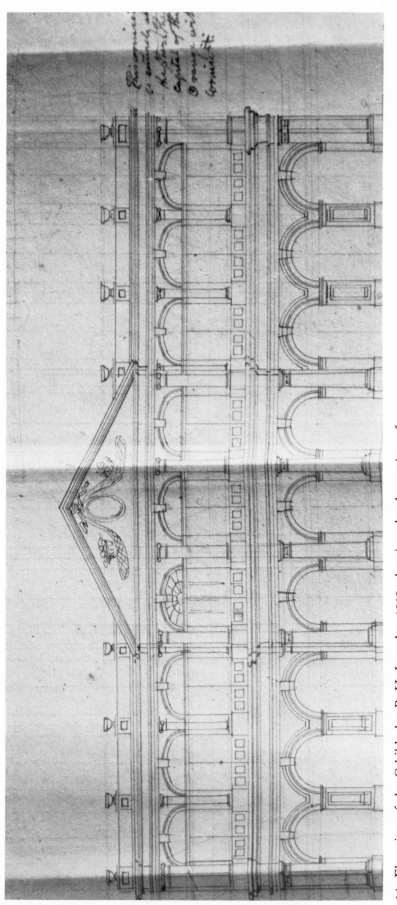

14. Elevation of the Cabildo by B. H. Latrobe, 1819, showing the decoration of the pediment that probably formerly contained the Spanish coat of arms. Maryland Historical Society.

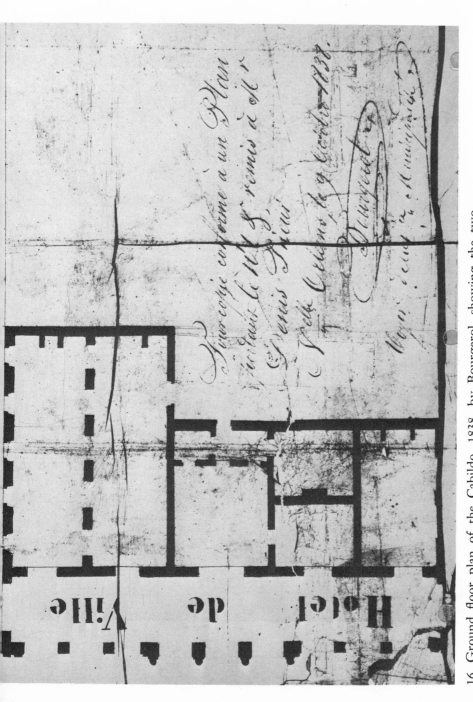

16. Ground floor plan of the Cabildo, 1838, by Bourgerol, showing the two large rooms of the old French *corps de garde* (right) incorporated into the new building. New Orleans Notarial Archives.

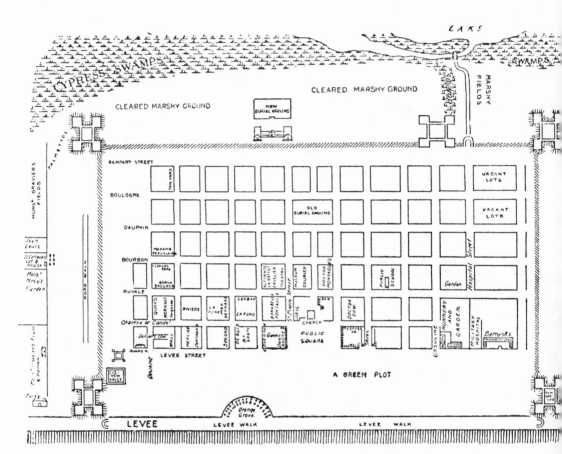

LAKE

CYPRESS SWAMP

SWAMPS

SWAMPS

CLEARED MARSHY GROUND

CLEARED MARSHY GROUND

NEW BURIAL GROUND

RAMPART STREET

TAN YARD

VACANT LOTS

BOULOGNE

OLD BURIAL GROUND

VACANT LOTS

DAUPHIN

MONSr GRAVIER'S FIELDS

PALMETTOS

Jean Louis

O'Conway Lot & House

Mons.r Percy's Garden

BOURBON

MADAME BEAUCLAIR

LODGED BERE

BARON BOUREN

ROYALE

HERCULE

RIVIERE

LA FONDA

LORD REYNARD

ZERBAR

LA FUNO

ACHIENTE LA BATTUT CAVELIER THEATRE

MUSEUM

COURIER

DOCTOR MONTAGNE

Garden

Hospital Street

PUBLIC SCHOOL

ST Peter Street

Chartre or Condé

QUAYS

MERCULE

DILLON H.

QUAID H.

MERCER

SECOND

DE BUY'S

BONNABLE FONTALLA

JAIL CHURCH

DOCTOR DOW

URSULINE NUNNERY AND GARDEN

MILITARY HOSPITAL

Barracks

LEVEE STREET

DOUANE

CUSTOM HOUSE

PUBLIC SQUARE

A GREEN PLOT

Orange Grove.

LEVEE

LEVEE WALK

LEVEE WALK

MISSISSIPPI DESCENDING.

17. Plan of New Orleans in 1793, redrawn from the Journals of Mathias James O'Conway, showing the Charity Hospital (upper center) and the public school (lower right) as well as other projects and properties of Almonester. *Records of the American Catholic Historical Society of Philadelphia*, X (Sept., 1899), 285.

R. Y. P.
___

642

Traslacion y entierro de los huesos del Sor Dn Andres Almonester y Roxas al Rosario de esta Sta Yglesia Cathedral.

Por orden de S. M. C. el Señor Dn Carlos 4.° (que Dios gue) y á Solicitud del Yllmo Sor Diocesano, Dn Luis Peñalver y Cardenas, digno primer Obispo de esta Provincia de la Luisiana, se desenterro del campo Santo comun de los fieles, y á Cathedral el cadaver del insigne Bien-echor de esta Sarita y Cathedral, Dn Andres Almonester y Roxas, fundador del Bien obra del insigne Bien-echor de esta Sarita y Cathedral, Dn Andres Almonester y Roxas, fundador del Bien obra-Orleans; cuyas obras piadosas, que hay en la referida Ciudad; cuyas obras que hay en la referida Ciudad, son no solamente utiles a la Religion, sino tambien á la Humanidad. fue natural de Mayrena de Alcor, Pro- vincia de Andalucia, en España, Arzobispado de Sevilla. fa- llecio en veinte y cinco de Abril del año proximo pasado de noventa y ocho, y hoy once de noviembre de noventa y nube, con asistencia del mencionado Yllmo Prelado, y todo su Clero, se dio honorifica Sepultura, con la posible Pompa funeral á los mencionados huesos del ya expresado Difunto; y para que conste, lo firme ✠

Fr. Antonio de Sedella
Cura del Sagrario

___

643

Queda sepulta- dos al pie de la grada de marmol del Altar de la Sma Virgen del Rosario de esta Yglesia Cathedral.

19. The Ursuline Convent, with Almonester's chapel of 1787 shown at left. From a plan of New Orleans by Jacques Tanesse published in 1816. Richard Koch Collection.

20. Detail showing the Charity Hospital location, from a plan of New Orleans copied in 1808 by Joseph Pilié. Tulane University Library.

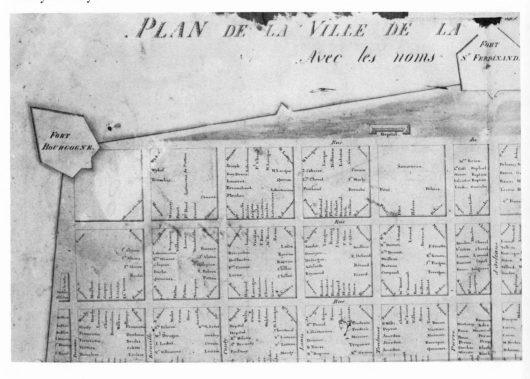

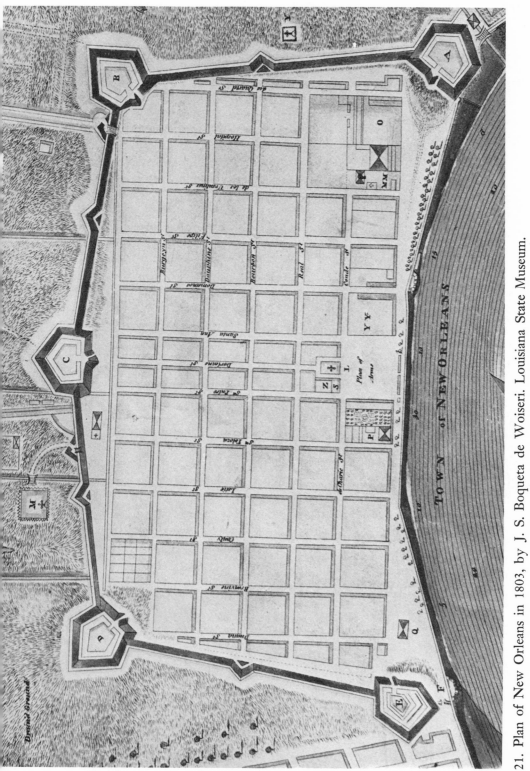

21. Plan of New Orleans in 1803, by J. S. Boqueta de Woiseri. Louisiana State Museum.

22. The *corps de garde* of the Cabildo as restored in 1969. The floor and the
major part of the walls and arcade are from the French colonial structure of the
1750s, incorporated into the Cabildo building in 1795. Louisiana State Museum.

The *sala capitular* or council chamber of the Cabildo as restored in 1969.
siana State Museum.

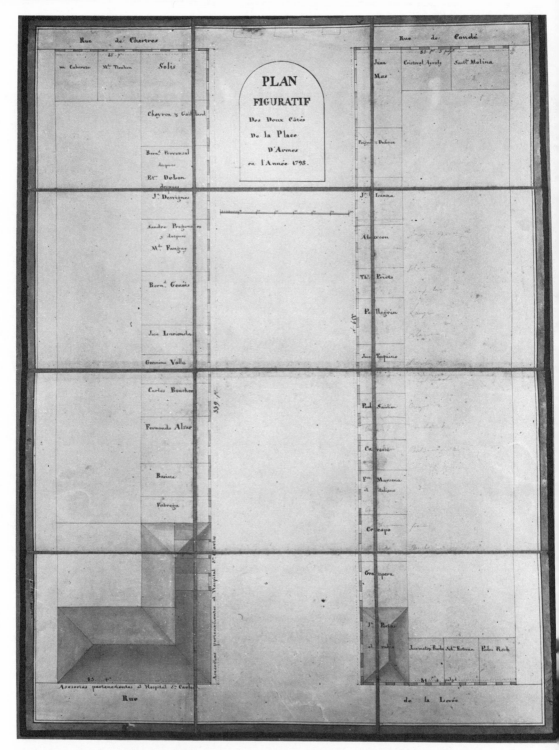

24. Plan showing Almonester's properties on the two sides of the Plaza de Armas at the time of his death in 1798. The names are probably those of the tenants. Almonester's residence is shown at the lower left. Pontalba Family Papers, Tulane University Library.

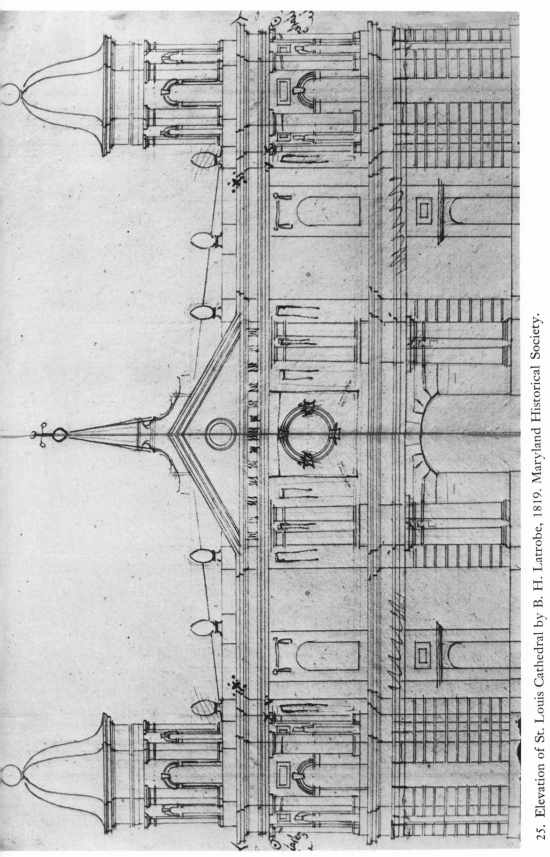

25. Elevation of St. Louis Cathedral by B. H. Latrobe, 1819. Maryland Historical Society.

Symbols of Chiefly Authority
in Spanish Louisiana

—————◆◆—————

JOHN C. EWERS

$\mathcal{T}$HE problems of establishing and maintaining friendly relations with Indian tribes were ones which confronted all those European powers which sought to gain footholds in the New World. Indian alliances were never won by force or by promises alone. They had to be purchased with trade goods and presents. This paper is concerned with the roles of a few extraordinary presents bestowed upon prominent Indian chiefs by Spanish officials in Louisiana in the Indian diplomacy and culture of the times.

When Spain acquired Louisiana the major tribes south of the Platte River—Pawnee, Osage, Wichita, and Comanche—were already known to Spanish officials in New Mexico and Texas, although primarily as enemies. Before Spain ceded Louisiana four decades later she extended her diplomatic and trade relations to those and to more than a score of other tribes who inhabited the vast drainage basin of the Mississippi west of that great river—tribes as far north as the Mandan in present North Dakota. This in itself was no small accomplishment.

To ease the transition from French to Spanish rule in Louisiana Spanish officials took pains to assure the Indians, who had had relations with the French, that there would be no fundamental change in the white man's relations with them. Not only would trade be encouraged, but the Indians would continue to receive the presents to which they had been accustomed. Indeed, the Spanish went so far as to try to impress upon those tribes who had been loyal to France that the Spanish and French were really the same people.

In his instructions to Captain Don Francisco Riú, leader of the first official Spanish expedition up the Mississippi from New Orleans, dated March 14, 1767, Governor Antonio de Ulloa wrote:

> Since it may happen that one must honor the chiefs of certain tribes who come to the fort, as has always been practiced, by giving them the medal of the king, a report will be given to the government of the tribes which come there, with information of the names and relations of the principal and secondary chiefs, in order that these medals may be sent. This is to be understood in regard to the tribes which can come anew to offer their friendship, since the old tribes have them from the time of the French government. And so far as they are concerned it is the same as though the medals were those of our king, for the Indians have been told so, in order that they might understand that no innovation is being made in anything.[1]

In October, 1769, Ulloa's successor, General Don Alexandro O'Reilly, summoned nine chiefs of tribes living within sixty leagues of New Orleans to his home. He assured them that the Spanish king "did not wish to demand of them any other gratitude than their constant fidelity." Then, impressively, he "arose from his chair to place about the neck of each one of the chiefs the medal which hung from a silk ribbon of deep scarlet color. He first had them kiss the royal effigy, and then with his bare sword he touched them on both shoulders and chest and made over their heads the sign of the Cross, and finally gave each an embrace and his hand, whereupon they again showed such admiration that it was evident how pleasing to them was the ceremony and that it was the first time they had seen it."[2]

The Spaniards, like the French, were keenly aware that the ritual and pageantry of formal ceremonies made deep and lasting impressions upon Indians who witnessed or participated in them. Written instructions were given to men who were to serve as the king's representatives in presenting symbols of chiefly allegiance and authority to newly contacted tribes, carefully detailing the ceremonies to be conducted and even the words to be spoken on those occasions.

---

[1] Louis Houck, ed., *The Spanish Régime in Missouri* (2 vols., Chicago, 1909), I, 11–12.

[2] Lawrence Kinnaird, ed., *Spain in the Mississippi Valley, 1765–1794* (3 vols., Washington, 1946–49), I, 101–102.

Jacques Clamorgan's June 30, 1794, instructions to Jean Baptiste Truteau, commander of the first expedition up the Missouri of the newly formed Commercial Exploration Company of St. Louis, were very specific: not only must Truteau present the chief of the distant Mandan Indians "a medal which the governor sends him in order that he may make strenuous efforts to establish peace with all neighboring nations and to live in friendship with us," but Truteau must give the Mandan chief the "most beautiful" of the three Spanish flags he was to carry upriver to present to chiefs of different tribes.

Truteau also was instructed:

> On his arrival among the Mandanas, he shall proceed to convoke a council among the chiefs, which he shall hold in the name of the Chief of the Spaniards, announcing to them that the latter sends them a flag of his nation, and a medal which bears the likeness of his Majesty, the great Chief of the Spaniards, protector and friend of all red men, who loves the beautiful lands, free roads, and a serene sky; he shall tell them that the flag which they receive is the symbol of an alliance and of most sincere friendship which he is able to give to the Mandanas nation, and that the medal ought to be the symbol of an eternal memory, that the Chief of the Mandanas ought to believe in the sincerity of the Chief of the Spaniards; finally that the sons of the Mandana chiefs are also the sons of the Chief of the Spaniards, that he will ever protect them from all those who may wish to harm or injure him.[3]

Actually it was the Welshman John Evans who gave the first and probably the only flags and medals to the Mandan in the name of "their Great Father the Spaniard" two years later. But Spain failed to exploit her brief foothold in the Mandan villages, and both the trade and allegiance of those Indians reverted to the British.[4]

Spain's greatest success in Indian diplomacy during her four decades of rule in Louisiana resulted from more subtle maneuvering than the cases previously cited. For nearly two decades officials in New Orleans, Natchitoches, San Antonio, and Santa Fe sought to make peace with the warlike Comanche. Divided into several strong, autonomous divisions, those nomadic, mobile warriors had long been a thorn in the side of the Spanish in both New Mexico and Texas. It was not until 1786 that Don Juan Bautista de Anza, governor of New Mexico, made peace with

---

[3] Houck, ed., *The Spanish Régime in Missouri*, II, 170–171.

[4] Abraham P. Nasatir, *Before Lewis and Clark: Documents Illustrating the History of the Missouri, 1785–1804* (2 vols., St. Louis, 1952), II, 495–496.

them. Painstakingly he elevated the status of Ecueracapa (Leather Coat or Iron Shirt) to that of head chief of all the Comanche, promising him both a medal and a staff of office to be displayed in all the Comanche camps as symbols of his chiefly supremacy. On July 15, 1786, Governor Anza formally "decorated Captain Ecueracapa with his Majesty's medal." And "in order that this insignia might be displayed with the greatest propriety and luster, he presented him with a complete uniform and another suit of color."[5]

These examples indicate that the important symbols of chiefly authority bestowed upon tribal leaders in Spanish Louisiana were not one but several. In addition to those mentioned in the foregoing accounts—medals, flags, uniforms, and staffs of office—they also included *patentes*, or commissions. Let us consider each of these in a little more detail.

MEDALS. These were symbols of allegiance and authority bestowed upon Indian chiefs by the French and English in North America long before Spain acquired Louisiana. Spanish officials in Louisiana presented large medals only to the principal chief of each tribe, and smaller ones to chiefs of second rank. The medals were silver, and bore upon one face the likeness of the reigning Spanish monarch. The Spanish also made a point of furnishing red silk ribbon for the suspension of the medals from their wearer's necks. By the year 1787, if not earlier, the Spanish also recognized a third grade of chiefs by presenting gorgets to them. I have found no detailed description of these Spanish gorgets.[6]

I have found a single reference to a gold or gilt Spanish medal given to an Indian of Louisiana, the notorious Omaha chief Black Bird, who was probably the only true despot among the tribes of Louisiana during the Spanish period. Black Bird achieved dominance of his tribe by administering poison (said to have been a crude arsenic obtained from traders) to his rivals, effectively eliminating all would-be contestants for Omaha tribal leadership. He regarded himself as the greatest of all Indian chiefs, and demanded a gold medal of the Spaniards. Because his tribe was strong, and stategically located astride the Missouri above the mouth of the Platte, where it could easily prevent St. Louis traders from proceeding upriver to trade with more distant tribes, and because the English were also actively wooing the allegiance and trade of Black Bird and his tribe, Governor Carondelet provided a gilt medal for "the great Maha chief, in order to flatter him most."[7]

[5] Alfred Barnaby Thomas, ed., *Forgotten Frontiers: A Study of the Spanish Indian Policy of Don Juan Bautista de Anza, Governor of New Mexico* (Norman, 1932), 300–320.

[6] Houck, ed., *The Spanish Régime in Missouri*, I, 268–269.

[7] Nasatir, *Before Lewis and Clark*, II, 185, 420.

FLAGS (*pabellones*). Some at least of the flags given to prominent chiefs by the Spaniards in Louisiana bore the cross of Burgundy, perhaps in red on a white field. They were large enough to be flown from a staff in front of a chief's lodge. Some may have been of silk, but obviously not all of them were, because Black Bird complained to Spanish traders that their English rivals gave "only silk flags, which would cause them to despise ours."[8]

Flags, of course, were less substantial than medals, but the Spanish do not appear to have replaced them with any regularity. On February 5, 1779, Fernando de Leyba wrote Governor Gálvez from St. Louis that the chiefs were "very urgently asking me for flags." He reminded the governor that flags had been distributed "only once since our establishment in this colony. . . . As it is their custom to have the flag always flying above the cabin of the head chief, there are tribes which have only a flag pole and on it usually some rags full of holes and patches."[9]

COMMISSIONS (*patentes*). This was a printed or hand-lettered certificate of an individual Indian's chiefly status. Sometimes, if not commonly, these commissions were supplied by the governor to his field officers with the name of the Indian recipient omitted so that they could fill in the names of the Indians to whom they were presented. That the illiterate Indians prized these documents even if they couldn't read them is remarkable only to the scholar who fails to understand the veneration in which they were held among the Indians. In 1787 the Caddo head chief requested that his old *patente* be replaced by a new one, because it had been damaged by water and torn.[10]

UNIFORMS. These were colorful coats and hats of military or semimilitary design. The coats may have been of different colors, and quite likely the facings were of contrasting colors. There were repeated references to their decoration with (metal) lace embroidery (i.e., galloons). Don Pedro Bautista Pino tells us that the coats given to the Comanche by the Spaniards in New Mexico were "made of blue Querétaro, with red lapels for the big chiefs." Apparently they were fashioned from fabrics woven in Querétaro, Mexico. He also stated that three-cornered hats were given the Comanche to be worn with these coats. Earlier references simply mention hats with feather plumes.[11]

When Great Sun, head chief of the Tawehash, was on his deathbed

8 Houck, ed., *The Spanish Régime in Missouri*, II, 189.

9 Kinnaird, ed., *The Spanish in the Mississippi Valley*, I, 329–330.

10 *Ibid.*, II, 235.

11 H. Bailey Carroll and J. Villasana Haggard, eds., *Three New Mexico Chronicles* (Albuquerque, 1942), 135; Kinnaird, ed., *Spain in the Mississippi Valley*, II, 199; Houck, ed., *The Spanish Régime in Missouri*, II, 52.

in 1784 or 1785, he "asked to be buried in his Chief's headdress and coat with the Spanish Royal flag." I suspect this was the final disposition of many chief's uniforms given to Indians by the Spanish in Louisiana—they continued to be worn by their chiefly recipients even after death. Perhaps historical archaeologists, if they are aware of this Indian custom, may recover at least the buttons and metal lace ornaments from the graves of some of these chiefs, provided of course these Indians were buried in the ground rather than exposed to the elements on elevated scaffolds or in trees.[12]

STAFFS OF OFFICE (*bastónes*). These were canes with ornamented gold or silver heads. The *bastón* must have been both an old and a peculiarly Spanish symbol of chiefly authority. It was employed in Spanish-Indian relations in East Texas as early as 1690. On May 25 of that year General Alonso de León presented to the head chief of the Nebedache village "a staff with a cross, giving him the title of governor of all his people." The chief "accepted the staff with much pleasure, promising to do all that was desired of him, and the company fired three salutes."[13]

In the course of re-establishing Spanish rule in East Texas in 1721, the Marqués de Aguayo gave silver-headed canes, as well as suits of clothes, to those chiefs whom he recognized as captains in a number of villages of Caddoan-speaking Indians.[14]

After the governor of Louisiana, through his lieutenant in Natchitoches, Athanase de Mézières, assumed responsibility for diplomatic relations with the southern Plains tribes north of the Red River, he followed the precedent of the Internal Provinces of Mexico in presenting staffs of office to those Indians whom he recognized as *capitanes* or *gobernadores* of their tribes or villages. Those chiefs appeared to prize their *bastónes* as highly as they did their medals.[15] Nevertheless, the Spanish governors of Louisiana do not appear to have furnished staffs of office to the chiefs they recognized among the tribes farther north, who had had no diplomatic relations with the Spaniards of Mexico prior to 1763.

[12] Robert E. Bell, Edward B. Jelks, and W. W. Newcomb, *A Pilot Study of Wichita Indian Archeology and Ethnology* (n.p., 1967), 277.

[13] Herbert E. Bolton, ed., *Spanish Exploration in the Southwest, 1542–1706* (New York, 1916), 416.

[14] Eleanor Claire Buckley, ed., "The Aguayo Expedition into Texas and Louisiana, 1719–1722," *Texas Historical Association Quarterly*, I, no. 4 (1898), 46, 47, 49.

[15] Herbert E. Bolton, ed., *Athanase de Mézières and the Louisiana-Texas Frontier, 1768–1780* (2 vols., Cleveland, 1914), I, 73–74, 132–133, 157, 201–202, 211, 262; II, 85, 86, 94, 185, 252.

Throughout the period of Spanish rule in Louisiana the medal, flag, and commission appear to have been the three symbols of chiefly authority most widely distributed among Indian tribes from the Red River northward as far as Spanish explorations were carried up the Missouri—i.e., to the Mandan villages.

The governor in New Orleans assumed responsibility for providing these symbols and for their discriminate and limited distribution among the Indian tribes by his regional representatives in Natchitoches, Arkansas Post, and St. Louis, as well as by licensed trader-explorers of the Upper Missouri. Correspondence between regional officials and successive governors indicates that the former had to justify to their superiors their requests for medals, flags, commissions, uniforms, and/or staffs of office, and that sometimes their requests had to be repeated before favorable action was taken upon them in New Orleans. A full year might transpire between the regional official's request for and the actual presentation of these symbols to the chiefs for whom they were requested.

As an anthropologist, I am particularly interested in the effects the distributions of these symbols of chiefly authority and allegiance may have had upon the beliefs and actions of the Indians—both those few individuals who received them, and the many members of their tribes who did not. Granted that the illiterate Indians left no records testifying to their regard or disregard for these symbols. Nevertheless, some of the writings of the whites who presented these objects to chiefs in the field provide revealing insights into the Indians' attitudes toward them.

Especially revealing are some observations by Jean Baptiste Truteau, the St. Louis fur trader, who first presented Spanish medals, flags, and commissions to the Arikara and Cheyenne chiefs far up the Missouri in present South Dakota, in the middle years of the last decade of the eighteenth century.

When Truteau attended an important council in the earth lodge of Crazy Bear, chief of the first village of the Arikara, on July 7, 1795, he observed that this chief had placed his flag before the door of his lodge and his medal around his neck.

"At the furtherest end of the hut, exposed on a mat, [was] the letter patent which his Spanish Father had sent him by me, having placed before it some live coals on which was burned a certain kind of dried grass the smoke of which produces a very strong odor, and which they use as we use incense."

Truteau went on to explain: "They hold such things as medals, flags, and letters in such deep veneration that whenever these are taken from their wrappings, they are smoked and hold the most important place at their feasts."[16]

In other words these Indians accepted these gifts not merely as secular symbols of allegiance and authority, but as sacred objects to be preserved in wrappings, ritually unveiled, and displayed with the same reverence they had employed in the care and manipulation of their most cherished traditional medicine bundles. Doubtless the incense Truteau smelled was the odor of burning sweetgrass, which was employed by the tribes of the Upper Missouri "in any ceremony or ritual to induce the presence of good influences or benevolent powers."[17]

That the Indians regarded these objects as personal medicines possessing powers to bring good or bad fortune to their recipients is also attested in Truteau's field observations of that summer of 1795.

The previous spring Truteau had formally presented a medal, flag, and commission to La Lance, a young man among the Cheyenne, whom the most important men of that tribe had chosen as "most worthy to wear the medal and to be made the great Chief of their Nation." Upon his acceptance of these symbols La Lance had promised to "do all the good which had been recommended to him, in the letter which his Father, the Chief of the White Men, had sent him." But La Lance failed to carry out the Spanish admonition to keep the peace with neighboring tribes. Not only had he stolen horses from the Mandan and Hidatsa, but he had murdered a family of Sioux who were living at peace among the Cheyenne.

The Indians believed, Truteau observed, that "the medal, the flag and the letter, who were great spirits, had become angry" with La Lance, for three of his children had died, and lightning had struck the lodge of his brother and reduced it, the brother, his wives, children, dogs, and horses tied before the door to ashes.

Truteau continued: "This accident happening to befall this man, above all others, known to have broken his promise to the White Men, and not having behaved in the manner imposed upon him, in the presence of all the esteemed ones of his Nation, had a terrible effect on the minds of all these Nations and confirmed anew their belief that the White Men were great spirits and all powerful."[18]

Nearly two decades earlier (November 21, 1776) Francisco Cruzat informed Governor Unzaga that the Sioux of the Mississippi were "very

[16] Nasatir, *Before Lewis and Clark*, I, 305.
[17] Melvin R. Gilmore, "Uses of Plants by the Indians of the Missouri River Region," *33rd Annual Report*, Bureau of American Ethnology (Washington, 1911), 66.
[18] Nasatir, *Before Lewis and Clark*, I, 309–310.

angry because of the death of five chiefs who had come down to see us and ask for the medal which had been granted them."[19] Might not this misfortune have been *one* reason why the English were more successful than the Spanish in winning the allegiance of the powerful Sioux?

Nevertheless, the great majority of Indian leaders in Louisiana appear to have coveted these visible symbols of Spanish recognition of their status as tribal leaders of distinction. These symbols not only distinguished them from their own warriors, but caused them to be respected by strangers—both members of other tribes and white traders and settlers.

How then did the introduction of these symbols affect the Indian political system? We know that the traditional Indian polity among the Plains tribes tended to be both democratic and highly competitive. Men rose to the chieftaincy through their deeds, and retained their leadership only as long as they could maintain it in competition with other vigorous achievers. Chiefs did not enjoy life tenure, and their positions were not hereditary. Furthermore, the number of chiefs recognized by the tribe was not limited. Generally, among those tribes who were divided into bands, each band had at least one chief.

The introduction of the white colonial policy of recognizing only a few chiefs in each tribe resulted in the elevation of some chiefs at the expense of others. Once these few chiefs were recognized they tended to remain in office for many years, in many cases for life. The hierarchy of chiefs of the large medal, the small medal, and the gorget tended to crystallize the system. Ambitious young men found little opportunity for advancement. Consequently, young men who found their way to power within their tribes blocked by intrenched incumbents had reason to become both frustrated and jealous of the chiefs as well as resentful of chiefly authority. Yes, the generation gap was *not* invented in this country during the 1960s!

The new system imposed by the whites also engendered jealousy within the chiefly hierarchy—of the wearers of the small medal or gorget toward the wearers of the large medal, while the latter looked to the whites to help them maintain their positions. Undoubtedly there must have been factionalism within the tribes of the Great Plains before the 1760s, but the system of external recognition of and discrimination among chiefs must have intensified rather than alleviated intratribal discord.

The best-documented cases of chiefly jealousy in the records of the

[19] Kinnaird, ed., *Spain in the Mississippi Valley*, I, 236.

Spanish period in Louisiana refer to the Great and Little Osage, who comprised the largest and most aggressive Indian confederation between the Arkansas and the Platte, and whose combined force numbered some 1,200 warriors.

On March 18, 1776, Francisco Cruzat in St. Louis wrote Governor Unzaga seeking his help in solving a problem of the relative recognition to be given two jealous Osage chiefs, both of whom coveted a medal. Traders had told Cruzat that the man previously regarded as second in rank actually had a larger following than the first chief. Cruzat's predecessor had given the second chief a coat and hat, and the Spanish official feared that if he was denied a medal he would show his displeasure by stealing horses from neighboring towns and insulting the traders. Eventually the first chief was given a large medal, and the second a small one—more than three years later. Doubtless this Spanish solution to the second chief's problem did not satisfy him.[20]

Nine years later, during the spring of 1785, Governor Esteban Miró, desirous of ending the prolonged intertribal warfare between the Osage and the Caddo, brought Tenihuan, great chief of the Caddo, and two Osage chiefs to New Orleans. There he publicly decorated both Osage chiefs with the small medal and obtained the promise of the older one, Brucaiguais, to make peace with the Caddo.

Later that year Miró sent a small medal, suit, and hat to another Osage leader, whom he wanted to bring to New Orleans to impress with the marvels of the city. Brucaiguais was so jealous that another man of his tribe should have that privilege that he renewed open warfare upon the Caddo and effectively prevented his rival from going down the Arkansas to New Orleans.

Governor Miró then ordered Brucaiguais to be brought to New Orleans as a hostage for the good behavior of the Osage Indians. When the governor's order reached Arkansas Post it was found that Brucaiguais was near death. Nevertheless, he was degraded from his rank, and his medal, commission, and flag were sent to the governor in New Orleans.[21]

This stripping of an uncooperative chief of his symbols of authority must have been an exceedingly rare case. I have found no other example of it in the records of Spanish Louisiana.

Intertribal jealousies also became intensified when the members of some tribes were led to believe that other tribes were receiving preferential treatment from the Spaniards.

[20] *Ibid.*, I, 229–230, 299, 305, 330.
[21] *Ibid.*, II, 171–172, 182–184, 196–197, 253–256.

In 1780 Antonio Gil Ybarvo reported from Natchitoches that the Tawehash were so irritated when they saw loads of Spanish goods transported to the Tonkawa and Tawakoni while their trade was virtually cut off that they "are destroying at every step my flags, staff of command, and medals, saying they cannot live on the luster of these." Ybarvo feared that these angry Indians would also show their displeasure by attacking Natchitoches.[22]

Some fifteen years later Jacques d'Eglise made the mistake of showing members of the small Ponca tribe the five medals and five flags he was taking up the Missouri for the Mandan chiefs. This "sight brought about a great jealousy between these two nations" and it also occasioned "bad words" against the Spanish.[23]

As a means of establishing and maintaining intertribal peace the bestowal of symbols of authority along with verbal admonitions to the recipients to make friends with other tribes were of relatively little avail. Intertribal warfare against traditional enemies was too much a part of Indian life to be ended so quickly or easily. Repeatedly—in 1773, 1786, and 1792—the Spaniards had to resort to the stronger measure of prohibiting trade with the Osage, thus cutting off their ammunition and other supplies, to try to stop them from raiding other and less powerful tribes. But this measure too was of little avail. When the Spanish officials prohibited their own traders from doing business with the Osage, English and later American traders were only too happy to take their places.[24]

If the bestowal of these symbols of chiefly authority upon the Indians disrupted tribal political organizations, encouraged both individual and tribal jealousies, and failed to end intertribal warfare, why did the colonial powers, and later both the United States and Canada, continue to make use of this means of diplomatic negotiation with the Indians? Perhaps the best answer may be that this was both an economical and a rather effective means of eliciting Indian allegiance.

Some twenty-six years after Governor Anza made peace with the Comanche in 1786, Pino wrote of the advantages to New Mexico of the practice of giving presents to that very warlike tribe on the Louisiana-Texas-New Mexico frontiers:

> We would never have believed the benefit that has accrued to
> the province from this practice if we had not seen it. A continued

22 *Ibid.*, I, 391–392.
23 Nasatir, *Before Lewis and Clark*, I, 291.
24 Kinnaird, ed., *Spain in the Mississippi Valley*, I, xxiv; II, 183–184; III, 107.

state of peace and friendship of the greatest importance in checking other tribes has been the result of the small number of presents
given them. At first the Comanches thought they had to recipro-
cate. They brought all the fine pelts they could collect in order to
exceed the munificence of our presents. When they were informed
that favors given them in the name of our king should not be returned, they were greatly astonished. Thus they were placed
under obligation to us; their gratefulness continued to increase, and
their esteem for the King of Spain, whom they call the general
chief [*capitan grande*], has likewise increased. In order to get an
idea of the esteem in which they hold the king, one needs only to
note that any appointments they receive from their government
are ignored unless they are confirmed for our officers in the name
of the general chief.[25]

This diplomacy must have inspired among the Indians of many
tribes strong feelings of attachment to and regard for the individual
head of state—whether this was the *capitan grande* in far-off Spain,
or in later years the Great White Father in Washington, or, for
Canadian Indians, the Great Mother (Queen Victoria).

We know that shortly after the flag of the United States was first
raised in St. Louis, Lewis and Clark embarked on their long overland
journey to the shores of the Pacific Ocean. Their baggage included
both large and small medals bearing the likeness of President Jefferson,
commissions, and uniforms, which they presented to Indian chiefs of
different tribes on the Missouri in very solemn ceremonies in which
the chiefs were informed of their new father in Washington and his
interest in their welfare. Even before these famed explorers began their
historic trek, Pierre Chouteau was on his way to Washington with a
delegation of Osage chiefs to meet and talk to that new White Father.

The United States continued until 1889 to give so-called "Indian
peace medals," bearing the likenesses of successive presidents, to tribal
chiefs. By that time the western Indians were confined to reservations
and the United States was coming to regard white Indian agents rather
than red chiefs as the persons primarily responsible for the management
of the Indians.

It was different north of the forty-ninth parallel. There Indian chiefs
continued to receive medals bearing the likeness of the British monarch,
as well as uniforms. I recall that as recently as World War II young
Blood Indians in Alberta volunteered for military service, not because

---

[25] Carroll and Haggard, eds., *Three New Mexico Chronicles*, 135–136.

their country was in danger, but because, as they said, "their king needed them."

There may be a moral to this little study—one which has some relevance to the solution of our current Indian Problem. Over the past eighty years our Indians' feelings of close personal relationship with our head of state may have become weakened by the interposition of a large and impersonal Bureau of Indian Affairs, which in turn is but a small part of a huge Department of the Interior which is more concerned with land and resource conservation and management than it is with Indian problems.

As recently as February 11, 1969, a task force established to study the Indian and the Bureau of Indian Affairs submitted its findings to the White House. Its first and major recommendation reads: "A meaningful and determined reorganization of the administration of Indian affairs, together with the providing of an effective Administration thrust to go forward to the opportunities of tomorrow and not simply solve the problems of yesterday, can only be accomplished by moving the Bureau of Indian Affairs to the Executive Office of the Presidency, for the objectives of Indian affairs in 1969 require nothing less than the priority, the mandate and visibility which the President himself can give them."[26]

In the light of history this recommendation may appear much less novel than its wording in the future tense would suggest. It is not an attempt to recapture through governmental reorganization that intimate association between the Indian and his head of state which existed in the very heart of our country 200 years ago, when Indian chiefs wore the likeness of their *capitan grande*, "protector and friend of all red men," over their chests, suspended from scarlet silk ribbons?

[26] Alvin M. Josephy, Jr., "The American Indian and the Bureau of Indian Affairs—1969," *Hearings, Subcommittee on Indian Education, Committee on Labor and Public Welfare, U.S. Senate*, 91st Cong., 1st Sess., pt. 2, app. (Washington, 1969), 1447.

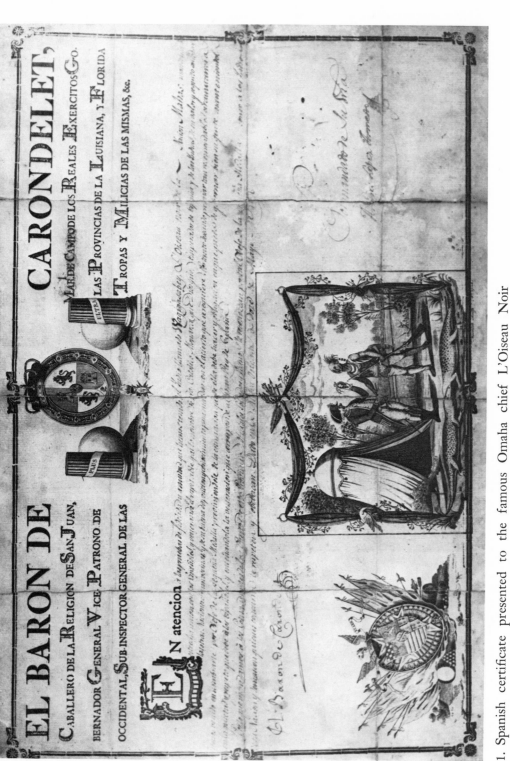

1. Spanish certificate presented to the famous Omaha chief L'Oiseau Noir (Blackbird) in 1796. It bears the signature of the Baron de Carondelet, governor of Louisiana. Nebraska State Historical Society.

2. Payouska (White Hair), chief of the Great Osage, by Charles B. J. F. de Saint-Mémin. The chief wears the large medal and handsome officer's coat presented to him by the United States when he visited Washington in 1804. New-York Historical Society.

The Indomitable Osage in Spanish

Illinois (Upper Louisiana) 1763-1804

CARL H. CHAPMAN

𝒯ʜᴇ Osage Indians were the most important of the tribes living in the western part of Spanish Illinois (Upper Louisiana) during the Spanish rule. They played several roles in the unfolding of the historical scene in the central Mississippi-Missouri Valley area and the prairies to the southwest. They were suppliers of hides and furs to St. Louis and Arkansas Post; they were barriers to overland travel and trade between the Spanish territory bordering the Mississippi and Missouri rivers and that of Mexico and New Mexico; they were buffers against the English during the American Revolution. They were indomitable in their position of power.[1]

[1] Much of the information in this paper has been extracted from an earlier unpublished study, "The Origin of the Osage Indian Tribe: An Ethnographical, Historical and Archaeological Study" (Ph.D. dissertation, University of Michigan, 1959); an abstract appeared in *Abstracts of New World Archaeology*, I (1960). Data were obtained from original archaeological survey and research as well as historical and ethnographical sources. During a thirty-year period of research, most of the Osage Indian village sites recorded in historical manuscripts and maps between 1770 and 1804 have been located. The earlier research by University of Missouri Archaeological Research expeditions in 1940–41 provided most of the site locations. Participants were Professor J. Brewton Berry, Carl H. Chapman, James J. Lowe, John P. Mack, and Professor Jesse E. Wrench. Fuller information about the sites was obtained archaeologically and ethnohistorically in 1961–63 through National Science Foundation grants for the study of "Osage Prehistory," NSF Grants G18585 and GS 13. The last chapter of the archaeological research, which resulted in the location of Fort Carondelet and a better picture of the Little Osage occupation, was made possible through grants by

Dominance of the Osage was necessary in upholding Spanish claim to the whole western area and to the utilization or exploitation of the prairies between the Illinois Spanish possessions and Mexico. Realizing this fact, the Spanish governors at New Orleans early sought to establish a hold over the Osage. When they failed through the chiefs, the Spanish attempted first to subdue the Osage by withholding trade and then by a war of annihilation. When neither lack of trade nor war provided the answer, other measures were adopted. The building of Fort Carondelet in their midst, and the placing of all trade rights in the hands of the Chouteaus of St. Louis, who planned and commanded the fort, seemingly established the necessary controls over the Osage. This was more fiction than fact, for the Osage continued their free reign of the prairies almost unchecked, but the governor at distant New Orleans was satisfied with the arrangement.

In order to comprehend the basis for the Spanish concern in the manipulation of the Osage, it is useful to know something about the area nominally under their control, the location of their villages, their way of life, and their political and ceremonial organization.

The location of the Osage villages is important because they were the base of operations of the tribe, and, though not permanent abodes, were returned to for a number of months of the year between hunting, gathering, and war expeditions. The mode of living makes possible a better understanding of the large extent of the area over which the Osage maintained some degree of control. Osage life was a regular hunting-gathering ceremonial cycle adapted both to the needs of the tribe and to those of the fur traders who supplied some of the basic materials of everyday existence. Failure to understand the limited power of the chief and the tribal importance of the mourning-war ceremony, with its concomitant war party performed at least once each year, explains why Spanish officials considered the Osage perfidious and determined on a war to exterminate them. The lucrative fur trade with the Osage and their manipulation by fur traders sheds light on the establishment and disappearance of Fort Carondelet and the effectiveness of the fort and the trade rights in controlling the tribe.

---

the National Park Service, Missouri River Basin Salvage Program, and the Archaeological Research Division of the Department of Anthropology, University of Missouri-Columbia, for archaeological research in the Kaysinger Bluff Reservoir area. Information obtained while the writer was acting as an expert witness for the Justice Department, Lands Division, Indian Claims Section, 1961–67, was also helpful in the location of Osage sites and hunting territories.

THE SETTING: OSAGE VILLAGE SITES AND
HUNTING TERRITORY, 1763–1804

Information bearing specifically on the location of Osage village sites and hunting territories in the period 1763–1804 has been obtained from published and manuscript materials and surveys conducted on foot. Particularly important was the study both of old maps on which Osage village sites and territory were shown, and modern maps, with the aim of equating the old map locations with the present-day physical-geographical locations by certain identifiable points of reference on each. Then a search of the area on foot for actual site evidences and finally the excavation of the site when evidences were located completed the site identifications.

The Osage appear to have had their village sites and hunting territory in the area between the Missouri and Arkansas rivers during the entire period 1763–1804. As far as can be determined, the center of Osage occupation prior to 1714 was wholly in the upper Osage valley. About 1717 one group of Osage, referred to as the Little Osage, moved to the Missouri River near the Missouri Indian village, located near or on the pinnacles in the bend of the Missouri River encompassing Saline County, Missouri. The Little Osage continued to live near the Missouri Indians until about 1777 and were completely separate from the Great or Big Osage, who lived on the upper Osage River. The Little Osage returned to the upper Osage River valley near the Big Osage between 1777 and 1794. It appears that during this time the Big Osage had become frequent users of the Arkansas River drainage, perhaps due in part to seeking hides on the prairies and in part to trade on the Arkansas when restrictions were placed on trade up the Missouri River by the Spanish authorities. When the Little Osage returned to their old homeland, they too began to hunt in the Neosho and Verdigris river valleys to the west.

After the Spanish officially declared war on the Osage in 1793 and then rescinded the declaration to accept Auguste Chouteau's plan to subdue the tribe in 1794, Fort Carondelet was established for that purpose. The buildings of the fort were not completed until 1795.[2] The

---

[2] Lawrence Kinnaird, ed., *Spain in the Mississippi Valley, 1765–1794* (3 vols., Washington, 1946–49), III, xxi, 143–144, 149, 155. For descriptions of the fort as it was supposed to be built see Louis Houck, ed., *The Spanish Régime in Missouri* (2 vols., Chicago, 1909), II, 100–110. Zenon Trudeau, the lieutenant governor, writing from St. Louis to the Baron de Carondelet, Apr. 18, 1795, told of the success of Fort Carondelet and of the pleasure of the Osage at having the fort in their midst. Abraham P. Nasatir, *Before Lewis and Clark: Documents Illustrating the History of the Missouri, 1785–1804* (2 vols., St. Louis, 1952), I, 320–322.

Osage came to the fort to trade, and evidences of an Osage camp (23VE-2: 23 = Missouri; VE = Vernon County; 2 = number of the site in the system of marking sites used by the Archaeological Survey of Missouri) have been found there.[3] There was one report that an Osage band or village under the leadership of Clermont moved to the Verdigris River in 1795 or 1796. About one-half of Chief White Hair's village in Missouri moved to the Arkansas drainage in 1802 under the leadership of Big Track in order to continue trading with the Chouteaus when trade rights were given to Lisa on the Osage River. The earlier Clermont village site has been located near Claremore, Oklahoma.[4]

When Louisiana was purchased by the United States in 1803, two Osage villages were still located on the upper Osage River (the Carrington and Hayes sites, 23VE-1 and 23VE-4—see 1 and 4 in figure 1), and two Big Osage villages, Clermont's (Clamors) and Gros Cote's, were in the Arkansas River drainage (see figure 2). Confirmation of the continued separation of the Big Osage is in the instructions sent to Peter Chouteau (agent of Indian affairs in Upper Louisiana) on July 17, 1804: "You will take the earliest opportunity for healing the breach between the Osage nation and the party under Big Track, and endeavor to prevail on the latter with his partisans to return to the nation and to live in harmony."[5]

Archaeological evidence of the Osage campsite locations has aided in confirming the cartographical and manuscript evidence. The Missouri Indian village site prior to 1723 has been located on the Pinnacles, in Van Meter State Park, Saline County, Missouri, and on the University of Missouri-Columbia Lyman Archaeological Research Center and

---

[3] See "Control of the Osage: The Establishment of Fort Carondelet" below. All the information on the fort has been brought together there. Locations of the fort and of the Osage villages are pinpointed by number on a map of the upper Osage River (Figure 1).

[4] Trudeau, in a letter to Carondelet, July 21, 1795 (Nasatir, *Before Lewis and Clark*, I, 343–346), noted that one Osage chief with forty men had been to the Arkansas and intimated that they might have done evil there, and a little over a month later, Aug. 30, 1795, in another letter to Carondelet, he said that a Big Osage dwelling of the father-in-law of Clermont had been destroyed by the Natchitoches and that a war party of 100 men had left in pursuit. Brown and Co., *History of Vernon County, Missouri* (St. Louis, 1887), 196, recorded that a split had occurred in the Big Osage in 1795–96 and that one group had settled on the Arkansas River. See also A. Timourian, "Catholic Exploration of the Far West 1794–1835," *Records of the American Catholic Historical Society*, XLVIII (1937), 378. Through the use of historical references, old maps, a modern U.S. Geological Survey topographic map, the Claremore Quadrangle (Oklahoma) (1916 ed. reprinted 1947), and a reconnaissance on foot, the writer located the Clermont village site on September 27, 1961 (Figures 2 and 3).

[5] Clarence E. Carter, ed., *Louisiana Missouri Territory, 1803–1806*, vol. XIII, *Territorial Papers of the United States* (Washington, 1948), 32.

Hamilton Archaeological Field School land. A later Missouri village site (23SA-4) and the Little Osage village site (23SA-3) have been located upstream a few miles.[6]

Cartographic evidence often follows manuscript materials by some years, so it is not until after 1808 that maps show the village locations of the Osage accurately. A manuscript map by William Clark of about 1812 places the "Old Village of the Little Osage" (23SA-3) reasonably accurately on the Salt Fork of the Lamine River and shows a Big Osage town on the "Cooksfield River" (23VE-1 on the Marmaton).[7] The Little Osage village in Saline County had been abandoned for perhaps as long as twenty-five years before the Clark map was drawn, and in Clark's time it was a well-known fact that the Little Osage had had a village on the Osage River fairly close to the Big Osage village on the Marmaton. Pike had visited both villages in 1806, and the locations and information about the villages had been printed in 1811.[8] Even so, not until 1822 was there a thoroughly accurate map showing the Osage village locations. This was the Edward Browne map drawn from the maps and information obtained by Richard Graham.[9] The earliest Big Osage village (23VE-3), noted on the map as "old village abandoned," was near a small stream and can be located readily on the modern topographic map, the Harwood Quadrangle.[10] The Little Osage village (23VE-4) is correctly placed on the Little Osage River and the Big Osage village (23VE-1) is shown on the Marmaton as "Old Village" (Figure 2). The Clermont village, located near Claremore, Oklahoma, is noted on the Browne map as "Clamors Village." It was the Browne map that made it possible to locate this village site accurately on a

[6] C. H. Chapman, "The Little Osage and Missouri Indian Village Sites ca. 1727–1777 A.D.," *Missouri Archaeologist*, XXI (1959), 1–67.

[7] An "Osage village, 2,500 souls" is shown on the Vermillion River (Verdigris River). It is Clermont's town. The map entitled "A Map of North America," signed by William Clark, is in the Coe Collection, Yale University Library.

[8] Zebulon M. Pike, *Exploratory Travels through the Western Territories of North America* (London, 1811); Donald Jackson, ed., *The Journals of Zebulon Montgomery Pike, with Letters and Related Documents* (2 vols., Norman, 1966), I, 306–313; Stephen H. Hart and Archer B. Hulbert, eds., *Zebulon Pike's Arkansas Journal* (Steward Commission of Colorado College and the Denver Public Library, 1932), 43–46.

[9] Manuscript map in color in the National Archives, RG 77, IR 46. An accurate copy (Figure 2) has been made of the portion of the map on which Osage villages are located. Edward Browne was a clerk in the map office in St. Louis. Similar information can be found in Clarence E. Carter, ed., *The Territory of Arkansas, 1819–1825*, vol. XIX, *Territorial Papers of the United States* (Washington, 1953), 392–394, 581–582, and map opposite p. 392.

[10] U.S.G.S. topographic map, prelim. ed., 1941 (Figure 1).

modern map and verify its location by an archaeological reconnaissance conducted on foot. Historic and archaeological materials were collected from it.

The location of the more permanent Osage villages during the period 1763–1804 can be determined wth great accuracy, and the most important village sites have been located and identified through ethnohistorical means.[11] For the first decade or two of the Spanish regime the Big and Little Osage villages were separated by quite some distance, the Little Osage village (23SA-3) being near that of the Missouri Indian tribe on the south bank of the Missouri River, and the Big Osage village on the upper reaches of the Osage River. After 1777 the Little Osage moved to a village location on the north side of the Little Osage River (23VE-4), and the Big Osage moved to the east bank of the Marmaton River (23VE-1). In 1795 or 1796 temporary Osage camps were established near Fort Carondelet (23VE-2) and on the Verdigris River (Oklahoma), and one of them, the Clermont or Claremore (Clamors) village was maintained as a permanent village by 1802. Both the Little Osage (23VE-4) and the Big Osage (23VE-1) villages continued in operation during and past the time of Spanish control of the Mississippi Valley, 1795–1816, but many of the Big Osage had moved to the Verdigris River, a branch of the Arkansas River, and by 1802 it was estimated that at least half of the Big Osage were living in the Arkansas River drainage.

Although the Osage were known to hunt and gather in the upper White River area of Arkansas and Missouri and as far east as the headwaters of the Gasconade River in Missouri during the Spanish regime, Osage hunting territory at this time was primarily in the western prairies of the present state of Missouri, in southeastern Kansas, and in northeastern Oklahoma. This extensive prairie area is a physiographic subdivision sometimes called the Cherokee Plains or Osage Prairies.

11 See nn. 1 and 6; J. B. Berry, C. H. Chapman, and J. P. Mack, "The Archaeological Remains of the Osage," *American Antiquity*, X (1944), 1–11; C. H. Chapman, "A Preliminary Survey of Missouri Archaeology, Part I: Historic Indian Tribes," *Missouri Archaeologist*, X (1946), 16–27; Chapman, "Culture Sequence in the Lower Missouri Valley," in J. B. Griffin, ed., *Archaeology of Eastern United States* (Chicago, 1952), 145–147, fig. 64; Chapman, "Osage Prehistory," *Plains Anthropologist*, VII, no. 16 (1962), 99–100; J. P. Mack, "Archaeological Field Work at the University of Missouri," *Missouri Archaeologist*, VIII (1942), 19–20; C. H. Chapman, "The Hayes Site, 23VE-4," MS in "Part II: Preliminary Archaeological Investigations in the Kaysinger Bluff Reservoir Area" (1965), on file in the American Archaeology Division, Department of Anthropology, College of Arts and Science, University of Missouri-Columbia; and Figure 1.

To sum up, from about 1717 to 1777 the main areas occupied by the Osage were the upper Osage River, the drainage of the Lamine River, and the south bank of the Missouri River in what is now Saline County, Missouri. The hunting territories during this period probably extended as far east as the Gasconade River. The next period, 1777–1804, saw the concentration of Osage activity in the upper Osage River valley and in the Neosho and Verdigris branches of the Arkansas River. During this period the hunting territories were primarily to the west and southwest of village locations which were already on the upper reaches of the Osage River. In the last decade of Spanish rule there was a shift of population and hunting territory to the Neosho and Verdigris rivers.[12]

OSAGE POLITICAL ORGANIZATION
AND THE MOURNING-WAR CEREMONY:
FACTORS IN OSAGE DEPREDATIONS

Perhaps the major source of difficulty in the relationships of the Spanish with the Osage was the lack of understanding of Osage culture by the Spanish rulers. Conversely, the understanding of Osage customs and mores was the main factor in the successful control of their activities by the Chouteaus. Two aspects of Osage culture were especially important to know in dealing with the tribe: (1) their political organization, particularly the power held by the chiefs, and (2) the lack of control by chiefs over war parties deriving from special ceremonies, the most important being the mourning-war ceremony.

The Osage chief held a hereditary position in the sense that he was selected from a particular extended family within a specific clan. New chiefs were usually selected from the sons or grandsons of the deceased chief, but might come from any close kin.[13] The prime duty of these hereditary chiefs was to enforce peace within the tribe. The chief's house was a sanctuary for Osage people and for any foreigners who might seek refuge. In the usual European meaning of chief, the Osage chief's power was very limited. In most instances the chief was the leader rather than the ruler of the council in regard to decisions con-

[12] C. H. Chapman, "The Aboriginal Use and Occupancy of Lands West of the Mississippi River by the Osage Indian Tribe, and Village Locations and Hunting Territories of the Osage from Time Immemorial to 1808 A.D.," information relating to case 105, Indian Claims Commission, filed in Indian Claims Section, Lands Division, U.S. Department of Justice (1960).

[13] Thomas Nuttall, *Travels into the Arkansas Territory, 1819*, vol. XIII, *Early Western Travels, 1748–1846*, ed. Reuben Gold Thwaites (Cleveland, 1905), 237.

cerning civil functions of the tribe. The general consensus of the council usually guided the chief's decision.[14]

The office of chief descended to the lineal male heirs of the chief in ordinary circumstances. If the heir or heirs were disqualified, the soldiers in council selected an acceptable new chief from the nearest kin of the former chief.[15] The council was made up of those who had been initiated into the seven tribal degrees, and thus included the top religious as well as sociopolitical leaders of the village or society.[16] The council was the true governing body of the tribe. This body of elders had no set meeting place, but selected the house of a prominent and generous man. Consequently a man could raise his prestige and position by entertaining the council, and by this means it is suspected that he could have some, if not a great deal, of influence in Osage government. This custom may explain in part how the Chouteaus became so influential among the Osage. The cost of feeding and entertaining the council would be small in proportion to the gains obtained by manipulating or influencing council decisions on hunting or war expeditions. Marriage into the hereditary group from which the chiefs were selected might have been another way to gain the "accredited ascendancy" attributed to the Chouteaus in the Osage tribe.[17]

The mourning-war ceremony of the Osage was a means of directing all violent emotional expressions into warfare and ceremony and was thus a psychological safety valve for the society as a whole. Underlying the mourning-war ceremony was a belief that the spirit of the dead Osage needed company for his trip to the hereafter. In order to satisfy the need for a companion, the scalp of an enemy, preferably, must be obtained and hung over the grave. Therefore, if he could afford it, a man who had lost someone dear, or a close relative, sponsored the mourning-war rite, which was the ceremony for the organization of a war party to obtain a scalp. After the scalp was obtained, a piece of it was given to the chief mourner, who planted bits of it at the head and foot of the grave of the one for whom the rite was performed.[18]

---

[14] Francis La Flesche, "The Osage Tribe," *Annual Report of the Bureau of American Ethnology for 1921*, 36, 67; also discussed in C. H. Chapman and E. F. Chapman, *Indians and Archaeology of Missouri* (Columbia, Mo., 1964), 109.

[15] La Flesche, "The Osage Tribe," 68.

[16] *Ibid.*, 47.

[17] Trudeau to the governor, Jan. 15, 1798 (Nasatir, *Before Lewis and Clark*, II, 538), noted that Auguste Chouteau "had found the means of diverting and dissuading them by good counsels and by means of the accredited ascendency which he has among both Little and Big Osage tribes."

[18] G. A. Dorsey, "The Osage Mourning-War Ceremony," *American Anthropologist*, IV (1902), 404–411; Francis La Flesche, *War and Peace Ceremony of the Osage Indians*,

The mourning-war ceremony got the Osage into much trouble and earned for them enmity, fear, and distrust. Frank Speck, who worked with the Osage at the beginning of our century, describes the reason for the ceremony precisely as "the ceremonial of securing an offering to pay for the entrance of a human soul into the future life."[19] It was believed that at death the soul went into dormancy until someone secured a scalp through the mourning ceremony war party. The setting off of the war party in a straight line at the end of the third day of the ceremony with intentions of obtaining a scalp of the first person or persons they encountered led to trouble. Friend, enemy, stranger, nearly anyone that happened to be in the line of march of the mourning-war party was likely to lose his scalp. No one could stop a mourning-war ceremony once it had been arranged, for it was essentially a religious and honor-bound operation that a man of prominence, conscience, and good will had to perform.[20] Furthermore, it was a means by which the young men in the society could gain honors allowing them to become prominent persons (Figure 4). Not even the power of a chief or a trader, not even the Chouteaus, could stop this custom that had become such an important tradition to the Osage. Thus war or, from the European viewpoint, murder on a limited scale was as much a part of Osage life as hunting. It was not until late in the nineteenth century that the scalp of an animal or the locks or beard of a hired individual were substituted for a human scalp in the performance of the ceremony.[21]

HISTORICAL RÉSUMÉ

From its beginning St. Louis was the logical headquarters for controlling the Osage trade and directing Osage affairs. This was recognized by the Spanish when they took over the Western Illinois in 1769 and included the Osage country in the District of Upper Louisiana.[22]

Bulletin 101, Bureau of American Ethnology (Washington, 1939), 87, 137; J. O. Dorsey, "An Account of the War Customs of the Osages," *American Naturalist*, XVIII (1884), 115–129.

[19] F. G. Speck, "Notes on the Ethnology of the Osage Indian," *Transactions of the Free Museum of Science and Art* (University of Pennsylvania), II (1907), 168.

[20] Charles E. Campbell, "Down among the Red Men," *Collections of the Kansas State Historical Society*, XVII (1928), 628, described the murder of a friendly Wichita chief by an Osage mourning-war party; La Flesche, *War and Peace Ceremony*, 142.

[21] La Flesche, *War and Peace Ceremony*, 142–143.

[22] Correspondence indicates that it was more difficult for the Spanish governor at New Orleans to keep communications open with the Osage from Arkansas Post than it was from St. Louis. See especially Nasatir, *Before Lewis and Clark*, I, 63–64, 536; Houck, ed., *The Spanish Régime in Missouri*, I, 73–74.

The English were across the Mississippi River to the east, and the Osage, who were thought to be hostile toward the Spanish, occupied the prairies on the edge of the vast territory of the Great Plains between the southwestern Spanish colonies (New Mexico and Mexico) and Spanish Illinois. Stories of the perfidy and great strength of the Osage circulated in the Spanish hierarchy. The Spanish rulers were frightened by reports that tribes friendly to the Spanish were being driven as far as San Antonio, Texas, by onslaughts of the Osage.[23] Fear of English encroachment on Missouri River trade and fear of Osage raids caused the Spanish rulers to adopt harsh measures affecting these Indians immediately after Spanish rule was established. The Spanish at first apparently made no distinctions between the Big and Little Osage, considering them both a single tribe, although their separateness by this time is certain.

In 1771 it was noted that the Missouri Indian and Little Osage villages were only eighty leagues distant from St. Louis on the Missouri River and that the Indians were being influenced by the English, who had given them presents and were trying to turn them against the Spanish. A Spanish fort, San Carlos, had been established at the mouth of the Missouri River in 1767 in order to cut off English trade upstream. In spite of these precautions English traders succeeded in bypassing the fort to the north, or in slipping past it, as in the instance of Ducharme, who traded with the Little Osage in the winter of 1772–73.[24] Ducharme, a Canadian, was captured, and in 1773 the Spanish ordered trade cut off completely with the Osage and Missouri Indians. It was mentioned in the documents concerning the capture of Ducharme that the Little Osage and the Missouri were subject to frequent attack by other Indians on behalf of the Spanish government, which was trying to destroy them.[25]

Sanctions against the Osage had begun almost at the start of Spanish rule, and the policy was to try to bend them wholly to Spanish will or to destroy them completely. This policy of the Spanish led to the crushing blows dealt the Missouri and Little Osage villages on the Missouri River by northern Indians (Sac and Fox) and caused the return of the Little Osage to their old homeland on the Osage River sometime after 1775.[26]

The American Revolution had an effect on the Indians in Spanish

---

[23] Grant Foreman, *Indians and Pioneers* (New Haven, 1936), 14.

[24] A full discussion of this incident is in Abraham P. Nasatir, "Ducharme's Invasion of Missouri: An Incident in the Anglo-Spanish Rivalry for the Indian Trade of Upper Louisiana," *Missouri Historical Review*, XXIV (1929), 8.

[25] *Ibid.,* 14.

[26] For fuller discussion see n. 6 and J. Spencer, "Missouri's Aboriginal Inhabitants, Part II," *Missouri Historical Review*, XXIV (1929), 28.

Illinois and may have been a stimulus for Spanish authorities to seek the removal of some of their villages to new locations. A report dated 1777 placed the Little Osage eighty-five leagues from St. Louis, one-half league from the shore of the Missouri River, and placed the Missouri Indian village upstream one or two leagues farther and on the bank of the river.[27] That location of the Little Osage village was on the Petitsas Plains (Tetsaw Plains). The 1777 report is the last verifiable mention of inhabited Little Osage and Missouri villages on the Missouri River near the mouth of Grand River. The village sites of the period about 1723–77 have already been tentatively identified and located.[28]

When Spain joined France in 1779 in the war against England, money, gunpowder, and cloth were passed secretly to the Americans through Spanish-American possessions, making this decade an extremely unsettled one for the Indians.[29] Certainly it must have been very confusing to the Osage as their allegiance and aid were sought through blandishments and presents from French and English traders and through coercive actions by Spanish officials. Since both France and Spain were helping the Americans in their fight for independence, England attempted to obtain all the Indian aid possible. The tribes in Upper Louisiana were kept stirred up and the situation was not much relieved by the end of the war in 1783. The struggle after 1783 was for the Missouri River valley Indian trade. The English traders continued to encroach upon this lucrative business by going overland from Canada to the upper Missouri.

Due to rumored depredations by the Osage, an ultimatum was given them by the Spanish in 1790 to send two chiefs to New Orleans as hostages to atone for any murders or damages committed by culprits not turned over to authorities. The Osage refused, and as trade with them had been cut off, they went to the Missouri River in 1791 and confiscated the goods of traders going upriver to trade with the Kansa. Whether they were the Big or Little Osage, or both, was not mentioned. The Big Osage went to the Kansa village and tried unsuccessfully to take the goods from the trader Pierre Chouteau (half-brother of Auguste Chouteau, one of the founders of St. Louis), whom they blamed for trade having been stopped.[30]

The Spanish attempted to incite all the tribes surrounding the Osage

[27] Houck, ed., *The Spanish Régime in Missouri*, II, 141–142.

[28] See n. 8 and B. Berry and C. Chapman, "An Oneota Site in Missouri," *American Antiquity*, VII (1942), 290–305, for full discussion of the Little Osage and Missouri Indian village site locations.

[29] Houck, ed., *The Spanish Régime in Missouri*, I, xx.

[30] Nasatir, *Before Lewis and Clark*, I, 49, 144, 149–150, 159.

to go to war with them and were successful in getting the Sac and Fox to send several war parties into Osage country. Five Osages were reported killed in these raids. By 1793 greater pressure was placed on the Osage. All trade on the Missouri River and its tributary, the Osage River, was cut off, war was officially declared, and the surrounding tribes were urged to war against them. In the same year the Delaware and Shawnee, who before 1790 had moved to Upper Louisiana near the settlement of Cape Girardeau, Missouri, were asked to assist in the war. The Iowa, Sac, and Fox were sent orders to refuse the Osage passage to trade on the Des Moines River. Everything was in readiness for a hard blow against the Osage by all the tribes surrounding them, including Indians as far away as Mexico. Many Indians were to be led by Europeans under secret orders of the Spanish rulers.[31]

Although war was thus declared in 1793, it did not take place that year, for the arrangements took so long that all was not ready until August, when the Osage were certain to leave for their fall hunt. It was postponed until 1794, which was to be the year of extermination of the Osage.[32]

In January of that year the Osage themselves struck the blow that decided the progress of the official war. A "war party of 100 men," participants in a mourning-war ceremony, appeared at Ste. Genevieve and killed a man. This so frightened the settlers that they raised a great clamor for peace. Shortly after the Osage raid Auguste Chouteau went to New Orleans to make proposals to the governor general for holding the Osage in check. He took with him six Osage chiefs to aid in convincing Carondelet that his proposed fort among the Osage would keep them under control, if at the same time he were given exclusive trade rights and command of the fort. The proposal was accepted early in May, 1794.[33] Perhaps one of the main reasons for the contract with Chouteau was the rumor that the French, under the direction of Genêt, were raising an army on the Ohio River to invade Spanish Illinois, and it was thought that the French and Americans would enlist the support of the Osage to wipe out the Spanish settlements.[34]

[31] For details see Houck, ed., *The Spanish Régime in Missouri*, II, 42–44, 49–53; Nasatir, *Before Lewis and Clark*, II, 530.

[32] See Kinnaird, ed., *Spain in the Mississippi Valley*, III, 144, 149, 155, for correspondence of Carondelet, Trudeau, and Delano. See also Houck, ed., *The Spanish Régime in Missouri*, II, 55–56, for Trudeau correspondence concerning the war.

[33] Trudeau to Gayoso de Lemos, Dec. 20, 1797 (Nasatir, *Before Lewis and Clark*, I, 526), reviews the actions concerning control of the Osage.

[34] See discussion by Kinnaird, ed., *Spain in the Mississippi Valley*, III, and Carondelet to Las Casas, 1795, in Houck, ed., *The Spanish Régime in Missouri*, II, 100–102.

The buildings at the new fort, named Fort Carondelet in honor of the governor general, were not completed until the fall of 1795. For nearly a year relative peace and quiet prevailed in Upper Louisiana. Peace had been established between the Osage and the Pawnee, Kansa, and Comanche. The most important event of the continued hostile activity against the Osage by neighboring tribes was the destruction of a Big Osage dwelling by the Natchitoches. In the dwelling was the father-in-law of Clermont, who was an important hereditary chief of the time. Since this event challenged the honor of the Osage tribal chief and called for his support of a mourning-war ceremony and a "war party of 100 men," the peace was broken. A war party left in pursuit of the murderers in spite of the attempts by Chouteau to stop it.[35]

The resumption of hostilities by the Clermont followers probably split the Big Osage into two groups. The Chouteaus had promised peace and were desirous of obtaining it at any price in order to continue their recently arranged lucrative trade monopoly with the Osage. Clermont's position as outstanding warrior and chief of the Big Osage no doubt made it necessary for him to support a mourning-war ceremony for his father-in-law; he could not do otherwise and still maintain his prominence in the tribe.[36]

It appears that the Chouteaus, finding it impossible to stop Clermont, undermined his standing through arrangements to give presents and medals to other "smaller chiefs" in order to raise their power and prestige in the tribe. The giving of medals, thereby creating new chiefs,[37] was the usual means of manipulating the Indians. It is very significant that in 1795 Pierre Chouteau ordered two large medals for two small-medal chiefs, White Hair and Little Chief, and a number of smaller medals, doubtless designed to influence the political situation among the Osage, were delivered in 1796. The record seems to be fairly clear that Clermont, on his return from the "war party of 100 men," could not resume his position of leadership of the Big Osage in Missouri. Therefore, he and his followers may have separated from the others and established the Arkansas unit on the Verdigris River.[38]

The Chouteaus held their exclusive trade privilege with the Osage from 1795 through 1801, and their power and prestige were increased

[35] See n. 2.

[36] Trudeau to Carondelet, Aug. 30, 1795 (Nasatir, *Before Lewis and Clark*, I, 346), noted that the Natchitoches had murdered Clermont's father-in-law. See also n. 4.

[37] On the importance of medals see John C. Ewers, "Symbols of Chiefly Authority in Spanish Louisiana," in this volume.

[38] Nasatir, *Before Lewis and Clark*, I, 326–327, 426, 430; Houck, ed., *The History of Missouri*, I, 193–194; and n. 4.

within the Osage units during this period. It was mentioned in 1798 that the Chouteaus had "accredited ascendancy" among both the Big and Little Osage, indicating that they had probably been adopted by important clans in which the hereditary chieftanship resided.

Due to a change in Spanish governors in 1802, Chouteau's grip on Osage exclusive trade was broken and transferred to Manuel Lisa and other traders at St. Louis. The possession and command of Fort Carondelet also were turned over to Lisa.[39] This caused another split in the Osage tribe, as almost half of the White Hair Osage in Missouri moved to the Arkansas drainage in order to continue trading with the Chouteaus, who still had trading rights there. This shearing away of Osage groups or villages illustrates the lack of political control over all Osage units by any individual chief. Villages were autonomous, with their own leaders and councils. If there was leadership of all Osage units by one chief, it must have been in war and ceremony, and it is doubtful that such leadership, if it existed, extended to more mundane matters after the ceremony was brought to a close.[40]

In spite of the war of extermination projected against the Osage during Spanish rule, carried on by surrounding tribes, and the restrictions in trade for long periods, the Osage prospered and expanded their contacts and territory to the south and west.

CONTROL OF THE OSAGE: THE ESTABLISHMENT OF FORT CARONDELET

The first real abatement of Osage Indian harassment of Indians and Europeans alike in Spanish Illinois and the Southwest came with the establishment of Fort Carondelet on the upper Osage River. The fort as a military establishment does not appear to be the real reason for the seeming control of the Osage, for the small garrison could have been overwhelmed at any time by the 1,200 or more Osage warriors sur-

[39] On the accredited ascendency of Auguste Chouteau see Trudeau to the governor, Jan. 15, 1798, in Nasatir, *Before Lewis and Clark*, II, 538–539. In a summary of trade licenses issued at St. Louis, 1799–1804, in the year 1802 the license to trade with the Big and Little Osage was given to Lisa, Sarpy, Sanguinet, and Benoit for five years. *Ibid.*, II, 592, 687–689.

[40] This second schism of the Osage is mentioned by Speck, "Notes on the Ethnology of the Osage Indian," 167; H. W. Ryan, "Jacob Bright's Journal of a Trip to the Osage Indians," *Journal of Southern History*, XV (1949), 512. Similar divisions of Plains Indian tribes are noted in M. W. Smith, "Political Organization of the Plains Indians," *University Studies* (University of Nebraska), 24 (1924), 68–73.

rounding it.[41] It is doubtful if the fort was anything more than a grandiose trading post and fur-trapper station used as a base of operations for fur trappers and Indian traders hired by the Chouteaus to man the installation. Having such a trading center filled with supplies practically on their doorsteps must have pleased the Osage and tended to keep them closer to their home-base villages.[42]

The closer relationships of the traders through longer periods of contact, intermarriage, and trade meant more exchange of presents and a greater distribution of trade goods and supplies, and thus a greater affluence for the Osage. It is surmised that in order to control the decisions of the Osage concerning hunting and war, the council was entertained frequently by the traders. Presents to council members and chiefs to gain influence and favor must have been welcome. For a while, no doubt, the directions taken by hunting and war parties were away from the Spanish settlements and Indian tribes friendly to the Spanish. Thus the Spanish record would show clearly that the Osage were being controlled.

Just what Fort Carondelet was like is in part conjectural, although detailed instructions for its construction were outlined in a contract dated May 18, 1794, to Auguste Chouteau, approved by the Baron de Carondelet:

> Ist. He will construct a fortified building (which will serve as barracks for the garrison) of the dimensions which appear on the annexed plan, and covered with tiles of brick or slate, and defended by four cannon and four swivel-guns. The buildings will be: a large warehouse, a lodging for the commandant, a powder-magazine built of brick or stone, a bakery, a kitchen, and privies— the whole surrounded with a strong stockade of six inches in thickness and sixteen feet in height (of which four feet shall be left in the ground) forming a square. It shall have four bastions, with the corresponding footbank, like the fort recently built at San Louis of Ilinoa; and shall be placed on the height or hill which commands the village of the Osages. The [guns on the] stronghold must [be able to] play on everything around them without the houses or cabins being able to offer the slightest obstacle.

---

[41] In Chouteau's contract it is stated that the Great and Little Osage count some 2,200 fighting men (Houck, Spanish Régime in Missouri, II, 106), but Trudeau in his letter to Carondelet, Apr. 10, 1793 (Kinnaird, ed., Spain in the Mississippi Valley, III, 148), notes that they have "a population of 1,250 men, young men, and warriors."

[42] Trudeau to Carondelet, Apr. 18, 1795 (Nasatir, Before Lewis and Clark, II, 320), tells how pleased and proud the Osages are to have the fort in their midst.

In approving the contract, the following change was approved by the Baron de Carondelet:

> I accept in the name of His Majesty the proposition which Don Augusto Chouteau makes in the foregoing memorial, for the construction of a fort among the nation of the Great Osages; and in view of the difficulty which has been laid before me, which may arise in procuring brick or slate for the roof, I consent to the buildings being covered with turf, according to the method that is practiced in Ilinoa, whenever the roof cannot be made otherwise.

The annexed plan is given in part in the following:

> Plan of the stronghold which is to be constructed upon the little eminence which commands the village of the Osages, at the expense of Don Augusto Chouteau, according to the contract which he has made with the Government in the name of His Majesty.
>
> The said stronghold shall be composed of two stories; the first shall be built of brick or stone, and the second story of pieces of timber two [sic] inches square, placed horizontally one above another, in the mode in which the Americans build. This stronghold shall form an exact square, of thirty-two feet on each side. The second story shall be placed diagonally, that is, in such manner that each face of it shall cut across and correspond to the angle of the first story, and each angle shall be in the middle of the face of the said second story. . . .
>
> The floor under the first story shall be at least three inches thick unless the contractor shall prefer to make it of brick closely joined or of stone laid in the same way. . . .
>
> The height of the first story shall be ten feet clear between the floors; and that of the second, nine feet in the same terms; the roof shall have a pitch of six to eight feet, and be covered with tiles of brick, slate, or stone, or with turf.
>
> The entire framework of the building shall be supported by four posts, raised at equal distances in the interior of the building; and on these, for its greater solidity, the cross-beams shall rest.
>
> Two embrasures, eighteen inches square, shall be cut in each face of the first story, in which shall be placed artillery on naval gun-carriages. . . .
>
> The door of the building which shall be of the most solid (planks) with its hinges, bolts, and locks of iron, shall be six feet six inches high and five feet wide. . . .[43]

[43] Houck, ed., *The Spanish Régime in Missouri*, II, 106–109.

In an earlier translation of some of the same information Houck notes that the logs of the upper story were to be ten inches square rather than two, and this is probably correct:

> The said stronghold is to be composed of two parts: The first shall be of brick or stone and the second of logs ten inches square laid horizontally one upon the other, as the Americans practice.[44]

In spite of the fact that twenty "soldiers" were stationed at Fort Carondelet during the period 1794–1802, no description of the fort seems to be in existence. Lisa, who took over the fort in 1802, failed to describe it, and Zebulon Pike, who was there just four years later in 1806, could find no evidence of it. It appears that the lack of information surrounding the location and description of the installation was an intentional, well-kept secret. The only apparent reason for such a secret would have been that the fort had not been built to the specifications laid out by Carondelet, and this may have been the case.

A history of Vernon County published in 1887 indicates that the location of Fort Carondelet was probably on Halley's Bluff, where early settlers had noted a stone wall and where cache pits had been cut into the solid rock of the bluff. "It was doubtless little more than a large log cabin trading house with perhaps a block house and one or two cabins, the whole surrounded by palisades, reinforced in places at least by a stone fence or wall." It was also surmised that the caches cut in the stone were "constructed by its garrison, as receptacles for their stores or the goods received from the Indians, and they may have been in the enclosure."[45]

Halley's Bluff has been reported by people in the region as the location of a historic Osage Indian village and burial ground. Indian burials were dug up on the bluff thirty years ago, and the items found with them (in the possession of one of the local residents)[46] are primarily European trade goods consisting of small white glass beads, copper bracelets, brass arrowheads, and a fragment of a native-made catlinite pipe. One of the grave diggers reported that the burials were fully extended, supine, and covered with rocks. It was judged from the description and the associated material that the graves had in fact been those of Osage Indians.

The University of Missouri Archaeological Research party searched

---

[44] Houck, *A History of Missouri*, II, 212.
[45] *History of Vernon County, Missouri*, 540, and Figure 5.
[46] Mr. C. P. McCumber was living in the frame house on Halley's Bluff in 1940–41.

the area pointed out as the place where the burials had been found and discovered bits of copper and brass kettles and a small cut-out brass arrowhead in a garden area, indicating that this was probably the location of an Osage Indian campsite. Several test trenches were dug in an attempt to locate the Osage burial ground, without success, but a test trench to determine the extent of the site and the possibility of subsurface evidences yielded an iron trade ax—reassuring evidence that in fact here was an Indian site of historic significance.[47]

Investigations were continued on Halley's Bluff in 1962 and 1963 in an attempt to locate the Osage burial ground area and to obtain more information on the nature of the Osage Indian campsite. Since historic information tended to point to the site as the location of the Fort Carondelet of 1795–1802, this possibility was also explored.[48] The entire area was scanned carefully during the winter and spring, when vegetation cover was at a minimum. The whole bluff area was searched on foot and plans were made to conduct excavations of several of the features that would possibly provide clues to the use of the area. Unfortunately the part of the bluff that had the most potential has been a favorite picnic spot for the past 100 years and much building of cabins and other changes have taken place there, making it difficult to find evidence of the flimsy Osage houses.

An interesting feature slated for excavation was found on the surface, approximately 150 feet from the edge of the bluff under which the cache pits had been dug. It appeared to be an embankment five to ten feet wide and about six inches in height, paralleling the edge of the bluff. A section of the embankment forty feet long was excavated. The excavation was carried five feet on either side of the embankment in order to make certain that any associated features might be found. It was soon apparent that the ridge or embankment owed its height to the addition of a sandy, light-colored soil. Beneath the added soil were two parallel trenches six to twelve inches wide but usually nine, dug to a depth of nine to twelve inches. The trenches were four feet apart. The dirt inside the trenches was often flecked with charcoal or soil that had been burnt red. No post molds or other evidence could be found that might have aided in the interpretation of the feature. Since the parallel trenches appeared to be in a straight line, tests were made at fifty-foot intervals to

[47] See n. 1.

[48] The field work in 1963 was conducted with the aid of a National Park Service grant for archaeological investigations in the Kaysinger Bluff Reservoir area. A manuscript report of the work on Fort Carondelet is in the files of the American Archaeology Division, Department of Anthropology, College of Arts and Science, University of Missouri-Columbia.

determine the full extent of the feature. It was found that a curved, rather than straight, line was being followed. It ran under a log cabin to the south, crossed a roadway, and continued into the yard of a modern house. The feature could be followed 300 feet north of the yard fence at the house but no farther, due perhaps to the fact that an old roadway which was eroded badly began to parallel the feature at this point. On the accompanying map the part of the feature that is relatively certain is shown by a double-dash line, and that which is purely a projection is shown by a single-dash line (Figure 5).

The possibility that the embankment and the subsurface parallel trenches were a part of the fortification of Fort Carondelet was considered. The fact that the rock outcropped less than two feet beneath the surface would have made it impossible for stockade posts to be set in the ground at this place. If a stockade had been made, it would have been necessary to devise some means of supporting it other than by the usual practice of sinking the stockade posts four feet into the ground. It was speculated that if indeed the feature were evidence of a stockade, the trenches could have been prepared to receive logs placed end to end, to which an X-type stockade wall could have been attached, the whole stabilized by covering the logs and the area between the X stockade with soil. Considering the possibility that the double trench–embankment feature might be evidence of the stockade of Fort Carondelet, other features were sought.

An important find made at the south edge of the projected feature was a large pit dug into the solid sandstone rock within the projected feature enclosure (Figure 5). The pit was similar in size and shape to those under the bluff to the north. It was dug under an overhanging ledge and was protected in front by a very large rock. It was completely hidden from view and access from either above or below, as the only access was by a narrow areaway between the bluff face and the large rock in front of it, to the west. This large dry storage bin was more than six feet in diameter and at least six feet deep. It was dry enough to have been used for the storage of powder and was so well protected that it could have been the powder magazine for Fort Carondelet. This discovery and idea prompted a detailed search of the area immediately above and below it.

A pathway was found which led from the top of the bluff, through the crack in the rock that was access to the pit, down to the base of the bluff where there was a spring, a source of water still used by campers. Not far from the spring to the north was a roadway leading from the bank of the Osage River to the top of the bluff. Although the roadway was relatively steep, oxen could have pulled carts or stone boats (sledges) up from the river. Due east of the pit and above it were large cut-sandstone foundation blocks stacked against the yard fence. A pile of similar foundation rock south of the house was uncovered, some of which had been used as foundation rock for the house. The rocks were of large size and perhaps of sufficient number to have been the foundation of the blockhouse of the type that Carondelet wanted as the main building of the fort. Preliminary excavation among the rock produced a gun flint. Encouraged by these findings a metal detector was obtained and used in the yard area of the house to avoid digging up the lawn. Fragments of brass and copper kettles, lead, and the lock plate of a flint-lock rifle were located with the detector. The lock plate was submitted to Mr. T. M. Hamilton, expert on identification of trade guns,[49] who judged that it had been made in the early 1790s.

These findings were more than coincidental. It was speculated from them that the main building of Fort Carondelet was possibly located near the present house on the bluff—the location is indicated by a dotted line on the accompanying map (Figure 5). This location overlooks the pit that could have been used as a powder magazine and the spring in the valley below. It also controls the river and the full length of the "stockade." The gun flint, the 1790 lock plate, and the pieces of brass, copper, and lead are the types of articles that should be found at a trading post–fort of the Fort Carondelet period. The cut-stone foundation blocks were much earlier than any known large house in the vicinity, adding credence to the speculation that they were part of the main building of Fort Carondelet.

A series of large pits cut into the solid sandstone, but partially protected by the overhanging bluff, were in a position overlooking the Osage River and west of the possible stockade (Figure 6). The remaining pits were only thirty to forty-two inches in diameter at the top and were bell-shaped and six to seven feet in diameter at the bottom. The pits were of the same shape as those found dug in the ground on the nearby Little Osage site (23 VE–4) (Figure 7). Perhaps the Indians were hired to dig them. Good examples of the pits are still present under a part of the bluff, though most of the original twenty-four or more have been destroyed by vandalism. Although accumulated trash was removed from five of the pits, all of it was relatively recent. Treasure hunters and relic hunters had cleaned them out many times before, according to

---

[49] Mr. Hamilton is the compiler of "Indian Trade Guns," *Missouri Archaeologist*, XXII (1960), and author of many articles on the subject.

local residents. The pits would have been good storage receptacles for furs obtained from the Indians during the winter hunting season. During the flood season in the spring the furs could have been rafted or boated to St. Louis. Furthermore, the pits and their valuable contents could have been protected easily by one man with a swivel gun stationed at the large rock immediately south of them, and the rock would have served as a protection against any attacks from the river.

Another significant feature discovered when tracing the extent of the pits under the bluff was a tunnel leading from the base of the bluff to its top. This tunnel was a natural crack in the face of the bluff that had been widened and cleaned out sufficiently for one individual to go through. Although the tunnel allowed access from the top to the base of the bluff where the pits were located, it could have been closed off quickly and easily and protected by one man (Figure 5).

That this section of Halley's Bluff is indeed the site of the long-lost Fort Carondelet is not absolutely established, but supportive evidence makes it the most likely conclusion. The location at a very defensible position that has, as well, the advantages of easy access to the river and the prairie, the protection and storage features, and the dated artifacts are convincing. If it was not Fort Carondelet, it must have been an important trading post of about the same period.

CONCLUSION

The Osage Indians were indomitable in maintaining their position of power in the prairies on the western border of Spanish Illinois throughout the Spanish regime in the Mississippi Valley. During the Spanish rule they maintained their hunting territory in what is now Missouri, Arkansas, Kansas, and Oklahoma, and they extended their actual control of prairies and lands to the southwest in Oklahoma by establishing a permanent village on the Verdigris River.

The Spanish rulers never understood the Osage culture, nor did they try to. They imposed restrictions on trade with the Osage and incited other tribes against them, but when they were unable to subdue them they accepted a more moderate method of control—a trade monopoly and a military installation.

Fort Carondelet was established by the Chouteaus primarily, it seems, as a grandiose trading post in the heart of Osage country. The Chouteaus of St. Louis understood and manipulated the Osage insofar as they could to their own advantage for trade. In so doing they provided Spanish rule with the relative stability, if not tranquility, that they desired on the western borders of Spanish Illinois. It turned out to be a desirable arrangement for all concerned—traders, Osage Indians, and Spanish rulers.

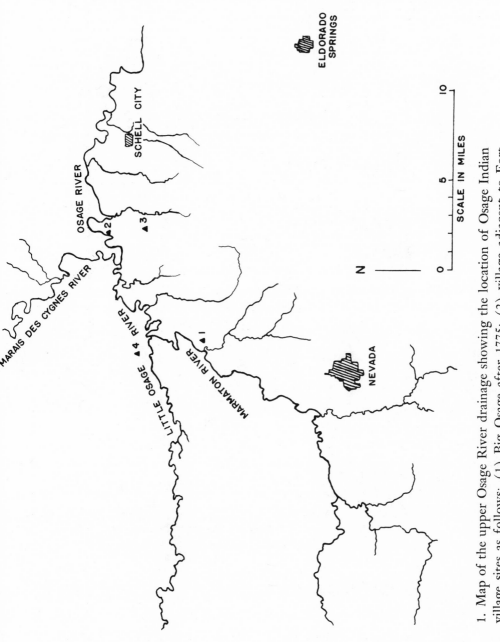

1. Map of the upper Osage River drainage showing the location of Osage Indian village sites as follows: (1) Big Osage after 1775; (2) village adjacent to Fort Carondelet 1795–1802; (3) Big Osage before 1775; (4) Little Osage after 1777.

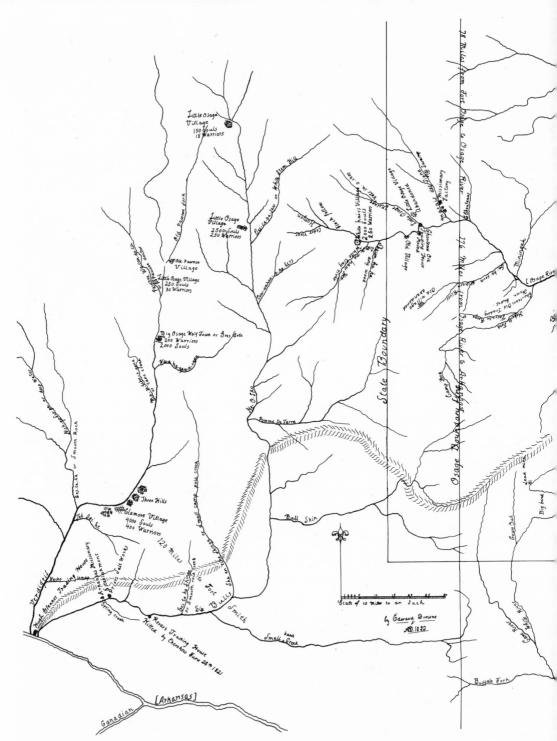

2. Copy of the main portion of the Edward Browne manuscript map of 1822.
Map Division, National Archives.

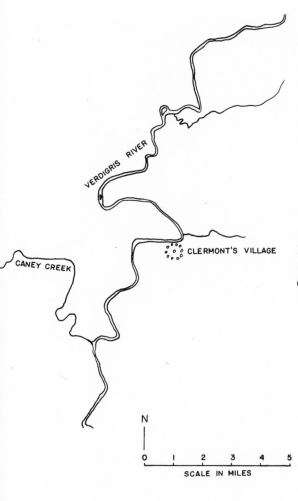

3. Map showing the location of Clamors (Claremore's or Clermont's) village in Oklahoma.

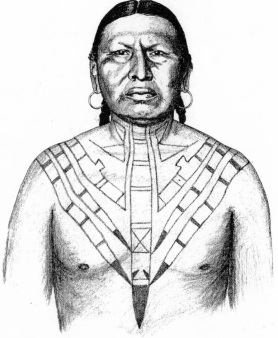

4. Drawing of Osage man showing tattooing earned as honors for participation in war parties. After La Flesche, *War and Peace Ceremony*, pl. 5.

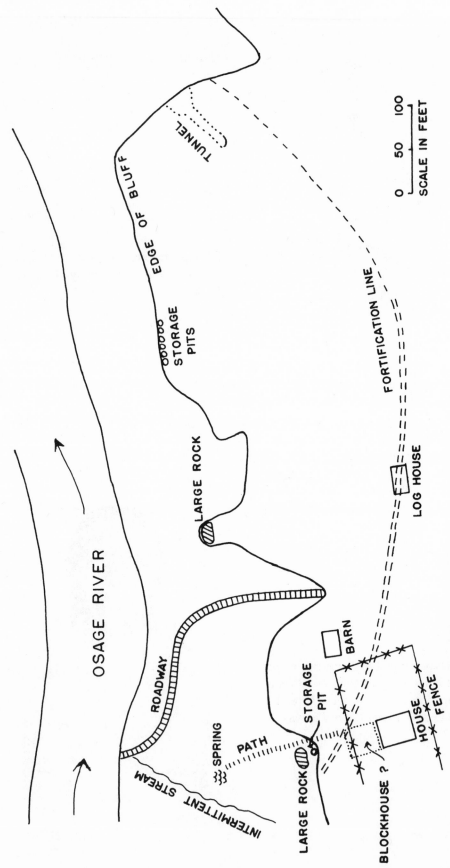

5. Sketch map of Halley's Bluff showing possible evidences of Fort Carondelet.

6. Pits carved in the solid rock under the edge of Halley's Bluff. They are similar in size and shape to those found dug into the ground on the Little Osage village site, 23 VE-4.

7. Pits dug for storage purposes by the Little Osage Indians at the Hayes site, 23 VE-4.

The Myth of the "Imbecile Governor": Captain Fernando de Leyba and the Defense of St. Louis in 1780

JOHN FRANCIS McDERMOTT

I

$\mathcal{T}$HAT Captain Fernando de Leyba was an "imbecile governor," a "Spanish Benedict Arnold," has been the most persistent myth in the history of St. Louis. The charges against the commandant were both baseless and base. It was in fact Leyba who saved St. Louis when it staggered under attack on the afternoon following Corpus Christi Day in 1780. But the tenacity of the myth warrants close examination and a search for its origin.

The case against Captain de Leyba was first set forth by Wilson Primm, a young attorney in St. Louis, in an oration delivered in December, 1831, before the St. Louis Lyceum and published early in 1832. Fifteen years later, at the celebration of the eighty-third anniversary of the founding of the town, Primm again presented his account, correcting a few details and extending his history to a later date.[1]

[1] The first version of Primm's "History of St. Louis" was published in the *Illinois Monthly Magazine*, II (Apr.–May, 1832), 312–321, 355–365; it was reprinted in the *Missouri Historical Society Collections*, IV (1913), 160–193, and in John Francis McDermott, *The Early Histories of St. Louis* (St. Louis, 1952), 105–130. The second version was published in the St. Louis *Weekly Reveille*, Feb. 22, 1847, pp. 1179–82, and in the St. Louis *Missouri Republican;* the latter text—the most complete—was reprinted by

The story that Primm developed from interviews with elderly St. Louisians told readers that

> when the rumor of an attack upon the town began to spread abroad [in 1779], the people became alarmed for their safety.
>
> The town was almost destitute of works of defence, but the inhabitants, amounting to little more than a hundred *men*, immediately proceeded to enclose it with a species of wall, formed of the trunks of small trees, planted in the ground, the interstices being filled up with earth. The wall was some five or six feet high. It started from the *half moon*, a kind of fort in that form, situated on the river, near the present *Floating Dock*, and ran from thence a little above the brow of the hill, in a semi-circle, until it reached the Mississippi, somewhat above the *bridge*, now on Second street. Three gates were formed in it, one near the bridge, and two others on the hill, at the points where the roads from the north-western and south-western parts of the common fields came in. At each of these gates was placed a heavy piece of ordnance, kept continually charged, and in good order. Having completed this work,[2] and hearing no more of the Indians, it was supposed that the attack had been abandoned. Winter passed away, and spring came; still, nothing was heard of the Indians. The inhabitants were led to believe that their apprehensions were groundless, from the representations of the Commandant Leyba, who did every thing in his power to dissipate their anxiety, assuring them that there was no danger, and that the rumor of the proposed attack was false. The month of May came, the labors of planting were over, and the peaceful and happy villagers gave themselves up to such pursuits and pleasures as suited their taste.
>
> A few days before the attack, an old man named Quenelle, a resident of St. Louis, had gone over to the mouth of Kahokia Creek, on a fishing excursion. While watching his lines on the

---

the *Republican* as part of a thirty-two-page pamphlet: *Report of the Celebration of the Anniversary of the Founding of St. Louis, on the Fifteenth Day of February, A.D. 1847* (St. Louis, 1847). I have quoted from this pamphlet as representing Primm's final word, though I have inserted four paragraphs from the 1832 printing, as will be noted. The author, born in 1810, may not yet have been admitted to the bar at the time of the lyceum lecture; he was to become a distinguished St. Louisan. For his life see William Clark Breckenridge, "Biographical Sketch of Judge Wilson Primm," *Missouri Historical Society Collections*, IV (1913), 127–159.

[2] As two among many instances of error demonstrating the unreliability of this "traditional" history, it may be pointed out that there were 226 males of military age (14–50 years) in St. Louis at the close of 1779 (if we are to believe the official census report), and that there was no "half moon" or fort of any kind, no entrenchment, no wall, until Leyba directed their construction in the spring of 1780. The whole account is refuted by the evidence presented in sec. II of this paper.

south bank of the creek, he heard a slight noise on the opposite side. Looking up, he beheld an acquaintance, who had formerly resided in St. Louis, but who had absconded from thence, on account of some crime which he had committed. His name was Ducharme, and he was afterwards ascertained to be one of the leaders of the attack upon the town. His sudden and strange appearance, the circumstances under which he had left St. Louis, and the rumor of the meditated attack, all these combined, induced Quenelle to refuse to cross the creek, at the invitation of Ducharme. He was confirmed in his refusal, by perceiving, a few moments after, the eyes of several Indians glaring upon him, from the bushes in which they were concealed. "Come over," said Ducharme, "I have something very particular to tell you." "No," said Quenelle, "your request is not intended for my benefit, or the gratification of your friendly feelings. Though I am old and bald, yet I value my scalp too highly to trust myself with you." So saying, he embarked in his canoe, and coming over to St. Louis, informed the Commandant of what he had seen.

The people became alarmed, but the Commandant, calling his informant an old dotard, ordered him to be put in prison. This proceeding had the effect of again calming their minds and banishing apprehension.

In the mean time, numerous bands of the Indians living on the Lakes and the Mississippi—the Ojibeways, Menomenies, Winnebagoes, Sioux, Sacs, &c., together with a large number of Canadians, amounting, in all, to upwards of fourteen hundred—had assembled on the eastern shore of the Mississippi, a little above St. Louis, awaiting the 26th of May, the day fixed for the attack. The 25th of May was the feast of *Corpus Christi*, a day highly venerated by the inhabitants, who were all Catholics. Had the assault taken place then, it would have been fatal to them; for, after divine service, all, men, women, and children, had flocked to the prairie to gather strawberries, which were that season very abundant and fine. The town, being left perfectly unguarded, could have been taken with ease, and the unsuspecting inhabitants, who were roaming about in search of fruit, could have been massacred without resistance. Fortunately, however, a few only of the enemy had crossed the river, and ambushed themselves in the prairie. The villagers frequently came so near them, in the course of the day, that the Indians from their places of concealment, could have reached them with their hands. But they knew not how many of the whites were still remaining in the town, and in the absence of their coadjutors, feared to attack, lest their pre-concerted plan might be defeated.

On the 26th, the body of the Indians crossed, and marched directly towards the fields, expecting to find the greater part of the villagers there; but in this they were disappointed, a few only having gone out to view their crops. These perceived the approach of the savage foe, and immediately commenced a retreat towards the town, the most of them taking the road that led to the upper gate, nearly through the mass of Indians, and followed by a shower of bullets. The firing alarmed those who were in town, and the cry, "To arms! to arms!" was heard in every direction. They rushed towards the works, and threw open the gates to their brethren. The Indians advanced slowly, but steadily, towards the town, and the inhabitants, though almost deprived of hope, by the vast superiority in numbers of the assailants, determined to defend themselves to the last.

In expectation of an attack, Silvio Francisco Cartabona, a governmental officer, had gone to Ste. Genevieve for a company of militia, to aid in defending the town, in case of necessity; and had, at the beginning of the month, returned with sixty men, who were quartered on the citizens. As soon as the attack commenced, however, neither Cartabona nor his men could be seen. Either through fear or treachery, they concealed themselves in a garret, and there remained until the Indians had retired. The assailed, being deprived of a considerable force by this shameful defection, were still resolute and determined. About fifteen men were posted at each gate; the rest were scattered along the line of defence, in the most advantageous manner.

When within a proper distance, the Indians began an irregular fire, which was answered with showers of grape shot from the artillery. The firing, for a while, was warm; but the Indians perceiving that all their efforts would be ineffectual, on account of the entrenchments, and deterred by the cannon, to which they were unaccustomed, from making a nearer approach, suffered their zeal to abate, and deliberately retired. At this stage of affairs, the Lieutenant Governor made his appearance. The first intimation that he received of what was going on, was by the discharge of artillery, on the part of the inhabitants. He immediately ordered several pieces of cannon, which were posted in front of the government house, to be spiked and filled with sand, and went, or rather *was rolled in a wheelbarrow*, to the scene of action. In a very preemptory tone, he commanded the inhabitants to cease firing, and to return to their houses. Those posted at the lower gate, did not hear the order, and consequently kept their stations. The Commandant perceived this, and ordered a cannon to be fired at them. They had barely time to throw themselves on the

317

ground, when the volley passed over them, and struck the wall, tearing a great part of it down. These proceedings, as well as the whole tenor of his conduct, after the first rumor of an attack, gave rise to suspicions, very unfavorable to the Lieutenant Governor. It was freely said, that he was the cause of the attack, that he was connected with the British, and that he had been bribed into a dereliction of duty, which, had not Providence averted, would have doomed them to destruction. Under the pretext of proving to them that there was no danger of an attack, he had, a few days before it occurred, sold to the traders, all the ammunition belonging to the government; and they would have been left perfectly destitute and defenceless, had they not found in a private house, eight barrels of powder, belonging to a trader, which they seized in the name of the King, upon the first alarm. These circumstances gave birth to a strong aversion to the Commandant, which evinces itself, even at this day, in execrations of his character, whenever his name is mentioned to those who have known him. Representations of his conduct, together with a detailed account of the attack, were sent to New Orleans by a special messenger, and the result was, that the Governor re-appointed Francisco Cruzat to the office of Lieut. Governor.

As soon as it was ascertained that the Indians had retired from the neighborhood, the inhabitants proceeded to gather and bury the dead, that lay scattered in all parts of the prairie. Seven were at first found, and buried in one grave. Ten or twelve others, in the course of a fortnight, were discovered in the long grass that bordered the marshes. The acts of the Indians were accompanied by their characteristic ferocity. Some of their victims were horribly mangled. With the exception of one individual, the whites who accompanied the Indians did not take part in the butcheries that were committed. A young man named *Calvé*, was found dead, his skull split open, and a tomahawk, on the blade of which was written the word "*Calvé*", sticking in his brain. He was supposed to have fallen by the hand of his uncle. Had those who discovered the Indians in the prairies, fled to the lower gate, they would have escaped; but the greater part of them took the road that led to the upper gate, through the very ranks of the enemy, and were thus exposed to the whole of their fire. About twenty persons, it is computed, met their death in endeavoring to get within the intrenchments. None of them within them were injured, and none of the Indians were killed, at least, none of them were found. Their object was not plunder, for they did not attempt, in their retreat, to take with them any of the cattle or horses that were in the prairie, and which they might have taken;

nor did they attack any of the neighboring towns, where danger would have been less, and the prospect of success greater. The only object they had in view, was the destruction of St. Louis; and this would seem to favor the idea that they were instigated by the English, and give good ground, when connected with other circumstances, to believe that Leyba was their aider and abettor. [There are many anecdotes of this war, which tradition has preserved, and it may not be uninteresting to record a few of them.[3]

A Mr. Chancellier had gone, on the day of the attack to the prairie, for strawberries, with his wife, two daughters, and an *American*, the first that had ever been in the country, in a cart, drawn by two horses. When they perceived the Indians, they immediately fled towards the town in the cart; Mr. Chancellier being seated before, and the American behind, in order to protect the women, who were in the middle. In their flight, the American was mortally wounded. As he was about falling out, Mr. Chancellier seized him and threw him in the midst of the women, exclaiming, "they shan't get the scalp of my American." He was at the same time struck by two balls, which broke his arm in many places above the elbow; his wife received a bullet through the middle of her hand, the elder daughter was shot through the shoulder, immediately above the breast, and the younger was struck on the forehead, but the ball glanced aside and merely stunned her. The moment Mr. Chancellier arrived at the gate, his horses dropped dead, pierced with a hundred wounds—but his family was saved.

Mr. Belhomme, in attempting to escape from the woods, where he had been hunting, into the town, had his thigh broken by a ball from an Indian. He managed to crawl to the great bend of the pond opposite the mill, and in the evening, when the Indians had disappeared, he began calling out for help. Finding this unavailing, he fired his gun, and continued firing until all his amunition was expended. The people in the town heard the gun, but were afraid the Indians were still lurking about, they dared not obey the signal of distress. The unfortunate man was found dead a few days after, having perished from loss of blood and hunger.

Mr. Julien Roy, being pursued by an Indian, who wished to take him prisoner, and finding that his enemy gained on him at every step, finally determined to give him battle. He turned around and taking deliberate aim, fired full at the savage's head. The Indian's jaw was shattered, and he fell. Mr. Roy ran up to him, and tearing his shirt, bound up the wound. The Indian was

---

[3] The passage beginning with the bracket and continuing through the next four paragraphs was included in the 1832 publication but was omitted from that of 1847. I have inserted it here to make Primm's account as complete as possible.

grateful, and guarded him through the ranks of his brethren to the town.

Many occurrences of like nature might be mentioned, tending to show that the ancient inhabitants of St. Louis, descended from the French, had, with the amenity and gayety of disposition, and courteousness of demeanor, which characterise them to this day, inherited a valor that was at the same time bold and magnanimous.]

Thus ended an attack, which, properly conducted, might have been destructive to the infant town, and which, from the number of the enemy and the danger incurred, was calculated to impress itself deeply upon the minds of those who witnessed it. It forms an era in the history of the place; and the year in which it occurred, has ever since been designated by the inhabitants, as *the year of the blow.*—"L'année du coup."

Leyba, aware that representations of his course had been specially forwarded to the Governor General at New Orleans, and fearful of the consequences, and unable to bear up under the load of scorn and contempt which the inhabitants heaped upon him, died a short time after the attack, suspected by many of having hastened his end by poison.

Upon his death, Cartabona performed the functions of government until the following year, when Cruzat returned to St. Louis, and assumed the command as Lieutenant Governor for a second time.

There can be no doubt that Leyba, like another Arnold, was seduced into defection from his duty, and that it was only the unflinching daring of the people of St. Louis, that saved this infant outpost from utter destruction.

The influence of Primm on later writers has been great. James Hall, in his *Sketches of History, Life and Manners in the West* (Philadelphia, 1835, pp. 165–182), simply reprinted the 1832 oration word for word without any acknowledgment whatsoever. Joseph N. Nicollet, who gathered his notes in St. Louis three or four years after Primm's account was first published, told essentially the same story and came to like conclusions. Leyba deserved "nothing but public contempt. . . . It is averred that the Spanish garrison took no part in this gallant defence. Lebas [*sic*] and his men had betaken themselves to the stone tower . . . he ordered the firing to be stopped . . . he died on receiving information that the Sacs, Foxes, and Iowa Indians were massacring the people on the plains." Nicollet succeeded in complicating the story when he declared that the "women and children, who could not take part in the defence, took shelter in the house of Auguste Chouteau" (a statement repeated in some later accounts).[4]

Primm struck a second blow at Leyba when he published in 1845, over the signature "P.," a copy of the "Chanson de l'Année du Coup" in the St. Louis *Weekly Reveille* (February 17, 1845, p. 249):

Ballad
of the Year of the Surprise

GOVERNOR

Courier, say, what is the news
That seems thy fancies to confuse?
What! have we lost the *Illinois?*
The English—do they the land enjoy?
Down hearted, thus! speak, courier, say
What great misfortune has happen'd, I pray?

COURIER

Oh, General, General, all is lost,
If not redeemed with speed and cost;
We've been by savages attacked—
They threaten, still, by others backed:
Ever so many, alas, were killed—
Unable to aid them—with grief we're filled.

When the enemy first appeared,

---

[4] Since Nicollet opened his description of the catastrophe by writing, "As I discover by the papers of the late Col. Auguste Chouteau, intrusted to me by the family . . . St. Louis was attacked by a party of Indians and British . . . ," it has been thought that Nicollet repeated Chouteau's own story, but in none of the extant Chouteau family papers is there anything to warrant this interpretation. The only known reference to this event by Chouteau is that in his testimony before the recorder of land titles in St. Louis on Apr. 18, 1825: "(Annee du Grand Coup) On the Sixth of May A D seventeen hundred and ~~seventy~~ [sic] Eighty, St. Louis was attacked by fourteen hundred Indians and Canadians—." Nicollet's historical sketch of early St. Louis was published posthumously in his *Report Intended to Illustrate a Map of the Hydrographic Basin of the Upper Mississippi River*, Senate Doc. 237, 26th Cong., 2nd Sess., 1843. The Nicollet quotations here are from McDermott, *The Early Histories of St. Louis*, 148–150; that from Chouteau's testimony, *ibid.*, 92.

It should be added that at the time of the attack Auguste Chouteau (still a bachelor) lived in his mother's house. The building historically known as his mansion had been erected by Pierre de Laclède for the Maxent, Laclède and Company trading post and had for years been rented to the Spanish government for the lieutenant governor's residence. It was only in 1788 that Auguste Chouteau bought and rebuilt the house. The women and children, Leyba declared in his report to Gálvez, June 8, 1780 (quoted hereafter), were placed in this government house under guard of twenty men commanded by Lieutenant Cartabona.

To arms we ran, no one afeared;
Townsmen, traders, grave and gay,
Bravely to battle and win the day;
But, by command, we were forbid
To quit the trench where our ranks were hid.

GOVERNOR

What did they in that moment—then?
Lacked they, all, the souls of men?
What! had ye not the great Leyba!
Where was the famous Cartabona!
Your Major, where was he, as well;
The Garrison, too, your force to swell?

Oh, that moment! what did they, then?
Lacked they, all, the souls of men?
Homeward cravens, come ye back;
Longer rouse not our scorn, alack:
Here we've, at least, within our wall,
To watch our standard—prevent its fall,
An officer prudent, bold and wise,
Who'll valiantly guard you against surprise.

Calvé, the petty tinkering knave!
Calls himself a warrior brave,
For having his nephew slain, alas,
Kinsmen and friends on the prairie grass,
Helpless, abandoned, to meet their fate
From the savages' fierce and furious hate!

Heartless Canadians! honor void;
Brothers and sisters, you have destroyed!
Cut-throats exult in your acts of night,
And, safety seek in your coward flight.

He prefaced these satirical verses attacking Leyba by writing that "notwithstanding the treachery of Fernando de Leyba . . . the attacking party was repulsed." After the attack, Primm continued, "a courier express was sent by the inhabitants to the Governor General of Louisiana, at New Orleans, with information of the events which had just occurred. The courier was the bearer, likewise, of the piece of versification which I give you below; and tradition says, that the venerable schoolmaster of the village, who composed it, received from the Governor General, in return, a handsome present." Though Primm may well have heard his mother and grandmother sing these words, as he avers, there is no proof that Jean Baptiste Trudeau [Truteau] wrote them—certainly this man often referred to as the "schoolmaster of St. Louis" was not exactly venerable in 1780, for he had been born in 1748. Nor is it likely that Governor Gálvez would have been pleased with the attitude taken toward his subordinate by the anonymous poet in St. Louis. Does it need to be said that there is *no* documentary proof to support this statement by Primm?[5]

In his revised edition of James N. Perkins's *Annals of the West* (St. Louis, 1850, pp. 242–251), John Mason Peck leaned largely on Primm, "an intelligent citizen of the place, and who has had access to every existing record, civil and ecclesiastical." He quoted at length from the 1847 history, including the last paragraph characterizing Leyba as "another Arnold" and adding a further judgment that he had "unquestionably" been an "imbecile governor."

Two unpublished letters from Peck to Lyman Draper reaffirm his published statements. On September 17, 1850, he wrote flatly: "Expresses had been sent by [Auguste] Chouteau and others to Ste. Genevieve for relief, and a party of men came from there, *after the fracas was over*. Another *Fact* is that *Leyba*, the Governor, was a traitor—very likely bought with British gold—& did all he could to prevent the people fighting as they did—Immediately after the enemy dispersed the Chouteaus and others sent off a deputation to New Orleans to impeach the Governor Leyba of treason to the Governor General—and in one month he died, suddenly—tradition says by poison from his own hands."

Six months later (March 20, 1851) Peck told Draper that he had his "facts" about George Rogers Clark at St. Louis from

> Colonel John O'Fallon of St. Louis, who was nephew and the "pet child" of Col. Clark, and heard him tell "the oft repeated tale" of his adventures in St. Louis in '79— It was that season, through French traders and friendly Indians, Clark got the intelligence of the projected attack on St. Louis, which was to have been that autumn, and *he* in his visits to St. Louis, gave Leyba warning, and offered his services with volunteers from Cahokia, Kaskaskia &c Leyba gave no credit to these warnings, politely declined all aid, affirmed the Indians were peacable & that this rumor of an attack deserved no credit. His behavior previous and

[5] The "Chanson" was reprinted by Primm as a note to his 1847 oration (pp. 25–26) with both French and English texts; there Primm attributed it to John B. Truteau by name. It has since been reprinted by William Clark Breckenridge in the *Missouri Historical Society Collections*, IV (1914), 295–302, and by James Malcolm Breckenridge, ed., in *William Clark Breckenridge. His Life, Lineage and Writings* (St. Louis, 1932), 192–198. Joseph M. Field, one of the editors of the *Reveille*, supplied the English translation.

at the time of the attack, fixed the impression on the minds of the people on both sides of the river that he was a traitor, and designed to have the place surrendered to the British. Immediately after the Indians & a few British retired, the Chouteaus and other leading French inhabitants dispatched a barge with an Express to New Orleans with an impeachment, or an account of his traitorous conduct in the attack. He shut himself up, and would see no one, & died as I have mentioned.[6]

In the face of such positive opinions it is little wonder, then, that Richard Edwards and Menra Hopewell, in *The Great West and Her Commercial Metropolis* (St. Louis, 1860, p. 267), the first book-length history of the city, should again repeat the lurid tale and the violent condemnation:

> The opinion has been advanced by many, that the governor, Don Fernando de Leyba, had an understanding with the English, and for some stipulated sum had agreed to let the savages surprise the town. Certain it was, that he had sold most of the powder belonging to the garrisons to some traders just before the attack, and used no reasonable precautions to prevent surprise; but, on the contrary, always repelled any idea of an attack on the town as an impossible event. These were ominous signs, and appeared to carry with them the dark burden of guilt; but these circumstances are only suggestive proofs against him. The positive proof is wanting. On the other hand, he was very feeble in health, and addicted to dissipation in so great a degree as to stupefy his understanding. One or both of these causes might account for his inaction, and why he did not make reasonable preparations for an attack which had threatened for so long a period. His sordid nature furnishes a motive for the sale of the powder. Be the facts as they may, there were suspicions afloat which have attached the foulest stigma

---

[6] The Peck letters are in the Draper Collection at the State Historical Society of Wisconsin. But Peck's story of O'Fallon's remembrance of George Rogers Clark's reminiscences is no more to be relied upon than Primm's reports of old folks' tales. It was Leyba, on May 9, 1780, who sent an "express" to Ste. Genevieve, and the party of men arrived at St. Louis four days later, thirteen days before the battle (see p. 342 below). On July 2, 1780, thirty inhabitants of St. Louis, including Chouteau, addressed a petition to Francisco de Cartabona, *ad interim* lieutenant governor of the Western Illinois, stressing the plight of the town and asking him to send a deputy to New Orleans to solicit aid from Governor Gálvez—but by this time Leyba was dead. The only "impeachments" of Leyba after the battle thus far found are two anonymous letters, one dated St. Louis, June 19, 23, signed "Virtutis, Veritatisque Amicus," and a second, not dated, signed "Le Peuple Des islinois." These will be presented in sec. III of this paper.

to his name and blasted it forever. He died a little more than a month after the attack—some say by poison administered by himself.

Elihu H. Shepard, who had lived in the city for more than fifty years when he published his book *The Early History of St. Louis and Missouri* (St. Louis, 1870, p. 25), dismissed Leyba with one scornful paragraph:

> That he was a sot was never questioned; that he had sold the powder of the garrison to some traders before the attack, was proved; and that he used but little precaution to prevent surprise, was apparent from his constantly repelling any idea of a possibility of a surprise. Suggestions were made that he had agreed with the English, for a stipulated sum, to let the savages surprise the town, but it was not necessary to furnish this proof to consign his character to ignominious oblivion and his name, as Governor, to lasting contempt.

The first voice raised in doubt of this "tradition" about Leyba was that of Sylvester Waterhouse, who contributed to Thomas Scharf's *History of Saint Louis City and County* (2 vols., Philadelphia, 1883, I, 204–210) the chapter on "The Affair of 1780." As a professor of history (at Washington University, St. Louis), Waterhouse approached the common popular version of this episode with scholarly caution. He found Leyba

> singularly deficient in the qualities which command political success. Devoid of tact and discretion, reputedly penurious and intemperate, he was subjected to an ordeal which conspicuously exposed his weaknesses. The difficulties which beset his administration were such as none of his predecessors had ever encountered. Doubtless his personal unpopularity led the people to magnify his faults. Public suspicion seems to be the only ground for many of the charges against De Leyba. But, in the absence of proof, repetitions of tradition cannot invest these apparent fictions with a title to a place in authentic history.

Waterhouse did not mention Primm but his summary of the affair is essentially that of the orations of 1832 and 1847. He endeavored to pass reasonable judgment on Leyba's abilities but came finally to condemnation of his actions during the attack, though he had no more documentary evidence than Primm had had.

The memory of Governor De Leyba has been covered with un-merited obloquy. His decisions, recorded in the Archives, show that he was a man of clear intelligence, business knowledge, and sound judgment. His insight into the principles of law, and his impartiality in the administration of justice, are unmistakable evi-dences of high qualities. Possibly something of his unpopularity may have been due to the indiscretions into which his alleged habits of self-indulgence betrayed him. The gravest fault of his official career was his neglect to fortify St. Louis. It appears from the testimony of Mr. Gratiot that Governor De Leyba was aware of the impending danger. In view of this fact, his remissness to prepare for defense was a culpable negligence of duty. But at the time of the massacre even the people themselves believed that the danger was past. If they were still anticipating an attack, they would hardly have neglected every precaution for their personal safety and have gone unarmed to their distant fields. However censurable may have been the Governor's failure to provide ade-quate means of defense, it seems scarcely just, at this juncture, to reproach him for entertaining a belief that was common to all the inhabitants of the village. Exasperated at the loss of their rela-tives, the people, with genuine French impulsiveness, not only ascribed the massacre to the criminal misconduct of their Gov-ernor, but also imputed to him many offenses and indiscretions of which there was not the slightest evidence that he was guilty. This narrative offers no palliation for the known faults of Governor De Leyba, but simply seeks to perform an act of tardy justice in vindicating his character from undeserved opprobrium.

In *St. Louis the Fourth City 1764–1909* (3 vols., St. Louis, 1909, I, 66–73), Walter B. Stevens quoted at length the account of the attack published by Father John O'Hanlon, who had served as a priest in St. Louis in 1848 (*Life and Scenery in Missouri. Reminiscences of a Mis-sionary Priest* [Dublin, 1890], pp. 45–52). But when one looks into the latter publication he finds that Primm has once more been repeated word for word without benefit of quotation marks or other acknowledgment.

It is not necessary to cite every instance of the repetition of the Primm story to demonstrate its pervasive influence, but as recently as 1960 a new book repeating old stories about early St. Louis offered a chapter entitled "A Spanish Benedict Arnold."[7]

Primm's account of the attack on St. Louis and of Leyba's part in it is wrong in almost every detail. He had *no* documents to support his alle-gations—only the faulty memories of men and women still living in 1831

---

[7] Ernest Kirschten, *Catfish and Crystal* (Garden City, N.Y., 1960), 63–68.

who had been alive in 1780. But his positive assertions were even more sharply restated by many of the succeeding local historians who denounced Leyba on no other basis than the old "tradition," for not one of them had a new scrap of evidence to present.

II

We have, then, serious charges persistently repeated against Captain de Leyba all advanced after his death: (1) he failed to provide for the defense of the town, (2) he traitorously disposed of the supply of powder, (3) he conducted himself improperly during the battle.

This "affair of 1780" has been discussed at varying lengths by Abraham P. Nasatir in "The Anglo-Spanish Frontier in the Illinois Country during the American Revolution, 1779–1783" (*Illinois State Historical Society Journal*, XXI [Oct., 1928], 310–322), and by James B. Musick in *St. Louis as a Fortified Town* (St. Louis, 1941, pp. 20–51). Many pertinent documents have been published by the editor of the *Missouri Historical Society Collections* in "Documents Relating to the Attack upon St. Louis in 1780" (II [July, 1906], 41–54),[8] by Louis Houck in *The Spanish Régime in Missouri* (2 vols., Chicago, 1909), by Nasatir in "St. Louis during the British Attack of 1780" (in George P. Hammond, ed., *New Spain and the Anglo-American West* [2 vols., Lancaster, Pa., 1932], I, 239–261), by Lawrence Kinnaird in "Clark-Leyba Papers [1778–1779]" (*American Historical Review*, XLI [Oct., 1935], 92–112), and by Kinnaird again in *Spain in the Mississippi Valley, 1765–1794* (3 vols., Washington, 1946–49).

When we look into these records, it becomes obvious that Leyba was neither an imbecile commander nor a Benedict Arnold, but, to the contrary, a competent governor and commandant who did everything in his power to prepare for the defense of the town against a long-expected attack and who conducted himself in a proper military manner during the action on May 26. He well deserved the promotion from captain to lieutenant colonel bestowed on him by high Spanish authority.

Let me recapitulate the military situation that confronted Fernando de Leyba when he arrived in Upper Louisiana in 1778. The town of St. Louis, it must be kept in mind, had never had any defensive works. It was a village that had grown up around the trading house of Maxent, Laclède and Company. French and Spanish colonial policy had main-

[8] These documents are in Canadian Archives, ser. B, vol. 97, pt. 2.

tained control over the Indians by means of annual presents and by cutting off trade with tribes that proved difficult. No Indians lived near St. Louis. No fort had proved necessary during the fourteen years of its existence.

When the Spanish prepared to take over this region following the secret treaty of 1762, planners far away, looking at the map, decided that the significant spot for control of the vast upper country was the mouth of the Missouri River: forts erected there would keep the British from entering the river and penetrating to the "Spanish" tribes. Accordingly, Captain Francisco Riú in 1767 was ordered up the Mississippi with an engineer, carpenters, masons, and a small military escort to build those forts and to command a newly created District of the Missouri, which did not include the settlements of the Western Illinois and to which, it was planned, the villagers of St. Louis would ultimately be removed. When Riú and Guy Soniat du Fossat arrived and had a look at the mouth of the Missouri, they discovered the obvious: bottomlands subject to annual overflow do not provide a satisfactory location for permanent installations. They so reported, but in the meantime, having specific orders, they built forts. The lesser one on the south bank of the Missouri, named "El Principe de Asturias, Señor Don Carlos," now became the principal fort, for it was on higher ground. On the north bank, where the floodwaters normally rose eight to ten feet, for the planned larger "Fuerte Don Carlos Tercero el Rey" a mere blockhouse was substituted, the timbers of which would have to be removed to the south bank when the spring rise came. Riú had brought up eight brass cannon for the forts; to garrison them he had thirty-eight men, four corporals, two sergeants, and a drummer. Second in command was Lieutenant Fernando Gómes. The Western Illinois continued under the command of Captain Louis St. Ange de Bellerive, now in the Spanish service.

By the time Captain Pedro Piernas was sent to take over command of the upper country, the authorities at New Orleans had realized the original mistake. The idea of a separate District of the Missouri was abandoned, Piernas was designated commandant and lieutenant governor of the Western Illinois (St. Ange was retained as a salaried consultant to Piernas), and St. Louis was made *chef-lieu* and the principal garrison point, with a token guard to be maintained at Fort Prince Charles. Government headquarters were now in the stone building Laclède had constructed for the trading post and his stone warehouse was let to the government for barracks. The entire military establishment under Piernas consisted of one lieutenant, one first sergeant, one second sargeant, one drummer, three first corporals, two second corporals, and twenty-five soldiers. Of these the lieutenant, one corporal, and seven men formed the garrison at Ste. Genevieve, and a sergeant and six men were assigned to Fort Prince Charles.[9]

Leyba, succeeding Francisco Cruzat, arrived in St. Louis as the third lieutenant governor and commandant on June 10, 1778, and took over on June 14. The war between Great Britain and the American colonies had by this time made the position of the Spanish west of the Mississippi a sensitive one, and confidential instructions issued to Leyba on March 9, 1778, instructed him to "endeavor to learn all the news occurring in the English part (of Illinois), concerning the war of this power with the colonists, the situation of both parties and their plans so as not to allow himself to be surprised in case of any unforeseen design." Furthermore, "if he [Leyba] should have any correspondence with any American chief of the American provinces, he shall observe the greatest secrecy, and report same to me [Gálvez]."[10]

In accordance with these orders Leyba almost immediately established a cordial understanding with George Rogers Clark, who on the night of July 4, 1778, took Kaskaskia and on the next day sent a party to Cahokia. On July 6, having occasion to write to Captain Joseph Bowman at Cahokia, Leyba congratulated the American on his "happy arrival at the Illinois, as well as on that of Commandant Clarke," and two days later wrote to Clark to say that "if the affairs of the government, of which I have taken charge only a few days ago, permit me, I shall come in person to congratulate you on your happy arrival at the Kaskaskias." Leyba added that a shipment of supplies for the Americans sent from New Orleans by Oliver Pollock had reached St. Louis and was being held for his orders.[11]

Some time late in July or perhaps early in August Clark paid his first visit to St. Louis. On July 21 Leyba had written to Governor General

[9] Piernas had made his first voyage up the Mississippi in 1769; however, his mission then was to relieve Captain Riú of command of the District of the Missouri and to transfer Fort Prince Charles to St. Ange, at this time Spanish commandant of the Western Illinois. Piernas arrived late in February and was again in New Orleans in October. That winter he was appointed lieutenant governor by Alexander O'Reilly and again left the colonial capital some time after mid-February, 1770. He took over command of the Western Illinois at St. Louis on June 18. St. Ange was retained as a paid adviser or consultant. In May, 1775, Piernas was succeeded by Francisco Cruzat. See in particular Piernas's report to O'Reilly, New Orleans, Oct. 31, 1769, in Houck, ed., *The Spanish Régime in Missouri*, I, 66–75; "General Instructions of O'Reilly to the Lieutenant-Governor of the Villages of St. Louis, San Genevieve, etc., dated February 17, 1770," *ibid.*, I, 76–83; and Unzaga to Piernas, not dated but clearly 1771, in Kinnaird, ed., *Spain in the Mississippi Valley*, I, 189–192.

[10] Kinnaird, ed., *Spain in the Mississippi Valley*, I, 260.

[11] Kinnaird, "Clark-Leyba Papers," 93–94.

Gálvez that he was "expecting this gentleman's visit from day to day; I shall show him all the courtesy I can. . . ." When Clark did arrive, he was "proud and pleased at the fine reception" given him by Leyba. "It is true," the latter wrote to his superior, "that there was a great consuming of powder at his arrival as well as at his departure." But there was much more than military salutes. Leyba entertained Clark "at meals and laid thirty covers on his first visit which lasted two days," he informed the governor general. "Dances were given for him both nights and a supper to the ladies and dancers, and lodging in my house with as much formality as was possible for me." Apparently Clark crossed the river more than once. Regularly he closed his letters to the commandant with "compliments to Madm. Lebau and my two young favourites the little Misses" or to "Madam Leyba and your Ladies" (one of whom was the captain's sister Teresa).[12]

This friendly understanding and close cooperation was to continue throughout Leyba's service at St. Louis. Clark wrote to Governor Patrick Henry from Kaskaskia on September 16, 1778, that "Mr. Leabau . . . interests himself much in favor of the States—more so than I could have expected. He has offered me all the force he could raise, in case of an attack by Indians from Detroit, as there is no danger from other quarters."[13] On May 30, 1779, at Ste. Genevieve we find Leyba addressing a letter of congratulation to his "cher amy" and proposing to visit him across the river the following evening.[14]

During this entire period Clark continued to pass to Leyba any in-

[12] Leyba to Gálvez, July 21 and Nov. 16, 1778, in Kinnaird, "Clark-Leyba Papers," 98, 102.

[13] James A. James, ed., *George Rogers Clark Papers, 1771–1781*, Illinois Historical Collections, VIII (Springfield, 1912), 69. Note that this was long before the declaration of war by Spain against England.

[14] George Rogers Clark Papers, MSS, Missouri Historical Society. In the same collection is a photostat (original in the Virginia State Library) of a list of "the following Articles [which] were furnished for the Entertainment of the Spanish Comd^t Viz^t

"1779	May 31	To bacon ham [11 lbs?] at 3# [shillings]	33.00
		To 1 Doz fouls	30.—
		To 8 [lbs?] Bacon @ 3#	24.—
		To 4 Doz Eggs	10.—
		To Spices	25.—"

The "bacon" was, of course, ham, not sides of bacon.
On May 26 Clark had written from Kaskaskia that he had just heard that Leyba had been for four days at Ste. Genevieve, and again on May 29 he sent over one letter about a meeting "next Wednesday" and a second one saying that he would be able to cross the river because of Colonel Montgomery's arrival ("Clark-Leyba Papers," 108–109). To this Leyba replied with the letter of May 30 just cited. The visit was made to Kaskaskia by Leyba the following day.

formation he received about British activities, and the Spanish commandant for his part induced St. Louisans to furnish on credit the supplies
that the American needed, going so far as to guarantee personally some
of Clark's paper.

But Leyba had more to do than establish good relations with Clark.
When he had had time to consider the defenses of the Spanish Illinois,
he called the attention of Gálvez to the insignificance of the fort at the
mouth of the Missouri, recommended a new one be constructed on the
bluff at Cold Water Creek (where Fort Bellefontaine was to be built in
1806), and another at the mouth of the Des Moines River, and recommended a force of 200 men to garrison the district:

St. Louis, November 16, 1778

Señor Governor General.
My Very Dear and Most Esteemed Sir: The Missouri River is
the main feature of this district. On its banks and on those of the
rivers emptying into it are settled all the Indian nations who carry
on the commerce of this place. Because of this, it is of the greatest
importance to guard its entrance. For this purpose, there is situated
on it (number 4) the fort, (only in name) of San Carlos, with a
garrison of six men and a corporal. The lowness of its situation,
and a beach in the form of a semi-circle of one-half league in
width, covered with trees which time has formed in front of the
aforesaid fort, are impediments to the observation from it of the
boats which enter and leave the aforesaid Missouri. Because of
this fact, and because of the ruined condition in which the fort is,
one may consider it as useless.
The best site in all this territory which is available for establishing a fort and near to it a great settlement is the one named
Aguas Frias on the height of *Del Monte de Pudra* (number 11),
which is precipitous on the side of the river, and elevated above
it twelve paces with two zigzag ascents situated on the sides. The
lieutenant governor of this district could be established in the
aforesaid fort with a garrison of two hundred men, distributed in
the following fashion: Twenty-five in Miseria [Ste. Genevieve],
an equal number at this post, and twenty at the entrance of the
Mua River, eighty leagues distant from this pueblo going up the
Mississippi. In that place it would be necessary to construct a
small fort enclosed with a stockade, and some building for the
shelter of the garrison. The principal object of this detachment
would be to impede the entrance which the English make through

the aforementioned Mua River in order to carry on trade with our Indian nations situated to the north, from whom they annually bring out furs to the value of fifteen to twenty thousand pesos.

There follow from this two no less serious disadvantages in addition to the aforementioned one of not closing this entrance. First, all the aforementioned Indian nations are devoted to the English. Second, through these Indians the English succeed in introducing their trade among the nations settled on the Missouri, a matter which, if totally accomplished, as they did part of last year, would reduce this settlement to the greatest misery. Furthermore, from the aforesaid settlement, a cruise could be made one or two hundred leagues further up the river where equal or greater contraband trade is carried on. The repeated seizure of contraband goods would check them and cause them to realize that this is not their home. To-day they come in, judge this place theirs, or believe that it has no owner. But for all of this, forces would be required capable of checking the attacks which all of the bandits who participate in the said commerce might attempt in spite of our just procedure.

Returning to the matter of distribution of the garrison, I say that the one hundred and thirty men remaining with the lieutenant governor should be stationed in a stone fort in the place mentioned [Cold Water Creek]. The fort need not be of the strong and expensive type constructed in Europe. The wall should rather be similar to that of the barracks in this place, with embrassures for a battery and a bank behind the parapet five feet in height. Such a work, in my opinion, would not represent a very great cost as there is stone easily available. The cost would be materially reduced if three or four soldiers who are masons were available. The fort would serve, first, to guard the entrance to the Missouri; secondly, to render aid to the post which might have need of it. To this end, and to be able to relieve the garrisons, it would be necessary to have two or three small boats.

The fact alone of transferring the commander of this district, the fort, and garrison to the site in question, would act as an inducement, so that from this town, from that of Miseria, and from the English district, there would come various inhabitants who would settle in the neighborhood. It would not be difficult to have families come from Canada, for I have been informed by some merchants who have just arrived that there are many who are desirous of leaving the clamor of war. They would join our ranks. If their poverty were such that they would not have means of undertaking the journey, I believe there would be many who would come if offered assistance.

The map of this district which I forward to Your Lordship has not been drawn with the semicircle and the circumferentor.[15] However, from what I have seen of the land and the river, as well as from information received from the most expert and able voyageurs in this country, I dare to assert that were it to be checked with the said instruments, there would not be found any great discrepancy either in the courses of the rivers or the situation of the places. In addition to this we had to confront the difficulty of mapping a territory unknown to us. Nevertheless, the measurements are exact. Your Lordship receives with the plan my good will and my limited ability, ever disposed to comply with anything that Your Lordship may design to demand of me in this or any other matter.

The plan and the explanation thereof are in French because of my poor writing and since there is not at this post anyone who can write Spanish even moderately well, unless it be a soldier, of whose services I have not availed myself because of the many errors which he makes.

I remain with all respect obedient to the orders of Your Lordship and beg that God may preserve your very important life the many years which I desire.

My dear Sir, your most affectionate servant kisses the hand of Your Lordship.

Fernando de Leyba [rubric]

Señor Don Bernardo de Gálvez[16]

To this able military report Gálvez replied on January 13, 1779, that he had no authority "to make such extraordinary outlays from the royal treasury. You are not ignorant of the fact that the funds available for this province are reduced to the salaries of the employees and daily pay of the troops. There must likewise be added to this difficulty the fact that the garrison of this colony is already insufficient to assign two hundred men to those settlements. I am therefore unable to consent to your proposal, but I shall communicate it to His Majesty in order that he may determine what is his pleasure." In the meantime, Leyba was reminded that he must "endeavor to prevent the entrance of the English into the aforesaid rivers, and see that they do not win over our Indians. This matter is expressly charged in the instructions carried by Your Lordship."[17]

15 This map was not found with document.

16 Kinnaird, ed., *Spain in the Mississippi Valley*, I, 310–312.

17 *Ibid.*, I, 230. The instructions referred to are the confidential orders of Mar. 9, 1778, which Leyba had brought with him from New Orleans (*ibid.*, 258–260). Leyba was, in fact, charged by his superior to "make every effort to win the good will of all the Indian tribes, not only those in the territory of His Majesty, but also those under

Gálvez had thus made it quite clear that Leyba must depend upon himself. Although Spain did not declare war on Great Britain until the summer of 1779 (the actual news of the state of war reached St. Louis on February 9, 1780), a threat of action came early from Detroit. Henry Hamilton informed Gálvez on January 13, 1779, that "the Rebel Americans having got footing in the Ilinois Country, and of course having opened a communication to the Colonies by taking Post there and at this place [Vincennes], I [had] thought it my duty to dispossess them as soon as convenient." He had therefore retaken Vincennes on December 17 and was now writing to Gálvez to protest against the furnishing of powder and other supplies to the rebels by merchants of Louisiana. He very definitely and boastfully implied a threat to St. Louis.

> Your Excellency cannot be unacquainted with what was commonly practiced in the time of your Predecessor in the Government of New Orleans, I mean the sending of supplies of Gunpowder and other stores to the Rebels, then in arms against their Sovereign — Tho' this may have been transacted in an underhand manner by merchants, unknown to the Governor, I must suppose that under your Excellency's orders, such commerce will for the future be positively prohibited—
>
> The several Nations of Savages who accompanied me to this Country may (if this traffic be continued) forget what instructions I have given them from time to time with relations to the subjects of His Catholic Majesty, but the native Inhabitants of the banks of the Ohio River, must be particularly jealous of strangers coming up thro their Country to supply the Rebels with whom they are at War. At the same time that I mention this to your Excellency, for the sake of individuals who might suffer from their ignorance of the English being in possession of this Post, and of the communication by Water to the Mississipi, I think it incumbent on me to represent further to your Excellency that the Rebels at Kaskasquias being in dayly apprehension of the arrival of a body of Men from the upper Posts accompanyed with the Savages from that Quarter, have declared that they will take Refuge on the Spanish Territory as soon as they are apprized of their coming—
>
> As it is my intention early in the Spring to take a Progress towards the Ilinois, I shall represent to the Officers commanding at

---

the jurisdiction of the English. He shall use for this purpose all the tact and good treatment possible in order to attract them to our dominions, but in such a manner as not to compromise himself, in order to avoid complaints on the part of England" (p. 259).

several small Forts and Posts for His Catholic Majesty, the impropriety of affording an Asylum to Rebels, in arms against their lawful Sovereign— If after so candid a declaration the Rebels should find shelter in any Fort or Post on the Mississipi, it will become my Duty to dislodge them, in which case their protectors must blame their own Conduct, if they should suffer any inconvenience in consequence.

Perhaps I may be favor'd with a letter from your Excellency before the arrival of the reinforcements I expect the next Spring, at the same time that the Officers acting under your Excellency's orders may receive notice how they are to act, whether as Friends or enemies to the British Empire—[18]

Leyba was well aware of a threat to St. Louis from the time of Hamilton's arrival at Vincennes. Both Clark at Kaskaskia and Francisco Vigo (who had been captured by Hamilton and released on his word to go directly to St. Louis without stopping at Kaskaskia or Cahokia) had quickly informed him of the event. Clark's letter to Leyba, which the commandant was forwarding to Gálvez, and Vigo's report in person would apprise the governor general of this new danger. Leyba wrote from St. Louis on February 5, 1779:

For my own part I tell your Lordship that this Almilthon is a depraved man who has countless Indians at his service and great ill will towards the Spaniards because, he says, they protect the rebels. He has been informed with great accuracy of the number of houses there are in this town, the garrison, and whether there is any fortification.

This affair has me somewhat on the alert. Sixteen men including the drummer are all the troops I have with me and I hardly have forty militiamen capable of bearing arms since at this season they are all trading on the Misury, hunting, or in that place [New Orleans]. Although the barracks are of stone they would be little protection since their parts are not protected by one another. Neither can one from within prevent the enemy from approaching its walls and they could make the breach they need to enter without the slightest risk. If the attack which he directed at Colonel Clark were only by royalist troops, there would not be the least fear, but the practice in Indian wars is to attack not where one should but where there is the least risk; and for that purpose this side is more desirable than the American because, in addition to the fact that they are 190 in number, they are in a good log fort with seven cannon.

[18] Kinnaird, "Clark-Leyba Papers," 103–104.

Nevertheless, if these towns under my command should be attacked through the influence of Sr. Almilthon, I shall do my best to leave the honor of Spanish arms untarnished. For this reason I am acting with the greatest vigilance, and I have given the few inhabitants who are present the orders which seemed necessary to me so that they should not be caught unprepared. I call the whole to your Lordship's attention so that you may be pleased to make arrangements which you think desirable for the safety of this district (incapable of receiving aid in its straits) and for the honor of the one who commands it.[19]

The reply of Governor Gálvez, could it have been received within a few days, would have given Leyba little comfort, for on March 23 the governor noted on the margin of the commandant's letter the substance of a reply: "From Colonel Clark's letter . . . and the report I received from Francisco Vigo, I learned of Mr. Hamilton's intentions. In view of this and what you tell me, I should say that I deeply regret not being able to aid you and that I hope your zeal and energy will not spare measures to avoid all conflict by remaining neutral to both parties so as to keep peace and harmony with them; and in case the aforesaid Hamilton attempts to attack you, you will be able to act in such a manner as to preserve the honor of our arms."[20]

Happily, this threat early in 1779 was lifted by Clark's forced march on Vincennes and his recapture of that town on February 24. Hamilton, instead of making a "visit" to St. Louis, went to Virginia as a prisoner of war. But this eliminated only one threat. The strategic importance of St. Louis covering the western frontier for the Americans and its unofficial but real assistance as a supply base for the rebels increased the hazard of war. To face this Leyba had his garrison of fifteen men and a drummer in St. Louis, a corporal and five men in the worthless fort at the mouth of the Missouri, and a lieutenant and twelve men at Ste. Genevieve. And Gálvez had made it amply clear that he would have no more soldiers.

The burden of defense, then, must rest on the militia, which included all able-bodied males between fourteen and fifty years of age.[21] The annual census figures as of December 31, 1779, reported 226 males in

[19] Clark's letter to Leyba was dated Kaskaskia, Jan. 23, 1779. Kinnaird, "Clark-Leyba Papers," 105–106.

[20] *Ibid.*, 105, n. 41.

[21] There is some uncertainty about the lower age. The census of 1779 (see n. 22 below) divided the groups of males on this basis; O'Reilly's instructions of Feb. 17, 1770, said that the militia would include "all the men capable of bearing arms, between the ages of fifteen and fifty years." Houck, ed., *The Spanish Régime in Missouri*, I, 81.

this age bracket in St. Louis.[22] Leyba reported to Gálvez on July 13, 1779, that the infantry company was "on the footing of one hundred and seventy-six men." A newly formed cavalry unit consisted of "forty-eight men, three sergeants, and three officers." This number, Leyba added hopefully, "will be larger when some youths who wish to enlist get horses." The infantry roll, dated November 9, 1779, shows 168 men and officers for this company. That for the cavalry (December 25, 1779), 3 officers and 48 men. In Cruzat's report of the militia (December 27, 1780) there were listed 220 officers and men in two companies of infantry.[23] The new lieutenant governor had then "incorporated into the second company the officers and men of the company of cavalry, partly because the latter is not provided with horses, and partly because when it is necessary for an expedition of mounted men to be made, the cavalry company provide themselves with horses of the habitants of this town, for the greater part of the cavalry company have no horses and have not the means to keep them at a daily expense in their stables."[24]

The enrollment of men in the militia did not automatically insure a disciplined military force. O'Reilly's instructions eight years earlier directed:

> The necessary enlistment in the militia must not be at all burdensome on the citizens. Each one shall continue in his trade, and no hindrance shall be offered him in leaving when it is advisable, but the men shall have to show the fitting respect for their officers and prompt obedience to their orders. They shall be assembled on Sundays when the weather permits, and the lieutenant-governor shall assign some good sergeants and corporals of those with him to drill each company, to train them in quarterwheeling and firing. But he shall avoid in these exercises the wasting of the king's powder. All the discipline and treatment of this troop shall be so mild that they will be greatly satisfied with the new formation.[25]

That occasional Sunday soldiering did not turn out a highly trained

[22] Total population of St. Louis: whites 500, slaves 189; for Ste. Genevieve, 408 whites, 290 slaves. Nasatir, "The Anglo-Spanish Frontier in the Illinois Country," 313.

[23] Leyba to Gálvez, St. Louis, July 13, 1779, in Kinnaird, ed., *Spain in the Mississippi Valley*, I, 347–348. Since the 1779 infantry roll (found in the Archivo General de Indias, Seville, *Papeles de Cuba, legajo* 213) and the cavalry roll for December, 1779 (*leg.* 193–B), have never been published, they are given in full detail in the appendix to this paper. These rosters must necessarily include the names of many of those engaged in the battle of May 26, 1780.

[24] Full information about the 1780 companies, with names and identification of members, was published by Houck in *The Spanish Régime in Missouri*, I, 182–196.

[25] *Ibid.*, 81.

force is clear from Cruzat's report in 1780. In order to teach the militia "to do their military service in the manner following the regular order as closely as possible considering the character of the population here and the fact that they are not in the least instructed in military matters," he had judged it necessary to name Benito Vásquez adjutant "to direct them and instruct them in the most essential parts of the royal military service."[26] This lack of military discipline is no reflection on the bravery of the militia defenders of St. Louis but it could endanger the turn of a battle. We shall see that at one point during the attack Commandant Leyba did have to restrain the men in the entrenchments.

Not only did lack of training and poor discipline create problems, but rivalry and jealousy also made difficulties for the commander. Leyba, on arrival at St. Louis, had almost immediately been confronted by discontent. No sooner did he install Benito Vásquez as sub-lieutenant in the one existing company of militia than Pierre Montardy, the sergeant, asked for his discharge. He "had served many years as a sergeant of the veteran troops of France," he protested to the commandant, and "since the establishment of the Spaniards in this colony, he had served in the same rank in the militia of this post. . . . he believed he had always served with merit." But now "as the sub-lieutenancy of his post had been given to Don Benito Vásquez (who had no other merits than that of having been a private soldier and a servant of Don Pedro Piernas), he wished to be given his discharge from the company."

Leyba soon after learned that there were others "who had their eyes on this post." But he handled the situation suavely. "I have pacified them all," he informed Gálvez, "telling them not to lose hope, because as the number of militiamen in this company was very large, I would propose to Your Lordship, that, if such were agreeable to you, it should be divided into two companies. In this case there would be three posts to fill. . . ." By the next summer he had received authorization for the creation of the second company, which he decided should be one of cavalry, and named Eugène Pourée (former lieutenant of infantry) captain, Louis Chevalier lieutenant, and Charles Tayon sub-lieutenant. He made Vásquez lieutenant of the infantry company and promoted Montardy to the vacant sub-lieutenancy.[27]

Finally, we must keep in mind that the militia, whatever its state of training, whatever its official numbers, was yet an uncertain army on

---

[26] *Ibid.*, 182.

[27] Kinnaird, ed., *Spain in the Mississippi Valley*, I, 314–315, 347–348. The roster at the close of the year named Louis Chanchelier (Chancelier?) as lieutenant. The uniform prescribed for the cavalry company consisted of "coat and breeches, red; cuffs, waistcoat, lapel and collar, blue; buttons, gilt."

which to depend, since it was composed of citizens free to go about their private concerns. At that time, for example, when Henry Hamilton was threatening to make his "Progress" toward the Illinois country, Leyba declared to Gálvez (February 5, 1779) that he had hardly forty militia available, since most of the townsmen were up the Missouri trading with the Indians or were away hunting or had gone south to New Orleans on business.[28] With twenty-four professional soldiers—and a drummer—and an uncertain quantity of untrained militia, Leyba would have to defend St. Louis and Upper Louisiana from all comers.

For much of 1779, after Clark had defeated Hamilton and secured the Eastern Illinois once more, St. Louisans and their commandant could relax, for retaliation by the English seemed unlikely. But Leyba's position (though he would not know it for many months) became truly hazardous when Spain broke off diplomatic relations with England in June, 1779. Immediately Lord George Germain, British secretary of state for the colonies, ordered General Frederick Haldimand, commanding British forces in Canada, to reduce the American and Spanish establishments on the Mississippi.

To Patrick Sinclair, lieutenant governor at Michilimackinac, was assigned the planning of an expedition for the coming spring. By February 17, 1780, the latter could report to Haldimand that a "Mr. [Emanuel] Hesse," a trader and former member of the Sixtieth Regiment, was to assemble the Menominee, Puant, and Sac and Fox Indians at the mouth of the Wisconsin River and to await there "the Nations higher up." Sergeant Phillips of the Eighth Regiment would be dispatched to him from Mackinac on March 10 with more Indians and with his final orders. Hesse would then proceed south. "The Reduction of *Pencour* [St. Louis], by surprise, from the Easy admission of Indians at that place, and by Assault from those without, having for its defense, as reported, only 20 men and 20 brass Cannon, will be less difficult than holding it afterwards," Sinclair wrote. However, "to gain both these ends, the rich furr Trade of the Missouri River, the injuries done to the Traders who formerly attempted to partake of it, and the large property they may expect to find in the Place will contribute. The Scious will go with all dispatch as low down as the Natches. . . ."

Later (May 29, 1780), Sinclair informed his superior that this party of "seven hundred and fifty men including Traders, Servants, and Indians" started down the Mississippi on May 2. "Captain Langlade with a chosen band of Indians and Canadians will join a Party assembled at Chicago to make his attack by the Illinois River, and another Party are

[28] Kinnaird, "Clark-Leyba Papers," 105.

sent to watch the plains between the Wabash and the Mississippi." After these parties had carried out their missions, Sinclair added in a postscript, Sergeant Phillips (made a temporary lieutenant by Sinclair) "will garrison the fort at the entrance of the Mississippi [Missouri?]. Captain Hesse will remain at Pencour, Wabasha [chief of the Sioux] will attack Misere [Ste. Genevieve] and the rebels at Kacasia. . . . All the Traders who will secure the Posts on the Spanish side of the Mississippi during the next winter have my promise for the exclusive Trade of Missouri during that Time. . . . The two Lower Villages are to be laid under contribution for the support of their different garrisons, and the two Upper Villages are to send Cattle to La Bay to be forwarded to this place [Michilimackinac] to feed the Indians on their return. . . ."[29]

This enthusiastically planned campaign did not come off according to expectation. On February 9, 1780, Auguste Chouteau arrived from New Orleans with the news of the declaration of war. By March 9 rumors had reached Leyba from the north that a large party of Indians led by a Frenchman (i.e., a Canadian) was preparing to attack or destroy the town.[30]

From a William Brown, taken prisoner by Menominees at St. Louis on May 26 and later interrogated by British authorities, we learn that one John Conn, near the close of March, came down the Mississippi with a report that an attack by Indians from the north was imminent.[31] "Upon the arrival of Conn the Trader," declared Brown, "The Spaniards began to fortify Pencour."

There is no document to identify the moment when Leyba began the construction of defenses for the town. From the church records it is known that the first stone of Fort San Carlos was blessed by the parish priest on April 17. But the planning of the defensive works and the persuading of the inhabitants to share in building them could well have begun at the time of Conn's arrival. In his report to Gálvez of June 8, 1780, Leyba noted that the corporal at the mouth of the Missouri on April 6 had advised him that "the savage nations, excited by

29 The paragraphs about Sinclair's plans are from "Documents Relating to the Attack upon St. Louis in 1780," 41–44.

30 Leyba to Gálvez, St. Louis, Mar. 9, 1780, in Nasatir, "The Anglo–Spanish Frontier in the Illinois Country," 313–314. See also a letter from Pierre Prevost to George Rogers Clark, Feb. 20, 1780, in James, ed., *George Rogers Clark Papers, 1771–1781*, 394–395, implying the organization of an attack.

31 "Documents Relating to the Attack upon St. Louis in 1780," 44–46. After hunting for a year at Natchez and Oyach (Ouachita?), Brown had wandered up to Vincennes two days before its recapture by Clark. From that place he had gone to Ste. Genevieve and in March (1780) had arrived at St. Louis.

the English, were approaching the post." Leyba had thereupon sent the captain of militia to bring back from the abandoned Fort Prince Charles (which had been entirely ruined by a most rigorous winter two years before) the five remaining cannon. A few days after retrieving the artillery, Leyba was warned by hunters from the rivers above St. Louis, who had left their camps "in order to help me," that "an army of Englishmen and savages was approaching St. Louis."[32]

During this period the commandant was planning what could be done to protect the village without incurring expense for the government at New Orleans, a difficult problem indeed.

> Having foreseen for a long time the embarrassment in which I would find myself in case of an attack by the English and savages, I formed the project to construct four towers or forts of stone at the four corners of this village—one on the north, the second on the south, the third on the east, and the fourth on the west—for the purpose of defending and [for] the security of this post. Consequently I assembled the inhabitants in a meeting that took place at my house. I pointed out to them the evident danger to which we were about to find ourselves exposed, in case of an attack by the English and savages, in a village open on all sides to the enemy and without defense; that the few people that we were would not be sufficient to preserve us from the furor of the barbarians unless we ourselves instituted a prompt remedy by making some fortifications. I put before them my project which they found apropos.
>
> Consequently I invited them to consecrate themselves and their families to this defense by cooperating each one according to his means. They have all devoted themselves to this with joy and good will and after each one had offered according to his means I collected one thousand *piastres*. Of this amount I gave 400 out of my own pocket in order to lighten the burden of these poor people. My own means did not permit me to make a greater effort because I have two daughters. These good people have exhausted themselves and have done the impossible in order to furnish among themselves the remaining 600 *piastres* and in addition about 400 working days.
>
> I commenced by ordering one of the towers to be erected on the west which would dominate the major part of this village. This tower was almost finished and a beginning made upon the second one located on the north. After having ordered the foundation to be excavated and the first stone placed, I calculated the expense of the first one. I saw, with pain, that all the contribution would

---

[32] Nasatir, "St. Louis during the British Attack of 1780," 243–251.

at most be sufficient to defray the expenses of only the first tower and that it was impossible to continue the other ones on account of the extreme poverty and misery to which the inhabitants have been reduced. They made their last efforts to furnish the 600 *piastres* by depriving themselves of the necessities of maintaining themselves and feeding their families.

All this expense, Leyba pointed out to his superior, as well as that for transporting the cannons to St. Louis, had cost the king's treasury nothing. Had it been possible, he continued, to build the other three towers, the town and the fields surrounding it could readily have been defended by "only a few troops and inhabitants."[33]

On May 9 Leyba was informed that the approaching army, "composed of 300 Englishmen and 900 savages," was within eighty leagues of St. Louis. He immediately ordered François Vallé at Ste. Geneviève to send, in two boats, sixty militia, and "to add to it the detachment which formed the garrison," all under the command of Lieutenant Francisco de Cartabona. This important reinforcement arrived on May 13. The commandant also called in, by an express, all the hunters scattered on the rivers within twenty leagues of St. Louis and forbade any at the post to leave town. "Therefore within four or five days I was re-enforced by about 150 men, all good shots, [all of] whom were lodged and fed at the expense of the inhabitants who did this voluntarily —until the thirty-first of May."

Leyba now ordered the captain of militia "to go out with forty men in three pirogues to reconnoitre the enemy as far as ten to twelve leagues from St. Louis." At the same time he sent two canoes with six men in each to "scout to a distance of about twenty leagues" from the town. The militia captain was to return in five days, but the smaller canoes "were to remain until they might see the army of the enemy and bring me certain news."

"While awaiting the arrival of the enemy army," Leyba continued in his report, "I speeded up the work on the tower and ordered the floor to be constructed. I ordered the five cannons which had been in Fort Charles to be put in place, and at the same time I ordered two *retranchements* to be dug—at each end of the village—one on the north and the other on the south where the enemy might enter. The one on the north was about twelve arpents in length starting from the Mississippi and following along the side of the tower; the one on the south

---

[33] Cruzat's plan, seven months later, for the defense of the town was principally a stockade. See Cruzat to Gálvez, Dec. 18, 1780, in the appendix below.

being about twenty arpents long, following like the first and defended by the tower."[34]

On the east bank of the river there was equal anxiety. On April 11, through Charles Gratiot, the board of magistrates at Cahokia expressed its distress to Clark at "the deplorable situation in which we find ourselves. . . . We are on the eve of being attacked in our village by considerable parties of savages and cannot work at the cultivation of our grounds, if we have not prompt assistance." Clark had gone down to the mouth of the Ohio to begin building a fort (April 19), but he was constantly in touch. On May 11 he wrote to Oliver Pollock that "the Illenois Settlement are much threatned by the British Gentlemen at Detroit they Count St Lewis their Seat of Government probably they will meet with the fate they have Once Experienced if they attempt it."[35]

On May 15 Colonel Montgomery and some of his officers crossed over to St. Louis to suggest a counteroffensive action to Captain de Leyba. Returning that evening to Fort Bowman, Montgomery reported to Clark:

Sir as the Bad nues of the Enemy Approaching in our Villiges encites me To Exert My Self With the hand full of Trupes I have to try to prevent there desines I thot it of An advantage to try to incorperate with the Spanish trupes Which desine I put in practus by Going over & consulting With the Commandant Feling how Nece[ss]ary it Was to Meete them and to Try to provent them from atacting the Villiges he Acaquest with me in a pinion that It Mite Be atended with Many advantages and proposed to furnish one hundred Men With Botes arms Artilerey Amonition & provisions & Every thing we stud in need of for The Expodition Which offer I could Not Refuse. I there fore intend to Start in a few days from this place With two hundred & Fifty men to try to Provent their hostaliteys on the inhabetents & should I Meate With them if the[y] prove two hard for us it is only to Retreate down Streeme But should their number Note be more than two for one Nothing but death Shall yeald the Surrender. I Recd your letter by John Duff & Should be glad to Complyed With your Request if the Bad nues had not Compelled Me to March with out loss of

[34] The entrenchments were respectively about 750 yards and 1,250 yards in length. Actual work on these trenches was directed by Pierre Picoté de Belestre, a former French officer who had remained in the Spanish service. See his letter to Governor Gálvez, St. Louis, July 14, 1780, in Nasatir, "St. Louis during the British Attack of 1780," 259–261.

[35] James, ed., *George Rogers Clark Papers, 1771–1781*, 410–412, 417, 418–419.

Time to the asistance of the inhabetents of Kaho [w]ho have Distinguished them Selves More like Vetrons than ondesiplened men and are Redy to turn out to a man to Go Any Where the[y] are Requested. I Have sent orders for Every tool to be Sent to you But the[y] ant of Much Acount. I have no Other nues to inform you of But what Mr. libas letter informed you of.[36]

With Colonel Montgomery was Captain John Rogers, recently arrived at Fort Bowman. He too reported this meeting to Clark on the same day.

Agreeable to your Instructions to me I have Set Down to Give you an account of my proseedings Since my arrival to this Place which has not been any thing Extrodenary I have taken Possession of the Fort which I found out of repair and very Dirty but have had it Cleand and Shall Put it in Some Poster of Defence

I was to day over on the Spanish Side with Col. Montgomry and some of his Off[s] who are now at thiss Place the Col. proposed an Expedition to the Commandant who Seemed to be fond of it and says he will send one Hundred men well Equiped under the Command of Col Montgomry but he the Col. has yet to send to Kaskaskias for my two Boats to Carry his Troops and no provision yet Laid in for an Expedition that I dout if the Enemy are on the way as Said they will be here before an Expedition Can take place.

The Col. intends to order me on the Expedition but in Consiquence of your Instructions to Me where in you Direct me to remain here till Orders to the Contrary from your self but at the Same time Left me to Consult the Sivell Govt what Method best to fall on for their Safety I shall not Go unless with the voice of the aforesaid Govt but I think it will be their Desire for me to Go my Men are Belited [billeted] out and appear well satisfied at Maintaining them

My Compliments to the Gentlemen[37]

As Captain Rogers foresaw, American delay in obtaining boats blocked this expedition. Within a week (on May 23) Leyba's reconnoitering party returned with news that it had seen the enemy within twenty leagues of St. Louis. Three days later came the attack:

The twenty-sixth of the same month of May our enemies attacked the fortifications on the north. The certainty in which they were of finding the post without any fortification caused them to

[36] E. G. Voorhis Memorial Collection, MSS, Missouri Historical Society.
[37] *Ibid.*

advance like madmen, with an unbelievable boldness and fury, making terrible cries and a terrible firing. At that moment my guard, who was on the fortification, very alert, gave me warning promptly. Although my orders were given in advance, everyone, without excepting anyone, hastened to the fortifications, half on one side and half on the other. There was not a single man left in the houses. The women and children retired into the governor's mansion, and I placed Lieutenant Cartabona, with twenty men, to guard it.[38] Although quite ill, I went to the tower with the rest of the garrison and with six *chasseurs* to work the cannon. I directed the artillery, and gave my orders in case of an attack on the fortifications. Although the tower was not all covered, and the parapet for the cannon was not in position, yet we used them successfully, and very much surprised the savages, who did not expect such a maneuver; and if it had not been for the rapidity with which I acted, together with all the people on the fortifications, it would have been the last day of St. Louis. Our soldiers and inhabitants have shown marvels of bravery while facing the most evident dangers for the defense of the fortifications, and even wished to make a sortie against the enemy, if I hadn't prevented them, because of the fear that they might succumb under the great number of the enemy, who awaited only this moment in order to force open and enter into the village.

What was most disconcerting in the attack, was the confusion and the lamentable cries of the women and children who could be heard from the *azile* [government residence] up to the place where the combatants were fighting and it was only due to heroic courage that the arms did not fall from the hands of the fathers of families, who signalized themselves with all imaginable valor on this occasion, in which one would not have believed that there was any hope of success for repelling the enemy on account of the great number who were opposed to us.

Notwithstanding our vigorous defense we could not avoid suffering great losses.

Seeing that they could not force our *retranchements* on account of our vigorous resistance, our enemies scattered themselves about the country, where they discovered a number of inhabitants and slaves who were working, sowing *maiz*. They destroyed the fields, killing and *sauvagaient* [acting as savages toward] all that they found: oxen, cows, horses, pigs, hens, and in general they did the

---

[38] It may well have been that Cartabona and a number of his men were in the attic of the governor's house, but certainly not hiding, for they could better spy out the close approach of the enemy and fire on them more effectively from that level than from the lower floor.

most terrible damage, but what was most pitiable and lamentable, was their massacring several persons, who were working in the fields, and who had not had sufficient time to take refuge in the *retranchements*. The list of these unfortunates who were killed and taken prisoner is herewith enclosed.

Alas! my governor, your paternal heart would have shed tears if you had been able to see with your own eyes a spectacle so emotional.

It was an affliction and general consternation, to see these poor corpses cut into pieces, their entrails *arrachez* [thrown out], their limbs, heads, arms and legs scattered all over the field. What a horrible spectacle, *mon général*. In detailing this to you, I find myself very deeply grieved with great pain. It is the *Champs de St. Louis* where was exercised, in less than two hours, the most unheard of barbarity. It was carried to excess without our being able to avoid it on account of the few people whom I had at my disposal, which altogether consisted of about three hundred: troops, militia, and inhabitants.[39] Judge, *mon gouverneur*, what kind of a fate was awaiting us, if Divine Providence, bravery and activity had not preserved us from the fury of those barbarians, animated by the English.

After the massacre, our enemies withdrew without being in a hurry, not having been able to win. Prudence did not allow us to pursue them, on account of the fear of leaving the post unprovided for and facing an ambush on the part of our enemies. Having sent out men to reconnoitre, I learned that the army had retired to twenty leagues from this post, ascending the Mississippi to the mouth of a river called the Illinois.[40]

With the enemy forced to withdraw, the battle of May 26 was a victory for the defenders, but what a sad victory it was for this town of fewer than 700 people! On June 8 Leyba reported fourteen whites and seven slaves killed, six whites and one slave wounded, twelve whites and thirteen slaves carried away prisoners. Farther away, "on the Mississippi," forty-six other whites had been made prisoners. The total count in the war losses of this season was even greater. In a petition of

[39] Martín Navarro (n. 41 below) gave the defending force as "twenty-nine veteran soldiers and two hundred and eighty-one countrymen."

[40] Leyba's report of June 8, 1780, from which I have quoted at such length, was dictated in French to his secretary, for the sick captain had not been able to write for at least a month, and he had no one to write Spanish for him. The translation is that of Nasatir in "St. Louis during the British Attack of 1780," 243–251. Martín Navarro's report to Joseph de Gálvez in Madrid (New Orleans, Aug. 18, 1780) is condensed from the Leyba letter. Houck, ed., *The Spanish Régime in Missouri*, I, 167–169.

the inhabitants of St. Louis to Cartabona, dated July 2, the writers listed "the massacre of eighteen people around St. Louis, six wounded and fifty-seven captured and robbed (as many within the environs of this post as in the farther distant places and dependencies), of nine *chasseurs* captured, massacred, and burnt alive in the Missouri by the Kans[a] Indians, and two private persons killed on the other side, all of which occurred in the affair of the twenty-sixth; besides the massacre of two inhabitants killed on St. Pierre's day by the Loup Indians, of six who had the same fate at Colonel Clark's habitation at the mouth of the *Belle Riviere* [together] with a *chasseur* detached from a bateau ascending from New Orleans."[41]

With all this sacrifice the pressure was not lifted from the people of St. Louis and their commandant. After the enemy withdrew Leyba continued on the alert. It was feared that Captain Langlade and his large party of Canadians and Indians, which had been expected from the direction of Chicago and the Illinois River, might at any moment "pounce upon this post a second time." For that reason Leyba would not dismiss any "foreign soldier" from St. Louis and ordered everybody, "old and young," subject to guard duty in the entrenchments.

About fifteen days after the attack, during which the enemy did not reappear, Leyba agreed with Colonel Montgomery to form an expedition to seek out the English and Indians on the Illinois. The Americans furnished 100 troops and 100 volunteers from the towns of the Eastern Illinois—Leyba 100 men under Pierre Picoté de Belestre. "The few

[41] Nasatir, "St. Louis during the British Attack of 1780," 255. Martín Navarro's report listed a total of fifteen whites and seven slaves dead, six whites and one slave wounded, and fifty-seven whites and thirteen slaves prisoners (Houck, ed., *The Spanish Régime in Missouri*, I, 168). Sinclair, reporting the battle to Haldimand on July 8, laid the defeat to treachery on the part of some of the Canadian traders. Hesse had been accompanied by "Winipigoes, Scioux, Ottawa, Ochipwa, Iowa, and a few of the Outgamies, Sacks, Mascoutins, Kicapous and Pottowatamies. . . . The two first mentioned Indian Nations would have stormed the Spanish Lines, if the Sacks and Outgamies under their treacherous leader Monsr Calvé, had not fallen back so early, as to give them but too well grounded suspicions that they were between two Fires. A Monsr Ducharme & others who traded in the Country of the Sacks kept pace with Monsr Calvé in his perfidy. . . . The Rebels lost an officer and three men killed at the Cahokias & five Prisoners. At Pencour sixty-eight were killed & eighteen Blacks and White People made Prisoners. . . . Many hundreds of Cattle were destroyed and Forty three scalps are brought in. There is no doubt can remain from the concurrent testimony of the Prisoners, that the enemy received Intelligence of the meditated attack against the Illinois . . ." ("Documents Relating to the Attack upon St. Louis in 1780," 48–49). In a note added to the interrogation of William Brown (attached to Sinclair's letter of July 8), mention was made of thirty-three scalps taken "on the West side. . . . A great number of Cattle were killed on both sides of the River and the Inhabitants were very much spared by all the Indians excepting the Winipigoes and Scioux. They only scalped five or six who were not armed for the Defence of the Lines [*sic!*]" (*ibid.*, 46).

inhabitants and boys residing at this post and who remain with me, forced me to keep the foreign militia . . . in order to be able to defend ourselves in case of emergency during the absence of our detachment." This joint force found the Indian villages abandoned and was able to do nothing more than burn their houses, destroy their crops, and leave a threatening message "in a phial suspended from a *poteau d'esclaves*," promising another visit in a couple of months with a much stronger army.[42]

During these weeks Leyba's sickness was growing rapidly worse. He closed what seems to have been his last letter to Governor Gálvez on June 20 by saying that "continuous suffering has obliged me to place the daily affairs in command of Lieutenant Cartabona." On June 28 he died and was buried on the same day in front of the altar in the parish church. In due time his report of June 8 reached New Orleans and the intendant Martín Navarro composed his report to Joseph de Gálvez, who on February 3, 1781, replied to Governor Bernard de Gálvez that "the King has been greatly pleased at the vigorous defense made by Captain Don Fernando de Leyba and Lieutenant Don Francisco Cartabona in repulsing the English Captain Esse, who intended to surprise them and dislodge them from the post of San Luis de Ylinoeses; and in proof of his sovereign gratitude he has decided to confer upon the first the rank of lieutenant-colonel and on the second that of captain. . . ."[43]

III

The record shows that Leyba was alert to danger, that he heeded the warnings floating into St. Louis, that he was in constant contact with the Americans across the Mississippi, that he made strenuous efforts to construct such defenses as resources permitted, and that he conducted the battle defense effectively. No document has ever been produced to support the charge that he sold gunpowder needed for the defense of the town, that he had been in traitorous correspondence with the British, or that he had accepted a bribe. No contemporary record has been uncovered which warrants calling him a sot, a penurious and avaricious man, a sordid, intemperate creature whose name should be forever held in obloquy. Yet the tradition, though given firm shape by Primm, was not invented by him. The lieutenant governor, well received in June,

[42] Nasatir, "St. Louis during the British Attack of 1780," 247–248, 251–252, 253, 260. Leyba gave the departure date as June 13, 1780, Picoté de Belestre, June 14.
[43] Houck, ed., *The Spanish Régime in Missouri*, I, 167–170.

1778, died two years later execrated by at least a few very vocal (though anonymous) citizens.

Leyba's unpopularity, deserved or not, is of record in two letters dispatched from St. Louis to Governor General Gálvez in New Orleans at the time of the disaster. Their anonymity need not concern us, nor the fact that the charges made are not substantiated: their passionate denunciation of the lieutenant governor marks the beginning of the tradition.

One of these letters, written June 19 and 23, 1780, and signed "Virtutis, Veritatisque Amicus," gives a report of the battle very similar to that set down by Primm. Leyba was held entirely to blame for the disaster. During the attack he hid in the "nearly useless" tower that he had forced the inhabitants to build. His own soldiers were heard to cry out for the government powder that had been sent to the Indians on the Missouri for the captain's private benefit. "The hatred that the people of this country and even his own troops bear for him is inconceivable," the writer asserted. "Sentiments of humanity, of conscience are not capable of keeping him safe from the most frightful curses and wishes. Never has an illness been so long, death so slow in coming, thunderbolts so tardy in overwhelming a sinner and wiping him out."[44]

The other anonymous letter to Gálvez, signed "Le Peuple Des islinois," is not dated but, since it contains no reference to the attack on St. Louis, was probably written shortly before that event and is therefore even more significant in this search for anti-Leyba feeling. In it the lieutenant governor is declared a man without conscience, without respect for the king's orders. He permits, we are told, the sergeant of the

---

[44] AGI, *Papeles de Cuba,* leg. 193–A. The entire letter is printed in the appendix. I cite this document not because it adds anything to the history of the affair of May 26 but because it expresses such strong revulsion to Leyba.

A petition to Cartabona, interim lieutenant governor, dated July 2, 1780, four days after the death of Leyba, intended for transmission to Gálvez, expresses much the same lament over the disaster and the same concern over the dangers to which the people of St. Louis were exposed, for it was a moment when they had reason to be greatly alarmed. Cartabona was begged to "paint to our Governor the horror of the situation of the Illinois and [to] send a deputy to him . . . [to] solicit the aid which is necessary for our preservation. . . . The Illinois country . . . is now at the moment of its ruin. Destitute generally of everything, the storehouses of the King are without gunpowder, without munitions of war, and entirely empty of merchandise sent by the King for the nations friendly to Spain. the [resources of the] inhabitants there are entirely exhausted, not to speak of a thousand small ruinous expenses which they have been obliged to make, in default of their indigent commandant, in order to prevent themselves from becoming the sad victim of the discontent and brutality of the Sac and Fox Indians, the only nation remaining to us who can serve us as a rampart against the enemies who surround us and are ready to strike." But in this petition, signed by thirty-one citizens of St. Louis, there are no recriminations against Leyba. *Ibid.,* leg. 113.

troops to maintain a "maison publique" (saloon? whorehouse?) outside the barracks, living there in concubinage. "The coadjutor of his agent" keeps a black concubine. Everywhere is disorder and debauchery. He is denounced as an absolute despot, a tyrant. The carpenter who made the coffin for Madame Leyba, coming to collect his due, is driven away with violence. Avaricious beyond example, for two years he has managed the presents for the Indians for his own advantage. He will hardly give visiting Indians bread to keep them from starving. By his conduct he has drawn upon himself not merely the hatred of the Indians, but that of the British Royalists and the Americans as well as that of his own people, whom he has forced to accept doubtful letters of exchange for more than 60,000 *livres*. He has so manipulated and controlled the Indian trade that he has built up a fortune of 248,600 *livres*.

Judicial costs under his rule are excessive. A man sues to collect 25 *livres* due him and finds, on winning his case, that he must pay costs amounting to 130 *livres* in deerskins. Every legal action is an opportunity to squeeze money out of the people. When the indigent Madame St. François has been condemned to pay 25 *livres* in costs, Monsieur Leconte offers to pay for her, but after Leyba has agreed to accept Leconte's offer, the commandant discovers that she is not literally destitute, as claimed, for she has stored in another house 400 weight of flour which she had purchased for 20 *livres* the hundred. The grasping Leyba now forces her to deliver the flour to him at the value of 12 *livres* the hundred. He is most to be feared, it is asserted, when he appears to do one a kindly service. He writes four lines to Colonel Clark for Madame Laurent about her Negro who has been poisoned by a slave on the other side of the river—and charges her 12 *piastres*. These are but a few of the specific charges brought against Captain de Leyba by this unidentified writer.[45]

These sweeping allegations, naming names and sums involved, cannot be proved true or exposed as false for want of documentation. Leyba may have been guilty, but there is no evidence of malfeasance in the colonial archives in St. Louis, nor is there a single reference in any state papers in New Orleans or in Spain thus far examined which shows he was ever reproved or even questioned about his procedures or that his successor was warned about irregularities in office.[46] But even though

[45] *Ibid.* A complete translation will be found in the appendix.

[46] Legal fees then (as now) were often excessive in relation to the sum involved in a suit, but they were established by law and were a matter of record. They cannot be interpreted as a special grab by the commandant in his position as judge. The inventory of Leyba's estate, made in July, 1780, does not show any evidence of ill-gotten gains,

we give Leyba a not-proven verdict or throw the case out of court for lack of evidence, the very existence of the accusations points to his unpopularity. We must ask how this came about. What was the situation that he faced when he arrived in St. Louis? What did he do that so set people against him?

On his arrival in the Western Illinois in June, 1778, the new lieutenant governor reported that he had been well received by all the inhabitants "with extraordinary signs of rejoicing." These signs, he wrote with some humor as well as polite flattery to Governor Gálvez on July 11, he did not attribute to his

> beauty, nor to the fact that they were dissatisfied with my predecessor, but only that in the creature they praise the creator. So public in his most remote district are the virtues with which your Lordship is adorned, when this point is touched upon, that although it brings joy to all, it surprises no one. This is the true reason for their joy: they believe that, since this district is commanded by a person chosen by your Lordship, they have whatever is necessary for their progress and happiness. In order that they may continue in this method of thinking, I have contributed not a little by the fact that I was of their opinion, and had good intentions to represent your Lordship as much as is advisable in this matter.[47]

An auspicious beginning. But this was the honeymoon of the new

---

since the three St. Louisans making the appraisal arrived at a total valuation of only 45,504 *livres* (his will and succession papers are in the French and Spanish Archives of St. Louis, nos. 2211, 2362, and 2581, MSS, Missouri Historical Society). Other charges against him seem equally exaggerated: for instance, that he should charge Madame Laurent 12 *piastres* (60 *livres*)—the equivalent today of at least $100—for writing a brief official letter is beyond easy acceptance.

Frederick L. Billon, who, as recorder of deeds in St. Louis in the later nineteenth century, had the early archives under his supervision, wrote "that when, long since, I first read all that had been alleged against De Leyba by the few early writers on St. Louis, I imbibed to a great extent the prejudices entertained against him; but after I had become familiar with his decisions on cases brought before him, and read his impartial and apparently just decisions in most of these cases, I became convinced that he had been a much vilified and abused man and grossly misrepresented, and when we consider the troubles and perplexities of his brief administration of the government, coupled with the irreparable loss of his young wife, leaving two motherless little girls to the care of strangers in a strange land, it should not excite surprise that he should become somewhat intemperate in his latter days, as is alleged against him by some of those early writers, although without proof." *Annals of St. Louis in Its Early Days under the French and Spanish Dominations* (St. Louis, 1886), 195–196.

[47] Houck, ed., *The Spanish Régime in Missouri*, I, 161. Leyba had arrived in St. Louis on June 10, after a ninety-three-day journey from New Orleans, and had taken over command from Francisco Cruzat on June 14. This letter, possibly Leyba's first to Gálvez from Upper Louisiana, was carried to New Orleans by Cruzat.

executive, those first pleasant months when the public waits to learn how much it will get and how little it will be asked to give. Leyba must have known that before long the day would come when his people would no longer be pleased with his efforts for the welfare of the district and the signs of rejoicing would turn to growls of dissatisfaction, when the rumblings of discontent would swell into loud complaint to higher authority.

What Primm and the writers who followed him seemed unaware of was the complexity of the problems that faced the administration of Upper Louisiana in the eighteenth century. For them, looking back with little benefit of records, the days of the first ancestors passed as those of a frontier idyll. These simple, impulsive French people lived a gentle, unobtrusive life far from the bustle of the modern world. They raised some crops, traded a bit with the Indians, danced and sang and played cards as gay-hearted Frenchmen do who refuse to take life too seriously. There was only an occasional unpleasantness to disturb the calm ways of this little, almost Eden-like democracy in the days before the Americans came. The year of the attack, the year of the high waters, the year ten boats went down the river together as protection against river pirates, the year the smallpox first struck the village— these were marked down on the tablets of their memories as highlights— these were the short and simple annals of a people who found life gay and uncomplicated, whose wants were few and easily satisfied. The only "government" needed was a little paternal guidance in settling not very important disputes between neighbors.

But in truth this was only an imagined world. Reality was something quite different. St. Louis was the farthest outpost of the Spanish empire in North America, a very small town but the seat of government for a vast territory. The Western Illinois, stretching to Canada and the Rockies, was important as a buffer to British advance westward. Leyba was sent to St. Louis not to be a kindly father to idyllic villagers but to administer the district effectively for Spain. His assignment was to see to its security, to prevent the intrusion of foreigners, to maintain friendly relations with the Indians, to stimulate the fur trade, to develop agriculture to the point where the district might be at least self-sustaining, and to encourage the increase of population.[48] All this the lieutenant governor was expected to accomplish at an absolute minimum of expenditure, for the whole colony of Louisiana was a heavy expense to the home government, with no compensating financial return.

[48] Special instructions of Gálvez to Leyba, Mar. 9, 1778, in Kinnaird, ed., *Spain in the Mississippi Valley*, I, 258–260.

Foremost among problems in the eyes of higher authority was the development of agriculture, for on this depended any increase in population to srengthen the colony. The town had been notorious from the beginning for its indifference to farming—its nickname, "Paincourt," applied as early as 1765, was recognition of its failure to produce enough crops for its own provisioning. Leyba's first examination of the country around St. Louis assured him, as he reported to Gálvez in November, 1778, that "there is not a foot of soil in this country which is not suitable for all kinds of crops, and there are many square leagues of beautiful meadows on the heights." But although any settler might have, free for the asking, as many acres as he could cultivate, Leyba quickly discovered that the men of St. Louis were "interested only in trading with the Indians, and neglect their farming. All are, or wish to be merchants." Consequently, "there is always a scarcity of food at this post." In fact, "the classes of people are so mixed up that one cannot tell who is a farmer and who is a merchant."

Recognizing that "self-interest is the motive force in all men," Leyba pointed out to the governor general that "these people are interested in commerce and not in farming because the latter gives them little or no gain, while the former supports them and even makes them rich. This same reason would incline them to farming if the flour which could be made here were disposed of in this very post." He then tried out on his superior an elegant scheme to make the farmers of St. Louis happy.

> Supposing that there were at this post a garrison of eight hundred men and that these lands supplied their bread, this troop, at the rate of a pound and a half daily, would consume per year 1,200 barrels of flour of 300 pounds each. Estimating the price of flour at twelve pesos, the cost of the barrel at one, and the freight at two, the total income for this post would amount to 18,000 pesos annually. It must be understood that in order to interest these settlers, it would be necessary for this amount to be paid directly to the people themselves, so that they would receive it as they delivered the flour. The reason is that its delivery to this post would entail more expense to them, partly because most of the settlers have no connections whatever here, and partly because of the risks there would be in connection with the persons whom they appoint as their agents.

The prospect of profit would cause the population to "increase greatly," thought Leyba, and soon the cultivation of hemp and flax, earlier proposed by Cruzat and "readily agreed to by everyone with the promise to set to work doing it," could be "contemplated."[49] But alas for dreams. Leyba was soon to hear, in response to his report on the defense of the district, that Gálvez could not spare even 200 men to garrison the upper country, let alone 800.

The best that higher headquarters could suggest was to urge the settlers to devote themselves, after grain, to the cultivation of hemp and flax, which would bring them "great benefits" because the king had ordered for their encouragement that these commodities (which could be produced very well in the Illinois country) would be free of all export and import duties. In view of their poverty Gálvez had proposed to the king that he advance them Negro slaves to stimulate this cultivation. The minister in Spain had replied that the king agreed to "take the best and most opportune measures for sending Negroes." Gálvez added: "It is necessary to await them. You will make known to those settlers these good intentions of our sovereign so that, in view of them, they may proceed to get ready for this raising of flax and hemp, which promises them profitable results, and, if possible, to undertake it before the arrival of the slaves promised by His Majesty."[50]

But the sovereign's good intentions came to nothing. Slaves were not forthcoming. All who awaited this aid before undertaking the cultivation of hemp put off a beginning. The proposed new money crops languished for lack of labor. Francisco Cruzat had, no doubt, been popularly awarded an *E* for effort when he made the proposal at the close of his term: the new lieutenant governor would inevitably be held responsible for the failure of the scheme. Bad weather at harvest time in 1778 ruined half the wheat. The prospects of the farmer were certainly not improved.

Dissatisfaction with a government program intent on forcing many of the settlers into farming when the fur trade seemed to promise better fortune with less effort inclined any who had capital or could raise credit to set up as a "merchant." But the possibilities of effective trade with the Indians were obviously limited, and the annual distribution of shares in the trade was always a major problem for the lieutenant governor. To whatever arrangements he made there were always repercussions. Leyba found, as others had before him and would find in later years, that the "person in command of this post . . . is so overwhelmed with requests for permits for the Missouri that, as it is impos-

[49] Leyba to Gálvez, Nov. 16, 1778, no. 255, in Kinnaird, ed., *Spain in the Mississippi Vaalley*, I, 312–313.

[50] *Ibid.*, I, 259, 314.

sible to satisfy them all, it is impossible not to make some enemies."[51] He had faced this situation—he thought successfully—in his first weeks in St. Louis. On July 21 he had reported to the governor general that on August 1 "traders will leave this post for the nations of the Missouri. I have divided this commerce up into small shares, thereby filling many needs. The details of this . . . appear to have greatly pleased the public, with the exception of those who, although not totally deprived of a share, expected a large one."[52]

Those who obtained substantial shares were no doubt pleased, but we can be certain that the less favored were considerably disgruntled, as becomes evident in the allegations made by the writer who undertook to speak for "Le Peuple Des islinois." But Leyba's greatest offense may well have been his own share in this commerce, as this letter writer avers. It must be emphasized that this allotment was legitimate and customary; its purpose was to provide additional remuneration to the lieutenant governor, who had only his regular army pay for his multiple duties. However, his partnership with Francisco Vigo obviously did not sit well with some St. Louisans.[53]

[51] Ibid., I, 313.

[52] Ibid., I, 299. Few details are available. Although many documents pertaining to the Missouri River area between 1765 and 1794 were published by Kinnaird in the three volumes of Spain in the Mississippi Valley and many for that region between 1785 and 1804 by Nasatir in Before Lewis and Clark: Documents Illustrating the History of the Missouri, 1785–1804 (2 vols., St. Louis, 1952), no full study has yet been undertaken of the history of the fur trade on the Missouri River during the Spanish domination—much essential documentation remains buried in the Archivo General de Indias at Seville and possibly in other Spanish archives. According to Nasatir, eight merchants of St. Louis (Francisco Vigo, Auguste Chouteau, Eugène Pourée dit Beausoleil, [François?] Delorier, Eugenio Alvarez, [Louis?] Perrault, [Jean Baptiste?] Sarpy, and [Jean] Motard) shipped to New Orleans in 1779 skins to the value of 161,227 livres ("The Anglo–Spanish Frontier in the Illinois Country during the American Revolution, 1779–1783," Illinois State Historical Society Journal, XXI [Oct., 1928], 323, n. 96). Were these the licensees of 1779? J. B. Martigny of St. Louis, on Oct. 30, 1779, wrote to Gálvez complaining that Leyba, "pour une somme considérable," had granted for 1780 all the posts on the Missouri to Auguste Chouteau, Silvestre Labbadie, and Gabriel Cerré (Nasatir, Before Lewis and Clark, I, 71). On this charge see Leyba's letters to Gálvez quoted on p. 360 below.

[53] The instructions issued to the first Spanish commandant, Captain Francisco Riú, in 1767, specified that "the commandant of the fort [District of the Missouri] shall choose one of the tribes who live near it, with whom the trade shall be reserved to him" (Houck, ed., The Spanish Régime in Missouri, I, 14). The custom was continued throughout the Spanish time. Lieutenant Governor Manuel Pérez in 1790 awarded the trade with the Kansa Indians to himself and Auguste Chouteau (Nasatir, Before Lewis and Clark, I, 135). According to new regulations drawn up at New Orleans in 1793 the trade was to be "free" to any merchant who would pay an annual fee of 20 pesos and was otherwise qualified for a share. One article provided that "each trading portion shall be drawn by lot in the presence of the commandant who will be the only one privileged to select the portion which may suit him best, but who will not have the

The white subjects of the crown thus posed problems not easy for the lieutenant governor to resolve without displeasing many. The Indian nations compounded his difficulties, for whatever action he took or failed to take affected the security and well-being of the colony and the enterprises of its members. Leyba's instructions had been to "make every effort to win the good will of all the Indian tribes, not only those in the territory of His Majesty, but also those under the jurisdiction of the English." He was to "use for this purpose all the tact and good treatment possible in order to attract them to our dominations."[54] This meant, first of all, "entertainment." That is to say, they must be ceremoniously received and "feasted" on state visits to the little capital in the wilderness. The word of the arrival of a new "father" had spread very quickly over the prairies and through the forests. On July 21, 1778, the commandant wrote to Gálvez that seven different nations had arrived in St. Louis to "welcome" him—Kickapoo, Sac, Maha, Mascuten, Missouri, and Great and Little Osage. "According to reports I have received, about a dozen more [tribes] are still to come."

Ordinarily this would mean only the chief and a supporting delegation, but "some nations have sent me word that they will leave their dogs to guard their villages, that is, that they will come with their wives and children." The Missouri, in fact, had done just this and had stayed for two weeks "eating us out of house and home." He pointed out that there "are only two ways of dealing with these people, either run them out with guns or feed them. For the former they give no cause, nor have we the forces to do so." He was therefore feeding them, but this was proving expensive. Part of the trouble arose from the war between the English and the Bostoneses: the Indians on the east of the Mississippi, not knowing to which party to turn, "come to this post under the pretext of asking advice on their troubles."

One serious result of this policy of conciliation was that the visitors "consume many rations of bread." In the six weeks since his arrival at St. Louis, declared Leyba, "the fewest that have been distributed in one day is fifty rations, and there have been days when it was two hundred."

---

privilege of changing it afterwards." In 1794, of the twenty-nine portions available Lieutenant Governor Zenon Trudeau chose for himself one-quarter of the Kansa Indian trade—this share permitted the entrance into the Indian country of goods to the value of 6,000 *livres* in silver (Kinnaird, ed., *Spain in the Mississippi Valley*, III, 191–198, 278–279). Instructions of Governor General Carondelet to Trudeau in 1792, however, had specified in that year that the 20-*peso* fee collected by the lieutenant governor should be retained by him in lieu of a share in the trade (Nasatir, *Before Lewis and Clark*, I, 152).

54 Kinnaird, ed., *Spain in the Mississippi Valley*, I, 259.

Yet a regulation drawn up by Piernas on January 4, 1771, specified a limit of 1,072 rations in any one year. Seven years earlier this might have sufficed, but the unsettled conditions now required a considerably larger allowance for the entertainment of Indian visitors, Leyba urged. Furthermore, the cost of flour for these rations was three times what it had been at the time Piernas had made his report.

It could have been little consolation to have Gálvez reply promptly on September 2 that he feared Leyba would have frequent visits from the Indian tribes during the war between Great Britain and her colonies and that they would consume many rations. But, as always, there were no funds. "I must tell you that I have not authority to increase the number of 1,072 rations, which you found stipulated in the papers of Don Pedro Piernas, because it is the same as stipulated in the regulation of the obligations of this province." He could only suggest that "for this reason you will try to prevent their exceeding this number, as with proper management you can see that they do not stay more than three or four days, and not two weeks as I note the Missouri nation has done." (Gálvez's formal close sounds almost ironic: "May God preserve you many years.")

From Leyba's letter of June 8, 1780, we know that the situation only grew worse: he now stated that in 1778 he had consumed 3,000 rations over the limit allowed by the king; in 1779, 3,800; and to date in 1780, 3,000. How were these paid for? No papers have been found, but Leyba must have been forced to issue to local citizens government promises to pay with his personal guarantee added.[55]

"Feasting" was for all visitors. For the notables there also had to be decorations discreetly awarded, for much depended on sustaining the prestige of the chiefs. On July 21, 1778, Leyba requested from Gálvez "four to six medals . . . as I have already distributed the two that Don Francisco Cruzat gave me, one to the second chief of the Great Osages, and the other to the first chief of the Little Osages. It is necessary to give one to the second chief of the Little Osages, not only because he was promised one by my predecessors, but also because he is an Indian much beloved by his people. I have told him in full council that he may come here in November to get it, and that I shall give it to him without fail. The other medals are to be kept on hand to be given out if some good Indian has to be rewarded or some bad one cajoled." In his reply on September 2 Gálvez noted: "I send you two large medals for the principal chiefs and shall send you small ones for secondary chiefs when they reach me, recommending that you give the former only to the

---

[55] *Ibid.*, 298–299, 305; Nasatir, "St. Louis during the British Attack of 1780," 248.

principal chiefs." Even these were in short supply, for on December 9 Leyba reported that he had not received the two large medals. But what he needed most was a pair of small ones, as they were the ones he had promised. It was not until the new year that Gálvez received from Spain the large medals he had requested, which he forwarded to Leyba on January 13. Leyba, however, was still begging on February 5 for the small medals for the secondary chiefs.[56]

The medals served as personal recognition of a chief by the Spanish "father." Prestige of the tribe also rested on the presence of the flag as evidence of the bond between the Indian nation and the white. "The chiefs of our nations of Indians," Leyba wrote to Gálvez on February 5, 1779, "are very urgently asking me for flags. I have told them that I would bring their requests to the attention of Your Lordship. I consider this to be just for the reason that, since your establishment in this colony, only once have they been provided with them. As it is their custom to have the flag always above the cabin of the chief, there are tribes which have only a flag pole and on it usually some rag full of holes and patches. Four or five would be sufficient for the present." This request, at least, Gálvez could fulfill: in his reply on March 23 he noted that he was sending six flags to be distributed as needed.[57]

Yet more important were the annual presents given to a chief for his distribution to the members of his tribe. "Each nation which arrives," Leyba pointed out to Gálvez in his letter of July 21, 1778, "even though a foreign one, must be given not only bread but also a present." For this purpose he was using goods which had been intended for some tribes that had not come to get them, but the supply was not sufficient. Before leaving New Orleans Gilbert Antoine de St. Maxent (in charge of Indian affairs for the colony) had told him that he would find a year's supply of presents waiting in St. Louis, but on arriving he found the presents few and of poor quality. On July 11 he had writtten to Gálvez that "the next year's presents for the Indians had not been received by me." On July 25 he had to report "that of those for this year I have received only a small part of that which M. Maxent [had promised to] put on my boat. He had assured me that the rest would be delivered by M. Lacled." However, Laclède's boat had arrived (Pierre Laclède had died at the mouth of the Arkansas River on the way up) without bringing the further supply of presents promised.

Necessity had forced Leyba, almost immediately after his arrival in St. Louis, to an unpopular action. Since the visits of the Indians required

---

[56] Kinnaird, ed., *Spain in the Mississippi Valley*, I, 299, 305, 317, 321, 330.
[57] *Ibid.*, 329–330.

very numerous presents, "in order not to make the Indians discontented" he had ordered "the merchants of this post to provide me with what may be needed for such presents." Up to this moment it had not been necessary to put this order into execution, "but I know that they are taking it with very bad grace on account of the scarcity and costliness of their merchandise this year." This was not a confiscation of the goods, for they would be replaced eventually by the government—but in the meantime the merchants would be without trade goods for the Indians and their opportunity for effective business greatly diminished.[58]

Above all, in keeping the Indians contented and the colony prosperous nothing was so important as a sufficient supply of trade goods. But the boats arriving from New Orleans brought little useful in the trade. Leyba wrote to the governor general on July 13, 1779:

> There have arrived here at this post from your city five boats, all loaded with rum, sugar, and coffee, which for these people are the world, the flesh, and the devil. . . . [But] there is no merchandise to furnish the Indian tribes, neither are there any furs, which are their money, coming into this town. Two boats are still to come. If these arrive as poorly stocked as the others, I do not believe the results will be happy. It is indispensable that our Indian tribes be provided with their accustomed goods. There are not enough in this post to supply the smallest of them. Even when we take to their villages what they need, Sir, they find reasons to make threats. If nothing is sent to them, as now will be the case because there are none, they will come furiously to this town to learn the reason for the lack of goods. On learning this, it is inevitable that they will turn their backs disdainfully on us and go to trade with the English (whose traders, even without this reason, make of our tribes a source of wealth). This will result in two disadvantages: no furs will come into our territory and the Indians will be won over to the English trade, which is certainly more profitable to them than ours. In order to see whether I could remedy this I sent some merchants to the other side to get goods for the Indians, but the English traders, from whom nothing is hidden and who see our need, asked such exorbitant prices that only a person who wanted to ruin himself would accept them. Their intention is to give the blow which I am trying to prevent, and for success in averting it I shall omit no measures which may occur to me. . . .

[58] *Ibid.*, 296–297, 300. The same situation existed the following year, for on Oct. 28, 1779, Leyba had to inform his superior that Maxent had not sent the presents for that year. "I have distributed all those I had on hand. Therefore nothing remains of this kind for the next year." The draft answer, dated New Orleans, Feb. 19, 1780, promised presents for the Indians "at the first opportunity" (*ibid.*, 361).

Three months later he informed Gálvez of the one measure he had been able to devise. In the imperative need for merchandise he had "permitted five traders of this post to bring in some goods from the other side." Again he was in trouble locally, for he could manage this only by making a special concession. "This has remedied our lack of goods with which to supply our Indian tribes; but inasmuch as they [the five traders] have bought them dearly, I have been obliged to permit them to take them to the tribes themselves. For this reason I have not, as last year, made a wide distribution of permits, but, as between two evils, I think I have chosen the lesser." The friendship of the Missouri River tribes might thus be preserved for another year, but what growling in the streets of St. Louis must have been heard![59]

Leyba was also under injunction, long before the declaration of war by Spain against Great Britain, to aid the Virginians discreetly in their struggle. In the summer of 1779 very soon after the taking of Kaskaskia and Cahokia, he not merely received George Rogers Clark as an honored guest but contributed importantly to his support. Three months later, however, he declared to Gálvez in a long personal letter:

> . . . the coming of the Americans to this district has ruined me utterly. Several inhabitants of this town, who put their property in the hands of the Americans to please me, find themselves in the same situation, and these losses are equally a matter of regret to me with my own since I consider myself the immediate cause of them. But what was there for me to do with your Lordship's orders except to come to their aid in view of the fact that even the principal leader, however many American documents he brought, had not a shirt to cover his nakedness. I accomplished this on my credit with all the inhabitants so that they might provide these Americans with whatever they needed.
>
> This measure relieved them from their affliction and I was left as hostage, since I became bondsman for ten thousand pesos (as is clear from the receipts that I have in various places in this post, which must be paid). On their part I was paid by two bills of exchange which Francisco Vigo took to that place [New Orleans], and they have not been paid. I do not think that those that go down there from my district could be many more since these inhabitants think that they are sufficiently afflicted and ruined; but I do think that there will be other new appeals begging me to pay the sums which I guaranteed. I acted in this way, my Governor, thinking to do a service for your Lordship and please you. The

[59] *Ibid.*, 346–347, 361. Letters of July 13 and Oct. 28, 1779. This appears to rebut the charge made by Martigny as quoted in n. 52 above.

result of this is that I am now overwhelmed with trouble not only for what I owe and cannot pay, but also by the chance that your Lordship may not approve my measures (this is what tortures me most) although all were intended to show you my blind obedience.

These inhabitants did not want to give up their goods even for Colonel Clark's receipts. They gave them immediately when I pledged mine. If I lose my credit by not being able to pay them, the service may be retarded as a consequence since it is certain that, if I need some unexpected aid for my troops, I shall not get it.

Finally, my Governor, my beloved wife, who came to this exile with so many hardships . . . when she saw her hopes [of returning to Spain] frustrated by the labyrinth of debts in which she found me involved, was overcome by such a great melancholy that after only five days of illness in bed, she passed from this to another life, without my repeated urgings that we could trust your Lordship's favor being able to relieve her. . . . Her loss makes me look upon that of my property as an affair of little importance. Therefore, in company with my weeping little daughters, I implore your Lordship's protection for the collection of these bills of exchange. . . .[60]

To cap the difficulties that arose in the normal administration of Upper Louisiana and the special problem of assisting the Virginians in their conquest of the Eastern Illinois came the threat of attack and the absolute necessity of calling upon the townspeople for a defense contribution of money and labor which they could ill afford. Completely exposed to any enemy, St. Louis for sixteen years had relied for its security on the colonial system of presents for the Indians and an adequate supply of trade goods. Now an invasion from Canada, organized, munitioned, and led by British officers, could overwhelm the town and destroy what little stake in the world the settlers had accumulated.

Without funds from New Orleans, without troop reinforcements, Leyba, as has already been pointed out, had to call upon the St. Louisans for a "voluntary" subscription of 1,000 *piastres* (to which he himself contributed 400) and for a donation of 400 working days for the digging of the entrenchments and the building of the tower, without which the enemy could sweep easily through the town, pillaging the houses, slaughtering the people, and driving off their livestock. He had to call the militia to duty—every male between fifteen and fifty years of age—to stand guard day and night. He had to bring into town all the hunters

---

[60] Kinnaird, "Clark-Leyba Papers," 111–112. Virginia money was almost worthless.

from outlying areas on the Missouri and the Meramec. He had to order to St. Louis a company of sixty militia from Ste. Genevieve. All these men served without pay. The "foreign" militia were quartered on the St. Louisans, both bedded and fed by them from their arrival on May 13 until the end of the month. There were indeed "a thousand ruinous expenses" which their "indigent commandant" had been forced to ask of them and there had been no time left to them to work at their normal occupations.[61]

It is clear, then, that there were many grievances—over the failure of government to assist in the development of agriculture though it was trying to force settlers into farming, over the distribution of the Indian trade, over the presents to the Indians and a satisfactory supply of trade goods which would keep the Indians friendly and the settlements safe, over the financing of the American war effort in the Eastern Illinois, over the inadequate military protection afforded by government and the financial and physical burdens laid directly on the settlers to defend their town—to augment the distresses and exacerbate the tempers of some or many St. Louisans. All this was topped by the disastrous attack of May 26, in which thirty-two St. Louisans and twenty-one of their slaves were killed, wounded, or carried away prisoner, and by the fear aroused or further enemy action. On whom better to lay the blame than the official in command?

How much personality may have affected public response we cannot say, for we know nothing of the temperament of Captain de Leyba. He may have been overbearing and difficult, though there is no detail to prove such behavior. It would be understandable, though not excusable, if his disposition had grown worse during the months of service in St. Louis, for to the problems of his office and worries over his financial involvements for the public good we must add his pain over the death of his wife, his ever-worsening health (at least as early as October 18, 1779, he wrote of his illness to Gálvez), and his anxiety about his two little daughters.

Here is the root of the tradition set down by Wilson Primm in 1831 in his lecture on the early history of St. Louis. Grounded upon a feeling of injustice, a sense of not being properly cared for, a reluctance to bear responsibility, upon ignorance and lack of understanding and fear, the

---

[61] Inhabitants to Cartabona, St. Louis, July 2, 1780, in Nasatir, "St. Louis during the British Attack of 1780," 254–257. On May 30 Leyba contracted with Gabriel Cerré to supply the Ste. Genevieve militiamen with rations for the duration of their service at St. Louis from June 1; each daily ration was to consist of six ounces of salted bacon (ham?) or eight ounces of fresh meat, one and a half pounds of bread, and one teaspoon of salt, at a cost of 2½ *escalins* each (*ibid.*, 13–14).

gossip of the day became reinforced by the faint remembrance of un-happy times and was accepted by later writers who found it easier to repeat what had been said before them than to examine the record criti-cally. Documents known today show that Captain de Leyba was effec-tive in his defense of St. Louis. None have been discovered which corroborate the allegations made against him.

Historical integrity is vital whether in the portrayal of a nation's great cities or of a wilderness settlement, and it is not quixotic to seek justice for one of history's minor characters.

APPENDIX

I

Virtutis, Veritatisque Amicus to [Governor General Gálvez], St. Louis, June 19, 23, 1780[1]

St Louis   19 June 1780

Monsieur—

Compelled by my compatriots, persuaded by my friends to send you the account of the sinister events which happened at St Louis, principal village of the Illinois, the twenty-sixth of June [May] 1780, I have consented to

---

[1] AGI, *Papeles de Cuba*, leg. 193–A; original in French. For help in the translation of this difficult letter I am indebted to my colleague Professor Betty Osiek of the Romance language faculty, Southern Illinois University; responsibility for the final ver-sion, however, is mine. One special problem has been bothersome. Several pages of the original (which neither of us has seen) were apparently damaged at the top, and a few lines appear trimmed at right-hand edges. But most vexing has been the uncertainty of page sequence. Dr. Nasatir had been kind enough to supply me with a handwritten transcript as well as a rough draft translation (never published); to complement these I obtained from Seville a microfilm of the original. Though a few lines are missing, I believe that the paragraphs down to the signature must run as I have given them, for they make a consistent sequence. After completing his letter (the punitive party had not yet returned to St. Louis), the writer four days later added a few paragraphs of latest "news." Last of all, as one of these additions, I have placed the long paragraph (a full page in the letter) about the Sac and Fox Indians, for I do not find any tie-in in detail with any other part of the document. Furthermore it is incomplete. In the letter of "Inhabitants to Cartabona, St. Louis, July 2, 1780" (Nasatir, "St. Louis during the British Attack of 1780," 254), the writers say, in brief reference to this incident: "De-spite their misfortunes, disgraces and sad remains of a dilapidated fortune, they [the inhabitants] were restrained from uniting and forming jointly a present which would serve for some time to preserve the friendship of the savages." Obviously this Friend of Virtue and Truth intended to say more than appears on his page. For present pur-poses, the sequence of the pages is not important, for the attack on Leyba is clear however they are read.

fulfill the desires of some and the will of others, only on the condition that, stripping off the mask of lies, I would expose the complete truth. In this narration I will not at all implore the clemency of the true nobleman; he does not glory in borrowed or assumed virtues, but only in those of his own character. The nobility of his extraction is a spur which drives him without pause to distinguish himself from the ordinary man, and not otherwise. I will implore then only the clemency of the false noble, who does not wish to agree that laws and justice are made for everyone, who unjustly claims the absurd privilege of being above the law, who believes that every good thing that he does is heroic and every bad thing he does is insignificant, who regards judgment of his own actions by right and equity to be a sacrilegious offense against the rights of his nobility. If his ancestors have left him property and a noble name, must it not therefore follow that he be the personal inheritor of their virtue, since the way of the things of this world is that the least virtuous action by a man of noble rank is exaggerated, and that his basest actions are constantly disguised; finding this prejudice as unjust as it is ridiculous, and moreover, knowing the justice of your tribunal [possibly one line missing here from top of second page] Knowing that all favoritism is here prohibited without exception, that all men are equal here, I shall expose everything with simplicity and solemn truth.

After a thousand repeated threats, multifarious pillaging by the Royalists [the British] and the barbarous tribes who are their followers, after a thousand secret warnings on the part of the latter, and by divers individuals attached to their party, which have been absolutely scorned; seeing us in negligent security and knowing us moreover to be without the munitions of war and partly scattered in our fields, this troop of savages, brought together at last by the distribution of presents, excited by the bad reception that has always been given them [here], and guided by the inhuman Royalists, presented themselves on the 26th of May to the number of 600 men in the vicinity of St Louis. While one part of them, scattered in the fields, massacred with all possible fury and barbarity the farmer and his animals, his sole resource, the other part by a false attack held a tight hand over the unprepared village, abandoned to itself without a chief, without any officer, or other resource for its defense except its own courage. The combat, furious and full of carnage, lasted five hours. 18 men on the Spanish side remained on the field of battle, scalped, entrails opened, cranium crushed, limbs mutilated, bathed in blood, and scattered here and there. 6 had been wounded and 15 made prisoners, not including 46 belonging to this district taken prisoner and pillaged along the Misissipi and three killed on the Cahokia side. Only three men of the [attacking] party [one line missing, top of third page] and in the entrenchments made by the efforts of the inhabitants one only heard desperate and repeated cries among the combatants: some who were there for the defense of their wives and children and the preservation of their modest fortunes, crying out at the top of their lungs for powder and bullets; others imploring for the defense of the country and the honor of their nation a leader who by his experience, his courage could lead them to victory; cries vain and useless; for during all the danger to which they had been exposed and the continuous fire of the enemy that they had endured, their commandant, seized by fear and terror, had shut himself up in an almost useless tower which had been erected by the strength and money of the unfortunate people. During the night of the 26th to the 27th one of the sentinels, placed at the north of the village in sight of the Misissipi, having perceived a drifting tree that he mistook for a canoe full of Indians, ran in a hurry to the government house to make his report; suddenly the sixty men designated to guard the women ran in a mass without an order to the border of the Misissipi; having perceived the floating tree which they likewise took for a canoe full of combatants, they all fired together; perceiving no change in the object of their vision, a fright as dangerous as it was general spread rapidly among them, running hastily and in disorder [word or two missing] from their leaders to the place where the wailing women were; some in this precipitous flight trying to hide their cowardice and passing over the bodies of the unhappy women who had seen their children almost crushed; others, after having spiked the cannons [word illegible] [one line missing, top of fourth page] government fired with small arms on a detachment sent by Mr Benito Basquez, officer of the militia and worthy of the post, for their defense, who, throwing themselves on their stomachs, were saved from the mortal blows which because of imprudence, disorder, and fear rained upon them [the militia] from all sides. During these horrors and in the midst of the shades of night many among the regular troops who were guarding the tower called loudly for the King's powder, which had been sent to the Missoury and distributed to the Indians for the profit of their captain. Others encouraged each other and at the same time, vomiting a thousand curses against their commandant, called him in a loud voice to put himself at their head and then asked each other what had become of him, whether he had gone to heaven to implore the help of God, or to hell to catch it for his disgrace. Several days after the departure of the Royalists with their prisoners, Colonel Clark, at the request of Mr Leyba, in order to come to our rescue, armed at the mouth of the Belle Riviere several barges and transported them to Kaos [Cahokia], a village near St Louis on the opposite shore [which had been] conquered by the Americans. Shocked by the murders and inhuman acts committed against our side, he proposed to Mr Leyba to form a company of 400 men, of which he would furnish ⅔ to overtake the common enemy and to punish them. This proposal was accepted at first but when it was necessary to furnish provisions and munitions, suddenly changing the decision, it was concluded after deliberation that it would be better to guard the village and let the American do it. Colonel Clark, recalled by express orders, although irritated by the unexpected change of Mr Leyba, who had called for his help, showing no sign of emotion or suffering, formed a body of volunteers of 230 persons, to whom he added eighty péorias, matchis, and Kaskakias who, always attached to the French, came to offer themselves to combat the tribes which were also their enemies. Mʳ Montgommery, colonel under the orders of Colonel Clark, who placed him at the head of this detachment, arrived with his little army on 13 June. Mʳ Leyba, for the moment won over by this example, forced by fear and excited by the entreaties of a ruined people who were inspired by vengeance, gave orders to form a corps of volunteers of 100 men at whose head he placed Mʳ De Beletre, formerly an officer of His Most Christian Majesty, who joined the detachment of Colonel Montgommery departing on the 14th of the same month. Directing their route toward the Ilinois River, which flows into the Misissipi 6 leagues above the Missouri and by which the enemy had withdrawn to go to Michillimakinac, a post belonging [word illegible] Royalists, where abound trade goods from Canada and where the merchants come to the same place with various peltries from the Misissipi, the Ilinois River, as well as from Lakes Superior, Michigan, Huron, from La Baye [Green Bay] near Fox River, which leads to the Wisconsin, which empties into the Misissipi, and from divers other places.

Since the beginning of all these sad events, because of weakness of character or because of a change that can be considered to be caused by fear or by the consequences envisaged from a bad administration, Mʳ Leyba has fallen into an illness which has so enfeebled and altered his health that he is despaired of. Already Mʳ De Cartabona, lieutenant and commandant at Sᵗᵉ Genevieve, has succeeded him in the government, and although he has made his will, we have learned nothing of it in particular, except that he has given over after his death to our Capuchin chaplain of this post 1000 *livres* in peltry without communicating the reasons to this prudent spiritual director.

Virtutis, Veritatisque Amicus

[one line missing, top of this page]

23 June 1780

Some traders from the Missoury have arrived at this post announcing to us a party of 800 Sioux who are joining with a party of the tribes of the Missoury in order to come to invade our village and put it to fire and sword.—

Others have confirmed to us the massacre of 8 hunters captured on the banks of the Missoury by the Kans[a], one of the Indian nations which inhabit it.—

We learn from various persons come from the environs of Detroit, a Royalist post located between Lake Erie and Lake Huron, that an army composed of 1500 to 2000 Frenchmen and Indians is on the point of beginning a march to come to destroy several considerable American settlements on the Belle Riviere and then to capture the Ilinois.—

Several inhabitants and [perhaps] almost all propose to abandon the Ilinois entirely; already several by express order have been diverted from this project, which they wish to carry out and which certainly they will not fail to effectuate if the country is not governed better, if a fort is not constructed here, and if at least 200 troops are not sent here to protect them from the incursions of the savages.—

Monsieur De Leyba, Captain and commandant of this post, is dangerously ill. The hatred that the people of this country and even his own troops bear for him is inconceivable: sentiments of humanity, of conscience are not capable of keeping him safe from the most frightful curses and wishes. Never has an illness been so long, death so slow in coming, thunderbolts so tardy in overwhelming a sinner and wiping him out.—[one line missing, top of last page] The Sacs and the Foxes, the only nations which, in spite of the bad reception that they have always received, remain attached to the service of the Spaniards, have arrived at this post with three inhabitants and three slaves made prisoner in the affair of the 26th of May by the Royalists, from whom they had forcibly taken them. Renouncing their self-interest, scorning the numberless presents of the Royalists, exposed to the fury of other barbaric tribes, they stopped a party of six hundred men who were coming to join the party which attacked us. Although such obvious marks of their attachment deserve our gratitude, although these tribes [form] one of the most numerous on the Misissipy [and are therefore] more able to do us harm, [two words illegible] in this case to serve us as a rampart against the enemies which surround us, to turn aside the blows which were on the point of being launched against us, and to prevent our complete destruction; in spite of all remonstrances on this subject by the best and most sensible citizens to our Commandant, he not only indulged himself by refusing to make a present worthy of the service of these independent Indians, but he even refused for three days to give them a supply of bread necessary for their subsistence. Shocked by such a procedure, the inhabitants, on the brink of ruin, feeling the need in which they found themselves of maintaining friendly relations with these tribes and besides knowing perfectly that if these two powerful nations returned to the Royalists, they would become infallibly the victims of their discontent and brutality, in spite of their miseries, their disgrace, and the sad remnants of their ruined fortune, it was determined in order to prevent their complete destruction to get together jointly a present which in proving the gratitude of their generous souls would preserve

11

Le Peuple Des islinois to Governor General Gálvez, [St. Louis, 1780][2]

To Monsieur, Don Bernard Degalvez, Governor & Captain General of the Province of Louisiana. &c. &c. &c.

Monsieur.

Although no voices, no piercing cries ordinarily reach the dwellings of the great, although the flatterers who surround them do not present the truth in its annoying aspect and never trouble them with it, we, convinced of the kindness of your heart and the justice of your love for an oppressed people, the enemy of falsehood and the friend of truth, are going to expose to you the misery of this people and reveal the behavior of its perpetrator, a man without humanity, without conscience, whose avaricious interest subjugates the senses and enslaves Reason, we mean M[r] Leyba, infamous commandant of the post of S[t] Louis.

Near you, integrity dares to condemn only fearfully, the equitable heart knows only friendship, justice, and peace as being pure and perfect, the old man dies peacefully, the poor contemplates his misery without fear, the rich man is his brother, the judge his friend, on the ruins of the poor the most avaricious trembles to [word illegible], justice and charity reign everywhere. Here, one only sees officials profaning the public welfare, greedy ravishers drunk with the blood of an oppressed people.

Your tribunal, although just, is strict; that in S[t] Louis is a sordid bench which justifies the guilty by its unique decrees and which enriches itself unjustly with the spoils of the poor. Finally, the kindness of the most tender father, the justice of the most honest judge, the virtues of the most perfect hero shine in the eyes of New Orleans in such a way that the inhabitants of the Islinois feel more deeply the weight of an overwhelming misery. We first taxed M[r] Leyba as a man without conscience, we could have added he was without any respect for the orders of his King, for disorder and debauchery reign absolutely and without fear among his troops. The sergeant, his former corporal, keeps a *maison publique* [saloon? whorehouse?] outside the barracks, living there in concubinage. The coadjutor of his agent without interference does the same thing with his negro woman. Almost every night the rest of his troops are disorderly, led on by the filthy heat of the most unrestrained concupiscence and debauchery.

Consequently and in gratitude this mercenary troop abandons to him without reluctance all the *piastres gourdes* provided its men as pay, and receives only merchandise or deerskins in return.

[2] AGI, *Papeles de Cuba, leg.* 113; original in French. For help with the translation of this not very literate letter I am indebted to Miss Odile Delente, a *française de France,* as we would once upon a time have said in the Mississippi Valley, a student at Southern Illinois University, Edwardsville; responsibility for the final version, however, is mine. It has not previously been published.

In old days, through the malversation of the commandant at the Natchez, that innocent people was massacred. The excessive behavior of this one [Leyba], if it continues, will expose the people of St Louis indubitably to the same afflictions since he shows a similar heart, torn by the passions of an unparalleled avarice. For two years he has turned to his own account the presents for the Indians sent by the King. Hardly does he deign to give them bread to keep them from starving. It is only after their appealing two or three times that he condescends reluctantly to listen to them. He has taken possession of the exclusive trade with the tribes which no longer enjoy their freedom; thence the implacable hatred felt by these brutal men, thence the slaughter of an innocent man at the saline at Ste Genevieve, and four or five men killed or wounded at the mouth of the Belle Riviere, thence finally the maltreatment to which many of these unfortunates are exposed on the Missouri, on the Missicipy, and even on the Ark[ansa]s river.

Besides the hatred of the Indians which he brought upon himself, he is also exposed to dislike by the English Royalists, and the allied Americans, and does not at all care about that of his own people. We have said the dislike of the English Royalists by threatening them and by receiving them as haughtily as possible, we have said the dislike of the Americans by cursing them every day for the loss of his letters of exchange, the amount of which was sixty thousand *livres* or more not paid. By harassing the unfortunate subjects subjugated to him, by making them pay [over] the moderate sum that charity advanced to them for a commerce which he himself [word illegible] or distributes through his creatures. We have added that he did not care at all about the hatred of his people. Whenever anyone asks to speak to him, if it is to get a legitimate and promised [trade] permit, it is only relcutantly, because he will be sent away and be obliged, neglecting his business, to return three or four consecutive days; if it deals with money matters, it is only fearfully because if the business concerns him, he is sure with expenses and damages to lose more than it is worth; or [be] unlucky [enough] to be sent away roughly, witness Mr Verdon [word illegible] who, on going to ask for his due for a coffin made for his [Leyba's] wife, was expelled violently by his order. If on the other hand the matter concerns a fellow inhabitant, it is equally fearfully, certain always to be duped, for if he loses, though deserving it sometimes, it is against his expectation, and already a poor man, he becomes more miserable by the forced sale of his furniture or some effects which he cannot live without to satisfy his debt. On the contrary, if he wins his lawsuit he is compelled to pay costs of justice which exceed the amount for which he sued; Mr Tinon, after having sued for twenty-five *livres* owed to him, notwithstanding he won, was condemned to pay one hundred and eight *livres* in peltry for the costs. Mr Leconte loses his lawsuit against two *engagés*, his two hired men are condemned to pay costs [amounting to] one year's salary, one gained only

369

seven *sous* and a few *deniers*, the other the same amount proportionally, and a thousand other examples more frequent and [word illegible] millions [?] that we could cite and from which we spare your kindness.

A judgment rendered cannot be appealed. Mr Labadie asks Mr Marie his neighbor to move his fence which entrenches one foot upon his property. The latter was condemned to do so, and in spite had his slaves cut down two fruit-trees on this bit of land. Against all rules, far from punishing Mr Marie, Mr Labady, his opponent, was condemned to pay one hundred and sixty silver *livres* costs without being able to appeal or claim his right.

Mr Auguste Chouteau, made responsible by Mr Maxant for the estate of the late Mr Laclede (which constitutes the Government house property), had it fenced by an inhabitant, Sieur Cotté, for eighty *livres* in peltry. The fence made by the latter, having been examined by agreement and condemned by arbiters, was taken away. Madame Chouteau, who did not have anything to do with all that, and who did not have any responsibility involved in it, has been forced to pay Mr Cotté this amount of eighty *livres* in peltry.

It is when Mr Leyba seems to be helpful that he is most to be feared. Mad^me Laurent learns that her negro had been poisoned by another negro on the English side, controlled at that time by the American Colonel Clark, being thereby deprived of her sole support and in poverty, overwhelmed by sadness, and bathed in tears, she went to Monsieur Leyba [to ask] that he condescend to write in her favor to Monsieur Clark in order to have her negro paid for or have the poisoner put to death. Mr Leyba, apparently affected by the misfortune of this poor woman, writes. Several days go by. No reply. Northing more is heard of Monsieur Clark or the negro. Madame Laurent receives only a statement from Monsieur Leyba for twelve *piastres gourdes* for having written four lines in her favor. Some time later, Mr Reynald, a surgeon, receives a bill for thirty-six *livres* in peltry for the like service provided to him by Mr Leyba in regard to a moderate sum owed to him in Ste Genevieve.

If we accuse Monsieur Leyba of cruelties, a thousand different persons, above all Mme St François, who is living in extreme poverty, will be able to testify. Condemned by the court of justice to pay twenty-five *livres* for costs, Mr Leconte offered to pay for her himself. Mr Leyba, after having accepted Mr Leconte in payment, learning that this unfortunate woman had four hundred pounds of flour at someone's house, for which she had paid twenty *livres* a hundred, suddenly had them fetched, compelling the said Dame St François to give them up to him at the rate of twelve *livres* a hundred although they had cost her twenty; she refused, alleging that this was the only thing she had to feed her children; that it was, besides, exchanging eighty *livres* for twenty-five and giving at twelve *livres* what had cost her twenty. She has been forced to give them up to him to satisfy Mr Leyba's [word illegible] and absolute power.

We could add, even assert that Mr Leyba does not fear more the anger of his King than that of the people he rules. As an absolute ruler and a despotic tyrant, besides the theft of the presents for the Indians, which we have already mentioned, against all the ordinances and regulations of his office and disregarding the welfare of a whole people, he has set up as a complete businessman, alleging, the better to mask his behavior, the scarcity of merchandise and to prevent the Missoury tribes from sending their peltries across the Missicipy, which they had done in the past but to which he had never paid attention, and began by sending to Michilimackinac a private representative to buy one hundred thousand *livres* worth of trade goods on his own account so that he could exploit alone the posts of the Missoury. Although the thing did not happen and the man was forced to come back because of a dangerous illness, Mr Leyba, sure of his deal, ran into excesses, after having suddenly and completely interrupted any commerce with the Cahokia people, commerce which had been previously tolerated and carried out by his officials after threats of confiscation and even executions of those threats against the right of these people, in order to be completely warranted to carry on the trade of the Missoury by himself, he went with Mr Labussiere, a rascal, a lawless, faithless, inhuman man, counselor of his actions and executor of his wishes, from house to house to investigate the amount of merchandise which could be there, he has forced without consultation or the approval of the husbands and with full consciousness of his own actions timid wives to give him a certificate reporting only so much goods or none at all, he has done more, himself examining, even rummaging in a trunk which contained the soiled linen of one woman in spite of her opposition.

Mr Leyba, seeing on the English Royalist side all speculations destroyed and fruitless, on another side seeing against his expectations the quantity of unpaid American notes, for a heart as ambitious as his, did not find sufficient the wealth that he extorted each year through judgments
To wit—

Acts, imprisonments[?], or confiscations, that we estimate at . . . . £ [*livres*] 20000

The profit that he made from the sale of flour bought at Cahos [Cahokia]. Estimated 2000

The profit from the oils and greases taken forcibly from the hunters (products which we are entirely deprived of) at the price of the tax established by his predecessors and resold at exorbitant prices estimated 6000

The profit on the sale of merchandise first shipped by himself on his boat, then on that sent to him by M^r

Vigo his agent and sold to Monsieur hortis Estimated	70000
The profit made on the capital and lucrative sales of the presents for the Indians for two years amount according to the estimation made	30000
The capital of one hundred and fifty packets sent by Mr Vigo to New Orleans the profit of which is estimated	15000
That of sixty-five thousand *livres* in American notes .	65000
to which we can add for his stipend for two years . .	7200
which forms a capital of . . . . £ [*livres*]	215200
which not yet being enough he then conceived the project of farming out the posts of the Missouri, consequently he delivered that of the Big Osages to Mr Ceré for seventy packets estimated	14000
Those of the Panis, of the Mahas, of the Othos, and of the Republic[an Pawnees] to Mrs Labadie and Chouteau for sixty packets estimated	12000
That of the Missouri[s] to Mr Quenel, a stranger in our part [of the Illinois], for thirteen packets and who only gave ten	2000
That of the Little Osages to Mrs Lami and Bissonet, inhabitants, for twelve packets estimated	2400
That of the Kans[a] offered to Mr Pappin for fifteen packets, given back and remained vacant until others accepted it, estimated	3000
Total . . . . £ [*livres*]	248600

After the recital of so many debasing actions for a military man, a judge, a commandant, committed against all ordinances, rules of state, against humanity, equity, and even conscience (although Mme Leyba declared publicly that we were wrong to complain against her husband, [for] even if he should lose everything, [if] his enemies should burn his property, he would lay by, would [word illegible] his fortune, that he would still enjoy his spoils openly and would get off with receiving only a slight remonstrance from his superiors), before any other tribunal, any other judge, to compel him to render deserved justice, one would display duty, religion, justice, the kindness of a great heart, and the virtues which distinguish it; but with you whose name itself is praise, it is sufficient for an unhappy people to expose its misfortunes and make you acquainted with their perpetrators by unveiling the vices that hide [under] their mask of virtue, [and] to ask God for the preservation of your life and that you never be deprived of it [are] our most sincere wishes and [we] subscribe ourselves with all gratitude, honor, and the most profound respect Monsieur.

Your very humble Servants
Le Peuple Des islinois

Militia Roster, Infantry Company, St. Louis, November 9, 1779[3]

Rank	Name	Birthplace	Occupation
Captain	Dⁿ Juan Bapᵃ Martigny	[Canada]	trader
Lieutenant	Dⁿ Benito Basquez [Benito Vasquez]	[Spain]	merchant
Sublieutenant	Dⁿ Pedro Montardy	[Illinois]	baker
First Sergeant	Nicolas Roy	France	boatman
Second Sergeant	Joseph Hortis [Joseph Alvarez Hortiz]	Spain	blacksmith
Second Sergeant	Franᶜᵒ Barera [François Barrere]	France	trader
First Corporal	Joseph Polo	France	boatman
First Corporal	Juan Bapᵃ Lapierre	Canada	farmer
First Corporal	pedro quenel [Pierre Quesnal *dit* Lafleur]	Canada	farmer
First Corporal	Carlos haut	Canada	carpenter
Second Corporal	Jacobo Noëles[?]	Canada	tailor
Second Corporal	Kery Denoyer [Kiery Marcheteau *dit* Des Noyers]	Canada	farmer
Second Corporal	Joseph Berdon [Verdon]	Canada	farmer
Second Corporal	andres Dupuis	Canada	farmer
Soldiers	Luis Bissonet [Bissonette]	Canada	
	Gamache	Canada	
	Picard	Canada	

³ AGI, *Papeles de Cuba*, leg. 213. This roster, with that of the cavalry company which follows, probably includes the names of all arms-bearing males of St. Louis who might have been involved in the battle of May 26, 1780. Though Señor Don Hilario Arenas Gonzáles, who searched the files of the *Papeles de Cuba* for me, was able to find the cavalry roster, as well as company rolls for July, August, September, and October following, he did not discover any monthly rosters for January, February, March, or April, 1780. The brackets enclose some suggested identifications. Many of these names reappear in the next annual report, Dec. 27, 1780, which was published by Houck in *The Spanish Régime in Missouri*, I, 182–196, where they are identified. The Cruzat report (1780) included ages not found in Leyba's 1779 roster.

Rank	Name	Birthplace	Occupation
	Baguet	Canada	farmer
	Joseph Part [Par?]	Canada	boatman
	Miguel pitre	Canada	hunter
	carlos Tibeau	Canada	boatman
	Dechennes [Deschenes]	Canada	farmer
	Bapᵃ Lacroix	Canada	boatman
	Nicolas chauret [Choret]	Canada	hunter
	Sᵗ Juan [St. Jean]	Canada	boatman
	Guillermo Leconte	Canada	boatman
	Agustin Lacombe	Canada	cooper
	reynardo Culiar [Cusiar?]	Canada	boatman
	franᶜᵒ Delorier	Canada	blacksmith
	carlos moro [Moreau]	Canada	farmer
	Joseph Peron	Canada	boatman
	Joseph Hebert	Illinois	hunter
	Juan Bapᵃ Bonet	Canada	hunter
	Genereux [Jean Baptiste Genereux]	Canada	boatman
	Joseph Calvé	Canada	farmer
	Joseph Calvé *bijo*	Illinois	farmer
	franᶜᵒ comparé	Canada	boatman
	franᶜᵒ Martin	Canada	hunter
	antonio sans Soucis	Canada	mason
	antonio Ladouceur	Canada	boatman
	Esteban Sumandre [Sumande?]	Canada	boatman
	Joseph Sumandre [Sumande?]	Canada	boatman
	Luis Lasoudray	Illinois	trader
	Jacobo Melot	Illinois	hunter
	gagnon Picard	Canada	boatman
	Tardif [Jean Baptiste Tardif]	France	musician
	Joseph moreau	Canada	farmer

374

Rank	Name	Birthplace	Occupation
	noël Brunet	Canada	farmer
	Jacobo Marechal	Illinois	farmer
	petit Jan [Jean Baptiste Petit?]	France	boatman
	paul Laderoute	Illinois	boatman
	montard [Jean Motard?]	France	silversmith
	Lapierre coudorge [Pierre Cudorge]	France	merchant
	Duchenes perrault [Jean Baptiste Perrault *dit* Duchene]	Canada	trader
	Joseph Perrault	Canada	merchant
	Simoneau [Charles Simoneau]	Canada	farmer
	Louis Perrault	Canada	merchant
	Serpy [Jean Baptiste Sarpy]	France	merchant
	Serpy [Silvestre Delor Sarpy]	France	merchant
	marié [Alexis Marie]	France	farmer
	Routier	France	merchant
	Labadie [Silvestre Labbadie]	France	trader
	Joseph M. Papin [Joseph Marie Papin]	Canada	merchant
	agustin Chouteau	New Orleans	merchant
	pedro Chouteau	New Orleans	merchant
	Cambas [Jean Baptiste Cambas]	France	carpenter
	Joseph Labrosse	Canada	farmer
	fran.co Bissonet [Bissonette]	Canada	farmer
	Luis Robert	Canada	farmer
	Robert *hijo*	Illinois	farmer
	Joseph Vasseur	Illinois	boatman
	Bonav Lamarche	Canada	trader
	carlos Moran	Canada	trader
	Jan M. Pepin [Jean Marie Pepin]	Canada	merchant, mason
	Tayon *padre*	Canada	farmer
	marly	Canada	boatman
	marly *hijo*	Canada	boatman

375

Rank	Name	Birthplace	Occupation
	Juan Lachapela	Canada	boatman
	Bap^ta cantara	Canada	boatman
	pedro choret	Canada	hunter
	Alexo Coté	Canada	farmer
	campo [Paul Campeau]	Canada	boatman
	Luis Ladouceur	Canada	boatman
	carlos Valet [Charles Vallé?]	Canada	boatman
	Dubancour Barsalou	Canada	boatman
	Luis Lafleur	Canada	mason
	pedro Noëlais	Canada	boatman
	Juan Luis Deruen [Jean Louis Derouin]	Canada	boatman
	Esteban Deruen	Canada	boatman
	Luis Deruen	Canada	boatman
	Jp^h Boduen [Joseph Bodoin]	Canada	boatman
	Bap^ta Dechamps [Deschamps]	Canada	boatman
	Bap^ta Dechamps *hijo*	Illinois	boatman
	Luis Ride	Canada	farmer
	Lorenzo Ride *hijo*	Illinois	boatman
	Luis Uno [Louis Hunot]	Illinois	boatman
	fran^co Labespera	France	boatman
	cadete Sabinac	France	boatman
	Luis Lemay	New Orleans	shoemaker
	amable Dion [Amable Guion]	Canada	farmer
	guillermo Lecompte	Canada	merchant, boatman
	marin Duralde	France	merchant
	Joseph parant [Parent]	Canada	trader
	Berger	Canada	hunter
	Jp^h Lemoine	Canada	trader
	Esteban	France	boatman
	Jp^h Tibeau	Canada	boatman

376

Rank	Name	Birthplace	Occupation
	Juan Bapª Malbo	France	baker
	Gaspard Rubio	France	merchant
	Larche	Canada	trader
	Rigoche [Ignace Rigauche]	Canada	trader
	Luis Dubreuil [Louis DuBreuil]	France	merchant
	antonio renard	France	sawyer
	franᶜᵒ Janrion	Canada	hunter
	nicolas Daniel	Canada	hunter
	Jacobo Sanguinet	Canada	merchant
	Sanmartin [Pierre St. Martin]	Canada	boatman
	Zuachin[?] Valet [Joachim Vallé]	Canada	hunter
	Luis frederic	Illinois	hunter
	Jpʰ Robidou	Canada	hunter
	Jpʰ Girard	Canada	boatman
	Vincente	France	boatman
	Luis Beaulac	Canada	boatman
	Larduese [Larduera? Laderoute?]	Canada	farmer
	moreau Dechamps	Canada	hunter
	constantin	Canada	hunter
	Bernier	France	boatman
	Biron [Etienne Biron?]	Canada	boatman
	Bergeron	Canada	cooper
	Dorion	Canada	butcher
	chevalier [Louis Chevalier?]	Canada	boatman
	antonio Valet [Antoine Vallé?]	Canada	boatman
	Juan Gibeault	Canada	boatman
	pedro amosty	France	boatman
	Luis Dodier	Illinois	boatman
	franᶜᵒ Grenier	Canada	boatman
	franᶜᵒ Bison	Canada	boatman

Rank	Name	Birthplace	Occupation
	Luis Lardues [Larduera? Laderoute?]	Canada	boatman
	Jpʰ Lardues [Larduera? Laderoute?]	Canada	boatman
	Jacobo Lardues [Larduera? Laderoute?]	Canada	boatman
	antonio Lardues [Larduera? Laderoute?]	Canada	boatman
	pedro Lardues [Larduera? Laderoute?]	Canada	boatman
	franco Demars	Canada	constable
	todos Santos laroche [Toussaint Laroche]	Illinois	boatman
	Jpʰ Vilard	Canada	boatman
	agustin hebert	Illinois	hunter
	Juan lamontagne	Canada	boatman
	franco hebert	Illinois	hunter
	Laurens	Canada	currier
	Luis Lachapelle	Canada	boatman
	pedro Gagnion	Canada	mason
	Jʰ Perin	France	boatman
	antonio Ribera [Antoine Rivière *dit* Baccané]	Canada	boatman
	franco marechal	Illinois	boatman
	Bapta amiot	Canada	hunter
	gabriel Dodier	Illinois	farmer
	Bapta henet	Illinois	boatman
	agustin Dodier	Illinois	boatman
	nicolas lange	Canada	boatman
	antonio Bellepeche [Antoine Oliver *dit* Bellepeche]	France	boatman
	pedro porcel [Pourcelly?]	France	boatman
	andres Ducharmes [André Fidecharmes]	New France	boatman
	antonio rotisseur	Canada	boatman
	Jpʰ Guillot	Canada	boatman
	Juan Bapta Cardinal	Canada	farmer
	Luis Berda	Canada	boatman
	miguel L'ami	Canada	trader

Militia Roster, Cavalry Company, St. Louis, December 25, 1779[4]

Rank	Name	Birthplace	Occupation
Captain	Dⁿ Euxenio Puré [Eugène Pourée *dit* Beausoleil]		
Lieutenant	Dⁿ Luis Chanchelier [Louis Chancelier]	[Illinois]	
Sublieutenant	Dⁿ Carlos Tayon [Charles Michel *dit* Tayon (Taillon)]	[Illinois]	
Sergeant	Joseph Labuciera [Joseph Labuxière]	Illinois	farmer
Corporal	Bapª Bivaren [Jean Baptiste Vifvarenne]	Illinois	mason
Corporal	Simon Cusot	New Orleans	farmer
Soldiers	Joseph Duchoquet [Duchouquette]	Illinois	farmer
	Juan Chanrrion	Illinois	farmer
	Carlos Forten [Fortin?]	Canada	boatman
	Joseph Chartran	Canada	hunter
	Bapª Buchard [Bouchard?]	Canada	hunter
	Carlos Bizet [Bissette]	Canada	farmer
	Luis Dubroll [Louis Dubreuil]	Canada	farmer
	Bapª Bacané [Jean Baptiste Rivière *dit* Baccané]	Illinois	farmer
	Luis Dufo	Canada	carpenter
	Antonio Bequet	Illinois	farmer
	Jacinto [Ride?]	Canada	trader
	Bapª Dechamps	Canada	farmer
	Joseph Tayon [Joseph Michel *dit* Tayon, Taillon]	Illinois	farmer
	Antonio Marichand [Antoine Marechal?]	Illinois	boatman
	Phe Probanché	Canada	farmer
	Joseph Liret	Canada	boatman

[4] AGI, *Papeles de Cuba*, leg. 213. See n. 3. Ages were included in this roster but it is not possible to read them with assurance on the microfilm copy supplied me. There is no evidence that this company functioned as cavalry.

Rank	Name	Birthplace	Occupation
	Antonio Chabalier	Canada	farmer
	Luison Barda [Louis Barada?]	Illinois	shoemaker
	Ygnacio Larrohe [Ignace Laroche?]	Illinois	trader
	Bap^ta Ortes [Jean Baptiste Ortes]	France	carpenter
	Luis Lacroix	Illinois	blacksmith
	Antonio Cadien	Acadia	farmer
	Joseph Chanchelier [Joseph Chancelier]	Illinois	farmer
	Antonio Marchand	Canada	hunter
	Fran^co Barrosié	Canada	farmer
	Migel Marié	Illinois	farmer
	Andrez Bizonet [Bissonette?]	Canada	trader
	Bap^ta Bizonet [Bissonette?]	Canada	trader
	Carlos Roy	Illinois	hunter
	Joseph Bequet	Illinois	boatman
	Antonio S^n Fransua [Antoine St. François?]	Illinois	boatman
	Pedro Bisonet [Bissonette?]	Canada	farmer
	Ph^e Bacané [Rivière *dit* Baccané]	Illinois	boatman
	Joseph Marichale [Marechal]	Illinois	boatman
	Luis Parant [Parent?]	Canada	boatman
	Antonio Reno [Renaud?]	Canada	boatman
	Joseph Lachanse	Canada	trader
	Gregorio Quersereau [Gregoire Kiercereau]	Illinois	boatman
	Nicolas Bocheneau [Beaugenou]	Illinois	farmer
	Basilo Bachor [Basile Basor]	Canada	hunter
	Joseph Langlua [Langlois]	Canada	hunter
	Nicolas Guillon [Guion]	Canada	blacksmith
	Carlos Bacané [Rivière *dit* Baccané	Illinois	farmer
	Pedro Duchuquet [Duchouquet]	Illinois	farmer
	Bap^a Henet	Illinois	hunter

v

Roster, Militia Company, St. Louis, July 5, 1780[5]

Captain	[Dⁿ Juan Bapᵃ Martiny]	P[resent]
Lieutenant	Dⁿ Benito Basquez	P
Sublieutenant	Dⁿ Pedro Montardy	P
First Sergeant	Nicolas Roye	CP	Detached at Paisa
Second Sergeant	Joseph Hortiz	P
Second Sergeant	Francᵒ Barrera	P
Drummer	Bapᵗᵃ Bienbenido	P
First Corporal	Joseph Polo	P
First Corporal	Pedro Quenel	P
First Corporal	Juan Bapᵃ Lapierre	P
First Corporal	Carlos Hot	P
Second Corporal	Jacobo Labé	P
Second Corporal	Andres Dupuy	P
Second Corporal	Joseph Berdon	P
Second Corporal	Juan Bapᵃ Vibaren	P
Soldiers	Alexos Marié	CP	Detached at Paisa
	Luis Rober[t]	CP
	Pedro Gañon	P
	Pedro Helias [Elias]	P
	Luis Breda	P
	Luis Honoré	CP	Detached at Paisa
	Pedro Duchene	CP	Detached at Paisa
	Pedro Plancha	P
	Nicolas Daniel	P
	Enrique Duchoquet	P
	Francᵒ Duchoquet	P
	Pedro Peltié	P
	Joseph Labuciera	P
	Esteban Derruen	P
	Alexos Nuesé [Luese? Loisé?]	P
	Jacobo Lasabloñera	P
	Carlos Chanrrion	P
	Pedro Roy	P
	Juan Gilber[t]	P
	Juan Bapᵗᵃ Brucieras	P
	Joseph Tecié	P

[5] AGI, *Papeles de Cuba, leg.* 2. The roster for July 5, 1780, signed by Martigny, Vasquez, and Cartabona, lists 3 officers and 260 noncommissioned officers and men formed into a single infantry company, the cavalry company having been found impractical. The roll provides only the information printed here. By August the militia had been re-formed into two companies with a total of 272 officers and men. In September the total strength was 318 and in October 322 (these rosters are also in *leg.* 2). These lists should not be read as a complete census of males of arm-bearing age, but rather as a list of such men present and available for duty.

Gregorio Quiersero	P
Jph Chartran	P
Jph Rubidu	P
Jph Girar	P
Pablo Cornollé	P
Pedro Bofrer[e]	P
Migel Blanco	P
Alexos Coté	P
Pablo Campo	P
Carlos Roy	P
Fran^co Berñé	P
Joseph Pety	P
Thomas Gorgé	P
Juan Gulmens[?]	P
Pedro McKens[?]	P
Jacobo Racie[?]	P
Juan Estampe	P
Pedro Sanmartin	P
Luis Chile	P
Pedro Rapen	P
Lorenzo Sorel	P
Pedro Larduera	P
Luis Larduera	P
Bap^ta Dufo	P
Todos Santos Larroche	P
Joseph Larduera	P
Antonio Larduera	P
Jacobo Fily[?]	P
Quiery Denoyé	P
Pedro Foché	P
Bap^ta Laforma[?]	P
Luis Lemer[?]	P
Belu Yngles[?]	P
Gabriel Dodié	P
Bap^ta Bequete	P
Gabriel Bequete	P
Lorenzo Ride	P
Luis Boduen	P
Jph Boduen	P
Amable Guion [*fils*]	P
Jph Leconte	P
Luis Honoré *Padre*	P
Bap^ta Richard	P
Luis Ride	P
Nicolas Leconte	P
Guillermo Leconte	P
Joseph Martiny	P
Jph Richard	P
Pedro Bergé	P

Joseph Guillot	P	
Joseph Dupuy	P	
Pedro Nolet	P	
Fran^co Villar	P	
Carlos Sanguinete	P	
Joachin Roy	P	
Antonio Belpeché	P	
Andres Fidecharme	P	
Agustin Dodié	P	
Pedro Bequet	P	
Antonio Salé	P	
Pedro Guitar	P	
Fran^co Alary	P	
Juan Pedro Porsely	P	
Fran^co Caiole [Cailhol]	P	
Fran^co Beron	P	
Antonio Ribera—*Padre*	P	
Ph^e Ribiera	P	
Bap^ta Ribiera	P	
Antonio Ribiera *hijo*	P	
Agustin Heber[t]	P	
Fran^co Marichar	P	
Joseph Lorens	P	
Joseph Dubé	P	
Pedro Durbua	P	
Joseph Bodry	P	
Luis Bolac	P	
Antonio Bensan	P	
Agustin Lacomble	P	
Fran^co Greñe	P	
Luis Crepo	P	
Antonio Lucere	P	
Bap^ta Moro	P	
Jacobo Fabo	P	
Nicolas Bogeneau	P	
Fran^co Doblen[?]	P	
Luis Frederico	P	
Joseph Tibo	P	
Simon Cusot	P	
Pedro Cusot	P	
Luis Malpet[?]	P	
Jph Ballancur	P	
Juan Cot [Col?]	P	
Simon Borné	P	
Fran^co Honoré	CP	Detached at Paisa
Fran^co Corno	P	
Pedro Chorret	P	
Bap^ta Cantara	P	
Juan Lachapela	P	

383

Pedro Bernié	P	
Saloman Petty	P	
Joseph Tayon	P	
Franᶜᵒ Lafranchis[?]	P	
Antonio Moran	CP	Detached at Paisa
Jph Viron[?]	P	
Luis feneto	P	
Franᶜᵒ Delero	P	
Jph Labro	P	
Luis Dubroy	P	
Pedro Simono	P	
Pablo Laderruta	P	
Franᶜᵒ Vizonet [Bisonet]	P	
Luis Vion	P	
Luis Chancro[?]	P	
Luis faché	P	
Jph Marchan	P	
Joseph Vasor [Basor]	P	
Basilio Basor	CP	Detached at Paisa
Luis Lapuente	CP	Detached at Paisa
Pedro Choteau	P	
Bapᵗᵃ Henet	P	
Juan Bapᵗᵃ Cambas	P	
Joseph Cavé [Calvé?]	P	
Jph Papen	P	
Silbestre Labadia	P	
Pedro Cudroche	P	
Pedro Berne	P	
Delord Sarpy	P	
Jph Langlois	P	
Bapᵗᵃ Lafranco	P	
Luis Blanchet	P	
Andres Bizonet	P	
Andres Arduen	P	
Andres Bequet	P	
Pedro Bisonet	P	
Luis Laflor	CP	Detached at Paisa
Bapᵗᵃ Visonet	P	
Carlos Tibo	P	
Nicolas Guion	P	
Pedro Liret	P	
Jph Par	P	
Franᶜᵒ Borosié	P	
Luis Harno	P	
Jph Lepir[?]	P	
Ygnacio Rigoche	P	
Bapᵗᵃ Dechan—*Padre*	P	
Bapᵗᵃ Dechan *hijo*	P	
Migel Pitre	P	

Antonio Rotison	P	
Jph Dechene	P	
Antonio San Susy	P	
Nicolas Chorret	P	
Todos Santos Paran[t]	P	
Pedro Debo	P	
Pedro Menar	P	
Luis Dubroy—*havitante*[?]	P	
Bap^ta Sabua[?]	P	
Bap^ta Depré	P	
Juan Bap^ta Hortez	P	
Loran Basedon	P	
Bap^ta Generoso	P	
Bap^ta Serré	P	
Antonio Hudet[?]	P	
Bap^ta Buché	CP	Detached at Paisa
Jph Hener[?]	P	
Luis Proto[?]	P	
felisberto Loran	P	
Pedro Hibon	P	
Luis Potié	P	
Carlos Moro	P	
Rene Depré	P	
Jph Lapierre	P	
Jph Fallar	P	
Fran^co Vigo	P	
Antonio Buden[?]	P	
Joseph Sanselier	P	
Jph Laporta	P	
Bap^ta Gotié	P	
Andres Primo	P	
Bap^ta Capitan	P	
Jph Belan	P	
Pedro Debien	P	
Luis Chatelero	P	
Pedro Langlois	P	
Antonio Quienel	P	
Juan Rotison	P	
Fran^co Delorié	P	
Jph Sumande	P	
Esteban Sumande	P	
Antonio Calbé—*Padre*	P	
Antonio Calbé *hijo*	P	
Jacobo Rober[t] Failar[?]	P	
Antonio Ladusor	P	
Luis Lasudray	P	
Antonio S^n Fransua	CP	Detached at Paisa
Jacobo Methode	P	
Juan Bap^ta Tardif	P	

Pedro Gañon mason	P	
Lorenso Michon	P	
Alexo Michon	P	
Noel Brunet	P	
Jph Marichar[?]	P	
Antonio Marichar	P	
Jacobo Marichard	P	
Nicolas Marichard	P	
Jph Ribet[?]	P	
Luis Amable Demarre	P	
Bap^ta Probanché	P	
Luis Huno	P	
Antonio Marcil	CP	Detached at Paisa
Joachin Balet	P	
Bap^ta Balet	P	
Fran^co Gaño	P	
Juan Maria Chouvin	CP	Detached at Paisa
Luis Berna *dho* [*dit*] Dufrene	CP	Detached at Paisa
Pedro Lapuente	CP	Detached at Paisa
Pedro Laderruta	CP	*Idem*
Antonio Brinete[?]	P	
Antonio Brunete *hijo*	P	
Bap^ta Castonque[?]	P	
Luis Laplanta	P	
Jph Depo	P	
Jph Laflanbuza[?]	P	
Jph Coté	P	
Juan Amiot	P	
Luis Chavaler	P	
Jacinto Sansile [St. Cyr]	P	
Jacobo Rober[t]	P	

V I

Casualty List, Battle of May 26, 1780[6]

Whites

Dead

Juan Colman
Thomas
Otro que se haió

[6] For this information I am indebted to Nasatir, "St. Louis during the British Attack of 1780," 249–251. I have given the names as he printed them from *leg.* 113. The names in square brackets are my interpretation of the Spanish versions, which no doubt were as badly inscribed as those in the militia rosters. I have not seen the original report by Leyba made two days after the battle and enclosed to Gálvez with his letter of June 8, 1780.

Ygnacio Larrosa [Ignace Laroche?—cavalry company]
Sn Juan [St. Jean—infantry company]
Sn Jorje
Vinere[?]
Calbe *hijo* [Joseph Calvé, *fils*—infantry company]
Pedro de Hetre [Pierre Deshetres]
Daban Caz [Dubancour Barsalou?—infantry company]
Francisco Huber [François Hebert *dit* Belhomme—infantry company]
Gladié [Pierre Gladu—see Billon, *Annals*, 202]
Amable Guion [infantry company]
Del——[?]

Total   14

Wounded

Th^e de Cab^{ra} Luis Sn Selier [Lieutenant Louis Chancelier—cavalry company]
Todos Santos Paran [Toussaint Parent]
Ma. Verguere
her two daughters
Peltié

Total   6

Prisoners

Juan Maria Cardinal [Jean Marie Cardinal—Billon, *Annals*, 199–200, listed
 him among the dead]
Pedro Carbila
Bap^a Bacané [Jean Baptiste Rivière *dit* Bacané—cavalry company]
Sn Juan [only one St. Jean in militia rosters—see list of dead]
Vigra
Moro [Charles Moro—infantry company]
Julian Roy [Julien Roy—killed according to Primm]
Goché Vequere [Bequet?]
Jph Sn Selier [Joseph Chancelier]
Lefebre
Santive[?]
Vean Cur who escaped

Total   12

Slaves
Dead

A. la Pierre	1
Mr. Serré [Gabriel Cerré]	2
Ma Choteau	1
Bonete	1
Dn Luis Sn Selier	1
Mr. Beletre [Pierre Picoté de Belestre]	1

Total   7

Wounded

Mr. Tayon [Joseph Michel *dit* Tayon]	1

387

Prisoners

Ma. Choteau	5
Mr. Serré	1
Mr. Paipin [Papin]	1
Ma. Heber[t]	2
Ma. Dodie[r]	1
Mr. Tayon	1
Mr. Dechen[nes]	2

Total   13

White Prisoners
taken on the Mississippi

Joseph Paran [Parent—infantry company]
Luis Dodie [Dodier—infantry company]
Sumanda [Etienne Sumande? Joseph?—both in infantry company]
Ignacio Heber [Ignace Hebert]
Sn Clu [St. Cloud?]
Pedro Leconte
Sancoman
Lecler
Yoy
Sn Esteban
Lachase [possibly Joseph Lachanse—cavalry company]
Larroche [Toussaint Laroche?—infantry company]
his three *engagés*
Probancias [Ph^e Probanché—cavalry company?]
his four *engagés*
Honoré *Padre* [Louis Tesson Honoré, *père*]
Honoré *hijo* [Louis Tesson Honoré, *fils*]
Sn Juan [once more!]
Ygnacio
Peltié
Goué [Gotié]
Yngles
Cadien [Antonio Cadien—cavalry company]
Tellier
three *engagés* of Mr. Buche
Juan Cardinal [possibly Jean Baptiste Cardinal—infantry company]
his ten *engagés*
Moron [Charles Moran—infantry company?]
Moro de Chan [Moreau Dechamps—infantry company?]
Constanten [Constantin—infantry company]

Total   46

[Billon, *Annals*, 197–198, listed Charles Bissette among the known dead. He belonged to the cavalry company.]

VII

Cruzat's Plan for the Defenses of St. Louis [Lieutenant Governor Francis Cruzat to Governor General Bernardo de Gálvez, St. Louis, December 18, 1780][7]

My Dear Sir: The condition in which I found the Ylineuses upon my arrival at this town of St. Louis, so different from what it had been in other times, caused me to reflect seriously upon devising an expedient which, in addition to being easy and economical for the royal treasury, might place in greater security the lives and goods of these unfortunate inhabitants, so extremely afflicted in the last catastrophe which they have suffered. Consequently I went there to examine the situation of the town for myself, accompanied by the most experienced persons of the country. Taking a bird's eye view of its position, I resolved, because of the following motives, to fortify it as I am going to outline to Your Lordship.

The manner in which the Indians of the north make war is, in comparison to all other barbarous nations, the most fierce and cruel imaginable. Everybody recognizes that humanity, respect for the rights of people, honor, or any of the other virtues which characterize men, have had no lodgment in the hearts of the peoples of whom I treat. The war they wage is a faithful picture of their barbarity and wild inclinations. No other laws govern them except the taking of man, woman, or child (which to them is the same) by surprise, for they hide behind a tree, or amidst the brush in order to take their lives, killing them cruelly by blows of a tomahawk or a knife. At other times crawling along the ground they creep up to a poor victim who is off his guard and then shoot him. It is a cause of wonder to see with what speed and destructive enthusiasm they heap their fury upon the poor victim when they see him fall to earth. The air rings with their shouts and cries of joy and the very resounding echo repeats the inhumanity of their deed and pierces the heart of the unfortunate who falls into their hands. As soon as they have laid hands on him they lift off the top of the scalp and, cutting the body into a thousand pieces, like ravenous tigers, they quench the violent fire which spurs them on by drinking the blood of the one they have just sacrificed.

Nothing I have said is comparable to the sufferings of a prisoner when his fateful destiny allows him to fall into the power of so fearful and tenacious enemies; for they burn the victim, who is tied to a post, or in a square, while they administer the most terrible torment and commit the blackest and most wicked atrocity that one could imagine. They make the prisoner eat pieces of his own body and cause him for a period of two or three days the most awful sufferings that could be conceived. It might be

[7] Kinnaird, ed., *Spain in the Mississippi Valley*, I, 408–410.

observed in passing that the women of the Indians are the most excited against the unfortunate prisoners, for they find amusement in seeing them tormented and they themselves invent the most horrible and inhuman martyrdom.

The Indians are never sufficiently courageous to attack a fort, trench, settlement, or party, unless their number be double that of their enemy. Their first attack, accompanied by weird cries, is so violent that, unless they are put to rout with an active and determined resistance, it becomes a difficult matter to combat the fury which sets them in motion. When this is abated, they are no longer men, but are like women, faint, and breathless. Having taken all these reflections into consideration, let us examine the other motives which have urged me to act.

1. Were a fort to be erected, it would not be sufficiently large to contain all the families, munitions of war, and provisions for their sustenance and defense.

2. Water would always be lacking, an indispensable necessity, for it would not be possible to sink wells, as the base on which this town is situated is rocky.

3. Were I to inclose myself with my meager number of troops in the fort, it would mean depriving the inhabitants of the protection which our Catholic sovereign (may God protect him) so kindly granted to his beloved subjects.

4. Wherever the fort may be made, it could never defend both extremities of the town because of its great extent. This is also the case with the royal tower of San Carlos which, although situated in the center of the line at the rear of the referred-to town, is only able with its great height to protect the country in that part, but not at the extremes.

5. Were a fort to be erected at La Granja [La Grange de Terre—Barn Bluff—the Big Mound—present-day northeast corner of Mound Street and Broadway], the promontory of land made by nature half a cannon's shot from the town, there would result the same disadvantage as from this one. Therefore, an entrance into it would be a simple matter, should enemies attempt it. Once penetrating therein they would reduce everything with fire and blood, as they are wont to do when they are conquerors, without respecting, as I have already said, the rights of humanity, or any other right which civilized nations hold sacred. These things we have already experienced in the fatal and awful disaster of the twenty-sixth of last May, as Your Lordship already knows.

6. Were trenches to be made (for I have found that those which the inhabitants had themselves made temporarily were rendered useless every day because of the rains and lack of cohesiveness of the soil in this country) it is evident that they would be insufficient to resist an assualt, and it would be impossible to man them with the few people I have.

7. Were I to make four towers as my predecessor Don Fernando de Leyba had projected, there would result greater inconveniences, and the enemies might with ease introduce themselves on a dark night into the town and thus take possession of it.

All these measures, and others that I omit, have been considered. The forces available to me are meager. I receive continued advices from every place of the preparations which, from the beginning of last summer, are being made by the English. They are calling together their friendly nations of Indians by means of lavish and continued presents, and all the other means which they make use of to carry into effect the premeditated enterprise of attacking us next spring with far greater vigor than they did this year. I therefore feel obliged (considering the charge that might be placed against me were I not to apply the greatest zeal and most efficacious means at my command, and all the means conducive to the preservation of the country confided to my care) to fortify the town all around with a stockade of ten feet in height, and six inches thick. The only part not to have it will be that fronting the river, for here it is fortfied by nature. This royal work I have already begun, and expect to have completed before the coming of our enemies.

I am sending this plan to Your Lordship by Don Agustin Choteau, the person commissioned by me to take charge of the referred-to fortification. Your Lordship will note that when the fort is completed and supplied with a sufficient quantity of munitions of war, which I now lack, for the firing of the cannon I have, and with guns, even though the number of my troops and militia be small, should I not succeed in preserving the country, I shall at least have the satisfaction of having defended it with the last drop of my blood. I have confidence in the courage and fidelity of all those who accompany me. They will follow my example, and sacrifice their lives, even to the point of losing them in the defense, for the honor and glory of the arms of our Catholic Sovereign, whom I trust the God of hosts will ever protect, in recognition of the justice of our cause. I feel confident and am persuaded that the provisions which I have made and now communicate to you will be acceptable to Your Lordship as the only remedy to keep us, if possible, from the perverse designs of our enemies, and cause their hopes to flee.

May God preserve Your Lordship many years.

St. Louis of Ylineuses, December 18, 1780.

Your most devoted servant kisses the hand of Your Lordship.

Fran^co Cruzat

Señor Don Bernardo de Gálvez

1. Fernando de Leyba to "Mon cher amy" [George Rogers Clark], Ste. Gene-vieve, May 30, 1779. E. G. Voorhis Memorial Collection, Missouri Historical Society.

Si les affaires de ce port m'avoient
permis de me détacher pour quelque
jour, j'aurois été vous faire une
embrassade, mais ce sera pour
mercredy prochain sur les six heures
du soir où j'aurai le plesir de vous
assurer de vive voix que je suis
avec toute l'estime et la considération
la plus parfaite

Mon cher amy,

[illegible lines]

S.te geneviève le 30 May 1779   Votre tres humble et
                                      très obeissant serviteur

M.r de Sartob comme vous
assure de ses civilités et
vous fait bien des
compliments et à tous
vos messieurs   Jean de Leypas

2. Colonel John Montgomery to Colonel George Rogers Clark, Fort Clark, Feb., 1780, reporting that Auguste Chouteau, on his way upriver ten days earlier, had brought news of the Spanish declaration of war. E. G. Voorhis Memorial Collection, Missouri Historical Society.

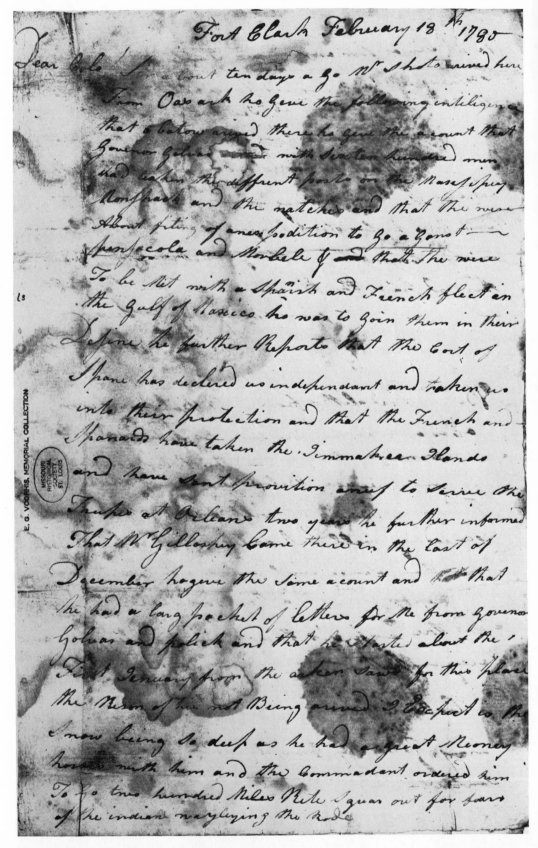

But Sir as soon as he arrives I will send you another
Express where I Expect to bee able to let you know
the hole particulars This Gentleman his brou[gh]t the a-
count is aman under a good Carecter and they are beleved
Beleves in What he has told them as well as if the
had seen it There is nothing in more I can [writ?] to you
But it is My Constant prayers to here of your Careing
on som Exposdition as things is so [bad?] Desperate here
And I have the Honour to scribee My Self
                    your Very Humble Sarvt

                              In Montgomery

NB Sir Recd a letter from Capt Robeson from
oers erk on his way down he desired Me to
inform you that he sued the Bluf acording to
To your derection Below the Mat of ohio for
Which he thinks it will answer the purpose
Exceeding well but as the River is Clear your
own Good Sence will inform you how Much it
necesary for to build a Gareson there pray Sir
Send the Express Back amediateley as I am
Very impatient   I M

To Colo Clark

pray Give My Compliments to all the
Gentle men

3. Colonel John Montgomery to Colonel George Rogers Clark, Fort Bowman, Cahokia, May 15, 1780, about the cooperation of Leyba on the proposed counter-expedition against the British. E. G. Voorhis Memorial Collection, Missouri Historical Society.

4. Captain John Rogers to Colonel George Rogers Clark, Cahokia, May 15, 1780, reporting his visit to the "Spanish side" with Colonel Montgomery and other officers. E. G. Voorhis Memorial Collection, Missouri Historical Society.

Dr Colonel — Kahows May 15th 1780

Agreeable to your Instructions to me I have set Down to give you an account of my proseeding Since my arrival to this Place which has not been any thing Extrodenary I have taken Possession of the Fort which I found out of repair and very Dirty but have had it Cleard and shall Put it in Some poster of Defence

I was to day over on the Spanish side with Col. Montgomery and some of his Offrs who are now at this Place the Col. Proposed an Expedition to the Comandant who Seemed to be fond of it and says he will send one Hundred men well Equiped under the Comand of the Col. Montgomery but he has yet to send to Kaskaskias for my two Boats to Carry his Troops and no provision yet laid in for an Expedition that I Dout if the Enemy are on the way as said they will be here before an Expedition Can take place.

he Col. intends to Order me on the Expedition but in Consiquence of your Instructions to Me wherein you Direct me to remain here till Orders to the Contrary from your self but at the same time Left me to Consult the sivell Cort what Methood best to fall on for their Safety I shall not Go unless with the voice of the aforesaid Cort but I think it will be their Desire for me to go my Men are Belited out and appears well Satisfied at Maintaining them My Compliments to the Gentlemin

I am Sir your Obdt Servt
John Rogers.

5. First and last pages of an undated letter [June, 1780?] from "Le Peuple des islinois" to Bernardo de Gálvez, governor of Louisiana. Archivo General de Indias, *Papeles de Cuba, leg.* 113.

Apres L'exposé de tant d'action utilisantes dans un militaire
on juge un Commendant, Et Commis des Contre toutes ordonnances,
Regles d'état, Contre L'humanité, L'équité, La Religion même (quoy que
M.me Leyba publiquement a declaré qu'on avoit tort de former des Plaintes
Contre Son Mari, quand bien même il perdroit entièrement Ses ennemis,
vieleroit Ses biens fonds, Reverseroit, tueilleroit Sa fortune, qu'il jouiroit toujours
publiquement de Ses Rapines et Bien seroit quitte que pour Recevoir
une Legere Remontrance de Son Superieur) a tout autre Tribunal a
tout autres juges, pour le forcer a Rendre justice Meritée on exposeroit
Le devoir, La Religion, La justice, La Bonté d'un grand Cœur et les Vertus
qui le Caracterisent, Mais auprès de vous Dont le Nom Seul fait
L'éloge, il Suffit a un peuple Malheureux de exposer Ses peines et de
Vous en faire Connoitre les auteurs en devoilant les vices que Cache
Leurs Masque de Vertus, de former au Ciel pour la Conservation de
Vos jours Et n'en estre jamais Privé les Vœux les Plus Sinceres Et —
de Le dire avec toute La Reconnoissance L'honneur! Et Le

Respect Le Plus Profond

Monsieur.

Vos tres humbles Serviteurs

Le Peuple Des istinois

A Monsieur Dom françois De Cartabona Lieutenant d'infanterie du Regiment De la Louisianne Lieutenant Gouverneur par interim de la partie occidentale Des Ilinois. &c. &c. &c.

Monsieur

Persuadés de Votre amour pour vos peuples, a deux Doigts de notre perte et à la veille De notre entiere destruction, nous Vous Supplions de vouloir peindre a Notre Gouverneur L'horreur de la situation Des Ilinois et de lui envoyer un Deputé, chargé d'aller auprès De sa Bonté Sollicter les Secours qui Sont necessaires a notre conservation. La Nouvelle Orleans conduite et dirigée par ce pere le plus tendre, forcée par ses Vertus n'est plus agitée que par le desir de combatre pour ses Droits, de deffendre son Sol, de fertiliser de ses Sueurs, et L'arroser de son Sang pour Lui conserver: Pretendant aux avantages de nos freres et voulant que ses Loix fassent notre Gloire et son Nom notre honneur, Desirant S'illustrer chez les Nations mêmes qui ne le connoissent pas, nous esperons que sa Tendresse, S'étendant jusques Sur nous, voudra bien nous couvrir de ses armes et de ses Voiles et nous envoyer de prompts Secours. Le pays des Ilinois auquel tente aujourd'huy par des efforts incroyables Les Anglois Royalistes, qui pourroit Devenir un des endroits de la colonie les plus florissants, presqu'étouffé au Berceau, Seroit au moins desarmé; Dépourvu generalement de tout, les magazins Du Roy y Sont sans poudre, sans nulles Munitions de guerre et entierement Vuides de marchandises envoyées par le Roy pour les nations affidées a L'Espagne. les habitants y Sont entierement epuisés; Sans comprendre mille petites depenses ruineuses qu'ils ont été obligés de faire, a Deffaut de leur commendant indigeant, pour s'empecher de devenir La triste victime du mecontentement et de la Brutalité Des Sauvages Sacs et Renards, Seule nation qui nous reste qui peut nous servir de rempart contre les enemis prets à frapper qui nous environnent, malgré leurs infortunes, leurs Disgraces et Les tristes restes d'une fortune delabrée, ils ont été contraints de S'unir et de former de concert un present qui fut en état pour quelques tems de leurs conserver L'amitié de ces Sauvages, de faire à leurs frais et dépens des fortifications, des retranchements, de faire lever Des Tours et de se livrer à des Veilles occasionnés par une garde continuelle qui les ont mis Dans L'impossibilité de se livrer aux travaux accoutumés et necessaires a La vie. Outre ces obligations ruineuses, outre le massacre de dixhuit personnes à l'entour de St. Louis, De six de Blessés, De 57 pris et pilliés tant aux environs de cepotte qu'aux endroits plus éloignés et Dependants, De neuf chasseurs pris, massacrés et Brulés Vifs dans le missoury par les Sauvages Kans, de Deux particuliers tués sur l'autre rive dans L'affaire du 26,

De deux habitants tués le jour de la S.t Pierre par les sauvages Loups, de six qui ont eu le meme sort a l'habitation du Colonel Clark a l'entrée de la Belle riviere avec un chasseur détaché d'un batteau montant de la Nouv.lle Orleans, nous nous voyons encore environnés d'enemis cruels et destructifs. une armée composée de 1300. hommes anglois et sauvages est sur le point de partir du Détroit et de se mettre en marche pour venir detruire plusieurs habitations ameriquaines dans la Belle riviere et s'emparer ensuite des Ilinois. huit cent Sioux doivent se reunir avec une partie des nations du missoury qui déja suivant le rapport de nos traiteurs ont a l'instigation de nos Ennemis arboré le pavillon anglois en place du pavillon espagnol pour venir investir notre village et le mettre a feu et a sang. nous attendons a chaque instant un parti de trois cent pour Nation de la riviere des Ilinois a quinze lieux de S.t Louis envoyés par nos memes enemis, soulevés par leurs presents prodigués et excités a venir frapper sur nous. nous apprenons que le Commandant de Michillimakinac a la tete de deux mille hommes français et sauvages qu'il a fait rassembler, s'apprete a venir fondre sur nous et faire un massacre general; déja les barques de cette endroit sont a Chicagou a l'entrée du lac michigan le transport de vivres et d'eprovisions de guerre necessaires pour cette barbare Expedition. Cernés de toute part par d'aussi cruels enemis, nous nous voyons hors d'etat, pour comble de Disgrace de faire nos foibles recoltes sans risquer notre vie. Telle est la misere et la Degradation des Ilinois qui ne subsiste plus que par les aumones qu'il recoit de quelques particuliers attachés a la gloire de leur prince — et qui s'epuisent.

Plusieurs canadiens avec leurs femmes et leurs enfants dans l'espoir d'une vie plus heureuse, forcés d'abandonner leur pays natal livré aux horreurs de la Guerre opprimé par ses nouveaux maitres, pour se soustraire a un Joug que leur cœur repousse, a des Liens qu'ils detestent, sont venus pour s'etablir en ces climats: Incertains de leur bonheur a la vie d'etant de calamites et ignorants la bonté de leur nouveau maitre sont a la veille d'affoiblir encore ces Etablissements par leur depart. Les anglais ne se content pas d'employer tous les moyens necessaires pour subjuguer le pays des Ilinois, ils poussent leur ambition Jusqu'a vouloir s'emparer du mexique. les coureurs des nations sauvages leurs ont donné la topographie de ce continent qui n'a été bien connu que par eux. ayant appris que le missoury courant ouest quart au nord Ouest et que les rivieres Kancé et platte qui sortent de dans prennent leur source; la premiere proche du village S.t Jerome de Taos, la seconde un peut plus haut que S.ta Fé, charmés de cette decouverte ils forment le hardy projet après la Destruction de ce pays qu'ils croyent certaine, d'etablir des forts sur ces rivieres qui serviront de retraite a des brigants qui iront commettre des pillages dans toute la province de S.ta Fé et qui meme en essayeront la Conquête; projet déja formé par la Cour d'angleterre, ainsi que le prouve la carte nouvelle des possessions anglaises en amerique qu'ils ont fait imprimer le 3. avril 1777. —

Après L'exposé auprés denotre Gouverneur detant demalheurs qui menaçent nos
Villages, lui avoir fait voir L'extrème indigence de Leurs habitants, les Dangers aux
quels ils Sont exposés et les Enemis qui les environnent: auprés detout autre pour le
forcer a envoyer les Secours prompts et neceffaires, onVous Suppliroit D'exposer le Devoir,
L'humanité, laBonté d'un grand cœur et les Vertus qui le Caracterisent, onVous
engageroit a lui faire voir une terre encore Teinte d'unSang rependu Sans regrets
pour la lui conserver, leSacrifice fait avec zéle denosfoibles Fortunes; mais auprés
Defous ce heros dont leNom Seul fait L'Eloge, il Suffit aun peuple Malheureux
D'exposer ses peines et ses Calamités, deformer au Ciel pour la conservation deSes
Jours et Nénêtre Jamais privés les vœux les plus Sincères et deSe dire avec
Toute Lareconnoissance, l'honneur et Le Respect leplus profond.

Ses tres humbles Serviteurs.

S.t Louis des Ilinois
Le 2. Juillet 1780.

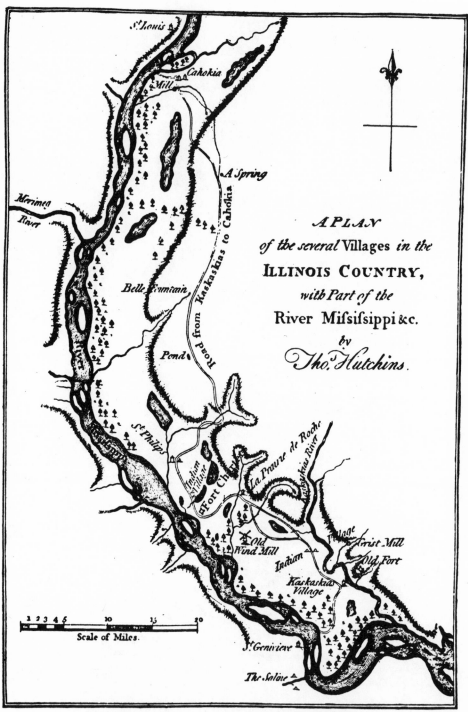

7. The Illinois country in the 1770s. From Thomas Hutchins, *A Topographical Description of Virginia, Pennsylvania, Maryland, and North Carolina* (London, 1778).

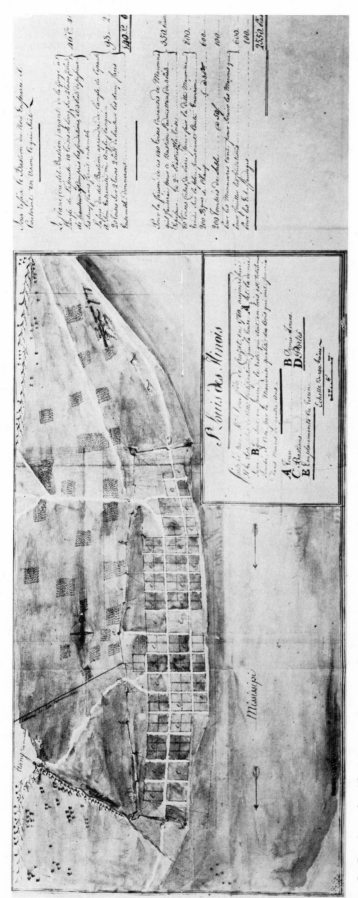

8. St. Louis as fortified by Lieutenant Governor Cruzat in 1780; sketch enclosed by Manuel Perez, lieutenant governor of Upper Louisiana, to Esteban Miró, governor of Louisiana, Dec. 2, 1788. Photocopy, State Historical Society of Wisconsin; original in Archivo General de Indias.

Contributors

C. Richard Arena, associate professor of history at Whittier College and director of the Richard Nixon Oral History Project, holds the Ph.D. from the University of Pennsylvania (1959). His interest in Louisiana colonial history is marked by his master's investigation at Tulane of the Spanish land tenure system, 1762–1803, and by his doctoral study of the Philadelphia–New Orleans trade, 1789–1803. Professor Arena has published articles on business activities in Spanish Louisiana, among other subjects, and is currently at work on a comparative study of land reforms.

John Francis Bannon, S.J., professor of history at Saint Louis University, received his doctorate at the University of California at Berkeley (1939), one more of those notable scholars trained by Herbert Eugene Bolton. Father Bannon has been chairman of the American Jesuit Historical Conference and of the Conference on Latin American History of the American Historical Association, and a founder and past president of the Western History Association. He was editor of the *Historical Bulletin* and served on the editorial board of the *Hispanic-American Historical Review, Arizona and the West,* and *Manuscripta.* Among his publications are *Colonial North America; Latin America—an Historical Survey; History of the Americas; The Mission Frontier in Sonora; The Spanish Conquistadores; Bolton and the Spanish Borderlands; Indian Labor in the Spanish Indies; The Spanish Borderlands Frontier;* and many shorter studies.

Carl H. Chapman, professor of anthropology and director of archaeological research activities at the University of Missouri at Columbia, spent his undergraduate years at the University of Missouri, studied for his master's at the University of New Mexico, and holds his Ph.D. from the University of Michigan (1959). He is chairman of the Advisory Council on Archaeology to the Missouri State Park Board, member of the Lewis and

Clark Committee for Missouri, Fellow of the American Anthropological Association and of the American Association for the Advancement of Science, and has been secretary, treasurer, or editor of publications for the Missouri Archaeological Society from 1946 to the present. His primary research interests have been the archaeology of Missouri and the Midwest and the ethnohistory of the Osage Indians.

JOHN G. CLARK earned a master's degree from the University of Kansas in 1960 and a doctor's degree from Stanford University in 1963. He is now professor of history at the University of Kansas, has served as visiting assistant professor of history at Louisiana State University, and in 1968 enjoyed a National Endowment for the Humanities fellowship. He has published an illuminating account of *The Grain Trade in the Old Northwest* (1966), a valuable Louisiana study, *New Orleans, 1718–1812: An Economic History* (1970), and *Towns and Minerals in Southeastern Kansas: A Study in Regional Industrialization* (1970). In addition, Clark edited *The Frontier Challenge: Responses to the Transmississippi West* (1971). He is now at work on an economic study of La Rochelle and other French Atlantic ports during the eighteenth century, as well as a second volume on New Orleans.

WILLIAM S. COKER (Ph.D., University of Oklahoma, 1965) has taught at Kansas State University, the University of Oklahoma, the University of Southern Mississippi, and is now associate professor of history at the University of West Florida at Pensacola. His special areas of interest are the history of Mexico and the Spanish period in the Old Southwest. He has published articles in the *Journal of American History*, the *Journal of Mississippi History, Historia Mexicana,* and other scholarly quarterlies. At present Professor Coker is writing a biography of Peter Bryan Bruin, a Revolutionary War officer from Virginia who migrated to West Florida in 1788, became a respected Spanish citizen, and eventually was one of the first judges in Mississippi Territory.

JOHN C. EWERS, senior ethnologist in the Smithsonian Department of Anthropology, has published so many papers and books on the Plains Indians and the West that it would take a dozen pages to list them briefly. Among his latest books are *Indian Life on the Upper Missouri* (1968) and his magnificent edition of Jean Louis Berlandier's *The Indians of Texas in 1830* (1969). To previous Southern Illinois University conference volumes he contributed an essay on "Fact and Fiction in the Documentary Art of the American West" (*The Frontier Re-examined,* 1967) and an account of Berlandier among the Comanches of Texas in 1828 (*Travelers on the*

Western Frontier, 1970). He is particularly excited now by three new studies: a book on Gustavus Sohon's pictures of Indians of the Northwest in the 1850s, a book about Plains Indian carving, and a complete revision of his first book, *Plains Indian Painting* (1939).

C. HARVEY GARDINER (Ph.D., University of Michigan) is research professor of history at Southern Illinois University, Carbondale. His research, which has repeatedly taken him to Mexico, Cuba, Japan, and Europe as well as to major Latin American collections in the United States, has been supported by the Guggenheim Foundation, the Folger, Huntington, and Newberry libraries, the American Philosophical Society, and the Fulbright Commission. In somewhat more than twenty volumes the following themes have occupied him as author and editor: the transference of Spanish culture to the New World in the era of the Mexican Conquest, the career and writings of William Hickling Prescott, and the travel literature of Latin America in the independent era. Present research concerns the Japanese in Latin America. Long residence in the Mississippi Valley, in both Missouri and Illinois, has led to a pleasurable identification with its history.

ROBERT L. GOLD, associate professor of history, Southern Illinois University, Carbondale, holds his Ph.D. from the University of Iowa (1964). Colonial Mexico, the Spanish borderlands, and nineteenth-century Latin American diplomacy are his favorite areas of research. In addition to articles and reviews in historical journals, he has published *Borderland Empires in Transition: The Triple-Nation Transfer of Florida* (1969). He has served as book review editor of the *Hispanic-American Historical Review* and as advisory editor of a Latin American travel series for Southern Illinois University Press.

A. OTIS HÉBERT, JR., director of the Louisiana State Archives and Records Service, has broad experience in Louisiana history. He holds a master's degree in history from Louisiana State University and has taught in the public schools and colleges of Louisiana for ten years. In 1960–62 he was associate editor of *Louisiana History,* the quarterly journal of the Louisiana Historical Association, and in 1963–64 he served as its managing editor. On June 1, 1966, he assumed his present position. His master's thesis was on the "History of Education in Colonial Louisiana." Among his other publications is an account of the "Calcasieu River" in *Rivers and Bayous of Louisiana,* and "Keeping Louisiana's Records," in *McNeese Review.*

JACK D. L. HOLMES, graduate of Florida State University, received his

Ph.D. in Latin American studies from the University of Texas at Austin in 1959, and is now professor of history at the University of Alabama in Birmingham. He is the author or co-author of sixteen books and more than a hundred articles in professional journals. His study of Manuel Gayoso de Lemos, one of the key Spanish governors in the Mississippi Valley during the final decade of the eighteenth century, received the Louisiana Literary Award as the best book published on Louisiana in 1965. He attended the Universidad Nacional Autónoma de México under a Mexican government grant in 1954 and since 1961 has done considerable research in Spain, Portugal, England, and France. A Fulbright research scholar to Spain in 1961 and 1962, he has also held grants from the American Philosophical Society, the American Association for State and Local History, and his own university research committee. He is editor and publisher of the Louisiana Collection Series, which brought out Dr. Holmes's *Honor and Fidelity*, a study of Spanish military organizations in the Mississippi Valley, and a *Guide to Spanish Louisiana, 1762–1806*. He edited the third volume in the Southern Illinois University Press's Travels on the Western Waters series, *Francis Baily's Journal of a Tour in Unsettled Parts of North America in 1796 & 1797*. He has participated in numerous historical conferences and symposia and is currently (1972) doing research on the role of the black man in Spanish Louisiana and the Floridas with the aid of a research grant from his university.

Most of the grandparents of NOEL M. LOOMIS were pioneers, from Josiah Loomis, who came to America in 1638, to John Miller, who was killed on the Great War Trail in present West Virginia in the 1790s, to Ben Miller, who owned the first licensed ferry in the Territory of Iowa, to P. M. Loomis, who got a homestead in the Cherokee Strip Run, to another John Miller, who was in the California Gold Rush. This background was important, for without it Noel Loomis would not have become interested in history. He was born in the Cherokee Strip and grew up as a printer and editor, working all over the West. A professional writer from 1929 on, author of short stories, articles, and novels, he published three historical studies: *The Texan–Santa Fe Pioneers* (1958), *Pedro Vial and the Roads to Santa Fe* (with Abraham P. Nasatir, 1967), and *An Illustrated History of Wells Fargo* (1968). He founded and until his death in the early fall of 1969 was the director of the annual Writers' Workshop at San Diego State College, where he had been an assistant professor of English since 1958.

JOHN FRANCIS MCDERMOTT's primary concern for many years has been the cultural history of the early Mississippi Valley. He has previously organized conferences on the French in the Mississippi Valley in 1956, 1964, and 1967. Research professor of humanities at Southern Illinois University, Edwardsville, from 1963 to 1971, he is author or editor of a number of books exploring this area that range from *Private Libraries in Creole Saint Louis* (1938) through *Frenchmen and French Ways in the Mississippi Valley* (1969) and *Travelers on the Western Frontier* (1970). He has recently acquired for the newly created Research Center for Mississippi Valley Culture at his university and plans to publish a hitherto unknown, book-length manuscript by Nicolas de Finiels, a French army engineer in the Spanish service, describing Upper Louisiana at the close of the eighteenth century. In 1965 the French government awarded him the Palmes Académiques for his studies of the French in America, and in 1970 he was named a Chevalier de l'Ordre National du Mérite. In the same year he was made a *miembro titular* of the Instituto de Cultura Hispánica at Madrid.

JOHN PRESTON MOORE, A.B., Washington and Lee University, M.A., Harvard, Ph.D., Northwestern University, is emeritus professor of history at Louisiana State University. He has published books on *The Cabildo in Peru under the Hapsburghs, 1530–1700* (1954) and *The Cabildo in Peru under the Bourbons, 1700–1824* (1966), and has edited a volume of letters from A. Dudley Mann to Jefferson Davis (1960) as well as made numerous contributions to scholarly journals. He was awarded a Guggenheim Fellowship in 1960 and received honorable mention for the Bolton Award in Latin American History. Professor Moore is now engaged on a biography of Antonio de Ulloa, the first Spanish governor of Louisiana.

California-born ABRAHAM P. NASATIR received his Ph.D. from the University of California at Berkeley in 1926 at the age of twenty-one. During his studies for the master's degree there he became interested in the history of the Mississippi Valley and wrote a thesis on "The Chouteaus and the Indian Trade of the West, 1763–1852." To pursue his investigations more thoroughly he went to Spain in 1924–25 on a Native Sons Fellowship and collected a "prodigious" amount of documentation which became the basis of his dissertation on "Trade and Diplomacy in the Spanish Illinois Country, 1763–1792." Ever since, he has pursued his studies and made his publications in that field. Subsequent years of working in the archives of Spain and France have enabled him to build up a personal collection of documentary materials surpassing 250,000 pages. Professor of history at California State University, San Diego, since 1928, he was chosen Distinguished Professor of the California State College System in 1965. He has served as president of the American Historical Association, Pacific Coast Branch, and as president of Phi Alpha Theta. He has published more than fifteen volumes and more than eighty shorter studies. Among these are *Before Lewis and Clark: Documents Illustrating the History of the Missouri, 1785–1804* (2 vols., 1952), *Spanish War Vessels on the Mississippi, 1792–1796* (1968), *Pedro Vial and the Roads to Santa Fe* (with Noel M. Loomis, 1967), and *Commerce and Contraband in New Orleans during the French and Indian War* (with James R. Mills, 1968).

CHARLES E. O'NEILL, S.J., professor of history at Loyola University in his native New Orleans, in the course of his historical studies has spent a number of years abroad working in European archives. He holds his doctor's degree (*summa cum laude*) from the Gregorian University in Rome, where he studied under Père Pierre Blet, a specialist on the church and the monarchy under the Old Regime. Dr. O'Neill has also studied under Professor Marcel Giraud of the Collège de France, who is noted for his extensive investigations and publications on the early years of French colonization in Louisiana. Father O'Neill's special field of study is the colonial Mississippi Valley and his long-term project is the gathering of Mississippi Valley mission documents. His years of research in European archives have resulted in an important volume entitled *Church and State in French Colonial Louisiana: Policy and Politics to 1732* (1966), for which, among other work, the French government named him a Chevalier de l'Ordre des Palmes Académiques. He is co-editor of a recently published catalog of Spanish colonial documents in a section of the Seville archives and he is working on a second volume of his study of church and state in Louisiana. He is a member of the Jesuit History Institute and in the spring semester of 1969 was guest professor of history at the Gregorian University.

SAMUEL WILSON, JR., a native New Orleanian and a graduate of the Tulane School of Architecture, Fellow of the American Institute of Architects, is a partner in the New Orleans firm of Richard Koch and Samuel Wilson, Jr., Architects. He has long had a special interest in Louisiana buildings, was a founder and first president of the Louisiana Landmarks Society, and has directed the restoration of a number of historic structures in his city. He edited B. H. B. Latrobe's *Impressions Respecting New Orleans* (1951) and is the author or co-author of numerous studies in his field including *Guide to New Orleans Architecture* (1959), *Bienville's New Orleans—a French Colonial Capital, 1718–1768* (1968), *The Vieux Carré, New Orleans: Its Plan, Its Growth, Its Architecture* (1968), and (with Leonard V. Huber) *Baroness Pontalba's Buildings* (1964) and *The Basilica on Jackson Square* (1965). To conference volumes on *The French in the Mississippi Valley*

(1965) and *Frenchmen and French Ways in the Mississippi Valley* (1969) he contributed substantial and valued essays on "Colonial Fortifications and Military Architecture in the Mississippi Valley" and "Ignace François Broutin," a notable engineer-architect in mid-eighteenth-century Louisiana.

Index